**Race Relations in
British North America,
1607– 1783**

Race Relations in British North America, 1607–1783

edited by

BRUCE A. GLASRUD
and
ALAN M. SMITH

Nelson-Hall nh Chicago

LIBRARY OF CONGRESS CATALOGING IN PUBLICATION DATA

Main entry under title:

Race Relations in British North America, 1607–1783.

Bibliography: p.
1. United States – Race relations – Addresses,
essays, lectures. 2. Afro-Americans – History – To
1863 – Addresses, essays, lectures. 3. Indians of
North America – Government relations – To 1789 –
Addresses, essays, lectures. 4. Slavery – United
States – History – Colonial period, ca. 1600–1775 –
Addresses, essays, lectures. I. Glasrud, Bruce A.
II. Smith, Alan M.
E184.A1R315   973'.0496073   81-18824
ISBN 0-88229-388-5   AACR2

Contents

Preface

THE RECENT CELEBRATION of the bicentennial of the United States led many Americans not only to ponder anew the reasons for the formation of this nation, but also to look at the premises upon which the nation was built. In 1776, when Thomas Jefferson and the other members of the Continental Congress argued for separation from England in the Declaration of Independence, they boldly declared that "we hold these truths to be self-evident, that all men are created equal, that they are endowed by their Creator with certain unalienable rights, that among these are Life, Liberty, and the Pursuit of Happiness." In that document they set forth the basic principles for what has come to be known as the "American Dream." However, many of those who signed the Declaration of Independence meant that all white men were equal before the law; they did not intend to include two large groups of people in the North American colonies, the Native Americans and the involuntary black immigrants from Africa.

This oversight was replicated again and again by historians of the colonial period throughout the ensuing two centuries. Most historians of British North America have focused relentlessly upon the exploits of the English and other European peoples in subduing a hostile continent. Little attention has been devoted to the other two peoples who inhabited Britain's mainland colonies. The Native Americans, or "Indians" as they were dubbed by Christopher Columbus, have often been perceived simply as obstacles to white settlement, or at best as "noble savages." Blacks have usually been considered only within the institutional context of the slave-labor system of the southern colonies. In short, the focus on the history of white Europeans has given rise to a bias of emphasis in which the lives of other American peoples have been treated as minor subplots to the major story line. Certainly there has been little attempt in most general treatments of colonial history either to emphasize or analyze the interaction among the three peoples of British North America.

This book, designed both as a supplement to traditional accounts of European expansion in British North America and as a separate study of the interactions between red, black, and white in the colonies, presents the writing of a number of historians who in recent years have attempted to understand the relationships among the peoples of early America. It is not our purpose to berate the systematic exploitation of black and red by white; rather we propose to examine the historical impact of the meeting of the three races in the British North American colonies of the seventeenth and eighteenth centuries.

The past decade has increased our knowledge of black and red Americans during the colonial era. Although several good monographs have been produced, most of the new scholarship has appeared in the form of articles scattered throughout many scholarly journals. This book draws together a selection of recent literature in the field from a variety of sources. Most of the eighteen selections appeared as short essays in historical publications, but there are also excerpts from longer studies. Some of the selections have been abridged for the sake of brevity. While we have sought to present the best scholarship in the field, our selections also have been governed by the overall plan of the book.

It is not our assumption that the cultures, or even the historical experiences, of the three races which inhabited colonial America were similar. Neither do we assume that there was a uniformity of experience or culture among all members of a particular race. Rather, it is our belief that the culture and experience of each race in America was affected in important ways by its contact with the others. The articles in this book consider red-white or black-white relations, rather than interactions among the three. The reason for this is twofold: first, because most studies focus either on red-white or black-white relations, and second, and to our minds most important, because in the United States a basic determinant of red and black history has been white power. Both red and black of necessity have reacted to white actions and to some extent have developed within the institutions and legal framework established by whites.

We have selected writings which concentrate on the interaction between races. The selections in Part One analyze the clash of cultures between the white English invaders and the red Americans, describe the process by which the former sought to impose their will upon the latter, and show the changes wrought in each culture by contact with the other. Part Two contains essays which deal with the emergence and development of the central facet of white-black relations in early America, the white exploitation of blacks through a system of slave labor. The articles in Part Three emphasize the way in which red and black attempted to resist their systematic exploitation by whites. Part Four examines the experience of red, black, and white during a revolution in which some white Americans gave lip service to the ideal of human equality, while in many cases continuing their exploitation of the other peoples of the new United States.

The book's focus on the colonial period permits one to observe the formation of several significant patterns of racial interaction which were to persist during the subsequent centuries of American history. During this period the mythology of white racism, based on an assurance of superiority by virtue of skin color and culture was fully elaborated. The pattern of white exploitation of the nonwhite peoples, motivated by economic desires and rationalized by racist attitudes, was well established.

Equally important, the patterns of nonwhite resistance were set during the colonial era. A white-red relationship developed which involved land seizure, wars, broken treaties, and the beginning of the reservation system. The institution of slavery, which locked in the relationships of blacks and whites, was fixed by the mid-eighteenth century in a form which would vary only slightly during the next hundred years. White uses of religion and law as a means of achieving racial domination had also become standard practice by the second century of English rule in America.

The American Revolution, with its ideological emphasis on the equality of all, brought some whites to question their racial assumptions while driving others totally to deny the humanity of nonwhites. Despite the pressures for change that the Revolution generated, little occurred to reorder existing social patterns. The peoples of the United States grew up separated and unequal, following patterns of interaction which were formed long before the nation was born.

We wish to thank the library staff at California State University-Hayward for their help in locating materials. The editors at Nelson-Hall kindly and patiently supported and encouraged our efforts. Pearlene Vestal Glasrud read and improved the entire manuscript.

Part 1

Native Americans and Europeans

THE ENGLISH COLONIZATION and settlement of the Atlantic coastal region of North America from 1607 to 1783 was, of course, a part of a larger European invasion of America which began with Columbus's famous voyage of 1492. Perhaps the most striking characteristic of the invasion process was the rapid decimation of the Native Americans by the white invaders. The native population of America north of the Rio Grande has been estimated to have been as high as twenty million before 1500, and it dwindled rapidly in the succeeding centuries. Generally, a depopulation ratio of nine out of ten Native Americans followed closely upon the initial contacts with the European invader.

So complete was the English destruction of the native population during the seventeenth and eighteenth centuries that little is known about the original inhabitants of North America east of the Alleghenies. The most notorious events in the stormy history of red-white relationships before the American Revolution are the major armed conflicts such as the attacks of Powhattan's Federation on Jamestown in 1622 and 1644, the Pequot War (1636) and King Philip's War (1675) in Massachusetts, and Pontiac's Rebellion in 1763. These wars, however, are merely among the most dramatic incidents in a broader red-white relationship marked by almost constant attack and counterattack. At the base of the conflict were the incompatible aims of two rival cultures.

Most European settlers came to British North America in the seventeenth and eighteenth centuries for the purpose of acquiring wealth through individual (and in some cases communal) possession of land. This basic fact meant that a pattern of intensive land cultivation and extensive permanent settlement rapidly came to characterize the English colonies in America. The settlers developed a society in which landholding was the prime value, the chief determinant of social standing, and the most important economic resource. Ultimately, land utilization was the key to the success of these European outposts in America, just as it was the key to the survival of the Native American.

This fact determined European attitudes towards Native Americans almost from the beginning of settlement. In some cases initial settlements, such as those at Jamestown and Plymouth, found themselves surrounded by native societies superior in numbers and in their ability to survive in what was to the Europeans an alien and hostile environment. Often there were early attempts on the part of Europeans to curb their appetite for land acquisition, and, in turn, some Native Americans attempted to accommodate the invaders and even to provide them with the food and knowledge which they needed to survive. However, as the numbers of European settlers grew, their demands for land became more importunate, and Indian fear and hostility mounted. Fueled by mutual misunderstanding between the two cultures, red and white clashed with increasing frequency. Individual quarrels tended to explode into intercultural battles. Native American attempts to expel the invaders, such as the Jamestown Massacre of 1622, were met with massive retaliation. Genocidal warfare became the dominant pattern in red-white relations.

The desire of some white leaders to maintain peace, the interest of both the white and red communities in profits through trade, the sporadic European attempts to proselytize for Protestant Christianity among the Native Americans, and occasional

Indian willingness to cede specified lands tended to act as a brake on the warfare. But the remorseless pressures for more land created by increasing European immigration continued the conflict. Already weakened by epidemics of European diseases against which they were defenseless, the Native Americans steadily lost their ability to resist. In the end superior numbers and a more efficient military technology usually determined a victory for white expansion.

By the time of the American Revolution much of the Indian population of the eastern portion of the British colonies, particularly New England and Virginia, had been almost completely dispossessed of the land. Many nations, such as the Virginia Indians and the Pequots of Massachusetts had been virtually exterminated by disease and warfare. Others had been pushed west of the frontier of white settlement. Still other "peaceful Indians" were isolated under white control and supervision in "villages" which were the forerunners of the modern reservation system. The patterns which were to govern the bloody history of red-white relationships in the United States were set well before the birth of the nation.

The Iroquois

Paul A. W. Wallace*

The European migrants who settled in the New York area during the seventeenth century had to deal with the powerful Iroquois. Comprised of five nations who settled along the northern tier of present day New York, the Iroquois included the Mohawk, Oneida, Onondaga, Cayuga, and Seneca. Struggles with the French, the Beaver Wars with the Hurons and other Indian nations, and pressures from the English eventually brought the decline of Iroquois influence. During the Revolutionary War some Iroquois supported the colonists, others the British, and many of the losers later settled in Canada. As Paul A. W. Wallace notes, the long range effects of the Revolution on Iroquois behavior were devastating: "People accustomed to think in continental terms were overwhelmed by the nagging frustrations of reservation life. There was widespread collapse of morale." The late Professor Wallace specialized in Pennsylvania and Indian history and included among his publications Conrad Weiser: Friend of Colonist and Mohawk, The Muhlenbergs of Pennsylvania, *and* Pennsylvania: Seed of a Nation.

THE FIVE UNITED NATIONS OF THE Iroquois called themselves "the Longhouse," a name that well describes both their geo-

*Paul A. W. Wallace, "The Iroquois: A Brief Outline of Their History," *Pennsylvania History* 23 (1956), 15–28. Reprinted by permission.

graphical relationship to one another, and the government of
their Confederacy. The Longhouse was composed of five independent peoples, each speaking a dialect of a common root
language, seated in a line of villages on a trail stretching
across northern New York from beyond Schenectady to the
Genesee River. From east to west—as the names of rivers and
lakes in that region remind us—they were the Mohawk,
Oneida, Onondaga, Cayuga, and Seneca nations. The Mohawks were known as "Keepers of the Eastern Door," the
Senecas as "Keepers of the Western Door." The Onondagas
tended the central council fire. These were the three Elder
Brothers. The Younger Brothers were the Oneidas (affiliated
with the Mohawks) and the Cayugas (affiliated with the Senecas); later also the Tuscaroras and Delawares[1] when they were
received into the Confederacy "on the cradle-board."

They had a federal council that met at Onondaga (Syracuse),
presided over by the head chief of the Onondagas, Atotarho; but
the political bond that held them was light. As in the typical
dwelling of the Iroquois—a long frame house with roof and
sides of bark and a corridor down the middle, inhabited by
several related families, each group with its own separate fire—
the nations of the League, though they sent representatives to
the Onondaga Council, retained each its own sovereignty virtually intact. An ingenious system of checks and balances, together with a modified form of the veto, made safe a maximum
of liberty for each individual nation. At the same time the periodic meetings of the Great Council at which the common interest of all the member nations was discussed, and the impressive
religious ritual associated with these gatherings, served to give
the Five Nations an underlying sense of unity stronger than the
many differences that divided them.

The course of Iroquois history, although to a partial view it has
often seemed confused and unreasonable, may be comprehended
easily enough if we first grasp its motivation and then follow its
main movements. To attempt such a view, we must sacrifice here
any close study of the innumerable filaments of Iroquois policy in
order to see better the general drift of their history.[2]

For convenience, let us consider Iroquois history under five heads, these roughly corresponding with five historic periods: (1) *The Founding of the Confederacy;* (2) *The Coming of the European,* with the economic revolution that ensued; (3) *The Great War for Survival,* sometimes known as the Beaver Wars because of its origin in conflict over the fur trade; (4) *Balance of Power,* a period during which the Iroquois maintained their position of importance on the continent by observing a policy of neutrality between the English and the French; (5) *Dispersion,* many of the Iroquois migrating, after the close of the Revolutionary War, to Canada where they reestablished the Longhouse on the banks of the Grand River,[3] while others remained in scattered reservations in the United States.

There is no documentary record of the founding of the Confederacy, that event having taken place before the coming of the white man, probably about the middle of the fifteenth century.[4] But the founding is described in a legend that has been transmitted orally among the Iroquois.

This legend, though undoubtedly in part a product of popular imagination and rationalizing, is important to us here both for the core of truth contained in it and for the influence it exerted in its elaborated form upon subsequent Iroquois history. It provided a patriotic incentive that helped to hold the Iroquois together, and gave to their wars something of the complexion of religious crusades.

Underneath the embroidery of myth, symbolism, and folk-tale, there is a foundation of honest historical broadcloth. The essential facts are there: the drawing together of five independent nations by slow degrees, through an intermediate process of local confederation, and against strong opposition, until under the influence of two great men, Deganawidah and Hiawatha, the union was completed and the Tree of Peace was planted on the shore of Onondaga Lake. The legend itself, with its wisdom and its poetry, seized the imagination of the Iroquois people, who took to heart the message it conveyed and derived from it a sense of national mission: to make the Tree of Peace *prevail.*

The Iroquois believed in the divine origin of the League. As the legend tells us, Deganawidah's mother was a virgin through whom the Great Spirit, in compassion for man, the victim of recurrent wars, incarnated his message of "Peace and Power." He converted Hiawatha to his ideal, and with the help of this disciple persuaded the Five Nations to organize effectively for peace. He left his people a body of laws which form the Constitution of the Confederacy.

The legend is full of vivid, unforgettable images, expressing man's perennial hope for a world in which, as a later Iroquois spokesman expressed it,[5] "The land shall be beautiful, the river shall have no more waves, one may go everywhere without fear." The Tree of Peace was not easily forgotten: a great white pine rising toward the sun for all men to see, with branches to shelter the war-weary, and white, healthy roots extending to the four corners of the earth.

What the Iroquois might have made of themselves if they had been given time to develop naturally under Deganawidah's laws, it is impossible to say. The coming of the European changed their whole mode of life and put them on the defensive. At first contact, the Iroquois recognized the superiority of the white man's manufactured implements over his own stone-age tools and weapons. A brisk trade sprang up between the two races. Soon the Indian found himself dependent on the white man's goods, not for comfort only but for survival.

The Iroquois were an agricultural people and good farmers. Their cornfields were rich. But the white trader would not accept corn in exchange for the guns, powder, broadcloth, hoes and axes that the Indian now relied on for subsistence and defense. The trader demanded furs, especially beaver, for the European market. The Indian, in order to buy what he needed, found it necessary to devote his best energies to hunting and the marketing of hides.

The change in the end affected all Indians adversely. To the Iroquois it brought almost immediately near-disaster. Though their population was not large—never more than about twelve thousand men, women, and children—intensive hunting on a national scale soon exhausted their hunting grounds. By 1640 scarcely a beaver was to be found between the Hudson River and the Genesee. The Iroquois, to save themselves, had either to find new hunting grounds or to capture a position as middlemen (like the Hurons, whose country was also denuded of beaver) in the trade between the white man and the far Indians in the north and west, where the best hunting lay.

These were not pleasant alternatives. The Susquehanna Valley and the rich hunting territories westward to the valleys of the Allegheny River and the Ohio, with which the name of the Iroquois has been associated from Pennsylvania's earliest colonial days, were not in 1640 accessible to them. The Longhouse was hemmed in by powerful and suspicious neighbors. The Mahicans on the Hudson were pressing them hard. To the south were the formidable Susquehannocks, jealous of their trade with the Dutch and Swedes at the mouth of the Schuylkill River. To the north were the Hurons, a large and powerful people, the greatest Indian merchants on the continent, through whose activities as middlemen the French at Montreal held a monopoly of the trade with the Indians north of the Great Lakes. The Neutral Nation, immediately west of the Senecas, was allied with the Hurons. This was the tough market the Iroquois had to break into or perish.

The greatest obstacle was New France. For political as well as economic reasons, the French were determined to suffer no breach of their monopoly of the northern fur trade. It brought wealth to the colony, and at the same time kept France's Indian allies dependent on her. As long as she held the monopoly, she could control her allies by the threat of denying them trade goods. Repeatedly the Iroquois sought to make a commercial treaty with the Hurons. The Hurons themselves were not averse to it, but the French intervened and put a stop to it.

Desperate, the Iroquois took to piracy, as the English had done on the Spanish Main. They raided French trade routes on the St. Lawrence and Ottawa Rivers, ambushing Huron fur fleets. So successful were these raids that the French in alarm reconsidered their policy. In 1645 they, with their Huron allies, made peace with the Iroquois.

It was just such a treaty as the Iroquois had hoped for, containing the right commercial terms. Deganawidah in his laws had laid down the principle that friends eat out of the same bowl. Kiotsaeton, Mohawk spokesman at the treaty, made this explicit: the Hurons were now to trade with the Iroquois.

Next summer a Huron fur fleet of more than eighty canoes—"the greatest fur fleet in the history of New France"[6]—came out of the north-west and, unmolested by the Iroquois, descended to Montreal. The Iroquois were allowed no part in the trade, though the high prices paid for furs at Albany might have made it worth the Hurons' while to give Iroquois traders a middleman's cut. Twelve bales of furs which the French did not have merchandise enough to purchase, went back to Huronia. The Mohawks, enraged at this open breach of the commercial terms of the Treaty, sent war belts to the Senecas and Onondagas.[7]

Vis à vis the French, the Iroquois were in a strong military position. The Longhouse flanked French trade routes to the west, and, in case of French attack, they had at their backs a range of wooded mountains into which they might retire by paths inaccessible to the enemy. Within easy reach of them, too, were the Dutch (later the English) to supply them with guns and powder. But the French made up by diplomacy whatever disadvantage they might have had in the matter of terrain. They tightened their hold on the nations surrounding the Iroquois.

In 1647 the Hurons made an aggressive alliance with the Susquehannocks, who agreed to lift the hatchet when the Hurons gave the word. It seemed to the Iroquois as if a trap had been closed about them. The Hurons went a step further. Taking advantage of the looseness of the political bond that held the Five Nations together, they sent an embassy to negotiate a separate peace with the Onondagas and Cayugas. Such a peace, if concluded, would have split the Confederacy apart, leaving the Mohawks and Senecas, at opposite ends of the Longhouse, to shift for themselves.

Thoroughly alarmed, the Mohawks and Senecas despatched forces to break Huron communications with the Onondagas and Susquehannocks, and together concerted further plans which took a little time to mature. The year 1648 passed with only inconclusive fighting. In the summer a large Huron trading fleet was brought successfully through the Mohawk blockade, with severe loss to the Mohawks.

In the autumn of that year, the Mohawks and Senecas quietly sent a thousand hunters up into the woods of Ontario. Some months later the hunters rendezvoused. At early dawn on March 16, 1649, they appeared suddenly out of the snowy woods before the Huron town of St. Ignace, stormed and took the place, and set it afire. Three of the inhabitants escaped, making their way to St. Louis, three miles away, where they gave the alarm. But by sunrise the Iroquois were before St. Louis, and by nine o'clock it, too, was in flames. A spirited Huron counter-attack decided the Iroquois not to press on against the principal Huron stronghold, Ste Marie. Instead, they returned to their own country.

But their work had been accomplished. Behind them, panic had overtaken the Huron people. They fled, burning fifteen of their villages as they went. Some spent a winter of near-starvation on Christian Island in the Georgian Bay. Others took refuge among the Petuns (Tobacco Nation), near neighbors to the south-west, or among the Neutrals about Niagara. A large number made their way to the country of the Eries. Some found shelter under the Tree of Peace, a whole village seating itself among the Senecas. Still another band made its way north to mingle with the Ottawas on Manitoulin Island. It was this last group, as we shall see, that in the end robbed the Iroquois of the expected fruits of victory.

The attack on Huronia was but the beginning. In the War for Survival, the Iroquois disposed of whole nations at a blow—not by massacring their people but by destroying their main centers of resistance and causing their dispersion. In this way the Petuns were destroyed in December, 1649, the Neutrals in 1650–51, and the Eries in 1654.

The wars with the Mahicans and Susquehannocks were a different matter. The Mahicans were good for the long pull. As early as 1626 they had driven the Mohawks from their lower Castle on the Mohawk River east of Schoharie Creek. The last

great battle, at Hoffman's Ferry, in which the Mohawks defeated the Mahicans, did not come until 1669. Peace was not
concluded until 1673.

The war with the Susquehannocks[8] dragged on for many
years. Living in populous towns, well fortified, they seemed to
be inexpungable. They had a fort on the Lower Susquehanna
River equipped with bastions and mounted artillery. Supported
as they were with guns and powder from Maryland, and possessed of a strong military tradition, they were not to be destroyed with one blow. In 1663 they turned back a Seneca force
of eight hundred men. They repeatedly raided the Iroquois country, and for years had the best of this desolating war. It was not
until the Marylanders had turned against them that the Susquehannocks were at last dislodged from their riverbank stronghold.
No adequate records have been preserved of this last Iroquois
conquest. But we know with certainty about the dispersion,
which was complete. Some of the Susquehannocks went south,
only to suffer further humiliation at the hands of Maryland and
Virginia. Others went north and were incorporated by the Iroquois, as some of the Hurons had been. A few were later allowed
to settle in the Susquehanna Valley again, at Conestoga, near the
present city of Lancaster.

The Beaver Wars, as we have seen, grew out of a struggle over
the fur trade, but soon passed beyond that. As wars for survival,
they were successful and decisive. The Iroquois emerged in
1675 as the strongest military power on the continent. They had
won title to a vast territory, including most of what are now the
states of New York, Pennsylvania, and Ohio, as well as much
of Maryland and Virginia. The Delaware Indians, formerly subject to the Susquehannocks, were now inherited as "props to the
Longhouse."

As commercial ventures, however, the Beaver Wars as a
whole were a failure. In particular, the dispersion of the Hurons
did not give the Iroquois the expected middleman's share in the
fur trade. The explanation is to be found in the activities of the
Hurons who joined the Ottawas on Manitoulin Island and later
moved with them to Michilimackinac. Hurons and Ottawas car-

ried on as vigorous a trade as ever with the French, from a more distant and less vulnerable base.

Failing in their northern commercial objectives, the Senecas, after the defeat of the Neutrals and Eries, spread out into the west and developed a profitable trade in the Ohio and Mississippi Valleys. Whereupon the Susquehannocks, as yet unsubdued, raided Seneca trading routes, forcing the Senecas to despatch a large part of their warriors—as many as six hundred at a time—to escort their traders home.

The expulsion of the Susquehannocks in 1675 rid the Iroquois of certain dangers only to expose them to others. The opening of the Susquehanna Valley brought them into close contact with advancing English settlements in Pennsylvania, Maryland and Virginia, and confronted them with several difficult problems.

To begin with, there was the problem of the Virginia, or as it was sometimes called, the Carolina Road. The Virginia Road was a warpath extending from the Five Nations country, through Pennsylvania, Maryland, and Virginia, to the country of the Conoys (Piscataways), Tuteloes, Tuscaroras, Catawbas, Cherokees, and other tribes with whom the Iroquois were associated in matters of peace or war. Warriors travelled it to punish those who had harbored the Susquehannocks. Sometimes these war parties fell into conflict with the settlers. It was a maxim among the Iroquois that their warriors, when passing through friendly country, should "eat out of the same bowl" with the inhabitants. In other words, they expected to find victuals in Virginia. The settlers near whose farms the path ran, not understanding this point in international etiquette, refused food to passing war parties. When the warriors helped themselves from the barnyard, the settlers took down their guns. At that point the natural law of reprisals took over.

To avoid such encounters, which the Five Nations deprecated as well as the Virginians and Marylanders, it was agreed in 1685 that the Virginia Road should be rerouted farther west, to the foot of the Blue Ridge. For a time all was well. Virginia discouraged settlement of the Piedmont in order to prevent trespass on the Indian highway. But, the path being still on the east side of the mountain, the westward thrust of population soon overran it, and the troubles began all over again.

Further negotiation resulted in the agreement of 1722, by which the Virginia Road was moved west of the mountain into the Shenandoah Valley, the Blue Ridge being accepted as the boundary between the English and the Iroquois. A similar problem beset the Pennsylvania frontier, where the Virginia Road, which for a time had run south through the lower Susquehanna Valley, was deflected ever farther west to avoid just such troubles as Virginia had had.

A more delicate problem for the Iroquois lay in the defenseless condition of the Susquehanna Valley after its former masters had been driven out. The crux of the problem was how to fill that vacuum before the English did, and to do it without bloodshed. The solution hit upon was to fill the valley with Indian refugee populations. It had long been a policy of the Iroquois, following Deganawidah's injunction to take strangers by the hand and welcome them under the Tree of Peace, to care for defeated peoples who appealed to them for sanctuary. We have seen them doing this with the Hurons and Susquehannocks. Now, in their time of triumph, the Iroquois had commiseration for Indians in the south who were having a rough time: the Shawnees and Conoys, for instance, whom the Iroquois themselves had been mauling; the Tuscaroras after the severe defeat administered to them by North Carolina in 1712; the Delawares driven by the Walking Purchase out of their homes in the Forks of the Delaware; the Nanticokes, who found themselves unwanted in Maryland. To all these dispossessed people the Iroquois offered asylum in the Susquehanna Valley. Colonies of them were placed at strategic points, usually at the junction of important trails or canoe routes. To superintend these "displaced persons," vice-regents or "half kings" were appointed, men like Shickellamy at the Forks of the Susquehanna (Sunbury) and Tenacharisson at the Forks of the Ohio. Sometimes—as when in 1766 a large band of Tuscaroras, with their sick and aged, came up from North Carolina to the Big Bend of the Susquehanna—the Iroquois despatched special agents to organize the removal and see to it that proper food and transportation were provided along the way.[9]

These little colonies or protectorates were moved up the river as the white settlements caught up with them, for the last thing the Iroquois wanted was a war with Pennsylvania or New York. Nevertheless these rearguard actions, though they were for the most part bloodless, were a reminder that the English colonies (whom the Iroquois, as they liked to tell them, had nursed through their infancy) had grown up to be dangerously acquisitive and importunate adults.

The Montreal Treaty of 1701, which marked a turning point in Iroquois history, came about as a result of the uneasiness felt by the Five Nations at the phenomenal growth and expansion of their English allies. They saw the need of a counter-balancing weight on the international scales.

We must go back a little in order to see more clearly the motivation of this treaty. In the year 1666 New France, in order to punish the Iroquois for their raids on her fur fleets, launched two expeditions under Courcelles and Tracy. The first was a failure; but the second, though it encountered few Mohawks (they having wisely vanished into the woods) burned villages and destroyed quantities of stored corn. Peace was made the following year, but it was soon broken. In 1687 Denonville's invasion of the Seneca country again caused little loss of manpower to the Iroquois, but the destruction of some 1,200,000 bushels of corn was crippling. In reprisal, two years later, the Iroquois secretly penetrated New France to the gates of Montreal and emerged from the woods to devastate the country for many leagues about. The expedition goes down in Canadian history as the Massacre of Lachine, because the Indians, unable to reach and destroy the enemy's stores of food, as the French had done, killed or captured the crop producers, which came to the same thing in the end—injury to the enemy's economy. A few years later the French launched another punitive expedition into the Iroquois country; and so the pendulum swung, from reprisal to reprisal, each side continually getting hurt, though never mortally.

What the Iroquois wanted was not war but a better share of

the fur trade. "In fine," wrote Lamberville of their war with the Miamis in the West, "they do not wage war save but to secure a good peace."[10] What the French wanted was freedom from Iroquois terror. "An extraordinary thing," wrote La Potherie, "that three or four thousand people should be able to make a whole new world tremble."[11] The Lachine affair had so frightened the Hurons and Ottawas that the French thereafter found them impossible to control. By this time the situation had reached a stalemate. The French had learned that they could not destroy the Iroquois. The Iroquois had learned that it would be unwise to destroy the French: they were a good counter-weight to the English. It was becoming apparent to both sides, French and Iroquois, that an accommodation was to be desired.

The English, getting wind of this *rapprochement,* did everything they could to stop it. They reminded the Iroquois that they were "subjects" of the King of England.[12] The merchants of Albany were apprehensive about losing their monopoly of Iroquois trade. The Province of New York feared losing Iroquois protection of the northern border. "Those Five Nations," wrote Governor Dongan, "are very brave & the awe & Dread of all ye Indyans in these parts of America, and are a better defence to us, than if they were so many Christians."[13] The middle colonies, fearing war with France, did not want to lose the support of Iroquois manpower. "If we lose the Iroquois, we are gone," wrote James Logan, Secretary of Pennsylvania, in 1702.

In the summer of 1701 what the English feared came to pass. At Montreal the Five Nations made peace with the French and their Indian allies. The French invited the Iroquois to trade with them at Detroit. In return the Iroquois promised, in case of a Franco-British war, to remain neutral. But the Iroquois were not deserting the English. While one embassy was on its way to treat with the French in Montreal, another was, quite honestly, renewing the chain of friendship at Albany. At Montreal, in return for the promise of their neutrality, the Iroquois stipulated that the French should respect that neutrality and, in case of a war with the English should, as far as the Iroquois were concerned, "sit on their mats" (i.e., not breach the Iroquois borders).[14]

During the early years of the eighteenth century, Conrad Weiser in Pennsylvania and William Johnson in New York did much to confirm the "Antient Union" of the Iroquois and the English. The Joncaires, father and sons, strove to preserve Iroquois neutrality. When at last the French and Indian War broke out, the Five Nations, true to their treaty with France, remained neutral. There were, it is true, some scattered acts of partisanship, as when Senecas took part in raids on the English settlements, or when Mohawks danced the war dance and accepted the hatchet from William Johnson. But officially Iroquois neutrality was maintained, and, on the whole, it worked to the advantage of the English colonies. The Iroquois exerted judicious pressure on their wards, Delawares and Shawnees, who had joined the French and struck the English. The chastisement administered to Teedyuscung, leader of the pro-French Delawares, at the Easton Treaty of 1758, was decisive. That treaty ended the Indian War in Pennsylvania and made Fort Duquesne untenable by the French.

After the fall of New France in 1763, the Iroquois quickly learned how sound their policy of keeping the balance of power had been. The English, freed of the French menace on their borders, ceased to court the Iroquois or to right their wrongs. Gross land scandals were imposed upon them without redress. "The Indians need not to expect even moderate Justice in this Country," wrote Sir William Johnson.[15] They had to submit to hard treaties, whittling away their territories, like the Fort Stanwyx Treaty of 1768.

The American Revolution found the Iroquois divided. After a period of neutrality, the Oneidas and many of the Tuscaroras sided with the "Thirteen Fires," while the Mohawks, Onondagas, Cayugas, and Senecas, under the leadership of Joseph Brant, sided with the British. After the war came their dispersion. Many of them followed Joseph Brant to Canada. Their descendants may still be found on the Six Nations Reserve (the Tuscarora being the sixth nation) near Brantford, Ontario. There are between seven and eight thousand of them, representing all the nations of the Confederacy, with a good sprinkling of Del-

awares and others who came into the Longhouse on the cradle-
board. Many have remained in New York and Pennsylvania: at
Onondaga, St. Regis, Tonawanda, Cattaraugus, Tuscarora,
Cornplanter. Still others have moved to reservations in the
West. Many of the Oneidas are now in Wisconsin.

The last decades of the eighteenth century and the first decades of the nineteenth were the unhappiest years in the history
of the Longhouse. Some of their fires had been put out and
others had been scattered. Power in international affairs was
gone from them. Their horizons had suddenly contracted.
People accustomed to think in continental terms were overwhelmed by the nagging frustrations of reservation life. There
was widespread collapse of morale.

Then came Handsome Lake, the Seneca prophet, with his
visions. He had walked the Sky Road, he said, and had talked
with three messengers from the Creator. The Creator was displeased with his *Ongwe-honwe* (Real People) for neglecting
their Indian heritage and sinking so far below the spirit of their
ancestors. Handsome Lake's words touched a chord among all
the Iroquois, the vibrations of which have not ceased to this
day. He had started a national religious movement that is still
strong.

Under these and other influences the Iroquois pulled themselves together and set their shoulders to the long task ahead:
without relinquishing their identity as *Kanonsionni,* People of
the Longhouse, to join the rest of the world in clearing the path
of brambles and briars for the advancement of all mankind.
Their success is attested by notable contributions they have
made in industry, the professions, scientific research, and the
arts. They are the best structural steel workers in America, and
for soldiering there are none to surpass them. Though their
population today is little more than it was in the seventeenth
century, they contributed to the armies of the United States and
Canada during the Second World War more than twice as many
men as they had assembled in their greatest days to crush the
Hurons. The white man may well be proud to eat out of the
same bowl with them.

Notes

1. William N. Fenton, "The Roll Call of the Iroquois Chiefs," *Smithsonian Miscellaneous Collections,* Vol. 3, No. 15, p. 54.

2. Certain of the main movements in Iroquois history have been individually treated in excellent analytical studies, such as the following: Charles Howard McIlwain's "Introduction" to Wraxall's *Abridgement of Indian Affairs* (Cambridge, Mass., 1915); George T. Hunt's *Wars of the Iroquois* (Madison, Wis., 1940); William N. Fenton's "Problems Arising from the Historic Northeastern Position of the Iroquois," *Smithsonian Miscellaneous Collections,* Vol. 100 (Washington, 1940); Anthony F. C. Wallace's "The Grand Settlement of 1701" (forthcoming).

3. A number of Mohawks settled also at Deseronto on the Bay of Quinte.

4. For a summary of the evidence on which this conclusion is based, see P. A. W. Wallace, "The Return of Hiawatha," *New York History,* October, 1948.

5. Thwaites, *The Jesuit Relations* (Cleveland, 1896), Vol. 21, p. 33.

6. George T. Hunt, *The Wars of the Iroquois* (Madison, Wis., 1940), p. 83.

7. See Hunt's *Wars of the Iroquois* for a full description of this affair.

8. Also known as Conestogas or Minquas—White Minquas, the Eries being the Black Minquas.

9. See letter from the Moravian missionary, John Jacob Schmick, at Wyalusing: "On the 18th [November, 1766] two chiefs, Newollike and Aehkolunty . . . brought a message from the Six Nations for our Indian Brethren to this effect: The Six Nations have received news by a Tuscarora messenger that a number of their people are on their way, but they do not know how they are to make out and provide for themselves. The Six Nations, therefore, request the Indians everywhere along the Susquehanna to receive these poor Indians, send canoes from place to place for them, and provide them with corn . . ." Bethlehem Diary, Archives of the Moravian Church, Bethlehem, Pa.

10. O'Callaghan, *Documentary History of the State of New York* (Albany, 1849), I, 133.

11. Bacqueville de La Potherie, *Histoire de L'Amerique Septentrionale* (Paris, 1722), IV, 147.

12. There seems to have been an honest misunderstanding here. The Iroquois, when they "gave" their country to the Governor of New York, meant

only that they placed themselves under English protection in case of a French invasion, not that they had surrendered either their sovereignty or title to their lands.

13.   September 8, 1687. O'Callaghan, *Doc. Hist. of the State of N.Y.,* I. 256.

14.   A full discussion of this episode is found in Anthony F. C. Wallace's forthcoming "The Grand Settlement of 1701."

15.   Johnson to Gage, Feb. 14, 1765. *The Papers of Sir William Johnson,* Vol. XI (Albany, 1953), 572.

Indian Agriculture
in the Southern Colonies

G. Melvin Herndon*

Survival for Indians in the southern colonies depended upon hunting and agriculture. Indeed, as G. Melvin Herndon, a specialist in colonial history from the University of Georgia, argues in "Indian Agriculture in the Southern Colonies," the Indians "taught the white settlers how to clear the land, what seeds to plant, what soils to cultivate and how to plant and cultivate their crops." Agriculture dictated patterns of settlement for the Indians and determined the duties and functions of members of the tribe. Land belonged to the tribe in common, and gifts of produce were usually given to important chieftains. Common stores were used by those who ran out of supplies or by neighboring villages which faced starvation for varying reasons. Herndon is the author of Tobacco in Colonial Virginia: The Sovereign Remedy, William Tatham and the Culture of Tobacco, *and* William Tatham, 1752–1819.

AGRICULTURE WAS A CONSPICUOUSLY essential part of Indian subsistence in southeastern North America. The natives were hunters, but they were also agriculturists. They lived in fixed habitations, tilled the soil, and subsisted as much, if not more, on their agricultural products than they did from those of the

*G. Melvin Herndon, "Indian Agriculture in the Southern Colonies," *North Carolina Historical Review* 44 (1967), 283–98. Reprinted by permission.

chase; scarcity of food in the winter, soil depletion, hostile Indian tribes, or white settlers forced the Indians to move about.

The early accounts contain numerous references to the "Indian fields" and villages. William Strachey mentioned Kecoughtan, Virginia, where a large concentration of Indians displayed great skill as husbandmen on land suitable for cultivation.[1] The German traveler, John Lederer, in 1670, found a group of Siouan Indians living near present Clarksville, Virginia, that put in an immense store of corn, and he observed that they always had a year's supply of provisions in reserve.[2] In 1775 James Adair wrote: "And their tradition says they did not live straggling in the American woods, as do the Arabians, and rambling Tartars; for they made houses with the branches and bark of trees for the summer-season; and warm mud-walls, mixt with soft dry grass, against the bleak winter."[3] From the experience of the Indians the colonists learned how to live in Colonial America. The natives taught the white settlers how to clear the land, what seeds to plant, what soils to cultivate and how to plant and cultivate their crops. There is little doubt that the Indian contributed much to the survival of the early colonists and to American agriculture.

The first task performed by the Indian farmer was that of clearing the land of trees and bushes. He usually selected the most fertile soil for cultivation, which was generally along river bottoms or near other bodies of water. The advantages for hunting and fishing probably had something to do with the selection of a site for planting, but no doubt the Indians understood the value of good soil. The method of clearing seems to have been the same from Virginia to Florida. Adair wrote that "In the first clearings of their plantations, they only bark the large timber, cut down the sapplings and underwood, and burn them in heaps; as the suckers shoot up, they chop them off close to the stump, of which they make fires to deaden the roots, till in time they decay."[4] This process is almost identical with that described by Captain John Smith, Robert Beverley, John Lawson, and Alanson Skinner.[5] Lawson noted that in North Carolina the best lands were not always used because of the size of the trees on them,[6] while Henry Spelman affirmed a more robust treatment than Adair: "the[y] cutt doune the greate trees sum half a yard aboue the ground, and ye smaller they burne at the roote pullinge a good part of barke from them to make them die . . ."[7]

The Indians usually built their villages of varying sizes in the midst of these clearings.[8] Smith says, "Their houses are in the midst of their fields or gardens, which are small plots of ground. Some 20 acres, some 40. some 100. some 200. some more, some lesse. In some places [there were] from 2 to 50 of those houses together, or but a little separated by groues of trees."[9] According to Strachey, the village of Kecoughtan contained about 1,000 Indians, 300 houses, and 2,000 or 3,000 acres of cleared land suitable for planting.[10]

Among the Algonquins, located from Virginia to the Neuse River, each family had its own carefully cultivated garden. This garden was commonly a small plot of ground 100 by 200 feet, and it furnished food until the large fields could be harvested. The large fields which supplied most of the food for the entire population lay on the outskirts of the village. Little houses or shelters raised upon platforms were built in the fields and were occupied by watchers, usually women or children, whose duty it was to keep the birds from injuring the crops.[11] This practice was also customary among the ancient Tumucua tribes in northern Florida.[12]

Lands belonging to the Indian tribes were divided into communities or petty provinces, each governed by its local chief, who was usually subject to a higher chief. To the greater chieftains the people paid tribute of corn, wild beasts, deer, and other gifts. The gardens of the principal chiefs among the Algonquins were cared for by the people, who met by appointment to plant and later harvest the crops. The Creeks paid their chiefs tribute by contributing a portion of their own harvest to the king's granary, which was a public treasury to which every member had a right of free and equal access when his own private stores were consumed. It served also as a surplus to accommodate travelers, to assist neighboring villagers whose crops had failed, and to afford provisions for expeditions against hostile tribes.[13] There was no fixed rule as to the size of a garden or cornfield an individual or family might plant. Each member of the village could clear as much land to cultivate as he pleased, and as long as it was cultivated his right to it was protected; if abandoned, anyone might acquire the right to use it. According to the custom or law, the land belonged to the tribe and no person could acquire an absolute title to any part of it.[14]

Tillage as practiced by the Indian differed from that practiced by the European. The field crops grown in England at the time of the discovery of America were largely broadcast seeded. Virtually every crop grown by the Indian was planted in rows and each stalk or plant hoed to keep down the weeds—one of several examples illustrating that American farm practices were influenced by Indian agriculture. Intertillage of such crops as tobacco, corn, and beans had been commonly practiced in America by the white man more than one hundred years before Jethro Tull wrote his *Horse Hoeing Husbandry* (1733) and had been in use by the Indians for centuries. In their common method of hill planting, the soil in the intervening spaces was not broken. The hills were from twelve to twenty inches in diameter and about three feet apart, and the soil in these hills was all that was stirred or loosened. As the tobacco plant or corn stalk grew, loose dirt was scraped around it thus keeping down the weeds and grass. Hilling may have been practiced for a more important reason, to prevent the plants from falling over during high winds and wet weather. Hilling promoted the production of buttress or bracer roots on the lower part of the stem in both corn and tobacco. The same thing cannot be accomplished by deep planting. Certain peculiarities about the structure and development of both of the above plants cause the main part of the root system to develop near the surface of the soil regardless of the depth of planting.[15] The hills were used over and over in successive seasons and became quite sizable mounds of earth. The early colonists followed the Indian method of seeding but often neglected the weeding and were frequently subjected to ridicule for their shiftlessness by the painstaking Indian squaws.

Later, in using animal labor for cultivation the colonists found it more feasible to kill the weeds and grass by breaking and stirring the intervening ground, and more modern methods of cultivation subsequently evolved. Thus the colonists provided the chief requisite for soil erosion by stirring the soil over the entire field. As long as an unbroken sod was retained between each hill, there was little danger of any significant amount of erosion. For this reason it appears that the Indians were able to grow corn on the same field longer than the white settlers. Recent tests have proven that row crops are not benefited by frequent cultivation if the weeds are kept out by other means, another instance where modern agriculturists have discovered that many of the farming practices of the Indians were based on sound principles.

The Indians practiced a rotation of fields rather than a rotation of crops. A field was "cropped" until it no longer produced profitable yields, then it was abandoned and new land cleared. The colonists followed the Indian example, as clearing new land was more feasible than fertilizing the old. Several years later the abandoned fields were frequently taken over by someone else or returned to cultivation by the original holder. So added to the several other Indian agricultural practices adopted by the white settlers was that of restoring fertility by resting land.[16]

The Indians could scarcely have avoided the beneficial effects of decaying organic matter on plant growth, yet, outside of New England, they appear to have made little or no use of any kind of manures. Smith wrote: "In *Virginia* they never manure their outworne fields, which is very few, the ground for the most part is so fertile: but in *New-England* they doe, sticking at every plant of corne a herring or two . . ."[17] On Roanoke Island Hariot observed:

> The ground they neuer fatten with mucke, dounge or any other thing; neither plow nor digge it as we in England, . . . [they] doe onely breake the vpper part of the ground to rayse vp the weedes, grasse, & old stubbes of corne stalkes with their rootes. The[se] which after a day or twoes drying in the Sunne, being scrapte vp into many small heapes, to saue them labour for

carrying them away; they burne into ashes. (And whereas some
may thinke that they vse the ashes for to better the grounde; I
say that then they woulde eyther disperse the ashes abroade;
which wee obserued they do not, except the heapes to be too
great: or els would take speciall care to set their corne where the
ashes lie, which also wee finde they are careless of.) And this is
all the husbanding of their ground that they vse.[18]

Again the colonists copied the Indian, even after the introduction
of a considerable number of livestock, which the Indian did not
possess. The colonist failed to fertilize his crops for the same
reasons as the Indian: scarcity of manures, the amount of labor
required, and, most importantly, the abundance of fertile land.

According to contemporary accounts, one of the most common characteristics of Indian agriculture was that the planting
and cultivation was done largely by the women, though the
amount contributed by the male varied somewhat in different
areas. In preparing a field for cultivation, the first task was to
clear it; this portion of the work belonged to the men. They
girdled and killed the trees, burned the brush and dead wood,
and then handed the field over to the squaws who broke up the
ground for the making of hills, using hoes made of wood, bone,
stone, or shell.[19] Smith related:

The men bestowe their times in fishing, hunting, wars and
such manlike exercises, scorning to be seene in any woman like
exercise; which is the cause that the women be verie painefull
and the men often idle. The women and children do the rest of
the worke. They make mats, baskets, pots, morters; pound their
corne, make their bread, prepare their victuals, plant their corne,
and gather their corne, beare al kind of burdens, and such like.[20]

According to Hariot, the men also helped prepare the ground for
seeding:

. . . a fewe daies before they sowe or set, the men with wooden
instruments, made almost in [the] forme of mattockes or hoes
with long handles; the women with short peckers or parers,
because they vse them sitting, of a foote long and about fiue
inches in breadth: doe onely breake the vpper part of the
ground. . . .[21]

It has been said that in North Carolina the women never planted the corn, and that among the Tunicas of the lower Mississippi valley all of the work was done by the men.[22] Some confusion on this point may have been due to the fact that in addition to the communal field there were small garden areas about most Indian villages which were maintained entirely by the women.

The Indians carried on their work much in the manner of the husking, quilting, and other "work frolics" that became common among the colonists.[23] The people of each village worked together in common fields, though the allotments of the different households were separated by a narrow strip of grass, poles, or some other suitable natural or artificial boundary. Among the Creeks, care of the fields was under the charge of an overseer, said to be elected: "He called the men to the square by going through the village blowing upon a conch shell or uttering a loud cry. Immediately they gathered with hoes and axes, and then marched in order to the field as if they were going into battle, headed by their overseer. The women followed in detached parties bearing the provisions for the day."[24] As a general rule the planting season for the out-fields began when the wild fruit had ripened, so as to draw off the birds and prevent them from picking up the grain.[25] The small garden plots in or near the village were planted earlier and provided the first harvest.

Work began at one end of the common field, in a plot of ground chosen by lot, and when the task on that one was completed, they moved to the next adjoining one, and so on until the entire field was planted.[26] Sometimes one of their orators cheered the workers on with jests and humorous old tales and sang some of their most agreeable tunes while beating a drum. At the end of a workday, all of the workers were usually feasted by the families for whom they had worked on that particular day.[27] Work usually ceased around noon for the day, and after the feast the afternoon was devoted to a ball game and the evening to dancing.[28]

The following is one of the better accounts of their manner of planting corn:

. . . beginning in one corner of the plot, with a pecker they
make a hole, wherein they put foure graines with that care they
touch not one another, (about an inch asunder) and couer them
with the moulde againe: and so through out the whole plot,
making such holes and vsing them after such maner [sic]: but
with this regard that they bee made in rankes, euery ranke differ-
ing from [the] other [by] halfe a fadome or a yarde, and the
holes also in euery ranke, as much. By this meanes there is a
yarde spare ground betwene euery hole: where according to discretion here and there, they set as many Beanes and Peaze: in
diuers places also among the seedes of Macócqwer [squash and
pumpkin] Melden [an herb] and Planta Solis [sunflower].²⁹

Corn was grown over a larger area of North America than any
other domesticated plant and is certainly one of the oldest in
America. It was the main dependence of all tribes south of the
St. Lawrence River and east of the Mississippi.³⁰

The Indians grew three or four varieties of corn. Hariot mentioned three types, two of which grew to be 6 or 7 feet tall, and
ripened in 11 or 12 weeks after planting; the third grew to a
height of about 10 feet and ripened in 14 weeks. Each stalk
might have from 1 to 4 ears on it, with some 500 to 700 grains
on each ear. The grains were about the size of an English pea
and might be of several colors, white, red, yellow, or blue.³¹
Near Jamestown Smith observed: "Every stalke of their corn
commonly beareth two eares, some 3, seldome any 4, many but
one, and some none. Every eare ordinarily hath betwixt 200 and
500 graines."³² They began planting in April, but the chief
plantings came during May and continued until the middle of
June. What was planted in April was harvested in August, that
planted in May was harvested in September, and that planted in
June was harvested in October. Perhaps the best description of
Indian corn was given by Beverley in 1705:

There are Four Sorts of *Indian* Corn, Two of which are early
ripe, and two late ripe. . . .
The Two Sorts which are early ripe, are distinguish'd only by
the Size, which shows it self as well in the Grain, as in the Ear,
and the Stalk. There is some Difference also in the Time of
ripening.

The lesser Size of Early ripe Corn, yields an Ear not much larger than the Handle of a Case Knife, and grows upon a Stalk between Three and Four Foot high. Of this are commonly made Two Crops in a year. . . .

The larger Sort differs from the former only in Largeness, the Ear of this being Seven or Eight Inches long, as thick as a Child's Leg and growing upon a Stalk Nine or Ten Foot high. This is fit for eating about the latter End of *May,* whereas the small Sort (generally speaking) affords Ears fit to roast by the Middle of *May.* The Grains of both these Sorts, are as plump and swell'd as if the Skin were ready to burst.

The late ripe Corn is diversify'd by the Shape of the Grain only, without any Respect to the accidental Differences in Colour, some being blue, some red, some yellow, some white, and some streak'd. That therefore which makes the Distinction, is the Plumpness or Shrivelling of the Grain; the one looks as smooth and as full as the early ripe Corn, and this they call *Flint-Corn;* the other has a larger Grain, and looks shrivell'd with a Dent on the Back of the Grain, as if it had never come to perfection; and this they call *She-Corn* . . .[33]

According to one scholar, "It may even be said that in four and a quarter centuries during which the white race has been growing maize almost nothing has been produced that can not be duplicated among the cultures of the aborigines. The most highly developed varieties of flint, flour, pop, and sweet types are little if any superior to individual types in native cultures, the chief advance having been toward uniformity."[34]

There were no conspicuous differences in the manner in which corn was harvested and stored. Among the Algonquins the women gathered the corn, each family receiving only what was grown on its own plot. The corn was picked and placed in hand baskets, emptied into larger baskets as each was filled, and later placed on mats to dry. When sufficiently dry, the corn was next placed in the house in piles and shelled by "wringinge the ears in pieces between their hands." The shelled corn was then placed in a great storage basket which took up a large part of the house. Late corn that had to be harvested while still green was frequently roasted and buried in the ground.[35] The corn might be stored in a crib raised on eight posts about seven feet above the ground[36] and curing hastened by fires built underneath. Thus the granary, public or private, might be a portion of the wigwam, a hole in the ground, or a storehouse raised above the ground.

The husks of an ear of Indian corn were thick, tough and coarse, fitted snugly, and extended well beyond the ear. To loosen and remove them was not an easy task and reached imposing proportions when multiplied by the number of ears to be husked. To ameliorate this task the Indians of eastern North America invented the homely husking peg, which the white man adopted. In its primitive form it was essentially a smooth, round rod of bone or hard wood about half an inch in diameter and three or four inches long. One end tapered down to a blunt point, and a shallow groove or two around it near the middle held a loop of cord or leather, through which one or two fingers were inserted to hold the tool on the hand. The blunt point of the peg was inserted into the snugly fitting husks at the tapered end of the ear, and by applying pressure on the husks held between the peg and the thumb of the hand holding the peg, the husks were peeled back and snapped off at the opposite end of the ear, thus freeing the ear from its husks.[37]

As to yields, one account reported 364 bushels of corn as the product of 13 gallons of seed;[38] another in terms of English measure—200 London bushels of a mixed crop of corn, beans, and peas from an English acre;[39] and a third estimated an average yield as 40 bushels per acre.[40] Corn, beans, and squash were frequently planted in the same field, another practice adopted by the colonists. The Indians domesticated several kinds of beans: the common bean, often referred to as the kidney or Indian bean; the lima bean; and the scarlet-runner bean. All three types were grown in the southern colonies. The early writers on the American crops frequently employed the phrase "beanes and pease." Just what was meant by the term "pease" is difficult to determine. It may have been used to indicate more than one specie of bean; at times it seems to have been used to mean a small bean.[41] Hariot speaks of two kinds of native beans, called by the English beans and peas respectively, though the latter seems to have been quite different from European peas.

> *Okindgier,* called by vs Beanes, because in greatnesse & partly in shape they are like to the Beanes in England; sauing that they are flatter, of more diuers colours, and some pide [piebald]. The leafe also of the stemme is much different. In taste they are altogether as good as our English peaze.
>
> *Wickonzowr,* called by vs Peaze, in respect of the beanes for distinctiõ sake, because they are much lesse; although in forme they little differ; but in goodnesse of tast much, & are far better than our English peaze. Both the beanes and the peaze are ripe in tenne weekes after they are set.[42]

Smith mentioned another type of pea which the Indians called "*Assentamens,* which are the same as they cal in Italye, *Fagioli.* . . ."[43] Beverly wrote: "They have an unknown Variety of them, (but all of a Kidney-Shape) some of which I have met with wild. . . ."[44] These wild peas may have been the marsh pea.[45]

There is also some uncertainty as to the various kinds of creeping vines cultivated by the Indians. Many of the creeper plants the white explorers had never seen, and those were named for the European plants which they most resembled. The evidence seems quite clear, however, that several kinds of squash and the ordinary field pumpkin were common food crops of the Indians. One observer described these plants as follows:

> *Macócqwer,* according to their seuerall formes called by vs *Pompions, Mellions,* and *Gourdes, because they are the like formes as those kindes in England. In Virginia* such of seuerall formes are of one taste and very good, and do also spring from one seed. There are two sorts; one is ripe in the space of a moneth [*sic*], and the other in two moueths [*sic*]."[46]

Beverley gave a more detailed description of the several kinds of creeping vines in Virginia. He mentioned muskmelons; several kinds of watermelons, red, yellow, and white meated, and some with yellow, red, and black seeds; pumpkins; two kinds of squash called ecushaws and macocks; and gourds, which the Indians never ate, but planted for other uses, such as use of dried shells for containers.[47]

There is a belief that muskmelons and watermelons were introduced to the Indians by the Europeans.[48] Captain John Smith made no mention of them in his descriptions of Virginia published in 1612, but in 1621 he reported that

A small ship comming in December last from the Summer-Ilands, to Virginia, brought thither from thence these Plants, viz. Vines of all sorts, Orange and Leman trees, Sugar Canes, Cassado Roots (that make bread) Pines, Plantans, Potatoes, and sundry other Indian fruits and plants, not formerly seen in Virginia, which begin to prosper very well.[49]

Melons appear several times in the accounts of the various Raleigh expeditions. Hariot mentioned melons and Captain John White in 1587 wrote of seeing melons of "divers sorts." While these sixteenth-century American melons may have been squash or pumpkins, there is nothing in the statements which would exclude watermelons. There is good presumptive evidence that the melons which were served raw might have been watermelons.

There is some controversy as to whether the sweet potato is of American or Asian origin. It is generally conceded that America was its original home. According to L. C. Gray, "sweet potatoes were in common use in the West Indies when the Spaniards discovered these islands. We have no account of their employment by the Virginia Indians at the time Jamestown was settled but they were cultivated by the Indians of northern Florida and eastern South Carolina."[50] Various roots, such as tuckahoe or wampee or koonti, used by the Indians were identified as potatoes by early explorers and settlers. Strachey says that potatoes had been given a trial in his time (1610–1612).[51] Smith mentioned white, red, and yellow potatoes among the products brought by the English from Bermuda in 1620.[52]

It is the opinion of Gray that "Tomatoes, Jerusalem artichokes, garden peppers, and sunflowers were among the less important contributions of the New World to agriculture."[53]

Tobacco was firmly established throughout the eastern and southern United States at the time of discovery. In the Southeast it is mentioned first in Jacques le Moyne's narrative of the Huguenot colony in Florida. In 1584 Arthur Barlowe noted tobacco growing along with corn in the fields of the Algonquin Indians of North Carolina.[54] In 1607 George Percy was shown a "Garden of Tobacco" by a Powhatan Indian.[55] Strachey offers the fullest account of Indian tobacco in Virginia:

> There is here great store of Tobacco, which the Saluages call *Apooke;* howbeyt yt is not the best kynd, yt is but poore and weake, and of a byting tast, yt growes not fully a yard aboue the grownd, bearing a little yellow flower, like a henn-bane, the leaves are short and thick, somewhat rownd at the vpper end: . . . the Saluages here dry the leaves of this Apooke over the fier, and sometymes in the Sun, and Crumble yt into Powlder, Stalks, leaves, and all, taking the same in Pipes of Earth which very ingeniously they can make. . . .[56]

At the end of the seventeenth century Beverley wrote:

> How the *Indians* order'd their Tobacco, I am not certain, they now depending chiefly upon the *English,* for what they smoak: But I am inform'd, they used to let it all run to Seed, only succouring the Leaves, to keep the Sprouts from growing upon, and starving them; and when it was ripe, they pull'd off the Leaves, cured them in the Sun, and laid them up for Use. . . .[57]

The native tobacco, *Nicotiana rustica,* was inferior to *Nicotiana tobacum* introduced into Virginia by John Rolfe from the West Indies; and, as Beverley noted, by the end of the seventeenth century the Indians of Virginia were depending mainly upon the English for their ordinary smoking tobacco. The colonists soon found the native Indian tobacco unsatisfactory to their taste and imported a new variety that truly became the "golden weed" for several of the colonies; but it must be remembered that it was the Indian who taught the colonists how to grow it.

Of all the hay and pasture plants of importance east of the Mississippi, there is scarcely one which was not introduced by the colonists. Many early explorers wrote of "goodly meadows," not knowing that the salt marsh grasses they saw growing along the coast were very inferior for forage. Had the Indian of the Southeast possessed horses and cattle before the coming of the white men, perhaps he might have developed an excellent hay crop from the wild rye that was found growing from the

Great Lakes to the Gulf of Mexico,[58] or from the several varieties of peas and beans.

If the natives of southeastern North America had been ignorant of agriculture, the colonization of American would probably have been delayed, for without aid from the Indians the planting of Jamestown might have failed. It was largely through the knowledge of agriculture learned from the Indians that the colony was enabled to survive the first few years. Perhaps the next greatest contribution of the Indians was the clearing of land for crops which the whites sooner or later took over, by force or other means. This speeded up the colonization by a considerable degree, for it would have taken generations for a small handful of colonists to clear enough land for survival. It has been said that the Valley of Virginia and sections of the Carolina Piedmont were without trees when the Europeans first came. Those sections and the areas used by the Indians for farming were practically the only breaks in the forests.

In some instances Indian agriculture was further advanced than that of the Old World. The colonists learned many valuable lessons in New World agriculture from the natives and several of their principles and practices have been proven sound by American agriculturists.

Notes

1.   Louis B. Wright and Virginia Freund (eds.), *The Historie of Travell into Virginia Britania (1612),* by William Strachey, gent. (London: Hakluyt Society [Second Series, No. CIII], 1953), 67, hereinafter cited as Strachey, *Virginia Britania.*

2.   Clarence W. Alvord and Lee Bidgood, *First Explorations of the Trans-Allegheny Region by the Virginians, 1650–1674* (Cleveland: Arthur H. Clark Company, 1912), 154.

3.   James Adair, *The History of the American Indians; Particularly Those Nations Adjoining to the Missis[s]ippi, East and West Florida, Georgia, South and North Carolina and Virginia . . .* (London: Printed for Edward and Charles Dilly in the Poultry [sic], 1775), 405, hereinafter cited as Adair, *History of the American Indians.*

4.   Adair, *History of the American Indians,* 405–406.

5.   Lyon Gardner Tyler (ed.), *Narratives of Early Virginia, 1606–1625,* unnumbered volume in J. Franklin Jameson (ed.), *Original Narratives of Early American History* (New York: Charles Scribner's Sons [19 volumes, 1906–1917], 1907), 95–96, hereinafter cited as Tyler, *Narratives of Early Virginia;* Strachey, *Virginia Britania,* 79; Louis B. Wright (ed.), *The History and Present State of Virginia,* by Robert Beverley (Chapel Hill: University of North Carolina Press, 1947), 143, hereinafter cited as Beverley, *Present State of Virginia;* Alanson Skinner, "Notes on the Florida Seminole," *American Anthropologist,* XV (January, 1913), 76.

6.   Frances Latham Harriss (ed.), *Lawson's History of North Carolina* (Richmond: Garrett and Massie, 1937), 84, hereinafter cited as Harriss, *Lawson's History.*

7.   Henry Spelman, "Relation of Virginia," in Edward Arber (ed.), *Travels and Works of Captain John Smith, President of Virginia and Admiral of New England, 1580–1631* (Edinburgh: John Grant, 2 volumes, 1910), I, cxi, hereinafter cited as Arber, *Travels and Works of Captain John Smith.*

8.   David Bushnell, Jr., *Native Village Sites East of the Mississippi* (Washington: Government Printing Office [*Bureau of American Ethnology Bulletin 69*], 1919), 32.

9.   Arber, *Travels and Works of Captain John Smith,* I, 363.

10.   Strachey, *Virginia Britania,* 67.

11.   Charles C. Willoughby, "The Virginia Indians in the Seventeenth Century," *American Anthropologist,* IX (January, 1907), 82–83, hereinafter cited as Willoughby, "Virginia Indians."

12.   John R. Swanton, *Early History of the Creek Indians and Their Neighbors* (Washington: Government Printing Office [*Bureau of American Ethnology Bulletin 73*], 1922), 360.

13.   G. K. Holmes, "Aboriginal Agriculture—The American Indian," in L. H. Bailey (ed.), *Cyclopedia of American Agriculture* (New York: Macmillan Company, 4 volumes [Second Edition], 1910), IV, 33, hereinafter cited as Holmes, "Aboriginal Agriculture."

14.   Lucien Carr, "The Food of Certain American Indians and Their Methods of Preparing It," *Proceedings of the American Antiquarian Society,* New Series, X (April 1, 1895), 163, hereinafter cited as Carr, "Food of Certain American Indians"; Willoughby, "Virginia Indians," 57.

15. Paul Weatherwax, *Indian Corn in Old America* (New York: Macmillan Company, 1954), 70, hereinafter cited as Weatherwax, *Indian Corn*.

16. It might be noted here that agriculturists now insist that resting land does not restore fertility; however, this was a common belief until the twentieth century.

17. Arber, *Travels and Works of Captain John Smith,* II, 952.

18. Thomas Hariot, *A Brief and True Report of the New Found Land of Virginia* (New York: History Book Club, Inc., 1951), unnumbered 17–18, hereinafter cited as Hariot, *A Brief and True Report.*

19. Carr, "Food of Certain American Indians," 164.

20. Arber, *Travels and Works of Captain John Smith,* I, 67.

21. Hariot, *A Brief and True Report,* unnumbered 17.

22. John R. Swanton, *Aboriginal Culture of the Southeast* (Washington: Government Printing Office [*Forty-second Annual Report of the Bureau of American Ethnology*], 1928), 691, hereinafter cited as Swanton, *Aboriginal Culture.*

23. Carr, "Food of Certain American Indians," 162.

24. John R. Swanton, *Social Organization and Social Usages of the Indians of the Creek Confederacy* (Washington: Government Printing Office [*Forty-second Report of the Bureau of American Ethnology*], 1928), 443.

25. Adair, *History of the American Indians,* 406.

26. Mark Van Doren (ed.), *The Travels of William Bartram* (New York: Dover Publications, 1928), 401.

27. Carr, "Food of Certain American Indians," 163.

28. Swanton, *Aboriginal Culture,* 691.

29. Hariot, *A Brief and True Report,* unnumbered 18.

30. Carr, "Food of Certain American Indians," 159.

31. Hariot, *A Brief and True Report,* unnumbered 15.

32. Arber, *Travels and Works of Captain John Smith,* I, 62.

33. Beverley, *Present State of Virginia,* 143–44.

34.   Guy N. Collins, "Notes on the Agricultural History of Maize," *Annual Report of the American Historical Association for 1919* (Washington: Government Printing Office, 2 volumes and a supplement, 1923), I, 423.

35.   Holmes, "Aboriginal Agriculture," 30.

36.   Harriss, *Lawson's History,* 12.

37.   Weatherwax, *Indian Corn,* 78–79.

38.   Arber, *Travels and Works of Captain John Smith,* II, 952. Smith was somewhat skeptical of this report: "All things they plant prosper exceedingly: but one man of 13. gallons of Indian corne, reaped that yeare 364. bushels London measure, as they confidently report, at which I much wonder, having planted many bushels, but no such increase. . . ."

39.   Hariot, *A Brief and True Report,* unnumbered 18.

40.   Holmes, "Aboriginal Agriculture," 31.

41.   Beverley, *History of Virginia,* 144.

42.   Hariot, *A Brief and True Report,* unnumbered 16.

43.   Arber, *Travels and Works of Captain John Smith,* I, 62.

44.   Beverley, *History of Virginia,* 144.

45.   John R. Swanton, *Indians of the Southeastern United States* (Washington: Government Printing Office [*Bureau of American Ethnology Bulletin 137*], 1946), 269, hereinafter cited as Swanton, *Indians of the Southeastern United States.*

46.   Hariot, *A Brief and True Report,* unnumbered 16.

47.   Beverley, *History of Virginia,* 142.

48.   Willoughby, "Virginia Indians," 84.

49.   Samuel Purchas, *Hakluytus Posthumus, or Purchas His Pilgrimes* (Glasgow: James MacLehose and Sons [20 volumes, 1905–1907], 1906), XIX, 147, hereinafter cited as Purchas, *Pilgrimes.*

50.   Lewis Cecil Gray, *History of Agriculture in the Southern United States to 1860* (Washington, D.C.: Carnegie Institution of Washington, 2 volumes, 1933), I, 4, hereinafter cited as Gray, *History of Agriculture.*

51.   Strachey, *Virginia Britania,* 38.

52. Purchas, *Pilgrimes,* XIX, 147.

53. Gray, *History of Agriculture,* I, 5.

54. Swanton, *Indians of the Southeastern United States,* 382.

55. Tyler, *Narratives of Early Virginia,* 16.

56. Strachey, *Virginia Britania,* 122–123.

57. Beverley, *History of Virginia,* 145.

58. Gray, *History of Agriculture,* I, 4–5.

Red Puritans: The "Praying Indians" of Massachusetts Bay and John Eliot

Neal Salisbury*

The initial relations between red and white in New England were characterized by conflict; this situation was brought on by white efforts to detach the Indians from their culture and introduce them to English culture, civilization, and religion. Puritan missionaries, often neglected by historians, played a prominent role in precipitating the conflicts. In the following article, Neal Salisbury, a member of the History Department at Smith College, concludes that missionary Eliot's "unrealistic objectives blinded him to the full dimensions of settler-Indian conflict, including his own role in that conflict." Salisbury has thoroughly studied the relations between Puritans and Indians in a doctoral dissertation written at the University of California at Los Angeles, "Conquest of the 'Savage': Puritans, Puritan Missionaries, and Indians, 1620–1680."

IN THE PRESENT REWRITING OF the history of white-Indian relations, religious missions demand particular attention. There has been an unspoken assumption among many historians that however violent and aggressive other whites may have been, the intentions of missionaries were consistently benevolent.[1] Recent

*Abridged from Neal Salisbury, "Red Puritans: The 'Praying Indians' of Massachusetts Bay and John Eliot," *William and Mary Quarterly* 31 (1974): 27–54. Reprinted by permission.

studies by Robert F. Berkhofer, Jr., and Francis Jennings have questioned this assumption. They make plain that Protestant missionaries showed little regard for Indian cultures while advancing the cultural values and, often, the political goals of the white conquerors.[2] In seventeenth-century New England, Puritan identity was not simply a matter of religious allegiance, but was firmly rooted in English and European culture. Accordingly, Puritan missionaries first directed their efforts at detaching the Indians from their "savage" culture and initiating them to the ways of "civilization," before introducing them to Christianity. In the words of John Eliot, the Roxbury minister who dominated the Massachusetts Bay missionary program through the 1670s, they must "have visible civility before they can rightly enjoy visible sanctities in ecclesiastical communion."[3] Prospective converts were to repudiate their identities as Indians and to act like English men and women.

In demanding this repudiation, the missionaries revealed that their values and their work lay within the larger matrix of English attitudes, policies, and behavior that was directed (both consciously and unconsciously) against all manifestations of Indian power and autonomy in southern New England.[4] To be sure, the small group of missionaries believed that their efforts and God's grace would enable the Indians to transcend their "savage" state, while most colonists implicitly assumed such a leap to be impossible or undesirable. But all agreed that native culture lacked intrinsic value and had to make way for English hegemony. Working within this basic consensus, the missionaries contributed to the expansion of English power and assumed that they were thereby "civilizing" the Indians without recognizing a possible conflict between the two processes. Focusing on Massachusetts Bay, this essay examines Eliot's program and its effects on the "praying Indians." It concludes that his unrealistic objectives blinded him to the full dimensions of settler-Indian conflict, including his own role in that conflict.[5]

The Massachusetts Bay Company's original policy, as well as the colony's early promotional literature, considered Indian conversion integral to the Puritan goal of establishing a holy commonwealth in the New World.[6] The colony's seal even depicted an Indian pleading, "Come Over and Help Us." But while a few individual converts were won in the first decade and a half, the overall problem was avoided.[7] This avoidance was not solely a result of apathy, oversight, preoccupation with other matters, or the great difficulties inherent in the task. Conversion, as defined by the Puritans, presupposed their domination of the prospective converts and the latter's isolation from outside influences. These preconditions, in turn, required that the colonists establish complete control over their claimed territory and that they eliminate any powerful "savage" contenders. Missionization officially began only after the Puritan colonies had carried out a war of extermination against the Pequots in 1637, and begun a war of attrition (waged diplomatically and economically as well as militarily) against the Narragansetts. The Narragansett campaign achieved its first significant victory in September 1643, when the English permitted the assassination of the sachem Miantonomo by delivering him into the hands of his Mohegan enemies.[8]

Massachusetts Bay then turned its attention to the weaker tribes within its own jurisdiction. In March 1644 five sachems of the Massachuset tribe submitted themselves, their people, and their lands to the colony. They also agreed to subject themselves "from time to time" to religious instruction. Perhaps, as Jennings has suggested, they took their cue from the fate of Miantonomo.[9] Three months later all Indians in the colony were enjoined to attend religious instruction on Sundays.[10] In the following year the General Court, reacting in part to severe criticism from England, noted the continuing paucity of converts and warned "the reverend elders" that more positive steps were about to be taken.[11] On October 28, 1646, after at least one failure, Eliot preached his first successful sermon to an Indian audience.[12] Apparently encouraged by this event, the General Court one week later passed a series of laws paving the way for a missionary program: the natives were forbidden to worship their own gods; two ministers were to preach to the Indians; and lands were to be purchased "for the incuragment of the Indians to live in an orderly way amongst us."[13] . . .

Eliot set out to "civilize" the Indians by regrouping them
into especially constructed "praying towns" where they would
be isolated from both settlers and independent Indians. Between
1651 and 1674, he modeled the fourteen praying towns of Massachusetts Bay on his utopian vision of a "Christian Commonwealth" governed according to the Bible.[14] During the formation of the first praying town at Natick, he promised to "fly to
the Scriptures, for every Law, Rule, Direction, Form or what
ever we do."[15] The system was to be administered by rulers of
tens, fifties, and hundreds, as Jethro suggested to Moses in
Exodus 18.[16] Twenty-two years later Eliot claimed that all the
praying towns were successfully operating according to this bib-
lical scheme.[17]

Although the adult males of each praying town elected their
local rulers of tens, fifties, and hundreds, their choices were
"approved by a superiour authority,"[18] namely, that of the
superintendent of subject Indians, a secular position created by
the General Court in 1656 and held in turn by Major Generals
Humphrey Atherton and Daniel Gookin. The superintendent,
together with a praying Indian "magistrate" (ruler of a fifty or
hundred), constituted a court with the jurisdiction of an English
county court. But the Indian member's function was at best
advisory, for the English superintendent designated the time and
place of all court sessions, and, more importantly, approved or
vetoed all decisions. The same superintendent exercised broad
discretionary powers over the towns' religious, moral, political,
and educational affairs.[19]

Each praying town had a legal code drawn up by Eliot and
consented to in some fashion by its original residents. The
codes' very existence indicated that tribal legal mechanisms
developed over centuries had suddenly been destroyed, while
the contents of the codes called for a radical uprooting of
native culture. Customs that conflicted either with the Bible or
with English values or prejudices were flatly prohibited. The
first law in the Natick code provided a five shilling fine for
idleness. The same code forbade husbands to beat their wives,
enjoined every man to set up a wigwam "and not live shifting

up and downe to other Wigwams," forbade women to cut their hair short or men to let theirs grow long, and prohibited the killing of lice between the teeth as was customary among New England Algonquians.[20] The code at Concord was even more complete, banning any use of body grease, the playing of traditional games, and numerous other customs. Indians here were also forbidden to tell lies and were required to "weare their *haire* comely, as the *English* do." For all these offenses, fines would be imposed.[21]

Despite many setbacks, the early years offered hope that the praying Indians could indeed be "civilized." Within its first year Natick boasted a fort, a meetinghouse, and several broad, straight streets. The abandonment of multifamily roundhouses and longhouses, with their clustered arrangements in villages, marked the weakening of a vital communal pattern.[22] Many customs were severely modified or disappeared altogether among the praying Indians. Never expressly forbidden their native dress, the converts were cut off from the traditional sources of furs by their new locations and their "civilized" life-styles. Eliot tried unsuccessfully to get the women to spin and weave but ended by relying on donations of clothing from England. To the Indians themselves, clothing became a visible distinction between the two ways of life. Thus a convert named Monotunk-quanit once refused to pray, assuming that his native clothing disqualified him from being heard by God.[23] The protective use of bear's grease on the skin and hair also declined as it, like the furs, became less accessible.[24] Gambling was somewhat troublesome for the missionaries at first because Indian debtors were converting and then refusing to pay up on the grounds that gaming was sinful. As a result, their creditors were developing a dim view of Christianity. Finally Eliot got everyone to agree that one-half of each debt should be paid, reminding the debtors that reneging on promises was also sinful.[25] In countless subtle ways the Indians' distance from their past was reinforced while they were as far as ever from being accepted as members of "civilized" society.[26]

In establishing these towns the missionaries followed, rather than preceded, white settlement. The effect of their work was to help clear the few Indians who remained, thus opening up still more land and assuring the settlers' safety. Eliot concentrated upon the seaboard area of the colony from the late 1640s through the 1660s, establishing five towns among the Massachusetts and one each among the branches of the Nipmucs and the Pennacook Confederacy. By 1670 this area had been secured, while settler-native tensions were mounting farther west in the heart of "Nipmuc country." Eliot went to work there, establishing seven more towns in five years.[27] This pattern is important for understanding why some Indians responded to the missionaries and others did not. By the time Eliot began preaching to a group of Indians, the group had typically passed through the earlier stages of English domination: it had been devastated by epidemics; it had sold or otherwise lost much of its land under the incessant pressure of English immigration; it had become economically dependent on the English; and it had submitted to the political authority of the colonial government.[28]

The Indians who responded to the missionaries, then, were not those who freely chose "civilization" over traditional ways, for those ways were already disappearing under the impact of the English invasion.[29] The sequence through which a tribe passed before receiving the missionaries was most dramatically demonstrated by the Massachusets. Cutshamekin was a sachem of this people, who had been powerful before the plague introduced by English fishermen in 1616 nearly exterminated them, exposing them to attacks from the Abnakis to the north. The first influx of the Great Migration posed a more general threat, and, to protect his people, Cutshamekin allied with the Bay colonists. By 1636 his ally-protectors had preempted most of his domain for the establishment of white settlements at Dorchester, Sudbury, and Milton.[30] In 1644 he was one of those who submitted to the government of Massachusetts Bay, a move enabling him to retain authority among his people except where it conflicted with the colony's.[31] The Massachusets thereby became the first Indians in New England to enter a new legal status, one in which they were neither independent nor assimilated into white society.[32] They had become, in effect, a colonized people.[33] In 1650 Cutshamekin acknowledged that his remaining authority was being challenged by the missionaries. Although neither English laws nor missionaries were overtly undermining him, his standing before his people and his ability to exact tribute from them were diminishing.[34] In the following year, when the first praying town government was instituted at Natick, Cutshamekin ended his long-standing resistance to Christianity and accepted a rulership in the new town. He and the missionaries thus enhanced each other's prestige, but for the sachem it was the only means of retaining authority within his shattered community.[35]

After the Massachusets, most Indian converts were Nipmucs. Although we know less about its prehistory, we do know that the tribe was politically fragmented at the time of the settlers' arrival. Instead of uniting around a single sachem, each village band paid tribute to one of its more powerful neighbors in exchange for protection from external enemies. The English attempted to substitute themselves as a new protector.[36] Their practice differed from traditional Indian tributary arrangements, however, in that the English claimed sovereignty over their subject tribes and endeavored to dominate their internal affairs.

These tribal histories illustrate what Eliot and the other missionaries knew to be a most crucial factor in winning converts: the sachems. "The *Sachems* of the Country are generally set against us," Eliot reported in 1650, "and counter-work the Lord by keeping off their men from praying to God as much as they can." Like Cutshamekin "they plainly see that Religion will make a great change among them, and cut them off from their former tyranny." Whereas the sachems previously collected tribute from unwilling subjects by intimidating them with great shows of anger, according to Eliot, "now if their *Sachem* so rage, and give sharp and cruell language, instead of seeking his favour with gifts (as formerly) they will admonish him of his sinne; tell him that it is not the right way to get money; but he must labour, and then he may have money, that is Gods Command, etc."[37] Whenever possible, the colonial governments and missionaries encouraged cooperative sachems like Cut-shamekin and Shawonon of the Nashuas, a branch of the Penna-cook Confederacy. When Shawonon died in 1654, the tribe divided over the succession. The General Court ordered Eliot and Increase Nowell to ''be sent unto them to direct them in their choyce, their eyes being uppon 2 or 3 which are of the bloud, one whereof is a very debaust, drunken fellow, and no friend of the English; another of them is very hopefull to learne the things of Christ; if, therefore, these gents may, by way of perswasion or counsell, not by compulsion, prevayle with them for such a one as may be most fitt, it would be a good service to the country.''[38]

These tactics reflected a realization that tribal coherence among southern New England Algonquians was dependent upon the loyalty of the members to the sachem. The intensification of agriculture in the Late Woodland cultural stage (from ca. A.D. 1000) brought population growth, more frequent and intense warfare, and greater political centralization to the tribes south of the Saco River. The result was a stratified social and political structure headed by a small group of lineages from which the political and religious leaders were drawn. Below was the rest of the tribe, followed by outsiders not fully adopted. Individual families paid tribute to the sachems in exchange for garden plots. But this structure by itself did not guarantee stability. Sachem successions were occasionally disputed, as in the case of the Nashuas, and sachems had to prove they were worthy of receiving their tribes' loyalty and tribute.[39]

Not surprisingly, the tribes most impervious to Christianity were those with the strongest leadership. Indeed, the challenge of responding to the English invasion accelerated the trends toward concentration of authority in the sachem and probably produced a more tough-minded, imaginative leadership than had previously been required.[40] Regardless of their *political* rela-tionship with the English, each of the great sachems of the mid-seventeenth century—Massasoit, Metacom, Ninigret, Un-cas—resisted the missionaries as threats to his tribe's survival. Massasoit's Wampanoags of Plymouth were allies of the colonies for half a century after the Pilgrims' arrival, while Uncas's Mohegans of Connecticut were virtually created under English protection after seceding from the Pequots on the eve of the 1637 war. Yet both sachems consistently and successfully rebuffed efforts to proselytize their subjects.[41] Massasoit's son, Metacom (King Philip), finally reversed his father's policy of alliance in the 1670s when continual English pressure, including that exerted by the missionaries, was threatening the very existence of his tribe.[42] . . .

Intratribal conflicts occurred frequently between converts and those loyal to traditional ways. One of Massachusetts Bay's first Indian preachers was poisoned by hostile tribesmen, and another was threatened with a similar fate.[43] Eliot's first followers were reviled by their peers for heeding his preaching and especially for cutting their hair.[44] Such incidents generally occurred when preaching had just begun and only a few Indians had publicly professed interest in Christianity. By the early 1670s, according to Eliot, the converts were the envy of the colony's Indians.[45]

The praying towns were even more threatened by opposition from the white population, whose protests revealed both the settlers' land hunger and their fear of proximity to "savages," even those striving to convert. . . . .

Direct opposition to the praying towns came principally from those settlers in immediate contact with them. Until the outbreak of war in 1675 the other English generally offered less resistance. This was due largely to the missionaries' success in presenting conversion as a positive solution to the problem of Indian "savagery." Christian Indians, by no means accepted as equals of Christian whites, were distinguished at least provisionally from those Indians who still pursued traditional ways. Not only were the converts adopting English clothing, houses, and ideas of private property, but they were potential allies in any future Indian war. As early as 1650 Eliot advocated that the praying Indians be allowed to have guns and ammunition with which to defend themselves against hostile natives.[46] Fears of "savages" with guns, however, prevented the enactment of this request until the 1660s, when their value as a buffer between the

English and the raiding Mohawks from the east became apparent. The Commissioners of the United Colonies then allowed *missionary* funds to be used to help arm the praying Indians.[47] Toleration of the praying towns was thus based on two important qualifications: the praying Indians were kept separate from the English settlements, and they could be useful in the war of "civilization" against "savagery."

With "civilization" a prerequisite for conversion, the Indians were expected to repudiate their past and to submit to the value system of the Puritans. Eliot and Gookin were thus more than religious instructors and supervisors. They were, in effect, social managers with an important role in English policy toward the Indians. Potential converts were isolated from the larger societies of both Indians and English, and placed in a position of political, economic, and cultural dependence upon the latter. While the towns may appear to have represented a traditional phase preceding full assimilation into white society, such assimilation was never considered as even a remote possibility. Instead, the praying Indians were relegated to a lower caste, yet expected to emulate white behavior.[48]

In one sense, the educational program carried out within the praying towns simply extended the traditional Puritan emphasis on purging the "natural" child and instilling the blessings of citizenship and Christianity through rigorous, disciplined training. This meant bestowing a basic education, particularly literacy, on all those presently or potentially within the covenant.[49] Until now this program had dealt with English, generally Puritan, children. Applied to the Indians, however, it acquired a radically new purpose—the inculcation of Puritan cultural and religious values in adults and children for whom those values were utterly foreign and meaningless.

The first necessity, as Eliot saw it, was to enable the Indians to read the Bible. Assisted by Indian translators, he transcribed the entire Bible into the Massachuset dialect of the Algonquian language. . . .

While most details of the Indians' system of belief are unknown to us, there is no reason to assume that it differed from those of tribal peoples in all times and places in providing a world view that securely integrated individuals with their societies, cultures, and natural environments.[50] Once this system and the community that supported it were shattered in New England, the Puritans' notion of man's alienation from God and His universe undoubtedly made more sense to many Indians.

The missionaries widened the distance between the two religions even farther through their choice of lessons. While Puritanism itself was a complex, many-faceted theology, the works translated for the Indians were those encouraging an inward, socially passive piety. . . .

The themes of guilt, fear of death, individual perseverance, distrust of other people, and literal, methodical rule-following were heavily imbibed by all devout Puritans. But white Puritans also had a sense of their church's militant heritage, and they participated in a dynamic lay culture. Unlike their Indian counterparts, their aggressiveness was culturally supported and encouraged, at times against Indians. The theology dispensed to the praying Indians, on the other hand, was the product of a foreign culture and its values were forthrightly ethnocentric. While encouraging the Indians to reject their own culture and to emulate the English, it denied the possibility of either assimilation or revitalization. The converts were left suspended between two cultures, with their own cultural expression carefully controlled from without.

As far removed as the praying towns were from tribal life, the missionaries felt that Indian children needed an even more sheltered environment. Like all children in Puritan New England, they were to enjoy the benefits of education, preferably through attending school.[51] If possible, Indian children were to receive an even more thorough education by being apprenticed as servants in English homes. Here they would be socialized through English family living, with the boys acquiring trades and the girls learning "good housewifery of all sorts." They would be taught to read English and would receive extra attention from their masters in the learning of Christian principles.[52]

But the program met with resistance from the start. By 1660 the United Colonies commissioners were trying to arouse the flagging interest of Indian parents by awarding them a new coat for each year of a child's apprenticeship. This did little to increase the number of apprentices, however, and the program remained largely unrealized, due to both the reluctance of Indian parents to part with their children and that of whites to accept the pupils into their homes.[53]

The Puritans' expectations for the schools were also illusory. Lacking dedicated instructors, Eliot had to make use of Indians whom he had trained at Natick. If the praying Indians were dependent solely on English teachers, Gookin noted in 1674, "they would generally be destitute."[54] Eliot also had to rely on native preachers, for whose training an Indian college was established at Harvard in 1654. The building constructed for the college had a capacity of just twenty students, but only three to five attended during the college's brief existence. . . .

The educational program with its religious orientation was only the first step for a praying Indian seeking sainthood. Any prospective church member—red or white—had to attend church, listen to sermons, and give a convincing account of his or her conversion experience. The similarity in procedures for white and Indian candidates was, however, superficial. Not only were the churches in Massachusetts Bay racially segregated,[55] but the path an Indian had to travel before converting was quite different from that of a white. Indian converts were expected to renounce their individual and collective pasts and to adopt a new identity created for them by representatives of an entirely foreign culture. As with other aspects of the missionary program, the converts' distance from both cultures, and their cultural subjugation to the English, were reinforced.

The missionaries' message was quite simple: all Indians were living in a state of sin, and repentance was necessary in order to be saved. "They must confesse their sinnes and ignorance unto God," Eliot's first audience was told, "and mourne for it, and acknowledge how just it is, for God to deny them the knowledge of Jesus Christ or any thing else because of their sinnes." And

although they did not yet know how to pray, they could at least
"sigh and groane and say thus; Lord make mee know Jesus
Christ, for I know him not." To aid their understanding of the
problem, Eliot's first sermon ran "through all the principall matter of religion, beginning first with a repetition of the ten Com-
mandments, and a briefe explication of them, . . . and so ap-
plyed it unto the condition of the *Indians* present, with so much
sweet affection."[56]

In recounting his first successful series of lessons—consisting
of sermons, question-and-answer sessions, and prayers—Eliot
emphasized his listeners' strong emotional responses. Near the
end of a particularly long meeting, he

> prepared to pray in their own language, and did so for a quarter of
> an houre together, wherein divers of them held up eyes and hands
> to heaven; . . . but one of them I cast my eye upon, was hanging
> downe his head with his rag before his eyes weeping; at first I
> feared it was some sorenesse of his eyes, but lifting up his head
> againe, having wiped his eyes (as not desirous to be seene) I
> easily perceived his eyes were not sore, yet somewhat red with
> crying; and so held up his head for a while, yet such was the
> presence and mighty power of the Lord Jesus on his heart that hee
> hung downe his head againe, and covered his eyes againe and so
> fell wiping and wiping of them weeping abundantly, continuing
> thus till prayer was ended, after which hee presently turnes from
> us, and turnes his face to a side and corner of the Wigwam, and
> there fals a weeping more aboundantly by himselfe.

An Englishman's two attempts to offer sympathy only provoked
new outbursts of tears. Finally, Eliot noted, "wee parted greatly
rejoicing for such sorrowing."[57] The next day another listener
came to Eliot, "wept exceedingly, and said that all that night
the Indians could not sleepe, partly with trouble of minde, and
partly with wondring at the things they heard preacht among
them."[58] After the next meeting two Indians came to Eliot, one
confessing "how wickedly he had lived, and with how many
Indian women hee had committed filthinesse, and therefore professed that he thought God would never look upon him in
love." Eliot reassured him that if he would give himself to Jesus
Christ, he would be shown mercy, "whereupon he fell a weep-

ing and lamenting bitterly, and the other young man being present and confessing the like guiltinesse with his fellow, hee burst out also into a great mourning, wherein both continued for above halfe an houre together at that time also.''[59] "If by a little measure of light such heart-breakings have appeared," Eliot asked after his third service at Nonantum, "what may wee thinke will bee, when more is let in?" "There is," he concluded, "the greater hope of great heart-breakings.''[60]

Eliot's hopes were realized during the conversion experiences of Indians in the years following. Relations of these experiences repeated the themes of renunciation of one's past and the need to be reborn as a Christian. . . .

These accounts contrast sharply with those of contemporary English conversions in at least two important respects. One is their lack of intellectual content. There is no indication that the converts understood either the Word, except as it applied to themselves, or the most basic tenets of Puritan theology. Nor is there any indication, in the face of most Indians' inability to read in either language, that the missionaries expected their saints' conversion experiences to measure up to those of the English in this respect. Perhaps not consciously intended so by Eliot, this difference could only confirm the gap between the two peoples in the eyes of most white Puritans. Also unlike whites, Indians had to reject their ethnic and cultural identity before converting. As Eliot told one audience, "Indians forefathers were stubborne and rebellious children . . . and hence Indians that now are, do not know God at all.''[61] Many of the converts responded by denouncing their parents for worshipping Indian deities and for heeding the powwows.[62]

The converts were especially vulnerable because their breakdowns constituted an abandonment of traditional Indian personality patterns. Although Eliot noted that some Indians were "naturally sad and melancholloy (a good service to repentance),'' New England Algonquians generally were "well known not to bee much subject to teares, no not when they come to feele the sorest torture, or are solemnly brought forth to die.''[63] It seemed that sadness, melancholia, and a propensity for tears were peculiar to Indians who converted. Although "the power of the Word" seemed to be the chief cause of conversion, the Reverend Thomas Shepard acknowledged the importance of a more relevant factor: "that mean esteem many of them have of themselves, and therefore will call themselves sometimes *poore Creatures,* when they see and heare of their great distance from the English."[64] Like the Oglala Sioux observed by Erik Erikson, the Algonquians who converted were those whose communal integrity had been compromised step-by-step—from the plague of 1616 to the treaties of political submission—and whose sources of collective identity and individual social stature had been destroyed.[65] The hostility arising from the humiliation and deprivation experienced at the hands of the English was turned inward, so that the converts blamed themselves and their culture for their failures. This "mean esteem . . . of themselves" was the price of admission to the missionaries' favor and, hopefully, to individual and cultural revival.[66]

One pattern in the praying Indians' religious behavior suggests that they may have sought, albeit unconsciously, to invest the imposed religion with traditional meaning. A strict adherence to external forms and rules, along with the limited intellectual content, indicates that they treated church services much as rituals in which the medium, more than the content, was the message. What is striking in accounts of praying Indian church services is not the theological proficiency of the converts but the enthusiastic participation of all—young and old, male and female—in catechizing, psalm-singing, praying, and other activities in which the members acted together or responded in predictable fashion.[67] When the pattern was broken and the individual was alone, in the conversion experience, he or she broke down. But even the relating of conversion experiences quickly acquired a uniform, repetitive quality. . . .

The formation of a praying Indian congregation was the ultimate goal in establishing a praying town. For its realization, several publicly related conversion experiences had to be approved by a group of elders. Beginning in 1652 Eliot unsuccessfully sought, through several carefully rehearsed days of confession, to have the Natick congregation certified.[68] In 1659 a compromise was finally reached. That "both Magistrates, Elders, and others" participated in the decision indicated its gravity for the colony as a whole. Before establishing a separate Indian church, the group concluded, the outstanding Indian candidates "should (for a season) be seasoned in Church fellowship, in communion with our English Churches." As for which church they would attend, "all with one mouth said that [Eliot's] Roxbury church was called of God to be first in that service of Christ to receive the praying Indians." After still another confession hearing, eight praying Indians were admitted to the Lord's Supper by a reluctant Roxbury congregation. Finally in 1660, nearly a decade after the founding of Natick—a decade in which some Indians had made half a dozen or more tear-filled public confessions of their past sins and present repentance—approval for the Natick congregation was finally granted.[69]

By 1660 the praying Indians' position within the Puritan church was apparent. The judges' reluctance signified the white population's distrust of the Indians and, perhaps, lack of confidence in the missionaries.[70] But the Natick congregation's delayed acceptance did not effect a tightening of standards so as to bring Indian conversions into greater uniformity with English ones. Such was not its purpose. Rather the whole process, including its duration, was a reminder that an Indian church required special supervision and was not a full member of the fellowship of New England congregations.[71] The "lower" standards prevailing for Indian conversions reinforced this point, and the elders' repeated insistence that the candidates lay bare their souls for judgment further confirmed the utter powerlessness of the Christian Indians.

The minority of Indians who converted to Christianity were responding to the crisis posed by English expansion into their lands. By the mid-1670s, the crisis had attained proportions which no tribe could continue to ignore.[72] Except for the Mohegans and the earlier converts, most Indians in southern New England joined in opposing the English in King Philip's War. Ironically, the war brought not only the defeat of the hostile Indians but the end of the missionary program as conceived by Eliot.

The settlers' latent distrust of the praying Indians flared as soon as the fighting began in the summer of 1675. Accusations of treason were hurled at the converts and, on some occasions, at the missionaries and their white supporters.[73] To be sure, there was foundation for some of the accusations. Most of the western Nipmucs, with less than five years' exposure to Christianity and geographically positioned to choose sides, opted to join the uprising.[74] But the accusers drew no distinctions, with the result that all Indians professing loyalty to the English cause were rounded up and placed on wind-swept Deer Island without adequate food and shelter.[75] As the English continued to flounder on the battlefield in the following spring, some Christian Indians were finally allowed to serve in the militia, especially as scouts. Their contributions were crucial in bringing about the eventual victory of the colonists.[76]

The praying Indians' military contributions did not lead to any new recognition of Indian rights and humanity. On the contrary, the war spelled the end of all remaining Indian autonomy in southern New England. Under terms of a 1677 law, those Indians who had not been killed, sold into slavery, or driven northward as a result of the war were physically restricted to one of the four remaining praying towns. The towns were no longer havens for those making conscious commitments to Christianity; they were reservations for an entire native population, now reduced, mostly as servants and tenant farmers, to a state of complete dependency on the English. Onto the lands formerly occupied by the Indians, both friendly and hostile, moved an onslaught of English settlers.[77]

If Eliot is judged in terms of the goals he set for himself, he must surely be accounted a failure. He had set out to transform the Indians into "civilized" saints. But the outbreak of war and the Nipmuc defection demonstrated that he had obtained a hold on only a few hundred of the several thousand Indians of Massachusetts Bay.[78] Even these could hardly be said to have lived up to his expectations. Yet Eliot's failure was of his own making. He demanded that Indians no longer be Indians, which most New Englanders of both races recognized as impossible and absurd. This simplistic vision led him to assume that the colonization of the Indians was merely a step toward their "civilization." In the end the reverse proved true. Eliot had provided the postwar government with a precedent for the waging of cultural warfare and for the management of a powerless minority.

Notes

1. In the case of 17th-century New England, even anti-Puritan writers have excluded the missionaries from their criticisms. See James Truslow Adams, *The Founding of New England* (Boston, 1921), 345n, and Herbert Wallace Schneider, *The Puritan Mind* (Ann Arbor, Mich., 1958), 38–41. The only exception in this century has been Vernon Louis Parrington, *Main Currents in American Thought, I: The Colonial Mind, 1620–1800* (New York, 1927), 84.

2. Berkhofer, *Salvation and the Savage: An Analysis of Protestant Missions and American Indian Response, 1787–1862* (Lexington, Ky., 1965), and Jennings, "Goals and Functions of Puritan Missions to the Indians," *Ethnohistory,* XVIII (1971), 197–212.

3. John Eliot to Jonathan Hammer, May 19, 1652, in Rendel Harris, ed., "Three Letters of John Eliot and a Bill of Lading of the 'Mayflower,' " *Bulletin of the John Rylands Library,* V (1918–1920), 104. See also *New Englands First Fruits* . . . (London, 1643), reprinted as Appendix D in Samuel Eliot Morison, *The Founding of Harvard College* (Cambridge, Mass., 1935), 421. *The Day-Breaking, if not the Sun-Rising of the Gospell with the Indians in New-England* (1647), reprinted in Massachusetts Historical Society, *Collections,* 3d Ser., IV (1834), 15, hereafter cited as *Day-Breaking;* Thomas Shepard, *The Clear Sun-Shine of the Gospel. Or An Historicall Narration of Gods Wonderfull Workings upon sundry of the Indians* . . . (1648), reprinted *ibid.,* 50, hereafter cited as Shepard, *Clear Sun-Shine;* Thomas Birch, *The Life of the Honourable Robert Boyle* (London, 1744), 320.

4. For a complete discussion of the matrix see Neal Salisbury, "Conquest of the 'Savage': Puritans, Puritan Missionaries, and Indians, 1620–1680" (Ph.D. diss., University of California, Los Angeles, 1972), *passim.* A differ-

ent approach can be found in Alden T. Vaughan, *New England Frontier: Puritans and Indians, 1620–1675* (Boston, 1965); he defends Puritan policy and argues that the consequences for the Indians were unavoidable, but makes little attempt to examine Puritan motives and actions critically.

5. While there were significant differences between Eliot's program and those of Martha's Vineyard and Plymouth, all Puritan missionaries worked within the basic consensus outlined here. See Salisbury, "Conquest of the 'Savage,' " chaps. 5–6. For some of the differences see *ibid.,* 172–175, 199, and Jennings, "Goals and Functions," *Ethnohistory,* XVIII (1971), 199–201.

6. Nathaniel B. Shurtleff, ed., *Records of the Governor and Company of the Massachusetts Bay in New England* (Boston, 1853–1854), I, 17, hereafter cited as Shurtleff, ed., *Mass. Bay Records;* "General Observations" in Allyn B. Forbes, ed., *Winthrop Papers* (Boston, 1929–1947), II, 118; Francis Higginson, *New Englands Plantation, with the Sea Journal and Other Writings* (Salem, Mass., 1908), 59, 107; [John White], *The Planters Plea. Or the Grounds of Plantations Examined, and usuall Objections answered . . .* (1630), in Peter Force, comp., *Tracts and Other Papers Relating Principally to . . . the Colonies in North America, from the Discovery of the Country to the Year 1776* (Washington, D.C., 1836), II, no. 3, pp. 7–31.

7. *New Englands First Fruits,* 421–431; Edward Hawes to John Winthrop, Jr., Mar. 26, 1632, in Forbes, ed., *Winthrop Papers,* III, 74; J. Franklin Jameson, ed., *Johnson's Wonder-Working Providence, 1628–1651,* Original Narratives of Early American History (New York, 1910), 79–80; James Kendall Hosmer, ed., *Winthrop's Journal: "History of New England," 1630–1649,* Original Narratives of Early American History (New York, 1908), II, 69; Roger Williams, *A Key into the Language of America,* ed. J. Hammond Trumbull in *The Complete Writings of Roger Williams,* 1 (New York, 1964 [orig. publ. Providence, R.I., 1874], 86–87.

8. Hosmer, ed., *Winthrop's Journal,* II, 134–136. The only recent published account of the Pequot War is Vaughan, *New England Frontier,* chap. 5, but see Francis Jennings, "The Invasion of America: Myths and Strategies of English Colonialism in the Conquest of the Indians" (MS.), chaps. 9–10. On early English-Narragansett relations see John A. Sainsbury, "Miantonomo's Death and New England Politics, 1630–1645," *Rhode Island History,* XXX (1971), 111–123, and Jennings, "Invasion of America," chap. 11. On the relationship of these events to the beginnings of missionization see Jennings, "Goals and Functions," *Ethnohistory,* XVIII (1971), 198–207.

9. Shurtleff, ed., *Mass. Bay Records,* II, 55, and Jennings, "Goals and Functions," *Ethnohistory,* XVIII (1971), 202.

10. Shurtleff, ed., *Mass Bay Records,* III, 6–7.

11. *Ibid.*, II, 134. For English criticism, see W[illiam] C[astell], "A Petition of W. C. Exhibited to the High Court of Parliament" (1641), in Force, comp., *Tracts,* I, no. 13, pp. 3, 9–11, and Thomas Lechford, *Plain Dealing: or, Newes from New-England. A Short View of New-Englands present Government, both Ecclesiasticall and Civil . . .* (1642), reprinted in Mass. Hist. Soc., *Colls.,* 3d Ser., III (1833), 90–93.

12. *Day-Breaking,* 3. For a complete discussion of the earlier session see Jennings, "Goals and Functions," *Ethnohistory,* XVIII (1971), 203–204.

13. Shurtleff, ed., *Mass. Bay Records,* II, 166, 176–179.

14. Eliot, *The Christian Commonwealth: Or, the Civil Policy of the Rising Kingdom of Jesus Christ* (1660), reprinted in Mass. Hist. Soc., *Colls.,* 3d Ser., IX (1846), 127–164, hereafter cited as Eliot, *Christian Commonwealth.*

15. Henry Whitfield, *The Light Appearing More and More Towards the Perfect Day. Or, A Farther Discovery of the Present State of the Indians in New-England, Concerning the Progresse of the Gospel amongst them* (1651), reprinted *ibid.*, 3d Ser., IV (1834), 131, hereafter cited as Whitfield, *Light Appearing.* See also Eliot, *Christian Commonwealth,* 135.

16. John Eliot, *A Late and Further Manifestation of the Progress of the Gospel amongst the Indians in New-England . . . Being a Narrative of the Examinations of the Indians, about their Knowledge in Religion* (1655), reprinted in Mass. Hist. Soc., *Colls.,* 3d Ser., IV (1834), 271, and Eliot to Hammer, May 19, 1652, in Harris, ed., "Three Letters of Eliot," *Rylands Lib. Bulletin,* V (1918–1920), 104–105.

17. "An Account of Indian Churches in New-England, in a Letter Written A.D. 1673 by Rev. John Eliot, of Roxbury," Mass. Hist. Soc., *Colls.,* 1st Ser., X (1809), 128.

18. Daniel Gookin, *Historical Collections of the Indians in New England* (1674), reprinted in Mass. Hist. Soc., *Colls.,* 1st Ser., I (1792), 177, hereafter cited as Gookin, *Historical Collections.*

19. William H. Whitmore, ed., *The Colonial Laws of Massachusetts . . . to 1672* (Boston, 1889), 163; Shurtleff, ed., *Mass. Bay Records,* IV, pt. i, 334; pt. ii, 34; Gookin, *Historical Collections,* 177–178; "Account of Indian Churches," Mass. Hist. Soc., *Colls.,* 1st Ser., X (1809), 128–129; Frederick L. Weis, "The New England Company of 1649 and its Missionary Enterprises," Colonial Society of Massachusetts, *Publications,* XXXVIII (1947–1951), 204–206; Yasu Kawashima, "Legal Origins of the Indian Reservation in Massachusetts," *American Journal of Legal History,* XIII (1969), 43–44.

20. *Day-Breaking,* 20–21.

21. Shepard, *Clear Sun-Shine*, 39–40.

22. John Eliot and Thomas Mayhew, Jr., *Tears of Repentance: Or, A Further Narrative of the Progress of the Gospel amongst the Indians in New-England* (1653), reprinted in Mass. Hist. Soc., *Colls.*, 3d Ser., IV (1834), 227, hereafter cited as Eliot and Mayhew, *Tears of Repentence*, and Gookin, *Historical Collections*, 181. For prehistoric dwellings and residential patterns see Williams, *Key*, ed. Trumbull, in *Writings of Williams*, 121; Gookin, *Historical Collections*, 149–150; Charles C. Willoughby, *Antiquities of the New England Indians with Notes on the Ancient Cultures of the Adjacent Territory* (Cambridge, Mass., 1935), 289–292; E. J. C. Brasser, "The Coastal Algonkians: People of the First Frontiers," in Eleanor Burke Leacock and Nancy Oestreich Lurie, eds., *North American Indians in Historical Perspective* (New York, 1971), 65; Harold E. Driver, *Indians of North America*, 2d ed. (Chicago, 1969), 124. On the effects of this change cf. Willian N. Benton, "Toward the Gradual Civilization of the Indian Natives: The Missionary and Linguistic Work of Asher Wright (1803–1875) among the Senecas of Western New York," American Philosophical Society, *Proceedings*, C (1956), 574.

23. John Eliot, *A further Account of the progress of the Gospel Amongst the Indians in New-England: being a Relation of the Confessions made by several Indians . . .* (London, 1660), 65; Shepard, *Clear Sun-Shine*, 46, 59; Gookin, *Historical Collections*, 152; Samuel Eliot Morison, *Builders of the Bay Colony*, rev. ed. (Boston, 1964), 300. For aboriginal clothing see Thomas Morton, *The New English Canaan* (1637), ed. Charles Francis Adams, Jr. (Boston, 1883), 141–145, and Willoughby, *Antiquities*, 279–281.

24. Gookin, *Historical Collections*, 153. For the uses of bear's grease see John Josselyn, *New-Englands Rarities Discovered* (1672), reprinted in American Antiquarian Society, *Transactions and Collections*, IV (1860), 149, and Nicholas N. Smith, "Wabanaki Uses of Greases and Oils," *Bulletin of the Massachusetts Archaeological Society*, XXI (1960), 19–20.

25. Shepard, *Clear Sun-Shine*, 58. See also "Account of Indian Churches," Mass. Hist. Soc., *Colls.*, 1st Ser., X (1809), 126.

26. Puritan accounts are strangely silent on praying town economic life, and this area needs much further research. For an ethnologist's findings on one activity see Frank G. Speck, *Eastern Algonkian Block-Stamp Decoration: A New World Original or an Acculturated Art* (Trenton, N.J., 1947), 30–32.

27. Gookin, *Historical Collections*, 189–196, and Vaughan, *New England Frontier*, 202.

28. Gookin, *Historical Collections*, 147–149, 179, 187; Frederick Webb Hodge, ed., *Handbook of American Indians North of Mexico*, Bureau of American Ethnology Bulletin 30 (Washington, D.C., 1907–1910), I, 816; II, 40–41, 74, 225, 344–345; Frank G. Speck, *Territorial Subdivisions and*

Boundaries of the Wampanoag, Massachusett, and Nauset Indians, Indian Notes and Monographs, no. 44 (New York, 1928), 88–122. John R. Swanton, *The Indian Tribes of North America,* Bureau of American Ethnology Bulletin 145 (Washington, D.C., 1952), 17–23; Vaughan, *New England Frontier,* 56, 195–196, 251–253, 291, 299; Laurence K. Gahan, "The Nipmucks and Their Territory," *Bulletin of the Mass. Archaeol. Soc.,* II (1941), 2; Charles Edward Beals, Jr., *Passaconaway in the White Mountains* (Boston, 1916).

29.   George W. Ellis and John E. Morris, *King Philip's War* (New York, 1906). Cf. Susan L. MacCulloch, "A Tripartite Political System among Christian Indians of Early Massachusetts," *Kroeber Anthropological Society Papers,* no. 34 (Spring 1966), 71.

30.   Speck, *Territorial Subdivisions,* 103. On the seizure of land for the establishment of Dorchester see Francis Jennings, "Virgin Land and Savage People," *American Quarterly,* XXIII (1971), 526–528.

31.   Shurtleff, ed., *Mass. Bay Records,* II, 55.

32.   Vaughan, *New England Frontier,* 189, and Yasu Kawashima, "Jurisdiction of the Colonial Courts over the Indians in Massachusetts, 1689–1763," *New England Quarterly,* XLII (1969), 532–534.

33.   Cf. Palmer Patterson, "The Colonial Parallel: A View of Indian History," *Ethnohistory,* XVIII (1971), 1–17.

34.   Whitfield, *Light Appearing,* 140–141.

35.   Henry Whitfield, *Strength out of Weaknesse; Or a Glorious Manifestation of the Further Progresse of the Gospel among the Indians in New-England* (1652), reprinted in Mass. Hist. Soc., *Colls.,* 3d Ser., IV (1834), 173, hereafter cited as Whitfield, *Strength out of Weaknesse,* and Vaughan, *New England Frontier,* 266. Cutshamekin had long been a target of Eliot's efforts, but was an inconsistent Christian before 1652. See Shepard, *Clear Sun-Shine,* 53–54, 55, and Edward Winslow, *The Glorious Progress of the Gospel, amongst the Indians in New England . . .* (1649), reprinted in Mass. Hist. Soc., *Colls.,* 3d Ser., IV (1834), 81, hereafter cited as Winslow, *Glorious Progress.*

36.   Gahan, "Nipmucks and Their Territory," *Bulletin of the Mass. Archaeol. Soc.,* II (1941), 2; Frank G. Speck, "A Note on the Hassanamisco Band of Nipmucks," *ibid.,* IV (1942–1943), 49; Hodge, ed., *Handbook of Indians,* II, 74; Swanton, *Indian Tribes,* 23.

37.   Whitfield, *Light Appearing,* 139.

38. Winslow, *Glorious Progress*, 81, and Shurtleff, ed., *Mass. Bay Records*, III, 365–366; IV, pt. i, 210.

39. Willoughby, *Antiquities*, 229, 278; Speck, *Territorial Subdivisions*, 16–30, 32–33; A. L. Kroeber, *Cultural and Natural Areas of Native North America*, University of California Publications in American Archaeology and Ethnology, XXXVIII (Berkeley, 1939), 143–145, 147, 150, 220; Brasser, "Coastal Algonkians," in Leacock and Lurie, eds., *North American Indians*, 65–66; William A. Ritchie, "Prehistoric Settlement Patterns in Northeastern North America," in Gordon R. Willey, ed., *Prehistoric Settlement Patterns in the New World*, Viking Fund Publications in Anthropology, no. 23 (New York, 1956), 76–77, 79–80; James B. Griffin, "The Northeast Woodlands Area," in Jesse D. Jennings and Edward Norbeck, eds., *Prehistoric Man in the New World* (Chicago, 1964), 255.

40. Speck, *Territorial Subdivisions*, 9–11, 16–32; Wendell S. Hadlock, "War Among the Northeastern Woodland Indians," *American Anthropologist*, N.S., XLIX (1947), 204–221; Anthony F. C. Wallace, "Political Organization and Land Tenure among the Northeastern Indians, 1600–1830," *Southwestern Journal of Anthropology*, XIII (1957), 306–307; Kroeber, *Cultural and Natural Areas*, 147–150. Cf. T. J. C. Brasser, "Group Identification along a Moving Frontier," 38th International Congress of Americanists, *Proceedings*, II (1968), 261–265.

41. For Massasoit see William Hubbard, *A Narrative of the Troubles with the Indians in New-England* (1677), ed. Samuel G. Drake as *The History of the Indian Wars in New England from the First Settlement to the Termination of the War with King Philip in 1677*, I (Roxbury, Mass., 1865), 47–48, hereafter cited as Drake, ed., *Indian Wars in New England*, and Winslow, *Glorious Progress*, 81. For Uncas see Gookin, *Historical Collections*, 192–193, 208–209; John Eliot to William Steele, Oct. 10, 1652, in "Letters of the Rev. John Eliot, the Apostle to the Indians," *New England Historical and Genealogical Register*, XXXVI (1882), 294; Whitfield, *Light Appearing*, 140.

42. See the statement by Metacom and his council on the eve of the war as related in John Easton, "A Relacion of the Indyan Warre" (1675), in Charles H. Lincoln, ed., *Narratives of the Indian Wars, 1675–1699*, Original Narratives of Early American History (New York, 1913), 10. See also Cotton Mather, *Magnalia Christi Americana; or The Ecclesiastical History of New-England; From its First Planting, in the Year 1620, unto the Year of Our Lord 1698* (1702), ed. Thomas Robbins (Hartford, Conn., 1855), I, 566; Ellis and Morris, *King Philip's War*, 23–24; Douglas Edward Leach, *Flintlock and Tomahawk: New England in King Philip's War* (New York, 1958), 21; George D. Langdon, Jr., *Pilgrim Colony: A History of New Plymouth, 1620–1691* (New Haven, Conn., 1966), 158.

43. *New Englands First Fruits*, 427, and Hosmer, ed., *Winthrop's Journal*, II, 69.

44. *Day-Breaking,* 22.

45. "Account of the Indian Churches," Mass. Hist. Soc., *Colls.,* 1st Ser., X (1809), 127–128.

46. Whitfield, *Light Appearing,* 143, and David Pulsifer, ed., *Acts of the Commissioners of the United Colonies of New England, 1643–1651, 1653–1679* (Boston, 1859), II, 122, 140.

47. John W. Ford, ed., *Some Correspondence between the Governors and Treasurers of the New England Company in London and the Commissioners of the United Colonies* . . . (London, 1897), 20; and Kellaway, New England Company, 218.

48. "Account of Indian Churches," Mass. Hist. Soc., *Colls.,* 1st Ser. X (1809), 126–127.

49. Edmund S. Morgan, *The Puritan Family: Religion and Domestic Relations in Seventeenth-Century New England,* rev. ed. (New York, 1966), chap. 4, and James L. Axtell, "The School upon a Hill: Education and Society in Colonial New England" (MS.), chaps. 1, 3–4.

50. Cf. Claude Levi-Strauss, *The Savage Mind* (Chicago, 1966), *passim.*

51. Pulsifer, ed., *Acts of the Commissioners,* II, 217, 261–263, and *Day-Breaking,* 22.

52. *New Englands First Fruits,* 423, and Gookin, *Historical Collections,* 219.

53. Pulsifer, ed., *Acts of the Commissioners,* II, 251, and Kellaway, *New England Company,* 108–109.

54. Gookin, *Historical Collections,* 183.

55. "Account of Indian Churches," Mass. Hist. Soc., *Colls.,* 1st Ser., X (1809), 126–127.

56. *Day-Breaking,* 4, 5.

57. *Ibid.,* 13–14.

58. *Ibid.,* 14.

59. *Ibid.,* 18. Cf. Whitfield, *Strength out of Weaknesse,* 182.

60. *Day-Breaking,* 17.

61. *Day-Breaking,* 10. See also Shepard, *Clear Sun-Shine,* 55.

62. Eliot, *Further Account,* 57, 71.

63. *Day-Breaking,* 17, and Shepard, *Clear Sun-Shine,* 60. See also A. Irving Hallowell, "Some Psychological Characteristics of the Northeastern Indians," in his *Culture and Experience* (Philadelphia, 1955), 132–133.

64. Shepard, *Clear Sun-Shine,* 41.

65. Erik H. Erikson, *Childhood and Society,* 2d ed. (New York, 1963), 153–154.

66. Cf. Robert N. Rapoport, "Changing Navaho Religious Values: A Study of Christian Missions to the Rimrock Navahos," *Papers of the Peabody Museum of American Archaeology and Ethnology,* XLI, no. 2 (1954), 52–56, 71–77.

67. Shepard, *Clear Sun-Shine,* 45, 51–52; Whitfield, *Strength out of Weaknesse,* 190; Gookin, *Historical Collections,* 169, 183.

68. Eliot and Mayhew, *Tears of Repentance,* 227–228, 243–245, 271–286.

69. Eliot, *Further Account,* 1–2, and *passim,* and Vaughan, *New England Frontier,* 269. Only one further Indian congregation was certified before the outbreak of war in 1675—at Hassanamesitt, or Hassanamisco, in 1671. See "Account of Indian Churches," Mass. Hist. Soc., *Colls.,* 1st Ser., X (1809), 124, and Gookin, *Historical Collections,* 185.

70. Cf. Kellaway, *New England Company,* 90.

71. Eliot wrote in 1654 that "in Church estate and affaires of ecclesastical polity they come on but slowly but in these matters they doo as they are ordered and guided by counsel, and not according to theire owne notions." Eliot to Hammer, June 29, 1654, in Harris, ed., "Letters of Eliot," *Rylands Lib. Bulletin,* V (1918–1920), 109.

72. Leach, *Flintlock and Tomahawk,* 14–22.

73. Mary Pray to James Oliver, Oct. 20, 1675, in the *Winthrop Papers,* Mass. Hist. Soc., *Colls.,* 5th Ser., I (1871), 106; Daniel Gookin, *An Historical Account of the Doings and Sufferings of the Christian Indians in New England* (1677), reprinted in Am. Antiq. Soc., *Trans. and Colls.,* II (1830), 455–467, 471–475, 482, 491–492, hereafter cited as Gookin, *Historical Account.* N[athaniel] S[altonstall], "The Present State of New-England with Respect to the Indian War" (1675) in Lincoln, ed., *Narratives of Indian*

Wars, 40–41; Drake, ed., *Indian Wars in New England*, I, 48–49, 95–96; "Letters of John Eliot the Apostle," Mass. Hist. Soc., *Proceedings*, XVII (1879–1880), 252; Birch, *Life of Boyle*, 434–435; *Records of the Suffolk County Court, 1671–1680* (Colonial Society of Massachusetts, *Publications*, XXIX–XXX [Boston, 1933]), II, 695–697; Leach, *Flintlock and Tomahawk*, 84–85, 148–151; Morrison Sharp, "Leadership and Democracy in the Early New England System of Defense," *American Historical Review*, L (1944–1945), 259.

74.   S[altonstall], *Present State of New-England*, 32–33; Gookin, *Historical Account*, 436; Leach, *Flintlock and Tomahawk*, 86–87, 100; Kellaway, *New England Company*, 116.

75.   Shurtleff, ed., *Mass. Bay Records*, V, 64, 84; "Letters of Eliot the Apostle," Mass. Hist. Soc., *Procs.*, XVII (1879–1880), 252; Gookin, *Historical Account*, 450–451; Leach, *Flintlock and Tomahawk*, 150–151.

76.   Gookin, *Historical Account*, 441–442; Increase Mather, *A Brief History of the War with the Indians in New-England* (1676), ed. Samuel G. Drake as *The History of King Philip's War* (Albany, N.Y., 1862), 143; Drake, ed., *Indian Wars in New England*, I, 178; Leach, *Flintlock and Tomahawk*, 152–153.

77.   Shurtleff, ed., *Mass. Bay Records*, V, 136–137; "Indian Children Put to Service, 1676," *New Eng. Hist. and Gen. Reg.*, VIII (1854), 270–273; Kawashima, "Legal Origins," *Am. Jour. of Legal Hist.*, XIII (1969), 44–45; Leach, *Flintlock and Tomahawk*, 245–246. For similar laws in the other Puritan colonies see Shurtleff and Pulsifer, eds., *Plymouth Records*, V, 203, 210; XI, 242–243, 252–255, and J. Hammond Trumbull, ed., *The Public Records of the Colony of Connecticut from 1665 to 1678 with the Journal of the Council of War, 1675 to 1678* (Hartford, Conn., 1850–1890), II, 285–286, 440; III, 309–311.

78.   Indian population figures can only be extremely speculative due to the lack of hard evidence. This statement is based on the estimates in Gookin, *Historical Collections*, chap. 7, and Leach, *Flintlock and Tomahawk*, 1–2.

Legal Origins of the Indian
Reservation in Colonial Massachusetts

Yasu Kawashima*

*The patterns of racial interaction which characterize modern
America often have deep historical roots. For example, the reservations on which many Indians live today had their origins not as
commonly supposed in the Indian wars of the nineteenth century,
but in events which occurred two centuries before that. In "Legal
Origins of the Indian Reservation in Colonial Massachusetts,"
Yasu Kawashima clearly shows that the reservation system began
in the seventeenth century as a creation of the forces discussed by
Neal Salisbury in the previous article. Despite the unsavory
effects of the reservation system, Kawashima argues that it
"served well not only as a useful means of regulating the natives
within the colony but also to protect the Indian land as the
minimum economic unit necessary for the Indians as a group."
Kawashima is a member of the History Department at the University of Texas at El Paso; among his publications are articles in the*
New England Quarterly *and the* Journal of Social History.

THE SYSTEM OF INDIAN reservations has its origins in the colonial period. In New England, as in some other regions of British
North America, the reservation, known commonly as "Indian

*Yasu Kawashima, "Legal Origins of the Indian Reservation in Colonial Mas-
sachusetts," *American Journal of Legal History* 13 (1969), 42–56. Reprinted by
permission.

plantation," "Indian village," or "Praying town," developed as an integral part of the entire colonial policy toward the Indians. In the process of the colonial expansion in Massachusetts, some of the natives were overrun and placed either in the reservations or in the English communities, while others were pushed farther westward or northward, still maintaining themselves as independent tribes on the border. By the turn of the seventeenth century, however, by far the greatest number of the natives were already living on the reservations scattered throughout the colony.[1] Consequently, the reservation had become a political, economic, and cultural center for the Indians and thus played a preponderant role in Indian-white relations during the colonial period.

Various attempts have been made to explain the reservation in New England. According to Roy H. Akagi, who regards the reservation strictly as a colonial device toward the management of Indian land, there were four distinct stages in its development. The first stage was the recognition and protection of Indian right and property; the second stage, the establishment of some kind of protectorate over the Indians; the third, the reservation or plantation for the exclusive use of the natives; and the last stage, the organization of Indian proprietors.[2] Ronald O. MacFarlane and others conceive the problem in a wider perspective and portray the reservation more broadly as an Indian community.[3] Beyond what has been observed on this subject, however, much remains to be done in order to comprehend the whole picture of the reservation. The present study is an attempt to give deeper insights into the colonial objectives and the nature of the Indian village in Massachusetts, mainly through the examination of colonial legislation.

The policy of confining the Indians to certain specific areas started in the early seventeenth century, when attempts were made, through the influence of John Eliot and the encouragement of the colonial government, to establish the Indian villages that were to be occupied by natives who had been converted to Christianity. Finally in 1652, the General Court passed an act providing that "if, upon good experience, there shall be a competent number of the Indians brought on the civilitie, as to be capable of a township upon their request unto the General Court, they shall have graunt of landes undisposed of, for a plantation, as the English have.''[4] During the 1650s the Indian villages increased so greatly in number and strength that the General Court in 1658 enacted to improve the village system with specific provisions for self-government. The colonial legislature provided that the Indian villages should choose their own magistrates, who would hear and determine all minor cases, civil and criminal, arising among the Indians. The native magistrates were given with their own villages exactly the same authority as that of the English counterparts. Moreover, the Indian magistrates were authorized to join together to constitute a higher court with jurisdiction comparable to that of the County Court. To such a court one English magistrate was to be added who would appoint the time and place of the court and give consent to the decision of the Indian judges. Cases involving capital punishment of plantation Indians and "all other matters beyond their cognizance" were to be heard before the Court of Assistants.[5] By the outbreak of King Philip's War, the progress of the "Praying villages" had been so remarkable that one such village, Natick, was actually given the title of "English town."[6]

King Philip's War, however, deeply affected all New England Indians, hostile and friendly, and marked a turning point in the development of the reservation. Both in Massachusetts and in Plymouth, the hope of the Praying villages was completely shattered, and the once promising reservations virtually became gatherings of what Frederick Jackson Turner calls "the broken fragments of Indians."[7]

Although the colonial policy regarding the Indians after the war did not contain the liberal plan of self-government, it nevertheless included a scheme for the Indian village. In May, 1677, the General Court of Massachusetts passed an act providing that all Indians who were permitted to live within the colony, "such as are called Praying Indians as well as others," should be confined to one of the four plantations of Natick, Punkapaug (Stoughton), Hassanimesit (Grafton), and Wamesit

(Chelmsford), with the exception of Indian children and servants living within the English communities.[8] Four years later the number of the Indian towns was reduced to three, and all Indians, except for apprentices and servants, were required to live in one of Natick, Punkapaug, and Wamesit, where sufficient land was available to all Indians in the colony. Those who violated the regulations and were found outside the reservations were to be sent to houses of correction or prisons.[9]

As the preamble of the law of 1677 significantly points out, the reservation after the war was reorganized in terms of the colony's peace and security. By stating that "The well-ordering and Settlements of those that remain, and are under Command, is a matter of great concernment to the peace and security of the Country," the law presented the foremost objective of the colony in administering the Indian reservation, considering "the welfare, and good education" of the Indians to be only secondary. The tighter regulations of the post-war period, therefore, made the previous Christian villages more secular.

Concerning jurisdictional problems of the reservation, however, the act of 1658, which had provided a large amount of "home rule" among the natives, did continue in effect in Massachusetts even after King Philip's War. Plymouth, before its incorporation into the Bay Colony in 1691, had also carried out a similar but more elaborate policy toward the Indian reservations.[10] Although little is known about the native courts, since the Indians kept few records, there is evidence from English sources that the colonists were much dissatisfied with the inadequate administration of justice by the natives.[11]

Thus in 1694, an act was passed "for the Better Rule and Government of the Indians in their Several Places and Plantations," which marked another turning point in the system of reservations in Massachusetts. Its fundamental principle, however, was basically the same as that of earlier laws. Designed to suppress drunkenness and other vices among the Indians on the plantations more effectively and to lead them hopefully into "civility and Christianity," the act empowered the governor, with the advice and consent of the Council, to appoint commissioners for the inspection and care of the plantation Indians. While the act provided nothing concerning the territorial problem of the reservation, it did set up many detailed rules to regulate the conduct of the natives. For instance, the law provided that any person selling liquor to an Indian was to be penalized forty shillings for every pint sold. When an Indian made an accusation of such a sale, if there were concurring circumstances, the guilt of the vendor was to be assumed. Any person could lawfully seize illegally possessed liquor from an Indian. Every Indian convicted of drunkenness was to be fined five shillings, or be publicly whipped not exceeding ten lashes.[12]

Under the act of 1694, the Indians on the reservations came under the jurisdiction of the white commissioners, who were authorized not only to exercise the power of justice of the peace over the Indians in all matters, civil and criminal, but also as the guardians of the Indians to handle all kinds of problems concerning the welfare of the village Indians. The governor was also given power to nominate and appoint constables and other necessary and proper officers among the Indians, who would assist the commissioners.[13] Based upon this act a number of white men were appointed during the early period of the eighteenth century.[14] The system proved to be highly effective in administering the Indian reservations, especially in handling legal matters. Although attempts were occasionally made to revise this act for more effective regulations,[15] it continued in use for fifty-two years until 1746, when finally superseded by another act.

The statute for "Better Regulating the Indians" of 1746, which found the laws in force becoming increasingly unsatisfactory for regulating the Indians on the reservations, in order to rule the reservations more effectively, provided that three persons should be appointed as guardians in each plantation of the colony. These officials, besides their proper powers as the justices of the peace, were authorized to lease the land not in use from the Indians so that the revenue could be used for the support of the Indian paupers. Once a year, the guardians were required to submit a report and their accounts to the General Court.[16] This act was to be effective for seven years until 1753, when it was renewed for another five years. In 1758 the act was once again renewed for another three years with a few minor changes. The preamble of the last act, "an Act in Addition to the several Acts for the Better Regulating the Indians," described the earlier act as "very beneficial to the Indians, and a further regulation is also necessary."[17]

Under the acts of 1746, 1753, and 1758, the justices came to be chosen by the General Court rather than by the governor as before and were to hold office during the continuance of the act under which they were appointed. In 1746, twenty-four guardians were selected altogether, three for each of the eight districts of Natick in Middlesex County; Stoughton in Suffolk County; Grafton in Worcester County; Yarmouth, Harvich, and Eastham in Barnstable County; Mashpee, Barnstable, Sandwich, and Falmouth also in Barnstable County; Plymouth, Pembroke, and Middleboro in Plymouth County; Martha's Vineyard; and Nantucket.[18] Although the powers of the guardians over the Indians were extensive, they were by no means absolute. A number of complaints had been directed to the General Court from the Indians against their own guardians, and in some instances the guardians were dismissed from the posts for their misconducts.[19]

On the whole, then, the system of Indian magistrates, which had originally been established to provide "home rule" in Indian villages, proved to be ineffectual as time went on and was finally abolished. The village Indians in the Provincial period consequently came to be placed under the control of white guardians. Although no colonial law provided any specific jurisdictional regulation for the plantation Indians, besides the power of the guardians, the practice of the ordinary courts reveals the general Massachusetts policy concerning such problems.

While there is no record of court cases in which the plantation Indians suspected of crimes in the white communities were actually sent back to their villages for trial, those who became involved in minor legal affairs at a place outside their reservations were tried by the regular justice of the peace of that region. For example, Nathaniel Harris, the justice of the peace in

Watertown in Middlesex County from 1734 to 1761, tried in 1737 an Indian, Samuel Abraham of Natick, who was charged with being drunk, found him guilty, and ordered him to pay a fine of ten shillings.[20] Reservation Indians were also placed under the jurisdiction of the two courts of the county in which they lived, which were directly above the justice of the peace and constituted the successor of the County Court of the seventeenth century. The Court of General Sessions of the Peace, with jurisdiction over criminal affairs, tried not only the individual Indians but also the natives on the reservations within the county. Similarly, the Inferior Court of Common Pleas handled all minor civil cases, including those involving the plantation Indians within that county.[21].

More serious cases involving the reservation Indians were tried before the highest court of the colony, the Superior Court of Judicature, as were those of the colonists themselves. This court, as a circuit court holding its sessions in nearly every county in the province at least once a year, heard various civil and criminal cases, both original and appellate, involving the plantation Indians.[22] Also, just as the rest of the colonial population, the plantation Indians charged with capital crimes came directly under the jurisdiction of the Court of Oyer and Terminer. This court was set up extraordinarily in various places in the colony to handle each specific case of capital crime, in order to obtain a more speedy execution of justice without the expense of the ordinary court procedure. Although this type of court was designed not only for the natives but for the whites as well, the Indian cases proportionally outnumbered those of the whites. Out of sixteen Courts of Oyer and Terminer held during the colonial period, eight courts were for the trials of Indian criminals, six of which were for those of reservation Indians.[23]

Such was the legal framework of the reservation in colonial Massachusetts. As we have seen, the colonial government started out to provide a great amount of autonomy, but, faced with the problem of maintaining the security of the colony more effectively, shifted its policy by putting more emphasis on control over the Indians on the reservation rather than on self-rule

among them. The fact that the colonial authorities did not provide any judicial system specifically for the Indian reservation,
except for the lowest level of the justice of the peace, seems to
indicate that the natives received almost equal jurisdictional
treatment to that of the whites. The colonial government in this
respect might have expected the eventual assimilation of the
natives.

In the administration of the reservation during the Provincial
period, the guardians were the most important officials in all
matters concerning the village Indians. They were not merely
the supervisors of the natives but were directly in charge of
Indian affairs within the reservations. The Indian officials, in
actuality chosen by the Indians themselves and confirmed by the
governor or by the General Court after 1746, did much routine
governing of their people under the direction of the guardians.
The records of the Indian town at Natick, for example, contain
numerous Indian names among the town officers during the
early part of the Provincial period.[24]

In addition to these officials on the reservations, the Superintendent of Indian affairs supervised all the reservations in
Massachusetts. Appointed by the General Court, he served as a
medium between the guardians of the Indians and the colonial
administration, and was to insure that the orders and acts concerning the natives were effectively carried out. In 1656, Daniel
Gookin became the first superintendent, holding the office for
thirty-one years until 1687, when he was succeeded by Thomas
Prentice, who held the office until 1709.[25]

The Indian reservation with such officials and governmental
structure should have naturally been regarded by the Massachusetts authorities as a useful device for controlling the Indians
and thus for keeping order within the colony. All colonial regulations concerning the reservation were, therefore, directed toward the preservation of the system. For this purpose, additional
rights and duties were imposed not only on the Indians but on
the colony as a whole. During King William's War and Queen
Anne's War, for example, special commissioners were appointed to protect Indian villages against the armed forces, to

notify all friendly Indians of their danger, to enlist as many natives as possible into military service, and to reward lands within reservations to those Indians who actually aided the colonists in the war.[26]

Even during peace time the reservations were protected against all kinds of encroachment. The "strange and foreign" natives who sometimes tried to establish themselves on the reservations were quickly ejected by the guardians or the native officers acting under the guardians.[27] The colonial authorities also endeavored, though not with complete success, to prevent any penetration of white settlers into the reservations.

In 1739, the Houssatonnoc Indians petitioned against one Elias Vanschoic, who molested and disturbed their land. The General Court, after a committee investigation, empowered the Inferior Court of Common Pleas of Hampshire County at Springfield to eject Vanschoic from the land, discreetly adding that if Vanschoic would give up the claim and leave the place quietly, he would be given "a full equivalent for two rights in the upper Housatonnock Town" or in some other unappropriated land in the province.[28] In a dispute between the towns of Dedham and Natick in the beginning of the eighteenth century, the General Court ruled that the Natick Indians should not be dispossessed of the land, based upon the reasoning that "although the legall right of Dedham thereto cannot in justice be denied, yet such have binn the incouragement of the Indians in their improvements thereof which, added to their native right, which cannot in strict justice be utterly extinct."[29]

The difficulty of the colonial government to prevent white squatters from encroaching upon the land in the reservation can be seen in a case of the Indian island of Chappaquiddick of Martha's Vineyard. It was reported that for a mere trifle, the squatters had purchased two thousand acres of valuable Indian land, erected nine houses, carried away five hundred cords of wood, and seized the Indian grazing and planting rights. In addition, these squatters secured more land by taking advantage of the Indians while they were gone for a whaling expedition. In 1761, the General Court took steps to prosecute the squatters, but without much success.[30] On the whole, however, it seems clear that Massachusetts at least tried hard to protect the Indian land from the encroachment of the squatters, although such policy was not always effective.

The selling of the land on the reservations led to more direct conflict with the preservation of the system. In 1737, for example, when one Jacob Lansing claimed a portion of the Houssatonnoc Indian land for the debt the Indians owed him, the General Court ordered him to purchase "an Equivalent in Lands elsewhere of the said Indians, he quitting his Pretensions to any Right in said Houssatonnoc." In order to prevent such problems in the future, the Court ordered public notice made to the effect that the government would not allow any person to purchase any of the Houssatonnoc Indian lands "without Leave first had thereof from the General Court."[31]

Transactions of reservation land between the natives themselves seem to have presented a more complicated problem. In 1738, when one of the Indian proprietors of the Hassanimisco plantation bequeathed his estate to his son, Antipas Brigham of Marlboro, the proprietors of the town petitioned the General Court that "order may be given by this Court for the effectual preventing such practices," because there were likely to occasion great inconvenience to the Hassanimisco proprietors. After an investigation by its committee, the General Court rejected the petition, and Antipas, nonresident of Hassanimisco, acquired a proprietor's right.[32] In another case, the petition of a Natick Indian, Joseph Ephraim, who claimed a proprietor's share of the Hassanimisco land based upon the fact that his father was an "Inhabitant or Proprietor of Hassanimisco" was rejected, but no clear explanation for this action was given.[33]

While Massachusetts carried out a consistent policy of territorial protection of the reservation, attempts were made to establish reservations with a plan for internal improvements. As early as 1735, the General Court empowered a three-man committee to establish a township for the Stockbridge Indians, not exceeding six miles square, and voted in the following year for building a meeting-house and school-house for the natives. Finally

Stockbridge was incorporated into an Indian town in 1739.[34] For another ten years, however, little progress was made. Thus in 1749, the General Court declared that "the Indians of the Housatonic Tribe, who were and have been settled as proprietors of lands within the township of Stockbridge, and their heirs and descendants, are and shall be distinct proprietary" and authorized Timothy Dwight to call a proprietors' meeting. After a careful investigation, Dwight ordered the division of land by which ten received eighty acres each, ten sixty acres, thirty-nine fifty acres, and one ten acres. Then the first meeting of the Indian proprietors was organized, and they managed their affairs under the supervision of the three guardians who were appointed by the General Court.[35]

Two years later, in order to speed up the progress of the town, the General Court voted £125 to be placed at the disposal of commissioners who had been appointed to investigate the reasons for tardy growth of the town. A survey was made of another tract of land four miles square, and any Indian who would remain for ten years on a hundred-acre lot was to be given title to it at the end of the term. One hundred acres were reserved for the use of a mission and two hundred acres for a school. A grant of £200 was to be made to the Society for Propagation of the Gospel in New England for a missionary and teacher among these Indians. Numerous committees were subsequently set up to consider ways and means of fostering the best interests of the town.[36]

Mashpee was another example of the so-called last stage of the colonial reservation, in which positive actions were taken for the welfare of the natives. In 1763, the General Court set aside "all the lands belonging to the Indians and mulattoes in Mashpee," wherein the natives were to be given a large part of the governing powers. The proprietors were empowered to meet annually in the public meeting-house to elect a moderator; five overseers, two to be Englishmen; a town clerk and treasurer, both English; two wardens; and one or more constables. The overseers had the power to regulate the fisheries in the district, to apportion to the Indians their lands and meadow, and to lease

such lands and fisheries as well held in common for a period not
exceeding two years.[37]

The experiments in Stockbridge and Mashpee then were quite
different from the other reservations, in which the whites controlled the activities of the Indians. For the first time since King
Philip's War, the reservations in Stockbridge and Mashpee were
beginning to enjoy a measure of autonomy as well as internal
improvements. But such were the exceptions. The majority of
the Indian reservations in the colonial period were under the
strict supervision of the white guardians, although the natives
enjoyed the exclusive territorial rights within their villages.

The native villages, even those that acquired considerable
autonomy, did not constitute, however, the "townships" of
colonial Massachusetts. The case of Stockbridge well illustrates
this fact. In the town election of 1763, Stockbridge was fairly
evenly divided between Indians and whites, with twenty-nine
Indian voters. But the natives lost the election only by three
votes and protested that the voting was unfair. After a careful
study of the situation by its committee, the General Court declared the election legal but recommended separation of the
Indians and the whites, so they could have separate elections.[38]
Nor did any reservation at any time send its representatives to
the General Court. Therefore, it is reasonable to assume that the
Indian reservations were outside the political divisions of the
colony and thus did not attain the status of township, the basic
political and territorial unit in colonial Massachusetts.

Although the Indians enjoyed many rights within their villages as the white men did in their respective towns, the natives
on the reservations as well as those in the whites' communities
were placed under some special regulations not applied to the
whites. The restrictions on selling of the land and regulations on
liquor are cases in point. Nor was the reservation during the
Provincial period economically self-sufficient. It was not uncommon for reservation Indians during the Provincial period to
work as day-laborers in the neighboring white communities.[39]
In the early seventeenth century, when the reservation encompassed a vast area, the natives were entirely self-sufficient on

account of their hunting, fishing, and farming. But as time went on, the situation became increasingly difficult, because the amount of Indian land diminished. The Stockbridge experiment, as we have seen above, was kept going only by constant support of the colonial government, but even with such subsidies, the town could hardly support itself successfully.[40]

As the name "Praying village" connotes, Christianity was much involved with the Indian reservation, particularly in the early part of the seventeenth century. Even in the later period, the role of the missionaries was by no means negligible. They not only propagated Christianity among the natives but also contributed to the orderly administration of the reservation. However, it cannot be claimed that the reservation in Massachusetts was strictly religious. Nor did the educational program established on the various reservations make much progress in benefiting the natives.[41]

Even for the native residents themselves, the reservation system might have been quite ambiguous and precarious, since the Indian traditions and customs were considerably modified on the reservations in accordance with the colonial needs. Before King Philip's War, Indian plantations were mostly based upon the tribal unit, but later reservations became more mixed in tribal composition. For example, Indian villages of Mashpee, Stockbridge, and Martha's Vineyard did, at one time or another, receive many natives of different tribes from outside.[42] Moreover, the population on the reservations during the Provincial period was constantly diminishing, while an increasing number of intermarriages between the natives and the whites or the Negroes took place within the reservation, undermining the uniquely Indian characteristics of the reservation.[43] Under such circumstances, the Indian plantations were in many respects simply turning into convenient living communities for the Indians and other minority groups.

It is difficult to determine exactly when the reservation system was terminated in Massachusetts. As late as 1861, there were still many Indian villages, such as Chappaquiddick, Gay Head, Mashpee, Herring Pond, Natick, Punkapaug, and Hassanimisco, although they had by then lost their importance as reservations as originally intended in the colonial period.[44] It can be said with certainty, however, that the Massachusetts reservation system began to deteriorate rapidly during the Revolutionary period. The act of 1758, "an Act in Addition to the several Acts for the Better Regulating the Indians," was to continue only for three years and does not appear ever to have been renewed. Furthermore, during the 1750s and 1760s, the General Court granted a great number of petitions by Indian proprietors to sell portions of their lands to the whites, a practice that tended to accelerate the colonists' penetration into the Indian reservations.[45]

In Natick, one of the most promising Indian towns in the early colonial period, the names of Englishmen were beginning to appear as town officers by 1734, the Indians were definitely a minority by 1764, and the natives lost their identity in the town by 1781, when Natick was incorporated as an English town.[46] The Indian village in Stockbridge, too, became merely part of the English town, when the General Court recommended, in the disputed town election of 1763, separation of the Indians and the whites so they could have separate elections. In Mashpee, the act of 1763, which provided a large amount of the governing power to the natives, was to be effective for only three years. Although the Indians continued to choose their own overseers under the act of 1763 even after it had expired, another act was passed in 1788 that reversed the situation and put the Indians and their land under strict supervision. By this time the native village had become only a component part of the Mashpee township.[47]

Such, then, was the nature of the Indian reservation in colonial Massachusetts. The reservation was not an integral part in the political system of the colony, because it came to be administered directly by the colonial government through the guardians, and few reservations attained the status of the English township. No doubt the reservation contained certain political, economic, and cultural elements, but its character cannot be clearly defined. This vagueness in colonial objectives concerning the reservation seems to indicate that the Massachusetts authorities did not intend the system to be permanent. The legislation enacted during most part of the period under review was mainly intended to utilize the reservation as a means to rule the dependent Indians in an orderly and effective manner.

Thus, all things considered, it seems probable that Massachusetts in some way or another expected the eventual assimilation of the Indians into the whites' society, and consequently, the gradual extinction of the Indian villages. The colonial government, which did not formulate any enduring judicial, political, or cultural policies concerning the reservation, might have regarded the reservation only as a preparatory step toward the assimilation of the natives. The policies, as seen most clearly in the colonists' attitude toward the reservation land, instead, tended to be negative in that the colony preserved the institution only as long as its existence continued to be necessary. By the time the United States inaugurated the federal reservation policy for the Indian tribes in 1786, the Massachusetts system of reservations had already served its purpose and virtually come to an end. It is a mistake, however, to conclude that the system in the Bay Colony was a failure. In spite of its limited scope, the Massachusetts reservation system nevertheless served well not only as a useful means of regulating the natives within the colony but also to protect the Indian land as the minimum economic unit necessary for the Indians as a group.

Notes

1. James Mooney, *The Aboriginal Population, North of Mexico*, 3 (1928); S. N. D. North, ed., *A Century of Population Growth from the First Census of the United States to the Twelfth, 1790–1900*, 158–162 (1909); Joseph B. Felt, *Statistics of Population in Massachusetts*, 142, 192, 195–196 (1845); Stella H. Sutherland, *Population Distribution in Colonial America*, 32–33 (1936); Evarts B. Greene and Virginia D. Harrington, *American Population before the Federal Census of 1790*, 15 (1932).

2. Roy H. Akagi, *The Town Proprietors of the New England Colonies*, 38–44 (1924).

3.   One of the earliest studies on the Indian reservation can be found in
James A. James, *English Institutions and the American Indian,* 19–22 (1894).
The best résumé of the reservation is Ronald O. MacFarlane, "Indian Relations in New England, 1620–1760: A Study of a Regulated Frontier" (Ph.D.
dissertation, Harvard University, 1933), 261–298, in which he discusses
many important aspects of the reservation including legislative and administra-
tive problems. Two most recent books on the Indian relations in colonial New
England, Alden T. Vaughan, *New England Frontier: Puritans and Indians,*
1620–1675 (1965) and Douglas E. Leach, *The Northern Colonial Frontier,*
1607–1763 (1966) briefly touch upon the Indian reservation. While Vaughan
emphasizes its religious aspect, Leach tries to grasp the reservation in terms of
the colonial land policy and the policy to maintain the peace and security.

4.   Nathaniel B. Shurtleff, ed., *Records of the Governor and Company of*
the Massachusetts Bay in New England, 1628–1686, v. 3, p. 381 (1853–
1854); Samuel E. Morison, *Builders of the Bay Colony,* 294–300 (1964).
Also in Plymouth in 1658, the authorities agreed to a system for setting aside
lands for the exclusive use of the Indians. Nathaniel B. Shurtleff and David
Pulsifer, eds., *Records of the Colony of New Plymouth in New England,*
v. 10, p. 199 (1855–1861).

5.   William H. Whitmore, ed., *The Colonial Laws of Massachusetts, Re-*
printed from the edition of 1660, with the supplements to 1672, 77 (1889).

6.   MacFarlane, (note 3), p. 265; William Biglow, *History of the Town of*
Natick, 28, 33, 45 (1830).

7.   Frederick Jackson Turner, *The Frontier in American History,* 46 (1920).

8.   Whitmore, ed., (note 5), p. 77.

9.   Whitmore, ed., (note 5), p. 289.

10.   Shurtleff and Pulsifer, eds., *Plymouth Records,* (note 4), v. 11, p. 253.

11.   Franklyn Howland, *A History of Town of Acushnet, Bristol County,*
State of Massachusetts, 259 (1907); Hugo A. Dubuque, *Fall River Indian*
Reservation, 46 (1907); Alexander Starbuck, *The History of Nantucket,*
County, Island and Town, 130–131 (1924); MacFarlane, (note 3), pp. 561–
562; *Massachusetts Archives,* v. 30, p. 353. Archives Division, State House,
Boston; *Dukes County Court Records,* v. 1 (1665–1715). This volume is not
bound in an orderly fashion. See the section for 1696 and 1697. Office of the
Clerk of the Courts, Duke County Court House, Edgartown, Mass.

12.   *Acts and Resolves, Public and Private, of the Province of the Massachu-*
setts Bay, v. 1, p. 150–151 (1869–1922).

13. *Acts and Resolves, Mass. Bay,* v. 1, p. 150; v. 11, pp. 147, 283, 343–344; v. 13, p. 597; v. 15, p. 286; MacFarlane (note 3), p. 283.

14. Massachusetts Executive Council, *Minutes,* v. 3, p. 366; v. 4, p. 43; v. 6, p. 475; v. 7, pp. 340, 369. Archives Division, State House, Boston; *Acts and Resolves, Mass. Bay,* v. 11, p. 147.

15. *Journals of the House of Representatives of Massachusetts, 1715 – 1761,* v. 2, p. 89.

16. *Acts and Resolves, Mass. Bay,* v. 3, pp. 306–307.

17. *Acts and Resolves, Mass. Bay,* v. 3, p. 679; v. 4, pp. 163– 164.

18. *Acts and Resolves, Mass. Bay,* v. 3, pp. 306– 307, 341; v. 4, pp. 163–164; v. 15, p. 110; v. 16, p. 241.

19. *House Journals (Mass.)* v. 31, pp. 113– 115, 118, 212, 277; *Acts and Resolves, Mass. Bay,* v. 13, p. 326; v. 14, pp. 52, 314; v. 15, pp. 121, 222; v. 16, p. 221; *Mass Archives* (note 11), v. 30, p. 405.

20. *Records of the Court of Nathaniel Harris, One of His Majesty's Justices of the Peace Within and for the County of Middlesex, Holden at Watertown, From 1734 to 1761,* 48–49 (1893).

21. *Records of the Court of General Sessions of the Peace of Plymouth County, 1719–1723,* pp. 55– 56, *1730–1749,* p. 148. Office of the Clerk of the Courts, Plymouth County Court House, Plymouth, Mass.; *Dukes County Court Records* (note 11), v. 1, see the section for the year of 1699; *Records of the Inferior Court of Common Pleas of Plymouth County, 1702–1773,* p. 348; *1727–1732,* p. 465; *1749–1755,* p. 489. Office of the Clerk of the Courts, Plymouth County Court House, Plymouth, Mass.

22. Such cases are recorded in *Records of the Superior Court of Judicature, 1686–1700,* pp. 19, 36, 93–94; *1700–1714,* pp. 92, 165, 234, 242; *1715–1721,* pp. 210, 215; *1721–1725,* pp. 104– 105; *1725–1729,* p. 106; *1725–1730,* pp. 124– 125; *1730–1733,* p. 120; *1740–1745,* p. 136; *1760–1762,* p. 189; *1763–1764,* pp. 48–49, 51, 52– 53. Office of the Clerk of the Supreme Judicial Court, Suffolk County Court House, Boston.

23. *Acts and Resolves, Mass. Bay,* v. 1, p. 12; Carroll D. Wright, *Report on the Custody and Condition of the Public Records of Parishes, Towns, and Counties,* 308– 309 (1889); Mass. Executive Council (note 14), v. 2, pp. 176– 177, 196, 419, 501, 569– 570; v. 3, pp. 494; v. 4, pp. 30, 479; v. 5, p. 526; v. 6, pp. 44, 631; v. 10, p. 644; v. 11, pp. 54, 652.

24. MacFarlane (note 3), at p. 265.

25.   Shurtleff, ed., *Records of the Mass. Bay* (note 4), v. 4, Part 1, p. 334; Frederick L. Weis, "The New England Company of 1649," Colonial Society of Massachusetts *Publications*, v. 38, pp. 204–206 (1959).

26.   *Mass. Archives* (note 11), v. 30, pp. 315a, 316a, 479; v. 63, p. 601; Mass. Executive Council (note 14), v. 2, pp. 249, 284; *Acts and Resolves, Mass. Bay*, v. 8, p. 56; MacFarlane (note 3), pp. 279–280.

27.   Shurtleff and Pulsifer, eds., *Plymouth Records* (note 4), v. 11, pp. 128, 183; MacFarlane (note 3), at p. 274.

28.   *Acts and Resolves, Mass. Bay*, v. 12, pp. 582–583; *Mass. Archives* (note 11), v. 31, p. 241; *House Journals* (note 15), v. 12, p. 181.

29.   Shurtleff, ed., *Records of the Mass. Bay* (note 4), v. 4, Part 2, p. 49.

30.   Mass. Executive Council (note 14), v. 16, p. 8; *Essex Gazette*, March 22, 1774; Ralph H. Records, "Land as a Basis for Economic Social Discontent in Maine and Massachusetts to 1776" (Ph.D. dissertation, University of Chicago, 1936), 195.

31.   *House Journals (Mass.)*, v. 14, pp. 220–221, 225; *Acts and Resolves, Mass. Bay*, v. 12, p. 332.

32.   *House Journals (Mass.)*, v. 16, pp. 103, 126; *Acts and Resolves, Mass. Bay*, v. 12, p. 494.

33.   *House Journals (Mass.)*, v. 13, p. 80.

34.   *Acts and Resolves, Mass. Bay*, v. 2, p. 991; v. 12, pp. 245–246, 332; *Mass. Archives* (note 11), v. 31, p. 244.

35.   *House Journals (Mass.)*, v. 15, pp. 70–72; *Acts and Resolves, Mass. Bay*, v. 7, pp. 130, 190, 251, 318, 320, 322; Akagi, *op. cit. supra*, note 2, at pp. 42–43.

36.   *Acts and Resolves, Mass. Bay*, v. 14, pp. 488–489, 567; *Mass. Archives* (note 11), v. 32, pp. 11, 12, 119, 203–212, 218–221; MacFarlane (note 3), at p. 294.

37.   *Acts and Resolves, Mass. Bay*, v. 4, pp. 639–640; William Apes, *Indian Nullification of the Unconstitutional Laws of Massachusetts, Relating to the Mashpee Tribes; or The Pretended Riot Explained*, 144–145 (1835).

38.   *Mass. Archives* (note 11), v. 33, pp. 256–257; *Acts and Resolves, Mass. Bay*, v. 17, p. 500; Robert E. Brown, *Middle-Class Democracy and the Revolution in Massachusetts, 1691–1780*, 42 (1955).

39. See, for example, *Records of the Inferior Court of Common Pleas of Plymouth County, 1702–1773*, pp. 57, 107, 348; *Records of the Court of General Sessions of the Peace of Plymouth County, 1719–1723*, p. 57.

40. *Acts and Resolves, Mass. Bay*, v. 14, pp. 597–598; v. 15, pp. 120, 122, 239.

41. MacFarlane (note 3), at p. 296.

42. John R. Swanton, *The Indian Tribes of North America*, 19–27 (1952); Frederick W. Hodge, ed., *Handbook of American Indians North of Mexico*, v. 1, p. 707; v. 2, p. 903 (1907–1910).

43. *Boston Weekly Post Boy*, Sept. 14, 1741; "Plymouth Church Records, 1620–1854," Colonial Society of Massachusetts *Collections*, v. 33, pp. 492–493; "Records of Boston Selectmen, 1701–1715," *Report of the Record Commissioners of the City of Boston*, v. 11, p. 226 (1876–1909); "A Description of Duke's County, Aug. 13, 1807," Massachusetts Historical Society *Collections*, Second Series, v. 3, pp. 93, 95; Carter Woodson, "The Relations of Negroes and Indians in Massachusetts," 4 *Journal of Negro History*, 50, 56 (1920); Lorenzo J. Greene, *The Negro in Colonial New England, 1620–1776*, 199 (1942).

44. *Massachusetts Documents Printed by Order of the Senate, 1861*, No. 96.

45. See, for example, *House Journals (Mass.)*, v. 29, pp. 21–22, 54, 60, 70, 140, 170; v. 30, pp. 16, 110–111, 129; v. 33, Part 1, pp. 197–198; v. 34, Part 1, p. 129; v. 35, pp. 353–354; v. 37, Part 2, pp. 180, 219, 351.

46. Biglow (note 6), pp. 28, 33, 45; MacFarlane (note 3), p. 265; Vaughan (note 3), p. 321.

47. *Mass. Archives* (note 11), v. 33, pp. 256–257; *Acts and Resolves, Mass. Bay*, v. 27, p. 500; Apes (note 37), pp. 144–145.

Indian Slavery

John Donald Duncan*

Whites not only tried to deculturate Native Americans, to incarcerate them on reservations, and to exterminate them in wars, they also used Indians as an unwilling source of labor. In the following article John Donald Duncan investigates Indian slavery in South Carolina, the only British North American colony to make extensive use of the labor of Native Americans. Indian slavery flourished during South Carolina's early years, but after 1719, the institution declined as South Carolinians turned to Africa for slaves. This happened "because the sources of supply dried up after protracted warfare climaxing in the Tuscarora War of 1711–1713 and the Yemassee War of 1715– 1717." Also, a decline in births and smallpox epidemics reduced the Indian population in South Carolina. Duncan teaches history at Armstrong State College. His doctoral dissertation written at Emory University explored "Servitude and Slavery in Colonial South Carolina, 1670–1776." He has published arti- cles in American Chronicle *and* Civil War Times Illustrated.

OF ALL THE BRITISH CONTINENTAL colonies South Carolina appears to have been "preeminent in the use and exportation of Indian slaves."[1] Several of the early travel accounts noted that

*Abridged from John Donald Duncan, "Indian Slavery," in "Servitude and Slav- ery in Colonial South Carolina, 1670–1776." Unpublished Ph.D. dissertation, Emory University, 1971, pp. 1–41. Reprinted by permission.

the Indians themselves practiced slavery, and the Spaniards perfected the institution in the West Indies and later on the mainland. Ironically among the earliest surviving laws of Carolina is a temporary law, probably 1671, that provided that "Noe Indian upon any occasion or pretense whatsoever is to be made a Slave, or without his owne consent to be car[r]ied out of our Country."[2] Soon the colonists and eventually the Proprietors themselves disregarded these rules.

Thus the Grand Council on September 27, 1671, citing theft of corn, night raids on the outlying plantations, conspiracy with the Spaniards to destroy Charlestown and withdrawal "from that familiar correspondence with our people," ordered "that an open War shall be forthwth. prosecuted against Kussoe Indians and their Coadjutors." Commissions were granted to two captains and Stephen Bull was ordered to take into custody "two Kussoe Indians now in this Towne."[3] Seemingly this was a strong case against the Kussoes, but at least one student has observed that "it would be interesting to hear their side of the story."[4] Actually, this first Indian War in Carolina was "hardly more than a raid," and five days later the Grand Council was ordering "every company who went out upon that expedition shall secure & maintaine the Indians they have taken till they can transport the sd Indians; but if the remaining Indians doe in the meane time come in and make peace and desire the Indians now prisoners, then the sd Indians shall be sett at liberty having first put such a ransome as shall be thought reasonable by the sd grand councill to be shared equally among the company of men that tooke them."[5] Transportation meant sale to the West Indies or the Northern colonies. The ransom, no doubt, was set at the market price of the Indians. In either case, the captors had nothing to lose. Unfortunately the fate of the captives is not known but a momentous precedent had been established. From that time onward there were to be exceptions to the prohibition against enslaving or exporting Indians.

In July of 1672, on a rumor that the Westoes were lurking at Sewee some thirty men were dispatched to intercept them.[6] In September of the following year the Council again ordered an expedition "to march against the said Indians to kill and destroy them, or otherwise to subject them in peace."[7] The outcome of these expeditions is not known, but it seems probable that if any Westoes were taken captive they were ransomed or sold as slaves.[8]

There were also other sources of Indian slaves. In July of 1674 the Grand Council was "credibly informed that the Indian Stonoe Casseca hath endeavoured to confederate certaine other Indians to murder some of the English Nation, and to raise in Rebellion against this settlement."[9] One student has pointed out that as only ten men were dispatched to settle the matter, "it could not have been a serious conspiracy."[10] In August of the same year the Grand Council authorized an expedition to pursue the Kussoe Indians who had reportedly murdered three Englishmen and "to take or destroy all or any of them, the whole matter being left to their advisement."[11] Apparently the method of circumventing the prohibition against enslavement and exportation of Indians was to rely on the interpreters, for as the minutes of the Grand Council stated:

> Mr. John Boon the English Interpreter, and Capt: Titus the Indians Interpreter came voluntarily before the Grand Councill and did declare that the Indian pr[i]soners which the Sowee and other [of] our Neighbour Indians have lately taken, are the Enemies to the said Indians who are in Amity with the English, and that the said Indian pr[i]soners are willing to worke in this Countrey, or to be transported from hence, upon which It is Conceived that the said Indian pr[i]soners may be transported by any who have or shall purchase them.[12]

The Proprietors were the next to offend. In an attempt to avoid "injuries, provocations, frauds & quarrels" all trade with the distant Indians was reserved to the Proprietors. Thus in October of 1674, Henry Woodward as agent for the Proprietory monopoly, made contact with the warlike Westoes along the Savannah River region and they promptly agreed to furnish the English with deer skins, furs and young slaves.[13] It is interesting to note that the temporary laws of 1671 and the agrarian laws of June 21, 1672,[14] prohibiting enslaving or exportation of

Indians were still on the statute books. Apparently, however, the Proprietors thought that allowing the Westoes to bring in distant Indians as slaves would not bring any "disagreeable complications," only "immediate profits."[15]

In 1680 the Proprietors considerably lessened their restrictions on the Indian slave trade. Specifically in May of that year they appointed a court "to hear and determine differences between the Christians and the Indians" with special instructions "to take speciall care not to suffere any Indian that is in League or friendly correspondence wth. us and that lives within 200 miles of us to be made slaves or sent away from the Country without speciall directions from us."[16]

Back in Carolina the Grand Council was informed on June 1, 1680, that the Westoes were killing and enslaving neighboring Indians[17] and sometime thereafter declared war upon that nation. Apparently the Charlestown government made no mention of this war to the Proprietors who, nevertheless, on February 21, 1681, wrote that they had been "informed you have had a war with the Westoes, but for what reason and the true & perticulr success hath ben we ignorant of And cannot but accuse you of great neglect."[18] Still later on a charge of intercepting an otherwise unidentified "boat of runawayes," the Carolina government confederated with the Savannah Indians in a war against the Winiah tribe.[19] In both cases the Westoes and Winiahs sent messengers to the Savannahs "to mediate for them," but they were intercepted and sold as slaves.[20]

In the meantime Governor Joseph West was replaced by Joseph Morton who was instructed by the Proprietors "to take all the Indians within 400 miles of Charles Towne in our protection as Subjects to the monarchy of England" and "not to suffer any of them to be made Slaves of."[21] One contemporary historian claimed that West was removed in part for "dealing in Indians," but later historians of Carolina have pointed out other reasons.[22]

Later the Proprietors took note of the three grounds of defense of the Charlestown government for enslaving and exportation of Indians, namely:

1 That the Savanas haveing united all their tribes are become powerfull that it is Dangerous to disoblige them.
2 That you have Warrs wth. the Waniahs, in wch. these people assist you.
3 That humanity Induceth you to buy their Slaves of them to keep them from being put to Cruell deaths.[23]

The Proprietors were in "no way satisfied" with these excuses and private letters they had received from Carolina told a different story. . . . [They] thought Governor Joseph West to be "a well meaning man" but one who had been "imposed on in this matter . . . to make this warr." Furthermore their consciences dictated that the Indian trade should not be allowed any longer. Only as an encouragement to soldiers in wartime or in other cases of absolute necessity "not at Present foreseen" could the traffic be tolerated.[24] . . .

Six weeks later the Proprietors wrote that Maurice Mathews and James Moore had "most Contemptuously disobeyed our orders about sending away of Indians" and had "contrived most unjust warr upon the Indians in order to the getting of Slaves & were contriveing new warrs for that purpose." This "sort of Insolent Disobedience could not be tollerated in our Deputyes wth. out rendring our Govermt. contemptible," and both men were ordered dismissed from the Grand Council.[25] . . .

In the fall of 1684 the Grand Council elected Joseph West to the governorship for a third time. Although the Proprietors had earlier reservations about him they were now "well pleased" with his election and even more so with his statement that the Indian dealers were "the great sticklers" against certain Proprietary election reforms which the Proprietors interpreted as a pledge "that you will not be swayed & governed by them as formerly." West was warned to appoint to office only "discreet sober Just & honest men and such as are affectionate to us." Men such as Maurice Mathews, James Moore and Arthur Middleton who had been removed from office "for disobeying our orders in Sending away the Indians" were not to be appointed to any office "untill We have some assurance of their better behaviour" and then only on the Proprietors' specific direction.[26]

In a 1685 letter to West and the Grand Council the Proprietors made some alarming observations, namely that

> the dealers in Indians bo[a]st they can wth. bole of punch get who they would chosen of the parliament and afterwards who they would chosen of the grand Councell, by which meanes they have heretofore gotten acts of parliamt. past that no man should sell armes &c to the Indjans upon penalty of forfiture of all his estate and perpetually punishment, which by Reason of their power in the grand Councell & parliament they caused to be observed by others but broak it themselves for their private advantage & escaped penalty.[27]

No longer could the punch bowl subvert their true meaning and intent. Thereafter Indian slaves were to be exported only in case of an actual Indian war, and "for the Incouragemt. of the English soldiers Imployed in that warr" the Commons House might allow soldiers "to make their best advantage of their prisoners."[28]. . .

Later in the year when the Proprietors realized that Mathews and Boone had been elected to the Grand Council and were still continuing to export Indians "not withstanding our soe often repeated orders to the Contrary," the new Governor Joseph Morton was directed to immediately dismiss the two from office. Furthermore, should they continue to violate the Proprietary rules, they were to be indicted and if found guilty were to receive appropriate punishment.[29]. . .

During the governorship of James Colleton the Proprietors made one last effort to suppress the Indian trade. In 1687, for example, blank deputations were sent out with the names of those who were "not for sending away the poor Indians" and those who were "affectionate to our Interests" to be filled in.[30] They were determined to break this "pnicious [,] Inhumane [,] barbarous practice wch. we are resolved to break [,] though In order to it Wee are forced to change all our officers there untill wee find men that will doe the thing."[31] That appears to have been their last gasp, for thereafter the Proprietors surrendered control of Indian affairs to the Carolinians.[32]

With a new administration of Seth Sothell beginning in 1690

the Carolinians passed the earliest surviving act "for Regulation
of the Indian Trade."[33] Unfortunately it has survived in title
only but that of September 26, 1691, established a monopoly of
the Indian trade for Sothell and his friends.[34] Eventually, however, Sothell was suspended from office and all laws passed
during his administration nullified.[35] His successor Phillip Ludwell found the Indian trade was "in a very great Disorder"
because of the skirmishes between the Indians and the white
traders.[36] Ludwell handled the affair well. All Indian traders
were ordered to remain in Charlestown, Indian chiefs were
brought to town for talks and no Indian was to be sent out on
any ship without a special license from Ludwell himself.[37]
When the chief of the Yemassee applied for the return of his
enslaved son, the Grand Council appropriated eight pounds currency to buy back the boy from one Phillip Mullins.[38] In October of 1692 Ludwell suggested to the speaker of the Commons
House that an act be passed "to hinder the shipping an Indians
out of the Province."[39] . . .

The Quaker Governor John Archdale was even more firmly
opposed to the Indian slave trade and, according to his own
account, he returned to Florida in 1695 four Spanish Indians
which the Yemassee had captured "about *Santa Maria*, not far
from *Augustine* . . designing to sell them for Slaves to Barbadoes or Jamaica as was usual."[40] . . .

In 1702 Governor James Moore got the Commons House to
vote an expedition against the Spaniards in Florida with "the
Encouragement to be free plunder and share of all Slaves."[41]
Later a representation of Assembly members from Colleton
County charged that the true design of the expedition was "no
other than catching and making slaves of *Indians* for private
advantage." Moore was also charged with granting commissions
to Anthony Dodsworth, Robert Mackbone and several others "to
set upon, assault, kill, destroy, & take as many *Indians* as they
possible [*sic*] could, the profit and produce of which *Indian*
slaves were turn'd to his private use." The representation further
charged that such "unjust and barbarous" undertakings would
"in all Probability draw upon us an Indian War."[42]

To recoup his fame and fortune Moore planned an even more elaborate expedition. According to his own account he raised at his own expense fifty white volunteers and with one thousand Indian allies the expedition set out for Apalachee about eighty miles west of St. Augustine in December of 1703. The first encounter was the "Strong and almost regular Fort" at Aya-vill[43] which was stormed at sunrise on January 14, 1704. After nine hours of fighting and a loss of three whites and four Indians the fort was taken. Moore's men had killed twenty men and had taken "26 Men alive and 58 Women and the Indians took about as many more of each Sort." The next day Moore and his men routed twenty-three Spaniards and some 400 Indians in a field battle.[44] One "particular account from our Indians" reported that 168 Indian men had been "killed and taken in the fight" and Moore later claimed that two hundred Indian men had been killed or captured.[45] Moore then swept through Apalache. One town made its peace but five others surrendered unconditionally. Moore obeyed his orders, as he put it, "to bring away with me, free, as many of the Indians as I can" but he complained that "the waiting for these people make my marches slow." Moore also claimed that he had not killed or enslaved a single Indian "but what were kill'd and taken in the Fight, or in the Fort I took by Storm."[46] An early report put the number of free Indians being brought to Carolina simply at 1,300,[47] and later Moore specifically claimed that he "brought away free 300 men and 1000 Women and Children."[48] The early source claimed that only 100 Indians were enslaved,[49] but Moore's later statement was that he had "kill'd and taken as Slaves 325 Men" and had "taken Slaves 4000 Women and Children."[50] As the expedition was financed through the sale of plunder and slaves and not by government appropriation, Moore could only lament that the free Indians, who were later settled on the Carolina frontier in the neighborhood of Savannah Town, "will make my men's part of plunder (which otherwise might have been 100£ to a man) but small."[51]. . .

The Charlestown government on July 19, 1707, provided a fine of sixty pounds currency for any Indian trader who confessed or was convicted by a jury of "selling any free Indian for a slave." If unable to pay his fine the trader was to receive "such corporall [sic] punishment as the judges of the general sessions . . . shall think fitt, not extending to life or limb." In addition such Indians illegally sold into slavery were declared free and their buyers were empowered to recover their purchase cost in a court of law.[52]

On February 14, 1708, the Charlestown government voted an expedition to enslave or destroy "the deserted Savannas or their confederates . . . with all the slaves and other plunder by them taken, to be proportionally divided." Indian allies were to be rewarded with one gun for every enemy Indian killed or captured. All slaves over twelve taken by Indians or whites were to be purchased by the commander of the expedition who was required to deliver them to the Public Receiver who in turn was to ship them off to the West Indies or sell them locally to anyone who posted bond so to do.[53] Unfortunately extant records do not appear to reveal the number of slaves taken during the expedition.

A little later in 1708 Indian agent Thomas Nairne claimed that "our Indian Subjects" had driven the Spanish Indians, or as he called them, the Floridians, to the islands of the cape and those "in quest of Booty" were now obliged "to goe down as farr on the point of Florida as the firm land will permitt." Reportedly they had already "brought in and sold many Hundreds of them, and Dayly now Continue that Trade so that in some years thay'le Reduce these Barbarians to a farr less number." Shifting his attention westward Nairne then noted that the Talapoosas or Upper Creeks and the Chickasaws were engaged in enslaving those French Indians in the Lower Mississippi region and that the high prices paid by the English traders encouraged them "to this trade Extreamly." Then, as if to disarm any forthcoming opposition, Nairne noted that "some men think it both serves to lessen their number before the French can arm them and it is a more Effectual way of Civilizing and Instructing, Then [sic] all the Efforts used by the French Missionaries."[54]

In 1703 Governor Nathaniel Johnson and His Majesty's

Council noted that Carolina traded with Boston, Rhode Island, Pennsylvania, New York and Virginia "to wch. places we export Indian slaves."[55] In 1710 it was also noted that South Carolina sent to New England, New York and Pennsylvania several commodities including "Slaves taken by the *Indians* in War."[56]. . .

The Tuscarora War of 1711–1712, although fought in North Carolina, brought many Indians to the southward to be sold as slaves. The conflict began rather quickly for as *The Boston News Letter* of November 26, 1711, reported, "the Cape Fear Indians had cut off about 20 Families of the Inhabitants" and "a party of English have been in pursuit of them and have kill'd and taken about 50." On learning of the news the South Carolina Assembly voted four thousand pounds for an expedition of about thirty whites and several hundred Yemassee and other Indians under the command of Colonel John Barnwell.[57] The campaign proved rather disappointing but before returning Barnwell "lured a large number of Indians to the vicinity of the Corree village near New Bern (and) permitted his own men to fall upon them unaware, capture many of them and hasten away to South Carolina to sell their victims into slavery."[58] From another source it is known that Barnwell's men killed between forty and fifty Indian men and took "near upon 200 of their women and children" as slaves.[59] The missionary at Goose Creek, Francis Le Jau, in his May 1712 report to the Bishop of London noted that the Yemassee had behaved "very well" in the Barnwell expedition and had "a great desire to have some Clergymen among them." However, Le Jau was so bold as to assert that the Indian traders had always discouraged such moves for "they do not care to have Clergymen so near them who doubtless would never approve those perpetual warrs they promote amongst the Indians for the onley [*sic*] reason of making slaves to pay for their trading goods." Moreover, the only slaves taken were "poor women and children; for the men taken prisoners are burnt most barbariously." At least this had been the case the year before when only "women and children were brought among us to be sold."[60]

Even more successful was a second expedition of 1712 sent out under the command of James Moore, Jr. "to bring those Murderers to due punishment . . . this is kill the Men and make the women and children Slaves."[61] *The Boston News Letter* of May 11, 1713, reported that Moore had with him "a few white men, and about 1200 Indians" and had in March of 1713 attacked the strongly fortified Indian Nehorookoh Port on Cokenneh Creek. Reportedly Moore had twenty-two of his men killed and "none of the English that are alive but had shot through their Cloath and others in their Bodies." In the end the English were triumphant for "on the Enemies side there were 640 kill'd, and we have taken 160 Prisoners and the Fort, so that we hope the heart of the Tuskeraro [sic] war is broken; the Indians have got a great many Slaves, but the white Men none."[62] *The Boston News Letter* of May 18, 1713, gave follow-up news. Under a New York dateline of May 11 it was claimed that Colonel Moore's forces had "wholly subdued" the Tuscarora Indians and had returned to South Carolina having killed or taken 800 Indians. Another item in the same paper from Philadelphia dated May 7 was more explicit in stating that Colonel Moore's forces had "totally reduced the Tuskarora Indians having kill'd abou[t] 500 and taken about 400 Prisoners, which they were Transporting to South Carolina in order to their being Sold for Slaves." Some may have been kept as slaves in South Carolina or at least their transportation was slow in occurring for it was reported that in the year following June 6, 1712, Carolina had exported only seventy-five Indians.[63] One student has claimed that no less than seven hundred Indians were enslaved during the Tuscarora War,[64] and another student has claimed at least eight hundred.[65] . . .

The Yemassee War of 1715–1717 brought many slaves to the Charlestown market. Thus *The Boston News Letter* of July 18, 1715, reported that from a sloop from South Carolina it has been learned that a Colonel Mackey "with a party of Men surprised a Body of Indians on a large Plain, kill'd near 30, and took above Forty Prisoners, most of which were sent for Jamaica." Francis Le Jau reported from Goose Creek in March

of 1716 that "Prince's father, head man of the Newaas, was
lately brought to our town by some of our men who surprised
him & his people in the town they were abuilding." Le Jau
believed that "his Men will be made Slaves but as for the old
man and his family" he had not heard "how they will be
disposed of."[66]. . .

The Yemassee War precipitated the passage of the Indian
Trading Act of June 30, 1716, which placed all Indian trade in
the hands of a public monopoly. Limited trading was permitted
among the Indians but it was hoped that eventually all trade
could be handled at three factories at Winyah, Congaree and
Savannah Town where the Indians might come to buy what they
wanted.[67] The public factors were first instructed "not to buy
any male Slaves, above the Age of fourteen years" and in no
case were they to knowingly buy "any free Indian, for a Slave,
or make a Slave of any Indian that ought to be free, that is to
say, Indians of any Nation that is in Amity and under the Protection of this Government." An appropriate brand was sent
each factor to mark "all Skins, Furrs and Slaves" and they
were instructed "to take the same Care of them, as if they were
your own private Interest."[68] Later the factors were instructed
to mark their slaves with gun powder and "not to inflict the
torture of a Brand on them." Apparently at the instigation of the
Commons House, the factors were "left at your Liberty to buy
at any Age not exceeding thirty Years."[69]

In Charlestown the board maintained a cashier and a store-
keeper who received and sold the public goods from the factors,
neighboring Indians and visiting delegations of Indians. In November of 1716 the board ordered that Colonel Theophilus
Hastings, chief factor to the Cherokee, be provided with
"Brands, Locks, Bolts, Shackles and such Necessaries as are
wanting . . . to provide the Publick's Goods, and Slaves when
bought in the Charikees."[70] A good investment it was for the
following year Hastings and thirty-one burdeners brought down
to Charlestown almost one thousand skins and twenty-one Indian slaves.[71]. . .

In the end the monopoly proved burdensome and lasted only

until 1719 and on a smaller scale until 1721.[72] Interestingly
enough, a group of English merchants engaged in the Carolina
trade petitioned the Board of Trade in 1720 to uphold the status
quo and requested that "none but deputies from the publick
should have power to buy Indian slaves from those Indians in
allaince with us as taken in warr, which deputies on the publick
acct. should be obliged to transport them to the Islands there to
be sold on conditions not to be sent to the contingent [*sic*]
again."[73] The Carolina Indian slave trade declined sharply
thereafter. . . .

As late as 1740 one commentator noted that "our Indians
sometimes sell the captured Spanish Indians to the Europeans as
slaves" but noted that "with them one cannot accomplish as
much as with the Negroes."[74] During the Cherokee War of
1760 *The South Carolina Gazette* of August 16, 1760, claimed
that the encouragement to be given for enlisting in a proposed
"regiment of 1000 to act against the Cherokees" was "greater
than has even been offered before in America." Included was
the provision that soldiers "will be entitled to 25£ bountymoney
for every Indian Man's scalp they take, and the property of
every Indian they take, will be vested as a slave, in the particular persons who take them."

If the records on the enslavement of Indians are skimpy and
sometimes confusing then the number or even percentage which
remained in Carolina or were imported into the province is even
more difficult to determine. Historians have long noted that
population statistics for the colonial period are inexact. Often-
time the colonial official deliberately exaggerated or understated
his statistics to strengthen some point. At other times the reports
were inaccurately based on the number of houses or families or
upon muster or militia rolls or upon poll or tax lists. Furthermore, more often than not slave population estimates gave no
breakdown between Indian and Negro slaves.[75]

Fortunately there were a few exceptions. Thus in 1724 the
missionary at Goose Creek estimated that his parish of St.
James had "about three hundred" white persons "f'm sixteen
to sixty" and "about two thousand Negroes & about an hundred

Slave Indians & as Near as can be guess'd fifty free Indian Families."[76] The reports of Thomas Hasell who served St. Thomas' Parish for a third of a century are even more revealing. In 1719 he estimated the slave population of his parish to be "between 8 and 900" Negroes and ninety-one Indians.[77] Ever thereafter his accounts show an increase in the number of Negro slaves and a corresponding decrease of Indian slaves. In 1720 there were "about 900 Negroes" and ninety Indian slaves[78] and in 1722 he estimated there were "Between 900 and 1000, Negroes and 90 Indian Slaves."[79] In 1725 the parish had "about 1600. Souls, besides a few Families of the Native Free Indians," specifically 128 families of 565 "free people or White, 950 Negro Slaves 62 Indian Slaves and about 20 free Negroes."[80] In 1725 Hasell reported his parish to have "abt. 950 Negro's & 60 Indian Slaves besides 16 free Negro's,"[81] but three years later there were about "1000 Negroes and 50 Indian Slaves, including Men Women & Children."[82] In less than ten years then the Negro slave population increased almost eighteen percent while the Indian slave population had decreased forty-five percent. In 1743, just before his death, Hasell estimated the Negro slave population of his parish to be 1,347. Either there were no Indian slaves in the parish or what is perhaps more likely the number was simply too small to note separately and may well have been included with "the Negroe Slaves."[83]

For the whole province there is a uniquely complete breakdown, namely that made by Governor Nathaniel Johnson and Council in 1708. Reportedly the province then contained 120 white servants and 3,960 free whites. There were 4,100 Negro slaves, that is, 1,800 men, 1,100 women and 1,200 children. Indian slaves totaled one-fourth of the total slave population or 1,400 with 500 men, 600 women and 300 children. Although these figures may have been fairly accurate they are perhaps misleading and Johnson and Council took note of the population changes that had occurred during the preceding five years. Specifically free white adults and white servants had decreased by 140 and eighty respectively but children had increased 500, a total increase then of 360. Negro slaves had increased by importation 500 and by natural increase 600, a total increase in the Negro slave population of 1,100. Furthermore, said the report, "Indian men slaves by Reason of our late Conquest over the French & Spaniards and the success of our Forces against the Appalaskye [Apalachees] & other Indian Engagemts. are within the Five years increased to the number of Four hundred & the Indian women slaves to four hundred and fifty . . . & Indian children to Two hundred."[84]

Some indication of the extent of Indian slavery is also given in the sale and runaway notices in *The South Carolina Gazette.* Thus in the ten years beginning in 1732, no less than four Indians, fifteen white servants and an estimated 3,343 Negroes were advertised for sale[85] and in the first twenty years of its existence the *Gazette* contained advertisements for the return of no less than fourteen Indians, 191 white servants and 679 Negro slaves.[86] Admittedly it is difficult to interpret these figures, but it seems obvious that by the 1730's Indian slavery had pretty much become a thing of the past in Carolina.

Apparently Indians were a sizeable percentage of the total slave population throughout the Proprietary period, but after 1719 Indian slavery began to decline. In the past many historians who have been influenced by the myth of the "noble savage" have explained this detail by emphasizing "the inability or refusal of the Indians to adjust to an existence so foreign to the ways of living of their people." In short "the culture of the Indian had made him a liberty loving individual, intolerant of restraint."[87] The great historian of South Carolina Edward McCrady practically dismissed Indian slavery by saying that the red men in bondage "pined, sickened, and died."[88] No such assertions can be made here. Much more likely slavery diminished because the source of supply dried up after protracted warfare climaxing in the Tuscarora War of 1711–1713 and the Yemassee War of 1715–1717. In addition an unexplained decline in the birth rate and epidemics, particularly smallpox, were contributing factors.[89] What Indians were kept as slaves in South Carolina appear to have been absorbed into the black community within a few generations.

Notes

1.   Almon Wheeler Lauber, *Indian Slavery in Colonial Times Within the Present Limits of the United States,* Studies in History, Economics and Public Law, Vol. LIV, No. 3, Whole No. 134 (New York, 1913), pp. 105–106, 240; Sanford Winston, "Indian Slavery in the Carolina Region," *The Journal of Negro History,* XIX (1934), 431, hereafter cited as Winston, "Indian Slavery," and M. Eugene Sirmans, *Colonial South Carolina, a Political History, 1663–1763* (Chapel Hill, 1966), p. 25, hereafter cited as Sirmans, *Colonial South Carolina.*

2.   W. J. Rivers, *A Sketch of the History of South Carolina* (Charleston, 1856), appendix, p. 353, hereafter cited as Rivers, *Sketch.*

3.   A. S. Salley, Jr., ed., *Journal of the Grand Council of South Carolina, 1671–1680 and 1692* (2 vols., Columbia, 1907), September 27, 1671, p. 8, hereafter cited as *South Carolina Grand Council Journal.* Manuscript Council journals from the South Carolina Archives are hereafter cited as SCCJ with appropriate South Carolina Archives citations.

4.   Anne King Gregorie, "Indian Trade of Carolina in the Seventeenth Century" (Unpublished master's thesis, Department of History, University of South Carolina, Columbia, South Carolina, 1926), p. 29, hereafter cited as Gregorie, "Indian Trade."

5.   *South Carolina Grand Council Journal,* October 2, 1671, p. 9.

6.   *Ibid.,* July 2, 1672, p. 38.

7.   *Ibid.,* September 3, 1673, p. 63.

8.   Gregorie, "Indian Trade," p. 29.

9.   *South Carolina Grand Council Journal,* July 25, 1674, p. 69.

10.   Gregorie, "Indian Trade," p. 29.

11.   *South Carolina Grand Council Journal,* August 3, 1674, pp. 69–70.

12.   *Ibid.,* December 10, 1675, p. 80.

13.   Gregorie, "Indian Trade," pp. 35–36.

14.   Rivers, *Sketch,* appendix, p. 358.

15.   Gregorie, "Indian Trade," p. 34.

16. "Instructions for the Commissioners appoynted to hear and determine differences between the Christians and the Indians," May 17, 1680, *Records in the British Public Record Office Relating to South Carolina* (5 vols., Atlanta and Columbia, 1928–1947), I, 99, hereafter cited as *S. C. Pub. Recs.* Volumes VI–XXXVI of *Records in the British Public Record Office Relating to South Carolina* were not published, but are available on microfilm and are hereafter cited as S. C. Pub. Recs.

17. *South Carolina Grand Council Journal,* June 1, 1680, p. 84.

18. Proprietors to Grand Council, February 21, 1681, "not sent but altered," *S. C. Pub. Recs.,* I, 104–115.

19. Proprietors to Governor, Grand Council and Parliament, September 30, 1683, *ibid.,* I, 256.

20. *Ibid.,* IV, 257.

21. Proprietors to Joseph Morton, [May 10, 1682], *S. C. Pub. Recs.,* I, 141–142.

22. J. Oldmixon, "The History of Carolina: Being an Account of That Colony, Originally Published in the History of the British Empire in America," B. R. Carroll, ed., *Historical Collections of South Carolina, Embracing Many Rare and Valuable Pamphlets, and Other Documents, Relating to the History of That State, from Its First Discovery to Its Independence, in the Year 1776* (2 vols., New York, 1836), II, 407, hereafter cited as Carroll, *Historical Collections.* David Duncan Wallace, *South Carolina, a Short History, 1520–1948* (Chapel Hill, 1951), p. 38; hereafter cited as Wallace, *South Carolina.*

23. Proprietors to Governor, Grand Council and Parliament, September 30, 1683, *S. C. Pub. Recs.,* I, 255.

24. *Ibid.,* I, 259–261.

25. Proprietors to Seth Sothell, November 6, 1683, *ibid.,* I, 266–267.

26. Proprietors to Joseph West, March 13, 1685, *ibid.,* II, 27–30.

27. Proprietors to Joseph West and Grand Council, March 13, 1685, *ibid.,* II, 33–34.

28. Proprietors to Joseph West, May 5, 1685, *ibid.,* II, 59–60.

29. Proprietors to Joseph Morton and Grand Council, September 10, 1685, *ibid.,* II, 89–90.

30.   Proprietors to James Colleton, March 6, 1687, *S. C. Pub. Recs.,* II, 181.

31.   Proprietors to James Colleton, October 18, 1690, *ibid.,* II, 293.

32.   Gregorie, "Indian Trade," p. 59.

33.   Thomas Cooper and David J. McCord, eds., *The Statutes at Large of South Carolina* (10 vols., Columbia, 1836–1841), II, 55, hereafter cited as Cooper, *Statutes.*

34.   *Ibid.,* II, 64.

35.   Sirmans, *Colonial South Carolina,* p. 50.

36.   *South Carolina Grand Council Journal,* May 28, 1692, p. 31.

37.   *Ibid.,* April 21, May 28, June 22, 1692, pp. 12, 31, 45–46.

38.   *Ibid.,* August 11, 1692, p. 55.

39.   Phillip Ludwell to Speaker of the Commons House, October 13, 1692, Frank Kirk, "Early Carolina Settlers Sold Indian Prisoners as Slaves," *The* [Charleston] *News and Courier,* August 9, 1936.

40.   John Archdale, "A New Description of That Fertile and Pleasant Province of Carolina: with a Brief Account of Its Discovery and Settling, and the Government Thereof to This Time, With Several Remarkable Passages of Divine Providence During My Time," Carroll, *Historical Collections,* II, 106.

41.   *Journal of the Commons House of Assembly of South Carolina* (30 vols. to date, Columbia, 1907–1962), August 28, 1702, p. 84, hereafter cited as SCCHJ. Manuscript Commons House journals from the South Carolina Archives are hereafter cited as SCCHJ with appropriate South Carolina Archives citations.

42.   Representatives of Assembly members from Colleton County., June 26, 1703, Rivers, *Sketch,* appendix, p. 455.

43.   Also spelled "Awivalla" and "Ayubale."

44.   "Extract of Colonel Moore's Letter to Sr Nathaniel Johnson 16th April 1704," S. C. Pub. Recs., XIX, 144–46. Internal evidence indicates that the letter was written between January 23 and 30, 1704. The letter was also published in *The Boston News Letter* of May 1, 1704, under the heading "South-Carolina Via New York."

45. James Moore to Proprietors, April 16, 1704, S. C. Pub. Recs., XIX, 141.

46. *Ibid.*, XIX, 143.

47. *The Boston News Letter,* May 1, 1704; "Extract of Colonel Moore's Letter to Sr Nathaniel Johnson 16th April 1704," S. C. Pub. Recs., XIX, 148 incorrectly transcribed the number at "300."

48. James Moore to Proprietors, April 16, 1704, S. C. Pub. Recs., XIX, 143.

49. "Extract of Colonel Moore's Letter to Sr Nathaniel Johnson 16th April 1704," S. C. Pub. Recs., XIX, 148.

50. James Moore to Proprietors, April 16, 1704, S. C. Pub. Recs., XIX, 143.

51. "Extract of Colonel Moore's Letter to Sr Nathaniel Johnson 16th April 1704," S. C. Pub. Recs., XIX, 147. Good accounts of the expedition are found in Herbert E. Bolton and Mary Ross, *The Debatable Land; a Sketch of the Anglo-Spanish Contest for the Georgia Country* (Berkeley, 1925), pp. 59–62, hereafter cited as Bolton, *Debatable Land;* and Verner W. Crane, *The Southern Frontier, 1670–1732* (Durham, 1928), pp. 79–80, hereafter cited as Crane, *Southern Frontier*.

52. Cooper, *Statutes,* II, 311.

53. *Ibid.*, II, 32–33.

54. Thomas Nairne to "your Lordship," July 10, 1708, *S. C. Pub. Recs.,* V, 196–97.

55. Governor and Council to Proprietors, September 17, 1708, *ibid.*, V, 205.

56. [James Glen], *A Description of South Carolina; Containing, Many Curious and Interesting Particulars Relating to the Civil, Natural and Commercial History of That Colony, Viz. the Succession of European Settlers There; Grants of English Charters; Boundaries; Constitution of the Government; Taxes; Number of Inhabitants, and of the Neighbouring Indian Nations, &c. The Nature of the Climate; Tabular Accounts of the Altitudes of the Barometer Monthly for Four Years, of the Depths of Rain Monthly for Eleven Years, and of the Winds Direction Daily for One Year, &c. The Culture and Produce of Rice, Indian Corn, and Indigo; the Process of Extracting Tar and Turpentine; the State of Their Maritime Trade in the Years 1710, 1723, 1740 and 1748, with the Number of Tonnage of Shipping Employed, and the Species, Quantities and Values of Their Produce Exported in One Year, &c. To Which is Added, a Very Particular Account of Their Exports of Raw Silk and Imports of British Silk Manufactures for Twenty-five Years* (London, 1761), p. 74, hereafter cited as Glen, *Description*.

57.   Crane, *Southern Frontier*, p. 159.

58.   R. D. W. Connor, *History of North Carolina* as quoted in Winston, "Indian Slavery," p. 432.

59.   Pollock's Letter Book, "a true copy of a letter to the Lords Proprietors dated Sept 20th 1712," William L. Saunders, Walter Clark and Stephen B. Weeks, eds., *The Colonial [and State] Records of North Carolina* (30 vols., Raleigh [place varies], 1886–1914), I, 875, hereafter cited as Saunders, *Col. [and St.] Recs. of N. C.*

60.   Francis Le Jau to the Bishop of London, May 27, 1712, Fulham Manuscripts of the Bishop of London. Transcripts of the original manuscripts made for the Library of Congress, S. C. No. 10, no pagination, hereafter cited as Fulham MSS.

61.   Francis Le Jau to the Secretary of the Society for the Propagation of the Gospel in Foreign Parts, August 30, 1712, Society for the Propagation of the Gospel in Foreign Parts. Transcripts of original manuscripts made for the Library of Congress, A 7, No. 27, p. 557, hereafter cited as S. P. G. MSS.

62.   A slightly different version is given in Crane, *Southern Frontier*, p. 161.

63.   Joseph Boone and Richard Berresford to the Board of Trade, June 1716, S. C. Pub. Recs., VI, 171–74. Duplicate information in "A demonstration of the present State of So. Carolina; delivered by the Agents to the Board June 1716," Carolina Papers. [George] Chalmers Collection of Letters and Documents Relating to the Carolinas, 1662–1795. 2 vols. Manuscripts Division, New York Public Library, I, 19, hereafter cited as Carolina Papers. Chalmers Collection.

64.   Winston, "Indian Slavery," p. 433.

65.   Rivers, *Sketch*, p. 255.

66.   Francis Le Jau to [Sec. S. P. G.], March 19, 1716, S. P. G. MSS, B 4, pt. I, No. 58, p. 219.

67.   An incomplete copy of the act is found in Cooper, *Statutes*, II, 677–80. The complete act is to be found in W. L. McDowell, ed., *Journals of the Commissioners of Indian Trade, September 20, 1710–August 29, 1718* (Columbia, 1955), appendix, pp. 325–29, hereafter cited as McDowell, *Journals, 1710–1718*.

68.   *Ibid.*, July 24, 1716, pp. 85–86.

69.   *Ibid.*, November 23–24, 1716, pp. 129–130.

70. *Ibid.,* November 23, 1716, p. 129.

71. *Ibid.,* June 11, 1717, p. 186.

72. Crane, *Southern Frontier,* p. 197.

73. "Memorial of several merchants trading to Carolina to Board of Trade," October 27, 1720, S. C. Pub. Recs., VIII, 226–227.

74. Klaus G. Loewald, Beverly Starika and Paul S. Taylor, trans. and eds., "Johann Martin Bolzius Answers a Questionnaire on Carolina and Georgia," *The William and Mary Quarterly,* 3d ser., XIV (April, 1957), 237.

75. General studies of the problem are Franklin B. Dexter, "Estimates of the Population in the American Colonies," *Proceedings of the American Antiquarian Society,* new ser., V (October, 1887), 22–50, and Evarts B. Greene and Virginia D. Harrington, eds. *American Population before the Federal Census of 1790* (New York, 1932). South Carolina statistics are given in Edson L. Whitney, *Government of the Colony of South Carolina,* Johns Hopkins University Studies in Historical and Political Science, 13th ser., I, II (Baltimore, 1895), appendix I, pp. 115–118, and Edward McCrady, *The History of South Carolina* (4 vols., New York, 1897–1902), I, appendix VII, p. 722, and II, appendix VI, p. 807, hereafter cited as McCrady, *History of S. C.*

76. Richard Ludlam to unknown addressee, April 16, 1724, Fulham MSS, S. C. No. 191, no pagination.

77. Thomas Hasell to Sec. S. P. G., August 1, 1719, S. P. G. MSS, A 13, pp. 297–298.

78. Thomas Hasell to Sec. S P. G., September 16, 1720, S. P. G. MSS, A 15, p. 66.

79. Thomas Hasell to Sec. S. P. G., March 20, 1722, S. P. G. MSS, B 4, I, No. 103, p. 388.

80. Thomas Hasell to "Your Lordships," June 15, 1724, Fulham MSS, S. C. No. 285, no pagination.

81. Thomas Hasell to Sec. S. P. G., August 26, 1725, S. P. G. MSS, A 19, No. 18, p. 100.

82. Thomas Hasell to Sec. S. P. G., June 4, 1728, S. P. G. MSS, A 21, No. 9, p. 106.

83. Thomas Hasell to Philip Bearcroft, March 17, 1743, S. P. G. MSS, B 10, No. 142, p. 327.

84.   Nathaniel Johnson and Council to Council of Trade and Plantations, September 17, 1708, *S. C. Pub. Recs.,* V, 203–4.

85.   See *infra*.

86.   See *infra*.

87.   Winston, "Indian Slavery," p. 440.

88.   Edward McCrady, "Slavery in the Province of South Carolina, 1670–1770," *Annual Report of the American Historical Association for the Year 1895,* House of Representatives Document No. 291, 54th Congress, 1st Session (Washington, 1896), p. 642.

89.   Winston, "Indian Slavery," p. 436.

Part 2

Africans and Slavery

VIRTUALLY ALL AFRICANS WHO entered the British North American colonies arrived as slaves; their condition fixed their status for life in colonial America. For whites the trip from Europe to America was fraught with danger and discomfort; for blacks, the dangers and discomforts were multiplied and often the voyage was deadly. Shackled, diseased, and ill-fed, they were crowded into unclean cargo holds where they occasionally slept "spoon" fashion. Many did not survive the trip, and their bodies were thrown into the ocean to be devoured by the sharks which continually followed the slave ships. Despite the desperate conditions of the journey, many black captives survived and adapted.

Taken from their homeland and transported first to the coast of West Africa and then across the Atlantic to labor in a strange environment, blacks adopted the basic elements of English culture while at the same time retaining aspects of their own background in a unique amalgam. As John Hope Franklin noted, "in the conflict of cultures only those practices will survive whose value and superiority give them the strength and tenacity to do so." At least two acculturative processes involved these survivors. Africans of different experiences borrowed from each other, and, concurrently, the interaction between whites and blacks changed the cultural patterns of both. With the new culture, distinctions arose, and blacks were either "outlandish," born in Africa, or "New Negroes," born in America.

The first black Africans were imported into the mainland colonies in 1619; during the next forty years their status varied, but few were able to escape some form of servitude. By the 1660s, the southern colonies began to develop an elaborate slave code to regulate the labor, status, and behavior of blacks. A century later slavery in the South was a mature institution which would change little in the ensuing years.

The growth of the institution of slavery matched the rising importation of blacks to meet the labor needs of a largely unsettled land. Virginia, in 1650, had about 300 blacks; by 1708 the number had increased to 12,000, and by 1756 there were 120,156 blacks. By 1750 Maryland held about 40,000 blacks. However, in both of these colonies whites were in the majority. The Carolinas, which developed black slavery from the time of their establishment in the 1660s, had a black majority within a hundred years; blacks outnumbered whites (90,000 to 40,000) in 1765. Georgia began without slaves in accordance with its charter, but whites protested, and by 1766 there were 10,000 whites and 8,000 blacks in that colony. It is also important to remember that during the colonial period slavery existed not only in the southern colonies but in the northern colonies as well, although the numbers there were much smaller. During the Revolutionary War, slavery would be abolished or the process of abolition begun in the northern colonies, while the South held on tenaciously to what had become its "peculiar institution."

Blacks came to constitute the primary source of unfree labor during the colonial period. European attempts to enslave Indians met with little success; and white indentured servants were unlikely to serve for life, especially with the availability of new territory where their status could be left behind even before their period of servitude had ended. Blacks, who seldom, if ever, were settlers by their own choice, carried their badge of servitude with them (their skin color), and could not escape it. Whites rationalized their use of blacks as slaves by arguing that blacks were inferior beings who would be helped by the imposition of white culture and religion. Thus the labor-intensive demands of frontier commercial agriculture and white prejudice created a two-layered society with a black base of slave labor.

The pattern was repeated in each region with variations only in the number of slaves and in the kind of work they performed. In the southern colonies most blacks worked on plantations. In the Chesapeake Bay region the major crop was tobacco; farther south rice and indigo were the staples. In the New England colonies most blacks worked on small farms or worked as house servants. In the middle colonies they often lived in the larger cities, such as New York, and were house servants or skilled laborers. The constant for British North Americans from Africa was black slavery.

Twenty Negroes to Jamestown in 1619?

Wesley Frank Craven*

The first blacks to land at an English continental colony did so in 1619 at Virginia. But Wesley Frank Craven demonstrates in "Twenty Negroes to Jamestown in 1619?" that, contrary to historical convention, neither the exact number of blacks nor the particular place at which they were sold is known. This leads Craven to ask whether we have "all been too much concerned with the question of the Negro's status at the time of his first identification with the country to be bothered with other questions." Craven, a member of the History Department at Princeton University, has written voluminously about the American colonies. Among his works are White, Red and Black: The Seventeenth-Century Virginian, The Dissolution of the Virginia Company, The Southern Colonies in the Seventeenth Century, 1607–1689, The Legend of the Founding Fathers, New Jersey and the English Colonization of North America, *and* The Colonies in Transition, 1660–1713.

THAT A DUTCH SHIPMASTER in 1619 brought to Virginia twenty Negroes, the first to reach this country, would appear to be one of the more firmly established facts of American history. Our

*Wesley Frank Craven, "Twenty Negroes to Jamestown in 1619?" in *White, Red, and Black: The Seventeenth-Century Virginian* (Charlottesville: University Press of Virginia, 1971), pp. 77–80. Reprinted by permission.

textbooks consistently assure us that this is true, as do also
many more specialized studies by well-informed scholars. Commonly, it is said that the Negroes were brought to Jamestown.
Actually, we do not know the exact number of these persons,
and there seems to be no certain documentary evidence that they
were carried to Jamestown at all.

Our textbooks say there were twenty because this is what
Captain John Smith said in his "Historie of Virginia." Robert
Beverley picked up the item from Smith, and in his own "History and Present State of Virginia," first published in 1705,
added the information that these were the first Negroes to be
"carried into the Country." And so begins the history of one of
those historical facts that become in time so well established
that no author bothers to burden his text with a footnote. Fortunately, Captain Smith had a way very often of citing his source,
which in this instance was a letter from John Rolfe to Sir Edwin
Sandys, and not only has the original survived but for nearly
forty years now its text has been readily available for consulta-
tion in any library possessing the third volume of Susan M.
Kingsbury's "Records of the Virginia Company." There one
finds not the "twenty Negars," as Smith paraphrased his
source, but a statement that there were "20. and odd Negroes."
Although this is an almost perfect example of the imprecision
with which a man in the seventeenth century might state such a
fact, the Oxford Dictionary leaves no room for doubt that the
phrasing must be read to mean somewhat more than twenty.
Whether it can be read as twenty-one, twenty-two, or even more
is a question that must be left to conjecture.

There is, it is true, additional evidence. It is found in a very
detailed census of the colony's population that was taken in
1625, the year immediately following the one in which the
Virginia Company had been dissolved, but this evidence serves
only to complicate the problem. According to the census, there
were then living in Virginia a total of twenty-three Negroes, of
whom two were children evidently born in the colony. Four of
the twenty-one adults, two men and two women, are listed as
having migrated to Virginia after 1619, the earliest in 1621,

another in 1622, and two as recently as 1623. Only in these four instances does the census, which may be readily consulted in Hotten's well-known "Lists" of emigrants to America, specify the time at which Negro inhabitants reached the colony, and so the remaining seventeen presumably represent the original group. Whether this means that John Rolfe's report of the number was mistaken, or whether several Negroes meanwhile had died, cannot be said. The death of one Negro at some time after April, 1623, is recorded in Hotten's "Lists," but apparently no other evidence bearing on the question has survived.

In view of the extraordinary effort that has been devoted to the search for every discoverable detail regarding the *Susan Constant,* or the *Mayflower* and its passengers, we perhaps should turn back to Rolfe's letter for such additional information as it provides. Although Rolfe seems to have left his letter undated, it unmistakably was written three months or more after the Dutchman's arrival at Point Comfort "about the latter end of August." There is no mention, or even a suggestion, that the ship subsequently had gone up to Jamestown. Rolfe describes the vessel as a man-of-war of 160 tons, names the commander as a Captain Jope, identifies "his Pilott for the West Indies" as "Mr. Marmaduke an Englishman," and reports that the ship had been engaged in a none-too-successful plundering expedition in the West Indies. It is in this connection that Rolfe gives the number of its passengers, declaring that the captain had brought into Point Comfort "not any thing but 20. and odd Negroes." His arrival in Virginia, as possibly also the fact that he had an English pilot aboard, is explained by a meeting in the West Indies between the Dutch ship and an English vessel named the *Treasurer,* which had sailed from Virginia for the West Indies earlier in the year and which belonged to the Earl of Warwick, a leading Virginia and Bermuda adventurer who may have been the heaviest English investor of his day in privateering voyages. It had been agreed by the commanders of the two ships, both evidently short of provisions, that they would sail together for Virginia. According to Rolfe, they had been separated in the passage, and the *Treasurer* had come into Point

Comfort three or four days after the Dutchman dropped anchor there.

Of much greater historical importance is Rolfe's report to Sandys, then the energetic and dedicated head of the Virginia Company, that Captain Jope had received the supplies he needed in a sale of the Negroes to Governor Yeardley and the Cape Merchant, resident agent or factor for the company's administration of its monopoly of the colony's trade, a post at that time held by Abraham Piersey. Whether the purchases were negotiated by the two men in their public or private capacities is not stated. It can be reported only that the census of 1625 shows eight Negroes among the servants belonging to Sir George Yeardley, who no longer was governor, and seven among those belonging to Piersey, one of them a child. To this must be added the fact that two adult Negroes, together with an infant child of theirs described as having been baptized, belonged to William Tucker, who in 1619 happened to be the commander at Point Comfort.

That Rolfe could have been wrong in some of his statements is indicated by one other document, evidently the only other document to make reference to the Dutchman's visit that has survived. It is a letter written by John Pory, best remembered as speaker of Virginia's first representative assembly in 1619, who wrote possibly to the Earl of Southampton, later governor or treasurer of the Virginia Company in succession to Sir Edwin Sandys. The letter was dated at Jamestown on September 30, 1619, for dispatch by way of a "man of ware of Flushing" then on the point of sailing for London. There can be no question as to the identity of the ship, for Pory explains its presence in Virginia as the result of "an accidental consortship in the West Indies" with the *Treasurer*. In closing the letter, he states that it is being entrusted to the ship's pilot, an Englishman named Marmaduke Rayner, who surely must have been Rolfe's "Mr. Marmaduke." Unfortunately, Pory found no occasion to mention the Negroes, or else he felt advised not to do so, and so we are left entirely dependent upon Rolfe's account of the transaction except for a more specific identification of the ship, the presumably correct name of its English pilot, confirmation for the approximate time of the transaction, and the possibility, though no more than a possibility, that the sale may actually have occurred at Jamestown.

The number of Negroes settled in Virginia in 1619 could have been much larger, for the *Treasurer* had reached Point Comfort with at least fourteen aboard. But the treatment given its master, Captain Daniel Elfrith, was quite different from that accorded the Dutch shipmaster. The leaders of the Virginia Company had become alarmed lest reports of Elfrith's use of the colony as a base for privateering against the Spaniard in the West Indies bring upon the company the king's displeasure, and there can be no doubt that this fear explains the denial to Elfrith of even so much as the victuals he sorely needed. He promptly had sailed for Bermuda, where he arrived with his ship reportedly in terrible condition and with fourteen Negroes aboard.

Elfrith's experience needs mention here for more than one reason. First, some historians have assumed that Elfrith may have disposed of one or more of his Negroes before sailing for Bermuda. It is possible, of course, that he did, but there is no evidence to confirm the assumption, either in Rolfe's report or in the not inconsiderable record resulting from a bitter controversy among the Virginia adventurers over the treatment Elfrith had received in Virginia. Secondly, this part of the story may help to provide a warning against the error, of which all too many of us have been guilty, in speaking of the Negroes carried to Virginia by the Dutchman as the first in an English colony. Actually, Elfrith's arrival in Bermuda brought the total number of Negroes in that colony to something like thirty, and the first of them had come to the islands as early as 1616. Finally, we might know more about this historic development in Virginia had not the courtesies extended by Governor Yeardley to the Dutch shipmaster come very close to raising precisely the same issue as did Elfrith's presence there—use of the colony for encouragement of privateering against the Spaniard. The issue has to be described as a hot one at the time, one contributing greatly to the bitter factional strife which helped ultimately to destroy the Virginia Company itself. Here, in other words, was a subject calling for the use of discretion in reports from the colony to London.

No doubt, the main question posed by our long-standing neglect of a readily available record that calls into question Captain John Smith's report of "twenty Negars" carried to Virginia in 1619 is one of attitudes. It would be easy to dismiss the question simply in the terms of one more example of the white historian's indifference to the Negro's place in our history, except for the fact that black historians have been hardly the less indifferent to a need every other ethnic group in our society has felt to demand that the record of its first identification with the country be explored fully. Have we all been too much concerned with the question of the Negro's status at the time of his first identification with the country to be bothered with other questions?

The Origin of Slavery in the United States—The Maryland Precedent

*Jonathan L. Alpert**

During the past two decades, historians have often asked and answered questions concerning the origin of slavery in the United States. Essentially they have argued either that prejudice or that economics caused slavery to emerge in the United States. And, in so arguing, most have looked at the growth of slavery in Virginia. But as Jonathan L. Alpert points out, "Maryland provides a particularly good focus to begin this consideration because it was the first province in English North America to recognize slavery as a matter of law." Alpert studied the legal process, and found that in Maryland, slavery "was a changing and developing legal concept." When he wrote this article Alpert was a student in the Charles Warren Program at Harvard University.

AMERICAN SLAVERY WAS ABOVE all else a product of the law. The "innocent legal relation"[1] was effectuated by legislatures and enforced by courts. But oddly enough the English common law did not allow slavery.[2] The closest approximation to slavery was villeinage, and even the villein was by no means a slave.[3]

---

*Abridged from Jonathan L. Alpert, "The Origin of Slavery in the United States— The Maryland Precedent," *American Journal of Legal History* 14 (1970), 189–221. Reprinted by permission.

In fact, the right of one person improperly held by another to seek redress in the King's courts had been recognized at least as early as 1346.[4]

The common law of England perhaps placed greater weight on the worth of the individual than any other legal system. Yet, even though fundamental individual rights were the foundation of the law, slavery was accepted in America. Its development was in response to various pressures. These pressures resulted in the creation of a unique legal institution. The justifications, growth and structure of slavery were transposed into legislation and judicial rulings and can be found incidentally in other legal records. Consequently any examination of slavery is incomplete unless the legal process is considered.

Maryland provides a particularly good focus to begin this consideration because it was the first province in English North America to recognize slavery as a matter of law.

The colony was established by feudal charter in 1632. Charles I granted to the Lords Baltimore all of the rights and powers which the Bishop of Durham ". . . . ever heretofore hath had, held, used, or enjoyed . . ."[5] The first colonists landed at St. Mary's in March, 1634.[6] Less than a year later the first session of the General Assembly was convened. During the early years of the Province a conflict existed between the Proprietary and the General Assembly concerning the power to initiate legislation, but by 1640 the issue had been resolved by permitting both to do so.[7] In 1637 a judicial system began to form.[8] There were a few courts baron and leet. The Proprietary himself developed three levels of jurisdiction. The county courts heard small civil suits and minor criminal cases. The Provincial Court heard more important civil suits and criminal cases and appeals from the county courts. Appeals from the Provincial Court were heard by the Upper House of the Assembly. The membership of both the Provincial Court and the Upper House consisted of the Governor and his Council.[9] Although few of the county court records have survived, most of the Provincial Court and Assembly proceedings are extant.[10]

Early legislation implicitly recognized the existence of slavery. "An Act for the liberties of the people" in 1639 provided that all Christian inhabitants, "Slaves excepted" should have the rights of Englishmen.[11] Further, "An Act limiting the time of Servants," also passed in 1639, expressly excluded slaves.[12]

These statutes raise two problems: What was the meaning of "slave" and who were the persons who were presumably being held in "slavery?" Although it has been suggested that "slave" had no legal meaning until late in the seventeenth century,[13] these two statutes belie that notion. The legislation clearly distinguishes slaves from servants. It also seems to indicate that even Christians may be slaves. Probably in 1639 "slave" as a matter of law simply meant a person who was obligated to serve his master for life. Although slavery may have been hereditary by 1640, perhaps it was not, because in 1664 legislation was enacted apparently to establish that characteristic.[14]

The recognition of slavery by 1640 was more important for the Indians than for the few Negroes then in the Province.[15] There were Indian slaves at this time.[16] In fact, the colonists often attempted to enslave Indians who in the interests of peaceful co-existence were not to be so treated. To prevent the stealing of "any friend Indian or Indians whatsoever," in 1649 and 1654 the General Assembly provided capital punishment for convicted Indian-nappers.[17]

Negroes were first mentioned judicially in an executory land contract recorded in 1642: ". . . the said John Skinner covenanted & bargained to deliver unto the said Leonard Calvert, fourteene negro menslaves, & three woman slaves . . ."[18] The seventeen slaves, however, may never have been delivered. But the use of the term "slaves" is significant. Not mere term servants were being purchased. Rather the delivery of slaves, at the least servants for life, was the promise which Skinner made. In 1644 mention is made of two Negroes who had been sold.[19] It is not stated whether or not these two Negroes were slaves because, unlike an executory contract in which it is necessary to clearly articulate the promises of the parties, there was no need for designation of the Negroes' status in reference to a past sale. Although there may have been a few Negro slaves in the colony as early as 1635–1640, there were also indentured Negro servants during this period.[20]

In 1653, "John Babtista a moore of Barbary," successfully petitioned the Provincial Court for his freedom. Babtista proved that Simone Overzee, who had "brought him in, did not sell him for his life tyme."[21] White servants were never sold for life.[22] Because Babtista had to prove that he had been sold for only a term, he was probably black. This indicates that some blacks at this time were being sold for life. But because Babtista had not been, sales for life apparently were not the unvaried rule. Consequently, slavery or life servitude existed contemporaneously with service for a term of years, with the status perhaps depending on the manner of the Negro's original sale or importation.

Whether or not a Negro was originally transferred to a Marylander for life or for a term, which of course determined his later status in the colony, may have been decided by the vendor on the basis of his original acquisition. In 1679, for example, a Negro named Charles Cabe petitioned for freedom, urging that he had been brought into the colony for only a twenty-one year term. He had apparently been purchased in England in 1656 for 25£ sterling, a rather high price for a mere term servant. The witnesses whom Cabe suggested be called would not support his story. They testified that they knew of "... only a fflying report from him and Likewise the seamen on board the ship they came ..." to Maryland on. The Provincial Court, without any recorded discussion, decided that "the said Charles Cabe is a Slave."[23]

If, on the other hand, the Negro came directly from Africa, there was probably no question but that he was obligated to serve for his life. He had made no contract or indenture concerning the length of his service for he could not even speak English. Further, the habit of the Europeans was to buy blacks from their fellow Africans, who did not dicker concerning the length of their product's service.[24]

In 1658, the same Simon Overzee who was involved in the *Babtista* Case was indicted in the Provincial Court for the murder of a Negro slave. The testimony indicated that the black, "commonly called Tony," had been chained up "for some misdemeanors," was released and ordered to go to work but refused, was then beaten with "some Peare Tree wands," had hot lard poured on him, then "rose up with a great shout," and was tied by his wrists to a ladder by an Indian slave. Several hours later Tony expired.[25] He had been purchased in 1656, had rarely been willing to work, had run away several times, and was felt to be somewhat of a menace to the community. Tony had only recently been acquainted with the benefits of English civilization. One witness testified: "I never knew such a Brute: for I could not perceive any speech or language hee had, only an ugly yelling Brute beast like."[26] Tony had been sold for life because that was the intention of his African vendors and original vendees. To hold an Englishman in service for four to five years could be profitable. However, several years were undoubtedly required merely to adequately train the fresh African import to his tasks. Tony was untrainable for two years. He finally died. Overzee, on the basis of a verdict which Semmes finds "impossible to agree with," was released.[27]

The fact that the court referred to Tony as a "Negro servant"[28] even though he was clearly a slave in the sense that he served for life, indicates that there may not have been a major conceptual distinction between term and life service. When it was necessary to make such a distinction, however, as in the case of the 1639 statutes, it was made. All slaves were servants but not all servants were slaves. Therefore, even though "servant" and "slave" may have been used almost interchangeably in the seventeenth century, this does not prove, as some historians have asserted,[29] that the terms lacked a juridical definition.

The basis of servitude was contract. One party agreed to serve another for a certain time. By and large imported blacks were not parties to any contract. They could be held and sold at the whim of their masters because they were not even parties to the basic social compact between Englishmen. As they became assimilated into colonial society, however, a new justification for holding them in servitude had to be developed. Some masters undoubtedly set their blacks free after they had received fair value for their investment.[30] But those who wished to retain their Negroes—and there must have been many of these[31]—had to develop a new justification for so doing. Consequently the paganism notion, which supposedly justified the holding of a non-Christian as a slave, was advanced to justify Negro slavery or perpetual servitude. Although a Negro's paganism may have been a factor in his original subjugation for life, it became more important as more Negroes were becoming "civilized" because a reason for their slavery had to be adduced.

The paganism justification went through three stages. At first, in the period roughly between 1634 and 1650, it was merely an unconscious factor in the reduction to life servitude of the Negro. Of primary importance was the fact that the black had made no original contract and was basically uncivilized. Whether or not he was going to be held for life depended upon the intent of the parties: an African black was not one of the parties.

The second stage, between 1650 and 1670, involved a period when the previously imported Negroes were becoming civilized and perhaps Christian. A justification had to be developed to continue in slavery those who were in slavery and to justify the imposition of slavery on fresh imports. This inspired the first legislation which unquestionably attests to the existence of Negro slavery. Although statutes had been passed in 1662 and 1663 which recognized the existence of Negro slavery,[32] the 1664 statute, which is often incorrectly cited to 1663,[33] was the first statute of its type in this country and conclusively established Negro slavery. Entitled "An Act Concerning Negroes & other Slaves," it provided:

> Bee it Enacted by the Right Honorable the Lord Proprietary by the advice and Consent of the upper and lower house of this present General Assembly That all Negroes or other slaves already within the Province And all Negroes and other slaves to bee hereafter imported into the Province shall serve Durante Vita [for life] And all Children born of any Negro or other slave shall be Slaves as their ffathers were for the terme of their lives And forasmuch as divers freeborne English women forgettful of their free Condition and to the disgrace of our Nation doe intermarry with Negro Slaves by which also divers suites may arise touch-

ing the Issue of such woemen and a great damage doth befall the
Masters of such Negros for prevention whereof for deterring
such freeborne women from such shamefull Matches Bee it further enacted by the Authority advice and Consent aforesaid That
whatsoever free borne woman shall inter marry with any slave
from and after the Last day of this present Assembly shall serve
the master of such slave dureing the life of her husband And that
all the Issue of such freeborne woemen soe marryed shall be
slaves as their fathers were And Bee it further Enacted that all
the Issues of English or other freeborne woemen that have already marryed Negroes shall serve the Masters of their Parents
till they be Thirty years of age and noe longer.[34]

This legislation legalized the *de facto* slavery which had been
recognized at least since 1639. There is no discussion of Christianity or paganism in the statute. Slavery was accepted apparently
regardless of the religious affiliation of the slave or potential
slave. This view apparently began to trouble the colonists, however, and led to the third stage of the paganism notion, which
lasted from 1670 until the date of the publication of this article.

It was only after 1670 that the colonists began to develop the
paganism rule as *the* justification for the enslavement of Negroes. Historians have accepted this *ex post facto* explanation
for slavery.[35] Previously, rather than a paganism justification,
there was a contractual one. Life service was not the instinctual
lot for the Negro, it was merely the condition under which he
entered the province. Some were, as pointed out earlier, able to
contract for indentured servant status. During the second stage,
the 1664 statute was enacted probably because the original basis
of life service, contractual and non-contractual, was under question. Some newly civilized black might well have said to his
master: "So you brought me in as slave. But I had nothing to
say about it so let me go." The *Cabe* and *Babtista* cases were
argued on the basis of the original agreement, not on any paganism or Christianity theory.

Therefore, in the third stage of the paganism evolution the
colonists first had to develop their justification for originally
holding Negroes for life and then, when that fiction began to
interfere with their future holding of the blacks, they had to

legislate it into oblivion. "An Act for the Encourageing the Importation of Negroes and Slaves into this Province" in 1671 is self-explanatory:

> Whereas Severall of the good people of this Province have been discouraged to import into or purchase within this Province any Negroes or other Slaves and such as have Imported or purchased any such Negroes or Slaves have to the great displeasure of Almighty God and the prejudice of the Soules of those poore people Neglected to instruct them in the Christian faith or to Endure or p⌐rmitt them to Receive the holy Sacrament of Babtisme for the remission of their Sinns upon a mistake and ungrounded apprehension that by becomeing Christians they and the Issues of their bodies are actually manumited and made free and discharged from their Servitude and bondage be itt declared and Enacted . . . That where any Negro or Negroes Slave or Slaves being in Servitude or bondage is are or shall become Christian or Christians and . . . Receive the Holy Sacrament of Babtizme before or after his her or their Importation into this Province the same is not nor shall or ought the same be . . . taken to be or amount unto a manumission or freeing Inlarging or discharging any such . . . Negroes Slave or Slaves . . . or their Issue . . . from . . . their Servitude . . . any opinion or other matter or thing to the Contrary in any wise Notwithstanding.[36]

Particularly fascinating is the fact that there were no cases prior to 1671 in which Negroes were freed because they had become Christian. The paganism justification coupled with the fear of possible release of converted slaves may have arisen spontaneously and entirely extra-judicially. . . .

As the paganism excuse was evolving the nature of slavery was changing. The 1664 "Act Concerning Negroes & other Slaves," which was cited in full above, established the hereditability of slave status. Although blacks who served for life may have passed their condition on to their progeny prior to 1664, this act established the two fundamental indices of slavery: life service plus life service for children. Because legislation is usually not adopted unless someone perceives a reason for the enactment, there was probably a need in 1664 to clarify the legal meaning of slavery and to clearly establish its incidents. As the original contractual basis of servitude was questioned by civilized and newly-civilized blacks, it was necessary to legislate life servitude apart from any contractual foundation. Further, there could be no original contractual basis for retaining the children of life servants in life servitude. Consequently, although black children may and probably were held as a matter of fact by their parents' masters prior to 1664, the statute established such holding *de jure*. . . .

In summary, by 1664 most of the slaves seem to be black and they will serve for life and their children will follow the condition of the father. The original basis of slavery—the contract of purchase and the black not being a party to the contract—has been superseded by legislation. Whether Negroes are or are not Christian does not matter and, after religion seems to become an issue, in 1671 Christian affiliation or lack thereof is declared a nullity.

Although "slavery" existed in Maryland from the time of the original settlement or shortly thereafter, it was a changing and developing legal concept. The previous section discusses the establishment of the legal institution of slavery as an isolated phenomenon. Such conceptual isolation for the purpose of explanation is not sound historical analysis. Slavery, which was at the first merely life service, developed within the context of a Maryland society in which servant status occupied an important place in the law.

The law was concerned with servants from the time of settlement. The titles of the earliest statutes which have survived are from the 1638 session of the Assembly.[37] Two of the fourteen acts passed at that session involved servants. One was for "limiting the time of service" and the other provided for the punishment of "ill" (probably misbehaving) servants.[38] Even the first recorded House Resolution involved servants: ". . . upon a question moved touching the resting of servants on Satturdaies in the afternoone, it was declared by the [lower] house that no such custome was to be allowed."[39]

Seventeenth century Maryland was sparsely populated.[40] There were few whites and even fewer blacks.[41] Much work needed to be done but there were not enough men to do it.

Because the price of tobacco rose and fell,[42] and land was cheap and easy to obtain,[43] the most valuable asset was the servant.[44]

> All the Planters in Generall affects the style of Marchants because they all sell Tobacco And their Chiefe Estates consists in the number of Their Servants who serve generally but for five or six years and then beceome Planters and call themselves Merchants but generally they are poore Their commodity (which is only Tobacco) not selling for more than One Penny p pound weight.[45]

When Maryland was founded and during the remainder of that century, the greatest need was for servants to assist in planting the colony.[46] Term servants and even more so life servants were the best forms of capital investment.

Servants therefore were brought into the Province with indentures which stipulated the length and incidents of their servitude.[47] Sometimes, however, servants came into the Province without written indentures. In such cases, under "An Act for all Servants Comeing into the Province with Indentures" of 1654,[48] they were to be brought before a county court to have their ages determined and the statutory time of servitude applied.[49] In one case, two servants were freed after they had served what they said was their time when the shipmaster who had conveyed them testified that he had lost their indentures.[50] The written indentures or contracts were usually for four to six years and the statutory periods of servitude never exceeded five years for adults.

Poorer colonists often indentured themselves to richer ones. These indentures were usually shorter than those which involved transporting the servant to the colony. For example, in Talbot County in 1664, a man and his wife agreed to serve two years to secure a discharge from their debts.[51] In 1661 in Charles County a widow arranged for her "daughter in Law" to serve a Thomas Baker for six years and for her three-year-old son to serve a Mr. Henry Addames for eighteen years.[52] In 1674 John Manning sued George Lordman in the Provincial Court because Lordman had agreed to serve one year but failed to do so. Manning won the suit.[53] In 1678 a man who had served one year per an agreement sued the estate of his late master because he had not been paid the stipulated 4,000 pounds of tobacco. The court awarded him 3,600 pounds.[54]

In fact, there were often more than pecuniary reasons for entering indentured servitude. During the seventeenth century a number of bachelors had presumably nubile maidservants. By 1712, the colonial leaders tired of meretricious servitude and empowered the county courts to inquire into the consideration of indentures. Entitled "A Supplementary Act to the Act of Assembly of this Province for the punishing the Offences of Adultery and Fornication," the statute stated, *inter alia:*

> Severall Lewd Women within this Province to Colour their Ill practices And to avoid being Separated from those that Entertain them doe frequently Enter into Feigned Articles Covenants or Indentures to serve such persons for a Terme who Claime them as their property for the Terme by them Agreed or pretended to be Agreed on when really such . . . Indentures have noe other Consideration but are purely devised by them to Elude the Law and Continue their wicked and Lewd Conversation.[55]

Even though a master had property rights in him, a servant still had certain personal rights. Though servants lacked the capacity to sue at law, they could petition courts for redress. In 1674, a servant complained ". . . of several injuryes done unto her by some persons of this Province and She being a Servant and not of capacity and ability to presente them at Law, Ordered that she be admitted in forma pauperis and that . . ." an attorney be appointed for her.[56] In 1677, James Disborrow claimed that he had entered the colony under an agreement to be an assistant to a merchant, but had been sold as a servant.[57] In 1675 a mother complained that her son was to be free at the expiration of her term under her indenture agreement. The Provincial Court decided the case in her favor.[58]

There were frequent petitions for freedom. For example, in 1660 in Kent County, in 1664 in Talbot County,[59] and twice in 1665 in Charles County.[60] Petitions for freedom were also filed in the Provincial Court in 1661,[61] twice in 1673,[62] in 1677, and twice in 1678.[63] The servants were quite often successful in these suits, but in the latter part of the century their petitions began to be disallowed because they were not in proper form or because of some other technical defect in the proceedings. The General Assembly, therefore, in 1698, in "An Act of Assembly for deciding differences between Masters & Servants," provided:

> No such Judgement shall be reversed for want of Judiciall process, or that the same was not tryed by Jury or any matter of form Either in its Entry or giving of Judgment, provided It appears by the Record that the parties defendant were Legally summoned & not condemned unheard.[64]

Servants could of course testify in court. There was servant testimony in a Charles County case in 1663.[65] Servant witnesses were also competent in a case involving a dispute concerning marital infidelity in 1657.[66] Servants also testified about petitions which they themselves brought and had the same rights as freemen in criminal cases.

Master-servant law was essentially contractual. The parties themselves could make certain provisions of the contract such as length of service; compensation, if any; support obligations; nature of service; and what personal possessions, if any, the servant would be allowed to acquire or keep. In the absence of stipulation by the parties, the law and the "custom of the country" fixed the obligations between whites.

From the beginning, however, the same law and custom did not in the minds of the colonists apply to blacks. Persons brought in as slaves were excepted from statutes limiting servants' times. The combination of the manpower shortage, a lack of any legal foundation for only term service to the exclusion of life service, and the stresses in the master-servant relationship combined to promote the development of slavery. The servant was the best capital asset; the best servant was one for life. The term-servant would carefully protect all of his rights because he would soon become a free man; the black man knew of no rights which he had and saw little prospect of freedom. Servants filed petitions for freedom with annoying frequency, blacks did not. At the beginning slavery or life servitude was seen only as another form of term servitude; this is what the almost interchangeable use of "servant" and "slave" means. Consequently there was no particular need to justify service *durante vita* while many pressures promoted it. When the time came for such justification Christianity was available.

In 1660 Mr. and Mrs. Bradnox, two of the wealthiest people in the Province, were tried for the murder of a white servant. The evidence indicated that the servant was beaten, that his spine was probably broken, and that he was refused all "Victualls or drinke . . . Soe that he drunck his own water . . ." The chief prosecution witness, a woman servant, was discredited by evidence that she had stated that, if she did not get the "upper hand" over Mrs. Bradnox, ". . . she would run a Knife into her Mistres['s] Bowells . . ." Mr. and Mrs. Bradnox, who were acquitted, also alleged by way of defense that the decedent had been sick and had died as a result of the disease.[67]

The life of the servant in colonial Maryland was not easy. In 1664 at least two of them committed suicide in Charles County alone.[68] A year previously a coroner's jury had found that "if it were possible that any Christian could bee beaten to death with stripes, wee thinke the aforesaid Servant was."[69] Perhaps this kind of mistreatment deterred whites from entering the Province as servants and promoted a system of involuntary labor.

Although the basic features of the involuntary labor system had been established by the 1664 statute, it was not yet the totally dehumanizing slavery which later developed. In 1665, for example, one Jacob Negro was indicted by a grand jury and convicted by a petty jury of petty treason, the murder of his mistress.[70] The procedures of inexorable justice were no different for Jacob than they would have been for a white.

In 1671, five servants of one John Hawkins were tried for his murder:

. . . being volluntaryly of their malice before thought . . . then and there with the said Axes feloniously and Traytorously upon his head strongly and stoutly did severally strike so that . . . the head broke giving to him a mortall wound . . .[71]

Two of the five servants were "John the Negro" and "Tony the Negro." . . . .The defendants were . . . informed that they could challenge any of the jurors if they wished to do so. There were no challenges. John the Negro, Sall and Speare were found guilty and, along with Warry, were sentenced to be hanged. Tony the Negro was acquitted. He was ordered, however, to be the hangman.[72]

The case is of note for several reasons. First, all five of the defendants are called "servants" even though John and Tony were probably bound to life service. The reason they are not referred to as slaves is that their legal position for the purposes of this trial would not be affected by their slave status. Secondly, the fact that they are black slaves does not appear to affect the outcome of the trial. At least from the record Tony and John received equal justice before the law.

The fact that even after slavery had been established Negroes continued for a time to receive equal justice is supported by another case. In 1667, a warrant was issued for the arrest of a free Negro, John Johnson, and two white men on suspicion of stealing Katackcuweitick's corn.[73] The three confessed the crime in court and were ordered to deliver "two barrells" of Indian corn to their victim as recompense.[74] Again the Negro was not singled out for any special punishment by the court.

In 1667 the General Assembly considered legislation which would forbid "Negroes or any other servants to keep piggs . . .[75] This implicit reference to Negroes as servants does not mean that they were not slaves. It is significant, however, that the General Assembly apparently did not feel that the use of the term "servants" alone would include Negroes. It was necessary to mention them specifically. The legislation failed of passage in any case because the Upper House commented:

> To the second part against allowing Servants to keep hogs It being in the power of every Master not to do it if not obliged by Indentures in England, and diverse Masters being obliged by Indentures to allow Servants to raise hogs against they are free, this House do think it Unnecessary to pass this Law & in the second part injurious.[76]

Masters were not usually obliged under English indentures to permit Negroes to keep hogs. Consequently, because there were no contracts with the blacks, they could prevent them from keeping hogs. And the blacks had no reason "to raise hogs against they are free;" they were not going to be free.

During this period, however, there were some free Negroes. A Negro John Johnson recorded his cattle mark in 1665, as did the other citizens of Somerset County.[77] This was probably the same John Johnson who participated in the corn larceny of 1667. Perhaps he needed the corn to feed his cattle, because the name of a Negro John Johnson appears again in the cattle marks recorded in 1670.[78] And in 1672 another Negro in Somerset County recorded his cattle mark: "John Cazara Negro servant to Mary Johnson Negro the relict of Anthony Johnson deceased with the said Marys Consent records his marke . . ."[79] In addition, there were some free Negroes in the late seventeenth century who had come to the colony as indentured servants. In 1676, for example, Thomas Hagleton, who was black, successfully petitioned for his freedom because he had agreed to only a four year indenture in England before he came to Maryland.[80]

Although there were free blacks in the Province, the law began to become more and more rigid as the necessity for special treatment of life plus hereditary servitude became apparent. In 1678 "An Act for keepeing holy the Lords day," provided that no person should work or fish on Sunday. Rather than providing that no "Negroes or other servants" should be permitted to work on Sunday, the Act provided that no master should suffer his "servants or slaves" to work or fish on Sunday.[81] This is perhaps a recognition that the two types of servitude, life and term, may be different for all and not just some purposes as a matter of law.

The legal dehumanization of the Negro began in 1678. All births, marriages, and deaths in each county were to be recorded. All that is "Except Negros Indians & Molottos . . ."[82] This statute, which contains the first legislative mention of mulattoes, does not specify whether or not the Negroes, Indians, and mulattoes, whose lives are not to be recorded, are slaves.

Either it must have been assumed that most of them were slaves and hence insignificant or else that even those who were not slaves were not worthy or important enough to have their names recorded in the white man's records. That this was at least a legislative change, although it may have represented existing practice, is made clear by a 1658 statute which had been enacted for the same purpose. The 1658 statute had provided that ". . . the names of *all* that shall be borne . . . [emphasis added]" were to be recorded.[83] In 1692 an act with the same title, same purpose and same exceptions as the 1678 statute was passed.[84]

The Maryland Wills Act of 1681 also involved a separate but not equal treatment of Negroes.[85] It provided that "Noe Negroes or other Slaves" be sold for the payment of the debts of the deceased if other goods were available.[86] Although this provision may have had the incidental effect of helping to preserve slave families, the purpose was to prevent the most valuable part of the estate from being dissipated. Another provision of the statute, which concerned orphans' slaves, also had this goal clearly in mind. That section provided that the Negroes would be appraised by the county court and then given "to the Guardians or Trustees." The guardians or trustees were to preserve the slaves while employing them to their own "use & benifitt." When the orphan became of age, his slaves were to be returned to him, but if any of them had "growne aged or otherwise Impotent or bee Lamed, & that the Increase will not make the original Stocke good as to number & ability of body . . ." then the guardian or trustee would have to pay the orphan the difference in value between when he first took the slaves and when he returned those that were left. Recognizing that these provisions were somewhat stringent and that persons might refuse to be guardians on such terms, the act goes on to provide that if no one is willing to take the slaves under these conditions, then the county courts may make the best terms possible so that the slaves ". . . may bee preserved for the orphans till they come to theire severall ages. . . ."[87]

Because a guardian or trustee is never allowed to waste trust assets, the stringent nature of this statute indicates that the peculiar nature of slave property dictated that slaves be put in a special juridical category.

Statutory provisions such as these are obviously inapplicable to term servants. They cannot "bee preserved" for an orphan beyond the length of their term. This recognition of the fundamental factual and legal differences between slavery and other forms of servitude must have promoted the special legal treatment which blacks were to receive. Further, this recognition of the factual and legal consequences flowing from slavery is not twentieth century hindsight. The colonists themselves realized it. Term servants are not handled as were "Negroes and other slaves" in the Wills Act of 1681.

In the same year in which the Wills Act was passed, the 1664 slave statute was repealed and replaced with new legislation. The new law continued the 1664 provision that Negroes and other slaves already imported or "hereafter to be imported" were to be held *durante vita*. The anti-miscegenation section of the earlier statute, however, was revised. The act recites the reason:

And for as much a[s] diverse ffreeborne Englishe or Whitewoman *sometimes* by the Instigation Procurement or Conievance of theire Masters Mistres or dames, & *always* to the Satisfaction of their Lascivious & Lustfull desires, & to the disgrace not only of the English butt allso of many other Christian Nations, doe Intermarry with Negroes & Slaves by which means diverse Inconveniencys Controversys & suits may arise . . . [emphasis added] [88]

The legislation provides that if a master, "by any Instigation procurement knowledge permission or Contriveance whatsoever . . ." permits any woman servant to marry a slave, then she is ". . . absolutely discharged manymitted & made free Instantly upon her Intermarriage . . . And all Children borne . . . shall bee ffree. . . ."[89] The statute also levies fines of ten thousand pounds of tobacco on masters who permit such marriages and on ministers who perform them.

The 1681 anti-miscegenation provision, as the earlier 1664 law, is more concerned with the possible legal consequences of interracial marriage than with the interracial marriage itself. The earlier statute on its face does not prohibit all interracial matches, only those between servants and slaves. The plain meaning of the 1681 statute is the same, although by 1681 the legislators are clearly thinking in terms of marriages with "Negroes & Slaves," not just marriages with "Negro Slaves."

The law was passed for two reasons. First, Lord Baltimore had returned to the colony in 1681. He had brought with him a servant girl by the name of Irish Nell, who had almost immediately married a slave. Rather than lose her to the slave's master, Lord Baltimore wished to have the earlier statute repealed.[90] Second, the General Assembly suspected that some masters would purchase or had purchased Negro slaves and white female indentured servants with the hope of enticing the servants into marrying the slaves. Under the earlier act, the girls would then become servants for the lives of their black husbands and their children would have to serve for thirty years, perhaps sufficient reason for masters to encourage miscegenation, contrary to the policy of the law.

The 1681 statute, as both earlier and later legislation, bespeaks the tendency of servant law to bifurcate. Entirely different legal and social consequences resulted from service for life than from service for years. The attempts of the law to deal with these consequences only resulted in more sharp distinctions.

The anti-miscegenation legislation adopted in 1692 is on all fours with this point. By that time the General Assembly realized that the 1681 statute, although it discouraged masters from promoting miscegenation, emboldened female servants to miscegenate because by so doing their terms of service would conclude. The 1692 statute forbids all interracial marriages and sexual relations:

> . . . any free born English or white woman be shee free or Servant and shall hereafter intermarry with any negro or other Slave or to any Negro made free, shall immediately upon such marriage forfeit her freedome and become a Servant during the

> Terme of seven years to the use and benefitt of the Ministry of the Poor . . . and if he be a free Negro or Slave to whom she intermarried, he shall thereby also forfeit his freedom and become a Servant to the use aforesaid during his naturall life [.] But . . . if the Marriage be without the Connivance or procurement of her Master . . . she shall finish her time of Servitude together with what damage shall accrew to her Master . . . by occasion of any Children that may happen to be begott . . . and the issues of such women shall likewise be Servants to the use aforesaid till they arrive at the Age of one and twenty years . . .

The statute also provides that any free woman who has a bastard by a Negro shall serve for seven years and, if the Negro is free, he shall serve for seven years "to the use aforesaid . . . and all such Bastard Children to be Servants . . . until they arrive at the age of thirty one years . . ." If a master instigates an interracial marriage, the woman servant is to be freed. In addition, the same penalties which white women incur are made applicable to white men who "inter marry with or begett with Child any negro woman . . ."[91]

This legislation is replete with examples of the differences between servant and slave status. A servant can be required to serve for an additional seven years. A slave cannot. The problems of servant-slave marriages seem to be resolved by the statute. Both the servants and the masters are discouraged from promoting them. The discouragement takes the form of extra service for the servant and no additional service for the master if he promoted the match. Neither the fear of additional servitude for the slave nor the hope of additional servitude for the slave's master would be inducements in their case. Consequently this statute, as the earlier ones, is not phrased in these terms.

What would particularly disturb the free black, however, who must have been daily confronted with the spectacle of the slave status of his race, was the fear of being reduced to such a status himself. Therefore the act provides that any "free Negro or Slave" who intermarries shall "become a Servant . . . during his naturall life . . ." In the context of the statute this does not mean that a slave shall become a servant for life. "Free Negro or Slave" means free Negro or *freed* slave because the fornication provision, quoted above, only penalizes free Negroes and not slaves. If this exegesis of the statute is incorrect and the intermarriage penalty does apply to slaves, its purpose was undoubtedly to discourage slaves' masters from permitting such matches and to encourage them to keep a watchful eye on the possible marital complications of their chattels. This was the first statute to reduce free Negroes to life servitude for certain acts. Later in the colonial period many colonies enacted legislation under which free blacks could be required for various acts to serve *durante vita*.[92]

Although by the middle of the eighteenth century it becomes clear that racial prejudice is a factor, the role of bigotry in seventeenth century Maryland legislation is difficult to assess. The anti-miscegenation legislation, however, stands at least for the proposition that the Marylanders felt there was something shameful, "a disgrace to all Christian nations," in black-white marriages. The essential historical problem is whether racism preceded and promoted slavery or whether it followed the institutionalization of slavery and merely supported the system. For this, as for all historical conundra, there is no simple solution. It should be sufficient to note, however, that these anti-miscegenation statutes would not have taken the form which they did unless there was some feeling that black was not white and that the two should not be joined in holy wedlock.

As for racism and the establishment of slavery, although a certain degree of racism was undoubtedly present, the processes of the law encouraged slavery and anti-miscegenation legislation. The essential element was from the first the protection of the masters' property interest. Although a notion of racial separateness contributed to the original basis of slavery—the lack of any saving contract between the master and the black which in the case of the white did not lead to life servitude—slavery was in essence a matter of law. It was the law and the legal institutions which provided the impetus.[93] That is, legal institutions reflected colonial attitudes as all legal strictures and structures are representative of the societies which establish them. . . .

The purpose of servant control legislation was to prevent servants from selling masters' goods, traveling without passes, and running away—the protection of masters' property interest. . . .

Seventeenth century servant and slave control legislation culminated in what might be referred to as The Omnibus Servant and Slave Control Act of 1699, which incorporated the basic means of subjugation that had been evolving during the century.[94] The early restrictions on servants may have applied to slaves. It was only after 1664, however, when the colonists began to realize that hereditary life servitude was fundamentally different from mere term servitude, that the slaves and Negroes begin to be specifically mentioned. As Negroes came into the colony in increasing numbers during the last quarter of the century, each successive act became harsher and somewhat more restrictive. The body of servant law that had developed with reference to white servants was easily extended by analogy to the new form of servitude which had arisen. The interest of masters in their servants was protected by the law. For white servants this interest never became absolute because such servants would eventually become free. But for the blacks, who were incapable of satisfying damages in the usual way in the currency starved economy, their status as property was to receive a most complete recognition in the law. Controls on white servants expired as white servitude itself gradually ended and a democratic mythology developed. Black servitude did not end and blacks were excluded from eighteenth century democratic theories. Therefore, the regulation of servants became the regulation of slavery. The precedent had been established. The development of law by analogy, which legislators and jurists find so appealing, was easy and simple.

Notes

1.   This is the name given slavery by its nineteenth century defenders. *See* W. Goodell, *The American Slave Code in Theory and Practice* (4th ed. 1853); G. Fitzhugh, *Cannibals All* (1857).

2.   Alpert, "The Law of Slavery: It Did Happen Here," 55 *A.B.A. Jour.* 544 (1969).

3. F. Maitland, *Domesday Book and Beyond,* 26– 107 (Norton Library ed. 1966). *See also Somersett v. Stuart,* 20 How.Eng.St.Tr. 1 (1772).

4. King's Bench, Coram Rege Roll, no. 343 (Hilary 1346), m. 103 d., as cited in 6 *Select Cases in the Court of King's Bench Under Edward III* 50– 52 (Seldon Soc. 1965).

5. The Charter is reprinted in 1 *Kilty's Laws of Maryland* (1779).

6. Strictly speaking, this is inaccurate. William Clayborne of Virginia had already established a trading post on Kent Island within the Province. He defied the provincial government for several years and one of the first Maryland statutes was a bill of attainder against him in 1638. 1 *Md. Archives* 21. Actually, the session at which the bill of attainder was passed took place during the official year 1637, because until 1752 each official year began on March 25th. To avoid unnecessary hairsplitting, all dates cited herein are to the historical year rather than to the official year.

7. Everstine, "The Establishment of Legislative Power in Maryland," 12 *Md.L.Rev.* 99, 120 (1951).

8. Steiner, "Maryland's First Courts," *American Historical Ass'n Annual Report for 1901* 213, 216 (1902).

9. 49 *Md. Archives* xiii. In spite of this rather peculiar situation, the Upper House reversed decisions of the Provincial Court with surprising frequency.

10. Gaps in the Provincial Court records occur primarily in 1641, 1642, 1645, and 1646. 49 *Md. Archives* viii. No county court records have been preserved for the 1630's and 40's and for the rest of the century they are very incomplete. 53 *Md. Archives* xiii.

11. 1 *Md. Archives* 41.

12. 1 *Md. Archives* 80. *See also* "An Acte lymiting Servants tymes," passed in 1661, which expressly excluded slaves. *Id.* at 409. Similar statutes with similar exclusions were also passed in 1662, *Id.* at 453, and 1666. 2 *Md. Archives* 147.

13. Handlin. "Origins of the Southern Labor System," 7 *William & Mary Q.* (3rd series), 199– 203 (1950).

14. "An Act Concerning Negroes & Other Slaves [1664]," 1 *Md. Archives* 533– 34.

15. For example, there is only one courtroom mention of a Negro in a nine year period in Charles County. *See* 60 *Md. Archives*.

16. *See* 41 *Md. Archives* 186, 190–91: 66 *Md. Archives* 226: 54 *Md. Archives* 191.

17. 1 *Md. Archives* 250, 346.

18. 4 *Md. Archives* 189.

19. 4 *Md. Archives* 304: ''The 24th July 1644. Received of Capt. Tho: Cornwaleys by the hands of Sir William Berkely Knight nine pounds sterl: and by the hands of Mr. Cutbert ffennick ninety seven pounds & halfe of beaver, and is for or towards satisfaction of a debt of fifty pounds sterl: for two negroes d/d [delivered] the aforesaid Capt. Cornwaleys. By me Rich: Bennett.''

20. 53 *Md. Archives* xiviii.

21. 41 *Md. Archives* 499.

22. Winthrop D. Jordan, *White Over Black—American Attitudes Toward the Negro* 1550– 1812 63 fn. 39 (Pelican ed. 1969).

23. 64 *Md. Archives* 121–22.

24. The Ashanti, for example, who appeared on the scene in the 1630's, traded blacks for guns. *See* Blanco, ''Wolseley's March to Kumasi,'' 1 *Mankind* 40 (April, 1969). *See also* Elizabeth Donnan, ed., 1 *Documents Illustrative of the Slave Trade to America* (1930).

25. 41 *Md. Archives* 190.

26. 41 *Md. Archives* 205.

27. R. Semmes, *Crime & Punishment in Early Maryland* 121 (1938): 41 *Md. Archives* 206.

28. 41 *Md. Archives* 204.

29. Handlin, *op. cit. supra* note 13.

30. *See* Susie M. Ames, *Studies of the Virginia Eastern Shore in the Seventeenth Century* 99– 100 (1940). Miss Ames cites examples of early manumissions as evidence of ''mutual good will'' between the races. Much more probable is the desire of most masters to keep their servants as long as possible. *See,* e.g., *Notes* 57– 59 *infra* & associated text.

31. *See,* e.g., *Notes* 72– 78 *infra* & associated text.

32. ''An Act concerning English Servants that Runn away in Company of Negroes or other Slaves [1663],'' 1 *Md. Archives* 489. In 1662, however, ''An Act Concerning Taxable persons,'' which levied a poll tax, had pro-

vided: ''And all Slaves whatsoever whether Male or female imported or borne in the Province att or above the age of Tenn years shall be likewise Esteemed and accounted taxable . . .'' 1 *Md. Archives* 449. The use of the word ''imported'' indicates black rather than native Indian slaves. In addition, the wording remained unchanged in a 1692 statute, which was long after most slaves were black and there had been a great influx of black slaves into the Province. 13 *Md. Archives* 538–39; 53 *Md. Archives* xlviii.

33.　E.g., James Curtis Ballagh, *A History of Slavery in Virginia* 39 (1902).

34.　''An Act Concerning Negroes & other Slaves,'' 1 *Md. Archives* 533–534.

35.　E.g., Handlin, *op. cit. supra* note 13, at p. 211.

36.　''An Act for the Encourageing the Importation of Negros and Slaves into this Province,'' 2 *Md. Archives* 272.

37.　Actually, this session took place during the official year 1637, but see Note 6 *supra*.

38.　1 *Md. Archives* 21. These statutes, however, did not become law because of the dispute with the Proprietary, Note 7 *supra* & accompanying text.

39.　1 *Md. Archives* 21.

40.　In 1634, there were 200 persons in the colony; in 1638, 700; in 1660, 12,000; 1665, 16,000; 1671, 20,000; 1701, 30,000. No figures for blacks are given for this period. 3 J. Scharf, *History of Maryland* 779 (1967 ed.). The Archives suggest slightly lower figures during the early part of the century and slightly higher figures during the later years: in 1650, 8,000; 1660, 11,000; 1670, 16,000; 1680, 20,000; 1690, 25,000; 1700, 32,000. 53 *Md. Archives* lviii.

41.　Up until the last quarter of the century Negroes came in only in ''ones and twos.'' 4 E. Donnan, *Documents Illustrative of the History of the Slave Trade to America,* 1 (1935).

42.　Tobacco was the staple crop of the Province. In 1666, the General Assembly debated a law for the cessation of tobacco growing because of a glut on the market. 2 *Md. Archives* 48.

43.　Land or headrights was given to men who brought servants and other persons into the Province. Also, servants received land at the expiration of their terms.

44.　53 *Md. Archives* xxxii.

45. *Md. Archives, Proceedings of the Council of Maryland* 1661– 1675, 265.

46. "Generally all the Inhabitants of the province being Labourers are imployed in planting tobacco . . . The Trade of this province Ebbs & flowes according to the rise or fall of tobacco in the market of England . . . and especially the Country is in want of servants & negros." 19 *Md. Archives* ("Answer of the (lower) house to the severall Quaries contained in the Ire of the Right honorable the Lords of the Council for trade & forreigne plantations . . . (1697)") 539–40.

47. *See,* e.g., an indenture recorded in the Talbot County Court in 1672. 54 *Md. Archives* 543.

48. 1 *Md. Archives* 352–53.

49. E.g., 54 *Md. Archives* 127, 465, 555; 53 *Md. Archives* 485, 501, 510.

50. 67 *Md. Archives* 420.

51. 54 *Md. Archives* 375.

52. 53 *Md. Archives* 182–83.

53. 65 *Md. Archives* 326.

54. 67 *Md. Archives* 272.

55. 38 *Md. Archives* 152–53.

56. 65 *Md. Archives* 279.

57. 67 *Md. Archives* 26.

58. 65 *Md. Archives* 475.

59. 54 *Md. Archives* 191, 375.

60. 53 *Md. Archives* 599, 624.

61. 41 *Md. Archives* 496.

62. 65 *Md. Archives* 179.

63. 67 *Md. Archives* 25, 227; *Md. Archives, Proceedings of the Provincial Court* 1678– 1679, 46.

64. 38 *Md. Archives* 117–18.

65.   53 *Md. Archives* 400.

66.   54 *Md. Archives* 116–19.

67.   41 *Md. Archives* 500–503.

68.   53 *Md. Archives* 502.

69.   49 *Md. Archives* 166.

70.   49 *Md. Archives* 486, 489–490. It cost the Province 1065 pounds of tobacco to execute Jacob. 2 *Md. Archives* 94.

71.   65 *Md. Archives* 2–3. The language quoted is from the indictment.

72.   65 *Md. Archives* 7–8. Requiring a released suspect to be hangman was not unusual. In another case, a servant, who had been convicted of a larceny, was released on the condition that he serve out his time and then become the "generall hangman" for the Province.

73.   54 *Md. Archives* 707. They were probably not taken into custody, however.

74.   54 *Md. Archives* 712. The trial took place in 1668.

75.   2 *Md. Archives* 75, 78, 91.

76.   2 *Md. Archives* 30.

77.   54 *Md. Archives* 741.

78.   54 *Md. Archives* 757.

79.   54 *Md. Archives* 760.

80.   66 *Md. Archives* 291.

81.   7 *Md. Archives* 51–52.

82.   "An Act for keeping of Register of Birthes Marriages and Burialls in each Respective County," 7 *Md. Archives* 76.

83.   1 *Md. Archives* 373.

84.   13 *Md. Archives* 529.

85.   "An Act for the better Administration of Justice in probate of Wills, granting Administrations Recovery of Legacys & secureing filiall portions," 7

Md. Archives 195. Interestingly enough, the Act states that ".. . our dependence upon England obleigeth us to make all our Lawes as neere as may bee Consonant to the Lawes of England . . ." *Id.* at 196.

86.   7 *Md. Archives* 197. A similar provision was again incorporated in the Wills Act of 1699. 22 *Md. Archives* 535.

87.   7 *Md. Archives* 199. A similar provision was re-enacted in the Wills Act of 1699. 22 *Md. Archives* 537.

88.   "An Act Concerning Negroes & Slaves," 7 *Md. Archives* 203.

89.   7 *Md. Archives* 204.

90.   Alpert, *op. cit. supra* note 2, at p. 546.

91.   "An Act concerning Negro Slaves," 13 *Md. Archives* 546, 547–48.

92.   *See* Alpert, *op. cit. supra* note 2, at p. 546.

93.   *See generally,* Thomas R. R. Cobb, *An Inquiry into the Law of Negro Slavery in the United States of America* (1858).

94.   "An Act relating to Servants and Slaves," 22 *Md. Archives* 546.

Black Puritan: The Negro in Seventeenth-Century Massachusetts

Robert C. Twombly and Robert H. Moore*

A black person in Massachusetts "felt the brunt of discriminatory laws but he was not without due process and never totally removed from participation in the white social and economic orbit" assert Robert C. Twombly and Robert H. Moore in "Black Puritan: The Negro in Seventeenth-Century Massachusetts." The authors note that due to their small numbers (2,000 in 1715) and to white prejudice, historians have tended to overlook blacks in the Puritan Commonwealth or to assume that they led desperate lives. But that was not the case; Puritan respect for the law gave blacks some advantages and protections not always available in the other British colonies. Twombly, a member of the history department at City College of City University of New York (CUNY), has also written on "Black Resistance to Slavery in Massachusetts." Moore is a member of the Department of English Language and Literature at the University of Maryland; among his other publications are School for Soldiers *and an article in* Contemporary Literature.

HISTORIANS HAVE ASSUMED that seventeenth-century Massachusetts was no different from other American colonies in its

*Abridged from Robert C. Twombly and Robert H. Moore, "Black Puritan: The Negro in Seventeenth-Century Massachusetts," *William and Mary Quarterly* 24 (1967), 224–42. Reprinted by permission.

treatment of Negroes.[1] It has been easy to overlook a colony where, as late as 1715, there were only 2,000 Negroes in a population of 96,000, and where whites seemed to hold racial views similar to those of other settlers. But an analysis of Negro life in the Puritan Commonwealth reveals the inaccuracy of this view.

Most authorities agree that Negroes first came to Massachusetts in 1638, but it seems clear to us that at least one Negro had arrived as early as 1633. Contemporaries estimated that there were between 100 and 200 in 1680 and 550 by 1708.[2] Although Negroes were numerous enough to be familiar in the everyday affairs of many communities by the 1660's, most Puritans regarded blacks as strange and exotic creatures. Despite the inconsistent terminology used to refer to Negroes,[3] Massachusetts whites held certain derogatory attitudes.

John Josselyn noted that some New Englanders thought Negro blackness resulted from the African climate, while others believed it came from Ham's curse. Blackness was commonly associated with evil. During the witchcraft hysteria many people claimed to have seen the Devil in the form of a "Blackman"; white women accused of having evil spirits were sometimes called "black witches." Blackness connoted ugliness as well as evil. "Sea-Devils," a fish found off the Maine coast, were popularly called "Negroes" because they were a very "ugly," "hideous" species, "having a black scale."[4]

If some derogatory attitudes found expression in metaphor, others appeared in social relations. Whites were insulted when compared closely with a Negro. "A Lieutenant of a Man of War," the perturbed Cotton Mather wrote, "whom I am a Stranger to, designing to putt an Indignity upon me, has called his *Negro-Slave* by the Name of COTTON-MATHER." Samuel Sewall recorded in his diary that "Mr. Cotton Mather came to Mr. Wilkins's shop, and there talked very sharply against me as if I used his father worse than a Neger; spake so loud that the people in the street might hear him." Such opinions sometimes led to bizarre actions. Josselyn wrote that fish did not respond to herring as quickly as they did for a "waggish lad at Capeporpus [Maine], who baited his hooks with the drown'd Negro's buttocks.'' Puritan racial attitudes do not seem appreciably different from those held by other contemporary white men.[5]

One might expect Puritans to have treated Negroes with an indignity matching their attitudes. But the real test of the colony's race relations must be based not on what whites thought and said but on what they did. How the Negro fared in day to day activity is the best indication of the nature of Negro life in the Puritan Commonwealth.

Central to the maintenance of order and stability in any society is the administration of justice. This was particularly true in Massachusetts where respect for the law was primary in the colonists' conception of a vigorous, stable, and godly society. A profound commitment to the law and the judicial process overpowered antipathetical racial views and assured fair and equal treatment, guaranteeing the basic legal rights of Englishmen to free, servant, and slave Negroes. These rights—including police protection, legal counsel, trial by jury, fair and considered hearings, and impartial justice—are very much expected in the twentieth century. In the seventeenth they were incipient concepts in much of the western world. But Massachusetts guarded these liberties jealously, applying them without regard for skin color. The Puritans did not hold advanced racial views but they did place a high priority on the universality of justice. Throughout the century Negroes and whites received essentially equal treatment before the law.

Important principles were observed even in minor offenses. . . . When, in 1653, ''a contravercy'' developed between John Smith of Plymouth and John Barnes's ''neager maide servant,'' the Plymouth court listened to ''whatsoever could bee saide on either side.'' Both were cleared of any misdemeanor, but they were admonished for public quarreling.[6]

Like whites, Negroes received police protection and were shielded from extralegal punitive action. When three Indians broke into the home of Angola, a free Negro, in 1672, he prosecuted. All three were given twenty stripes and ordered to remain in prison until they paid court costs.[7] . . .

Other incidents establish that Negro testimony was admissible as evidence against whites. In 1673 a defendant challenged a witness's legal right to testify, but the plaintiff replied "that the negro was of such carriage and knowledge that her testimony had been accepted several times before this." Later, in 1679, Wonn Negro testified against Bridget Oliver, who was suspected of witchcraft. In 1680 Mingo the Negro was a witness in a suit involving warehouse arson. Instances of Negro testimony for and against both races are numerous.[8]

It is also evident from the records that Negroes had access to legal counsel. In 1679 Hannah, a Negro servant, was convicted for stealing a box of "Chyrurgions Jnstrumts." From prison she persuaded three white men to post forty pounds bond for her release and petitioned the Suffolk County court for dismissal of her fines. Her appeal, a sophisticated legal argument, cited page and section numbers of the laws governing burglary. Although the jury dismissed it, Zachariah Chaffee, Jr., commenting on Hannah's appeal, noted the "refined distinctions" that could only have been "written by men accustomed to legal problems."[9]

An additional example of the many elements of justice accorded Negroes stemmed from the Salem witch controversy. In 1692 a warrant was issued for the arrest of Mary Black, a Negro owned by Lieutenant Nathaniel Putnam of Salem Village. Although maintaining her innocence, Mary was tried, convicted, and imprisoned for witchcraft. The next year, however, cooler heads had apparently prevailed, and Mary was not forgotten. Upon petition she was released from prison by proclamation of the Governor.[10]

These cases introduce important principles illustrating Negro legal rights. A Negro's word was admissible as evidence and his testimony could be as acceptable as that of whites. Charges against Negroes had to be documented and they received the thoughtful consideration of juries and magistrates. Negroes had police protection and were shielded from extralegal practices that would have denied them due process of law. They could appeal, use legal counsel, and receive gubernatorial pardons. . . .

Of the sexual crimes committed in Massachusetts, fornication, bastardy, and rape were most prevalent. According to the 1675 Laws and Ordinances of War—a compilation of previous statutes—rape, ravishment, and unnatural abuses were punishable by death. Fornication and other "dissolute lasciviousness" were penalized at the judge's discretion, taking into account the severity and circumstances of the case. Fornication, by both Negro and white, was a considerable problem in early Massachusetts, and the many recorded cases provide ample opportunity for comparative analysis.[11]

Essex County punished its Negro fornicators by whipping or fine, the choice sometimes being left to the offender. In 1660, Captain White's Negro Jugg was whipped; Grace and Juniper, convicted in 1674, were "to be fined or whipped." In 1678, two "neager" servants, David and Judith, chose to pay a fine rather than feel the lash ten and five times respectively. The whites in Essex County received similar treatment. Mary Dane, an indentured servant, was whipped. The same year, 1654, Elizabeth Osgood was given thirty stripes and her mate twenty-five. Most infringers, regardless of race, received from ten to twenty stripes or were ordered to pay from forty to fifty shillings.[12]

Representative of Suffolk County's treatment of fornicators was the case of Mary Plumb, a white, who was punished with fifteen stripes and court and prison fees for "Lascivious carriage by being seene in bed with a man." For the same offense, Phoebe Lovell received ten stripes or a forty shilling fine plus court costs. Negroes in Suffolk County got the same penalties. Joan and her partner, Jasper Indian, were given their choice of fifteen stripes or a forty shilling fine plus court costs. In a significant case, Robert Corbet, a white, and George, a Negro, both servants of Stephen French, received identical sentences in 1679 for committing fornication with the Negro Maria: twenty stripes and court costs. Fornication between the races was not punished any more stringently than that between members of the same race. In Suffolk, as in Essex County, the most common penalty ranged from ten to twenty lashes or a forty to fifty shilling fine plus fees of court.[13]

Although there is no evidence that it was practiced, racial intermarriage was not illegal until 1705. Before then most miscegenation was illicit. If it led to bastardy, penalties for both races were generally the same as for simple fornication. . . . In 1682, for example, Richard Prior gave thirty pounds surety to save Ipswich from maintaining his illegitimate child. The same year John Tucker was fined six pounds and ordered to pay an undisclosed amount for birth and support. In 1679 the court ordered John Hunkins to give his partner's father one shilling per week. When the races mixed the penalties were about the same: William Rane, father of a child by the Indian servant Ann, paid three shillings a week. For "haveing a bastard," the white Hannah Bonny was "well whipt"; her mate, Nimrod Negro, was also whipped and made to turn over eighteen pence weekly for his offspring. Illegitimate Negro children were generally awarded financial support in amounts similar to those paid to white and mixed offspring. In 1673 the Negro Silvanus provided two shillings six pence per week for his son's upbringing. . . .[14]

Rape, a more serious offense, could be punished by death. The two Negro cases in the published records reveal the severity dealt offenders. Basto Negro was convicted in 1676 of raping the three year old daughter of Robert Cox, his master. When Cox appealed Basto's death sentence, the jury substituted thirty-nine lashes and ordered him "allwayes to weare a roape about his neck, to hang doune two foot." If ever he was found without his rope Basto would feel an additional twenty lashes. Shortly thereafter John Negro confessed to "pulling Sarah Philips of Salem off her horse and attempting to ravish her." John's penalty for attempted rape was a five pound payment to Miss Phillips, prosecution and court costs, and banishment from the colony.[15]

Whites also received stiff penalties. John Man, perhaps the Marquis de Sade of his time, for "wanton and lascivious carriages . . . and cruell beating" of his indentured servant, gave two hundred pounds sureties until the next court, paid prosecution costs and court fees, and terminated his girl's contract.

John Kempe attempted rape on "3 yong girles [and] was censured to bee whiped both heare [Boston], at Roxberry and at Salem very severely and was Comitted for a slave to Lieft Davenport." Two other white rapists, William Cheny and Samuel Guile, were hanged until dead. . . .[16]

The average penalty for manslaughter was a twenty pound fine and the costs of prosecution, court, and detention. Depending on the circumstances, part of the fine went to the colony and part to the deceased's relatives.[17] Both instances of Negro manslaughter, originally indictments for murder against whites, were handled equitably. A 1684 defendant, "Robert Trayes, negro," wounded the "legg of Daniell Standlake . . . , of which wound, and cutting the legg occationed therby, died. . . ." Since he had meant to fire at Standlake's door, the jury decided that Trayes was "an instrument of the death of Daniell Standlake by misadventure," and sentenced the defendant to pay the deceased's father five pounds or be whipped. The second case, in which the servant Robin was accused, is of particular note, not only for its dealing with manslaughter but also for its clear statement of Negro legal rights.[18]

Robin was guilty of giving John Cheeny of Cambridge "a mortall wound on the head with a stick" in 1689. His punishment was light: charges of prosecution, fees of court, and costs of prison where he was to remain until he paid. Robin had pled not guilty, but what extenuating circumstances had brought about the easy sentence are not recorded. More important, however, is that after the jury had been selected Robin was allowed to "make . . . challange against any of them." In addition, one juror, feeling as Hawthorne had in 1660, that Negroes did not deserve "the same distribution of Justice with our selves," refused to appear. In reply the court fined him five shillings. Through this concrete act the court clearly stated that shirking jury duty was inexcusable and that due process extended to blacks as well as whites.

The only recorded case in which a white killed a Negro took place in Maine in 1694 when a master's continual mistreatment of his servant led to her death. In the South well before this time, as Carl Degler points out, masters were without "any fear of prosecution" if they killed slaves; the law "allowed punishment for refractory slaves up to and including accidental death. . . ." But the Puritans showed more restraint. Indicted by a grand jury on suspicion of murder, Nathaniel Cane was convicted of manslaughter for "Cruelty to his Negro woman by Cruell Beating and hard usage." His fine—ten pounds ten shillings—was light. Nonetheless, a master could not mistreat, abuse, or murder his Negro without threat of legal action.[19]

Arson, an infrequent but serious offense, brought harsh penalties. Severity was demonstrated early in the colony's history when in 1640 Henry Stevens fired his master's barn and had his indenture extended by twenty-one years. Throughout the century the penalties were stiff: Jack, a Negro arsonist, was hanged in 1681. Two Negroes implicated in the Maria arson case the same year were banished and Maria was burned alive, the only punishment of its kind in Massachusetts history.[20] Maria's fire had caused the death of a baby girl. She had deliberately destroyed her master's house and had not intended murder. But since she had caused a death by burning she in turn was burned. Her severe sentence may have been prompted by uneasiness over a rash of fires in the Boston vicinity. Social pressure may have induced the court to be unduly harsh in this affair but it was not stampeded. The strict sentence was a response to a specific situation and did not become a precedent for future dealings with either arsonists, murderers, or Negroes. But the case stands as an ugly blot on Puritan history.[21]

This review of legal cases indicates that throughout the seventeenth century the Negro received due process and only in isolated incidents, like the Maria case, was he given unusual treatment. But even on that occasion it is questionable to what extent skin color dictated severity. In general, the Negro held the rights of Englishmen before the courts. The legal apparatus did not undergo subtle shifts when Negroes came before it.

If the Negro's legal status was not circumscribed by pigmentation neither were his economic opportunities. Several black men, servant and free, accumulated real and other property; the color of their skin did not by definition render them ineligible for economic gain. Although most Negroes were members of the servant class and therefore at the bottom of the economic ladder, some were able to carve out an enviable niche in the white business world.

The story of Angola illustrates the possibilities. In 1653 he was owned by Captain Robert Keayne, who in his will in 1656 left Angola a two pound legacy. Then the free Negro Bostian Ken purchased Angola and set him free by bonding his property to Mrs. Keayne. In 1670 Governor Richard Bellingham sold a piece of land bordered "Upon the North East with the land of Angola, the Negro." Bellingham had given him this fifty-foot square piece in the late 1660's when Angola, paddling in a river, had rescued the Governor from his sinking boat. When he died in 1675 Angola's will confirmed his house, land, and other possessions upon his widow Elizabeth, her children, and her heirs forever. In the twenty years before his death Angola had paid his eighteen pound obligation to Ken and had moved from a servant with a two pound legacy to a free Negro of means.[22]

Bostian Ken, Angola's benefactor, was another prosperous Negro. In order to purchase his friend's freedom in 1656 Ken bonded his house and land in Dorchester plus four and one half acres of wheat. In 1662 he sold his one-third share of the fourteen-ton ship *Hopewell* to his "loving Friend Francis Vernon" along with "one barrell of liquor one barr of Sugar one Barr mackerell and one Barr Codfish." From 1656 to 1662 Ken dealt in considerable amounts of property.[23]

Most of the other seventeenth-century Negro landowners received their holdings from their masters. . . . Although the number of successful Negroes was small, they came from a total Negro population in the colony that was at most only two hundred at this time.[24]

A few Negroes were property owners, but the majority were house servants living with white families. Many resided in Boston but those in the outlying areas and the Boston blacks who traveled about broadened interracial contact. Most Negroes lived in their masters' homes, were often left alone, and could come and go as they pleased when not working. They were not restricted to the towns in which they lived and in many cases moved freely about the countryside.[25]

Freedom of movement opened up certain options. One option, running away, may have been a product of working class discontent; but running away was also encouraged by alternatives that lack of repression offered.[26] Freedom of movement permitted a certain amount of fraternization between races in the lower classes; the derogatory views of most whites did not preclude informal relations. Occasionally mutual activities were forms of antisocial behavior. In 1673, for example, "John Burrington, Edward Fish, Richard Hollingworths Negro Tom, Thomas [,] Clark Cliffords Servt," and a fifth man, stole saddles and bridles and "complotted to run away." About the same time "Gregory, Nath. Emerson, Arthur Abbot and a Negro" broke into a house, took wine, and improvised a drinking party. But not all interracial mingling was mischievous. For five years in the 1690's one of Boston's four chimney sweepers was "Jeremiah the Negro"; for one year, 1693, he was joined by "Negro Will," who along with Jeremiah brought token integration to Boston's public employ. During the smallpox epidemic in the 1680's Mary Heall, a seventy-four year old widow living alone, took the Negro Zanckey into her home to watch over his recovery. On another occasion, Jack, a runaway Negro, came to Anthony Dorchester's home. Jack was a stranger but Dorchester invited him in and made him welcome:

> . . . after asking for a Pipe of Tobacco which I told him there was some on the Table he tooke my knife and Cut some and then put it in his Pocket, and after that tooke downe a Cutlass and offered to draw it but it Coming out stiff I closed in upon him. . . .

Jack was overpowered and taken to prison, but Dorchester's initial hospitality is noteworthy.[27]

The colony's mechanisms of social control which permitted easy interracial contact did not make Negroes full fledged citizens or the social equals of whites, but neither were the blacks shunted to another realm of existence. The absence of rigid barriers in Massachusetts did not create a Negro utopia. But neither were Bay Colony blacks forced into a separate and demeaning world of their own. The Negro hovered on the fringes of full participation in social and economic life.

Overcoming the obstacles of nature was of immediate importance to the first generation of Puritans; in their attempt to construct a ''city upon a hill'' their first concerns were the problems of building communities, of keeping their children from barbarism, and of reproducing essential and familiar institutions. But as the generations passed, as trade increased, as the frontier receded, and as the complexities of a growing colony burgeoned, the Commonwealth's problems shifted. Social order and stability had been of major importance from the beginning but during the last two decades of the seventeenth century serious social introspection increased. Ministers warned that God was angry with the people; family structure, education, the churches, and other social institutions came under closer scrutiny. It was in this context that the colony passed her first laws to regulate the Negro's behavior.

Except for militia policy, no laws were passed applying only to Negroes until the 1680's.[28] Old and New England had fitted the black man into the social system without legally recognizing slavery or a slave caste. Within the broad guidelines of the Common Law and Puritan religious views Massachusetts had extended century-old rights of Englishmen to Negroes. But in the 1680's the colony began to place restrictions upon them. The new Negro policies were responses to three social concerns: a widespread anathema for the slave trade, a pervasive uneasiness about the colony's economic future, and a growing anxiety about the Negro's behavior.

In spite of the unpopularity of slaving, several Massachusetts merchants were active traders in the 1680's, selling Negroes in Virginia for three to five thousand pounds of tobacco per head. Public pressure could not prohibit businessmen from dealing with Southerners but it could discourage the practice at home. Fear of public reprisal forced John Saffin, John Usher,

James Wetcomb, and Andrew Belcher to import Negroes secretly in 1681. Fearing seizure, these merchants rerouted their Guinea trader from Swansea, Rhode Island, to Nantasket, Massachusetts, where, they wrote, "before you come in there take in such negroes . . . of ours and come up in the night with them, giveing us notice thereof wth what privacy you can. . . ." "Keepe your men Ignorant of your designe," the traders told their agent, and do nothing "prejudiciall to our mayne designe."[29]. . .

The first regulations on Negroes were clauses inserted into general laws prohibiting Negroes, mulattos, Indians, servants, and apprentices from buying or being served alcoholic beverages. Later in the 1680's the same groups were warned about stealing or giving away stolen goods and whites who induced thefts or received stolen merchandise were similarly promised punishment.[30]

No further legislation appeared until after the turn of the century. In 1703 Indian, Negro, and mulatto servants and slaves could be on the streets after nine in the evening only with masters' consent. After 1703 no Negro or mulatto could be manumitted unless his master gave fifty pounds surety for the servant's welfare. The first law was directed toward night-time unrest, and the second prevented masters from throwing elderly, unemployable servants on the town charge. Both were concerned with specific and observable social problems.

The most stringent new measure, "An Act for the Better Preventing of a Spurious and Mixt Issue" of 1705, drove a deep wedge between the races. Sexual intercourse and racial intermarriage were now specifically prohibited. Fixed penalties were imposed on both races. Fornication was no longer left to judicial decision; Negro offenders were banished and the white consort, male or female, assumed responsibility for the offspring. The law reemphasized the desirability of Negro marriages, presumably as part of an effort to minimize mulatto births.

The 1705 law also placed a four pound duty on Negroes imported into the colony, and set heavy penalties on violators. The new duty aimed to discourage the slave trade. Some Puritans wished to rid the colony of Negroes or prevent any more from coming but restrictions on importation did not rest on this basis alone. Seven years later, in 1712, the General Court prohibited the trade in Indians. Revulsion for the slave trade and suspicion of outsiders worked to prevent nonwhites from coming to the Puritan Commonwealth.

A five-part law in 1707 prevented free Negroes from harboring or entertaining nonwhite servants in their homes without masters' approval and ordered them to repair highways, clean streets, or perform other tasks equal in time and amount to military duty. Since free Negroes had "a share in the benefit" of common defense, they would also go to the parade ground "in case of alarm" and "perform such tasks as the first commission of the company shall direct. . . ." The several laws were supplemented by town ordinances which, throughout the eighteenth century, further limited Negro freedom of movement.[31]

The new Massachusetts statutes dealing with Negroes were responses to specific and observable colonial problems. The measures arose from what the Puritans thought were manifestations of social disorder. The legislation was not a premeditated program to debase the Negro, for the Puritans believed that their regulations were in the Negro's best interest. Some colonial leaders like Samuel Sewall and Cotton Mather wanted to incorporate Negroes more intimately into the colony's social and religious institutions; but men of narrower vision passed laws which overruled better intentions. The Bay Colony reluctantly accepted the black man's presence but believed by the 1700's that it precipitated social disorder. Legal restrictions on Massachusetts's Negroes neither followed from nor led to slavery. In the Bay Colony these restrictions were part of a hasty problem-solving endeavor that prevalent attitudes and predispositions made possible. The Negro felt the brunt of discriminatory laws but he was not without due process and never totally removed from participation in the white social and economic orbit. These advantages reflected an attitude that later enabled the Bay Colony to lead the way in constitutional prohibitions of slavery.

Notes

1.   Recent scholarship on early American slavery has ignored Massachusetts or assumed similarity with the South: Oscar and Mary Handlin, "Origins of the Southern Labor System," *The William and Mary Quarterly*, 3d Ser., VII (1950), 199–222, and Oscar Handlin, "The Origins of Negro Slavery," *Race and Nationality in American Life* (New York, 1957), 3–29, argue that discrimination developed because of the institutionalization of slavery. Carl N. Degler, "Slavery and the Genesis of American Race Prejudice," *Comparative Studies in Society and History,* II (1959), 49–66, reverses the Handlin thesis, attributing slavery to innate white discriminatory attitudes. Winthrop D. Jordan, "Modern Tensions and the Origin of American Slavery," *Journal of Southern History,* XXVIII (1962), 18–30, sees both slavery and discrimination as part of a worldwide debasement of the Negro. Other relevant works are: Jordan, "The Influence of the West Indies on the Origins of New England Slavery," *Wm. and Mary Qtly.* 3d Ser., XVIII (1961), 243–250; Lawrence W. Towner, " 'A Fondness for Freedom': Servant Protest in Puritan Society,"*ibid.,* XIX (1962), 201–219; Towner, "The Sewall-Saffin Dialogue on Slavery," *ibid.,* XXI (1964), 40–52; Jules Zanger, "Crime and Punishment in Early Massachusetts," *ibid.,* XXII (1965), 471–477; Emory Washburn, "Slavery as it Once Prevailed in Massachusetts," in *Early History of Massachusetts: Lectures Delivered . . . Before the Lowell Institute, in Boston* (Boston, 1869), 199–225; and Lorenzo J. Greene, *The Negro in Colonial New England, 1620–1776* (New York, 1942).

2.   William Wood's 1634 *New-England's Prospect . . .* (1764 ed.), in *Publications of the Prince Society,* III (Boston, 1865), 86; and Deloraine P. Corey, *The History of Malden, Mass.,* 1633–1785 (Malden, Mass., 1899), 415, refer to a Negro living in Plymouth at least as early as 1633. Population estimates are taken from Simon Bradstreet to the Committee of Trade and Plantations, May 18, 1680, in Elizabeth Donnan, ed., *Documents Illustrative of the History of the Slave Trade to America* (Washington, D.C., 1930–35), III, 14–15; Edward Randolph's Report to the Lords of the Committee of the Colonies, Aug., 1681, in Samuel G. Drake, *The History and Antiquities of Boston . . .* (Boston, 1856), 441; Joseph Dudley to the Council of Trade and Plantations, Oct. 1, 1708, in Cecil Headlam, ed., *Calendar of State Papers, Colonial Series, America and West Indies, June, 1708–1709* (London, 1922), 110; and Evarts B. Greene and Virginia D. Harrington, *American Population Before the Federal Census of 1790* (New York, 1932), 14.

3.   "Slave" was not precisely defined in seventeenth-century Massachusetts; its flexible usage permitted several meanings. The conventional definition was "one who is the property of, and entirely subject to, another person, whether by capture, purchase, or birth; a servant completely divested of freedom and personal rights." See W. A. Cragie, ed., *A New English Dictionary on Historical Principles* (Oxford, 1919), X, 182–184. The burden of this article is to demonstrate that Massachusetts never forced Negroes into this

status. Puritans also used "slavery" to describe prisoners of war and criminals, and the term functioned as a rhetorical device to indicate dissatisfaction with government or authority. "Slave" and "servant" were used interchangeably in reference to Negroes: John Noble and John F. Cronin, eds., *Records of the Court of Assistants of . . . Massachusetts . . .* (Boston, 1901– 28), I, 74; and John Josselyn, *An Account of Two Voyages to New-England, Made during the Years 1638, 1663* (Boston, 1865), 139– 140.

4. The long history of black men in the European experience and the development of white racial opinion has been admirably treated in Winthrop D. Jordan, "White Over Black: the attitudes of the American colonists toward the Negro, to 1784" (unpubl. Ph.D. diss., Brown University, 1960), Ch. I. Puritan racial attitudes are illustrated in Josselyn, *Two Voyages,* 143; George L. Burr, ed., *Narratives of the Witchcraft Cases, 1648– 1706* (New York, 1914), 309– 310, 312, 425; and William S. Southgate, "History of Scarborough, from 1633 to 1783," Maine Historical Society, *Collections,* III (1853), 92.

5. Dec. 10, 1721, in Worthington C. Ford, ed., *Diary of Cotton Mather* (New York, 1957), II, 663; Barrett Wendell, *Cotton Mather: The Puritan Priest* (New York, [1891]), 153, quoting Samuel Sewall, Oct. 20, 1701; Josselyn, *Two Voyages,* 159; Jordan, "White Over Black," Ch. I.

6. Nathaniel B. Shurtleff, ed., *Records of the Colony of New Plymouth in New England* (Boston, 1855– 61), III, 39. To demonstrate racial equality before the law we shall compare the several kinds of criminal and civil offenses committed by Negroes to similar cases involving whites. We have appraised all the published records (falling between 1650 and 1690) in which Negroes appear; those presented here are not atypical. We believe these cases accurately reflect the temper of the Negro's participation in the legal process.

7. The Angola case is in Samuel Eliot Morison, ed., *Records of the Suffolk County Court, 1671– 1680,* 2 vols., in *Publications of the Colonial Society of Massachusetts, Collections,* XXIX– XXX (Boston, 1933), I, 119. A comparable case involving a white woman brought a penalty of twenty stripes and the order to wear a paper "pinned upon her forehead with this inscription in capital letters: 'A SLANDERER OF MR. ZEROBABELL ENDICOTT,' " in George F. Dow, ed., *Essex Court Recs.,* I, 380. Norton and Peter appear in Robert E. Moody, ed., *Province and Court Records of Maine* (Portland, 1928– 64), III, 226. Carl Degler, on the Southern administration of justice to Negroes, says: "As early as 1669 the Virginia law virtually washed its hands of protecting the Negro held as a slave. It allowed punishment of refractory slaves up to and including accidental death, relieving the master, explicitly, of any fear of prosecution. . . . ," in "Slavery and the Genesis of American Race Prejudice," 61. Compare this situation also with the 1694– 95 Nathaniel Cane murder case cited in Moody, ed., *Maine Recs.,* IV, 34– 35.

8. See Dow, ed., *Essex Court Recs.,* V, 179; VI, 255; VII, 329– 330, 373, 410. For white testimony on behalf of Negroes see Noble and Cronin, eds., *Assistants Recs.,* III, 194.

9. Morison, ed., *Suffolk Court Recs.*, II, 1153–1157. Chaffee's remarks are in the Intro., I, xxv.

10. Charles W. Upham, *Salem Witchcraft* . . . (Boston, 1867), II, 128, 136–137.

11. The 1675 statutes are in Nathaniel B. Shurtleff, ed., *Records of the Governor and Company of the Massachusetts Bay in New England* (Boston, 1854), V, 49–50, Sections 13 and 14. Also see Jordan, "White Over Black," 119. Fornication and adultery were usually treated as one crime in the seventeenth century. Married men, engaging in sexual activity with women other than their wives, were often tried for fornication.

12. For Essex County Negro fornication cases see Dow, ed., *Essex Court Recs.*, II, 247; V, 411; VI, 73, 135; VII, 141, 411; for whites see I, 71, 80, 82, 337, 347, 404, 414, 420; III, 17, 61, 198–199; VII, 377–378, 398, 406, 410; VIII, 375, 377, 424. This list is by no means exhaustive.

13. Because the published records are incomplete, the only Suffolk County cases are from the 1670's. For Negro offenders see Morison, ed., *Suffolk Court Recs.*, I, 233; II, 991; for whites see, for example, I, 22, 80, 90–91, 114, 119, 185, 233–234; II, 885, 1012–1014, 1097–1099, 1102, 1153. The Courts sometimes required a couple fornicating before marriage to make public confession before the church. See I, 80, 90–91. In Maine fornicators usually received seven or more stripes or a fine ranging from fifteen to fifty shillings. See Moody, ed., *Maine Recs.*, IV, 268–269, 293, 340, 344–345, 358, 360, and 371 for examples.

14. As with fornication interracial bastardy was not punished more severely than bastardy between two members of the same race. For examples of penalties accorded illegitimate white births see Morison, ed., *Suffolk Court Recs.*, II, 1097–1099; Dow, ed., *Essex Court Recs.*, VII, 97, 187; VIII, 12–13, 279; Shurtleff, ed., *Plymouth Recs.*, I, 127. For illegitimate Negro births see Morison, ed., *Suffolk Court Recs.*, I, 113, 259; II, 809, 841, 1164; Dow, ed., *Essex Court Recs.*, I, 196, 323; VI, 137. Interracial bastardy cases are: Dow, ed., *Essex Court Recs.*, V, 409; VI, 23; VII, 410; Morison, ed., *Suffolk Court Recs.*, I, 185, 232; II, 809; Shurtleff, ed., *Plymouth Recs.*, VI, 177. Alice Metherill and Black Will are in Moody, ed., *Maine Recs.*, IV, 47–49, 64–66; V, 126, 169–171, 199–201; *York Deeds* (Portland, 1887–1910), VI, fol. 88.

15. Basto's case is in Noble and Cronin, eds., *Assistants Recs.*, I, 74, and Shurtleff, ed., *Mass. Recs.*, V, 117–118. John Negro is in Morison, ed., *Suffolk Court Recs.*, II, 1067.

16. *Ibid.*, II, 807; Noble and Cronin, eds., *Assistants Recs.*, I, 50, 199; II, 86; innocent whites are *ibid.*, I, 73, 158.

17. Shurtleff, ed., *Mass. Recs.*, V, 50, lists penalties for manslaughter and murder. White manslaughter cases are cited in Noble and Cronin, eds., *Assistants Recs.*, I, 54, 114, 188, 358–359.

18. The Trayes case is in Shurtleff, eds., *Plymouth Recs.*, VI, 141–142; Robin's in Noble and Cronin, eds., *Assistants Recs.*, I, 304–305, 321.

19. Moody, ed., *Maine Recs.*, IV, 34–35. We saw no published court records convicting Negroes of murder. But note the equality of sentence in this extract from Samuel Sewall's diary, June 8, 1693: "Elisabeth Emerson of Havarill and a Negro Woman were executed after Lecture, for murdering their Infant Children." Massachusetts Historical Society, *Collections*, 5th Ser., V (1878), 379.

20. The Stevens case is in Noble and Cronin, eds., *Assistants Recs.*, II, 100. The documents relating to Maria, her accomplices, and Jack have been brought together by John Noble. See *Publications of the Colonial Society at Massachusetts, Transactions, 1899, 1900*, VIII (Boston, 1904), 323–336.

21. Noble, *ibid.*, argues that Maria was hanged before burning, dismissing both Cotton and Increase Mather's assertions that she was burned alive. But Noble overlooked evidence that substantiates the Mathers' contentions: a Milton minister who had witnessed Jack's and Maria's execution noted in his diary on Sept. 22, 1681: ". . . two negroes burnt, one of them was first hanged." "Rev. Peter Thacher's Journal" in Albert K. Teele, ed., *The History of Milton, Mass. 1640 to 1887* (Boston, 1887), 646. Increase Mather wrote: Maria was "burned to death,—the first that has suffered such a death in New England." Mass. Hist. Soc., *Proceedings*, III (1859), 320. Edgar Buckingham's allegation that in 1675 Phillis, a Negro slave, was burned alive in Cambridge, in "Morality, Learning, and Religion, in Massachusetts in Olden Times," *History and Proceedings of the Pocumtuck Valley Memorial Association, 1880–1889* (Deerfield, Mass., 1898), II, 20, seems unsupported.

22. *Suffolk Deeds* (Boston, 1880–1906), II, 297; III, 78; VII, 22, 144; VIII, 298–299; Morison, ed., *Suffolk Court Recs.*, II, 598; *Report of the Record Commissioners of the City of Boston Containing Miscellaneous Papers* (Boston, 1876–1909), X, 25.

23. Bostian Ken (Kine, Kajne), also known as Sebastian and Bus Bus, probably took his surname from the Keayne family. It was common for a Negro, if he had a last name, to use his master's or former master's. *Suffolk Deeds*, II, 297; IV, 111, 113.

24. Property owning Negroes and master's gifts are *ibid.*, VII, 43; X, 278, 295; Dow, ed., *Essex Court Recs.*, II, 183; VIII, 434; *York Deeds*, IV, fol. 52; Ford, ed., *Diary of Cotton Mather*, I, 278; Henry A. Hazen, *History of Billerica, Mass.* (Boston, 1883), 170–171. Charles Taussig noted a Rhode

Island Negro couple that had accumulated a 300 pound fortune and in 1735 sailed back to Guinea where they were independently wealthy; see *Rum, Romance and Rebellion* (New York, 1928), 33.

25.   Horizontal mobility and freedom of movement are illustrated by the Maria case, discussed above; Dow, ed., *Essex Court Recs.*, VI, 255; VIII, 297–298; *Suffolk Deeds*, IV, x–xi; Ford, ed., *Diary of Cotton Mather*, II, 139; *Diary of Samuel Sewall*, Mass. Hist. Soc., *Coll.*, 5th Ser., VI (1879), 5; the travel account of an unknown Frenchman, *ca*. 1687, in Nathaniel B. Shurtleff, *A Topographical and Historical Description of Boston* (Boston, 1871), 48; James R. Trumbull, *History of Northampton* (Northampton, 1898), I, 376–377. Exemplifying freedom from masters' supervision is the case of a servant who persisted in wooing a young lady although repeatedly warned by *her* master to keep away. Both were later convicted for fornication. Dow, ed., *Essex Court Recs.*, VII, 141.

26.   Revolts were never a problem in Massachusetts but runaways were frequent. Closest to a slave revolt was an unsuccessful 1690 attempt by a New Jerseyite with abolitionist tendencies to induce Negroes, Indians, and Frenchmen to attack several Bay Colony towns. See Joshua Coffin, *A Sketch of the History of Newbury* . . . (Boston, 1845), 153–154, and Sidney Perley, "Essex County in the Abolition of Slavery," *Essex-County Historical and Genealogical Register*, I (1894), 2.

27.   On informal relations see Dow, ed., *Essex Court Recs.*, I, 287; V, 141; VII, 394–395; VIII, 297; Morison, ed., *Suffolk Court Recs.*, I, 249; II, 648–649; Robert F. Seybolt, *The Town Officials of Colonial Boston, 1634–1775* (Cambridge, Mass., 1939), 77, 79, 83, 85, 87; Joseph Dudley to Gabriel Bernon, May 20, 1707, in George F. Daniels, *History of the Town of Oxford Massachusetts* (Oxford, 1892), 26–27. The quotation is from Joseph H. Smith, ed., *Colonial Justice in Western Massachusetts*, (1639–1702) (Cambridge, Mass., 1961), 298–299.

28.   Massachusetts never formally denied Negroes the right to bear personal arms and specifically included them in the militia in 1652. But in 1656, without explanation, she reversed her policy, excluding Indians and Negroes from training. Shurtleff, ed., *Mass. Records*, IV, Pt. i, 86, 257.

29.   William Fitzhugh, King George County Virginia, to Mr. Jackson of Piscataway, in New England, Feb. 11, 1683, in R. A. Brock, "New England and the Slave Trade," *Wm. and Mary Qtly.*, II (1894), 176–177; Saffin, Usher, Wetcomb, and Belcher to Welstead, June 12, 1681, in *New-England Historical and Genealogical Register*, XXXI (1877), 75–76.

30.   Acts regulating alcoholic consumption are in the Records of the Council of Massachusetts under the Administration of President Joseph Dudley, "Dudley Records," Mass. Hist. Soc., *Proceedings*, 2d Ser., XIII (Boston, 1899,

1900), 252; Ellis Ames and Abner C. Goodell, eds., *Acts and Resolves of the Province of Massachusetts Bay, 1692–1714* (Boston, 1869–1922), I, 154; Moody, ed., *Maine Recs.*, IV, 51; Edward W. Baker, "The 'Old Worcester Turnpike,' " *Proceedings of the Brookline Historical Society* (Jan. 23, 1907), 29. Laws governing stolen goods are in Ames and Goodell, eds., *Acts and Resolves*, I, 156, 325; see also Greene, *The Negro in Colonial New England*, 130. The only other seventeenth-century statute aimed at Negroes was passed in 1680: that no ship of more than 12 tons should entertain any passenger, servant or Negro, without permit from the governor. *The Colonial Laws of Massachusetts. Reprinted from the Edition of 1672, With the Supplements through 1686* (Boston, 1887), 281.

31. The laws discussed in these paragraphs are in Ames and Goodell, eds., *Acts and Resolves*, I, 535, 578–579, 606–607; John B. Dillon, ed., *Oddities of Colonial Legislation in America* . . . (Indianapolis, 1879), 206–207, 211–212; *Report of the Record Commissioners of the City of Boston*, VIII, 173–177.

The Legal Status of the Negro in Virginia, 1705–1765

Adele Hast*

Despite the fact that much has been written about the origins of seventeenth-century slavery in British North America, little has been published on blacks in the eighteenth-century South. Adele Hast in "The Legal Status of the Negro in Virginia, 1705–1765," has rectified this fact for one southern region. Hast depicts the status of black slaves both as persons and as property and also examines the role of free blacks in eighteenth century Virginia society. She concludes that "the laws pertaining to Negroes in colonial Virginia of the eighteenth century reflected the attitudes of the white planter class toward the Negro race." When she wrote this article, Hast was a doctoral student in history at the University of Iowa.

THE VIRGINIA PLANTER, Robert Carter, made a will in 1726, leaving extensive holdings in land and slaves to his heirs.[1] His grandson, Robert Carter III, provided for gradual manumission of his slaves during his lifetime, beginning in 1791, and continuing after his death.[2] The two men reflect a change in attitude toward slavery. During Carter I's lifetime, Negro slavery was a firmly established and accepted institution, both in the social

*Adele Hast, "The Legal Status of the Negro in Virginia, 1705–1765," *Journal of Negro History* 56 (1969), 217–29. Copyright by The Association for the Study of Negro Life and History, Inc. Reprinted by permission.

thought of the planters and in fact. By the 1780's, after several economic crises and a revolution had intervened, a small group among the white planters began to question the wisdom and morality of continuing slavery.

The first half of the eighteenth century was characterized by the full development of Negro slavery as an integral part of the Virginia tobacco economy. The legal system reflected and legitimized the slave's social position which had developed by custom on the plantations. The laws governing the behavior and ownership of slaves between 1705 and 1765 revealed the attitudes of the planter class toward this lowest social group.

Slave owners had many complaints about their slaves' behavior. These complaints, however, were not attributed to the system itself; they were, rather, blamed on the character failings of the slave. Landon Carter, for example, repeatedly attributed delays in harvesting, repairing and other plantation work to "the Lazyness of our People", whom he viewed as "most ungratefully neglectfull".[3] The planters, with rare exceptions, did not question the morality or legitimacy of slavery during this period. In law, too, slave status was accepted *de facto*. Laws and their concomitant court actions not only regulated slavery, but perpetuated and strengthened the institution. The notion that slavery was regrettable did not generally emerge. Rather, the view prevailed that slaves were more imperfect than white men, and would constitute a menace to society in any status other than slave.[4]

The first Negroes brought into Virginia in 1619 were probably considered similar to indentured white servants.[5] However, sometime in the first half of the seventeenth century, Negro slavery began. In 1700, the white population of Virginia was estimated at 60,000, with 6,000 slaves.[6] By 1756, the population, based on tithe records, contained 173,316 whites and 120,156 Negroes;[7] the number of free Negroes was quite small, with only 3,000 in 1783.[8] With the slave population increasing at a more rapid rate than the white, slavery had greater dominance in Virginia life as the half-century progressed; in the flowering of the tobacco economy, slavery became indispensable. A revisal of laws in 1705 revealed the slave's legal status at that point. Until the 1760's, no significant changes in that status occurred. The fifty-year period saw a gradual withdrawal of the few privileges the Negroes had in 1705, and increasingly rigid control over their behavior.

Before the law, the slave was a person and a non-person simultaneously. As a person, his position in society was defined and his behavior controlled. He was held criminally liable for specific unlawful acts, and his punishment provided for. His rights before the law, extremely limited because of his slave status, were described. He was a titheable individual in the revenue arrangements of the colony, as his white owner was.

Viewed as a non-person, the slave was dealt with in law as property. He served as a source of revenue as an imported item. The Negro slave was part of his owner's estate, to be inherited as real or personal property, bought and sold without his consent, taken for payment of debts, and disputed over in court cases on ownership. He was accounted as part of the sale, purchase, or exchange of lands. The theft of a slave, as property of great value, was a felony.

This dichotomy in attitude toward the slave existed in fact as well as in law. The owner who was solicitous of his slaves' health, who transferred them from one plantation to another to keep their families together, could also engage in the slave trade, and divide his slaves among his children in his will.

Who was a slave in the eyes of the law? The 1705 revisal legitimized the practice of importing Negroes for slavery: all servants brought in by sea or land, who were not Christians in their native country, were to be accounted slaves, and "bought and sold, notwithstanding a conversion to Christianity afterwards,"[9] further, a slave's being in England was not sufficient to release him from his status. This proviso was intended to prevent conflict over free or slave status under English law.[10] By this Virginia law, the slave was a kind of servant, but clearly distinguished from the white indentured servant. Indeed, many of the laws governing the behavior of servants and slaves covered both groups. In such cases, the servile status was the basis of treatment. In most cases, however, the basis was racial, rather than social.

The exclusion of conversion as a means to freedom indicated a change in attitude toward slavery that had occurred before 1700. In its early years in Virginia, slavery was justified as permissible with heathen people. That such a basis no longer applied was evidenced by this law.[11] Further, a law to this effect had been in existence since 1667.[12] It was perhaps believed that such a provision would encourage the planters to Christianize their slaves.[13] However, the slave owners did not give much attention to the religion of their slaves during this period. Some of the owners had such a low opinion of the character of the slave that they felt conversion was worthless.[14] Others found it an impracticable goal.[15] Some planters did concern themselves with the religion of their slaves,[16] but such was not the general rule. In one of the parish registers, which listed all the children born each year, every white child was christened soon after birth. Very few of the Negro slave children were baptized—about five out of a total of about 150 newborns.[17]

The racial basis of slavery applied not only to the slave, but to his owner as well. Only a white Christian could have a Christian servant. The two most important criteria for determining a man's status were race and religion, in that order of importance. Negroes, mulattoes, or Indians, although Christians, and "Jews, Moors, Mahometans, or other infidels" could own slaves, but not Christian servants.[18]

This same law made slavery perpetual, for all children were to be bond or free, according to the condition of their mothers.[19]

Was there a way for a slave to become free at this time? Manumission was frowned upon, and in 1723, forbidden by law. The existence of such large numbers of slaves engendered a constant fear of insurrection. Although the owners lived with the institution of slavery without questioning it, they felt their view was unilateral, that the slaves were not content with their position, and would escape it by violence, if they could. A population of free Negroes would compound the danger. In 1712, after the Council learned that a planter in Norfolk County had freed sixteen slaves and given them a large tract of land, the councillors asked the General Assembly to pass a law against such manumissions because of the potential danger.[20]

Even William Byrd II, one of the few critics of slavery during this half-century, opposed manumission. In 1736, he commended the plan of Georgia's founders to exclude slavery, and wished the Parliament "to put an end, to this unchristian Traffick."[21] Yet, he was a member of the Council of 1712 seeking a law to forbid the freeing of slaves.

Prior to the passage of such a bill, relatively few slaves were freed; those that were, had to be transported out of the colony, by law.[22] In 1710, a special bill was passed, setting free one slave, to allow him to remain in the colony; his freedom was a reward for revealing a slave conspiracy.[23] Manumissions were thus used to prevent insurrection, at the same time that they were feared as aiding slave revolt.

The law of 1723 forbade the freeing of any slave, on any pretense, "except for some meritorious service," as judged by the governor and Council. No longer could an owner manumit a slave privately; if he did so, the church-wardens of the parish were to sell the slave. Such cases were brought before the county courts, where the owners were ordered to show cause why the freed Negroes "should not be sold according to an act of Assembly in that case made and provided."[24]

After 1723, only a few slaves were freed, individually, in accordance with the law. The judgment of the owner as to meritorious service was accepted by the Council; one petition stated that she "had a great regard" for her slave "on Account of several very acceptable Services done by her" and provided for manumission in her will.[25] The Council approved.

The Negro slave, then, was born into a status he had little chance of changing. What kinds of relationships were sanctioned among Negroes, and between the two races? How did the planter view family life among the slaves? Legislation in this area showed two goals concerning slaves—a desire to keep the two races separate, and, at the same time, a wish to increase the numbers of slaves by propagation rather than importation. The moral code applied to the white population was not pertinent to the slave; he was viewed as a creature apart from and inferior to the white society.

Legal marriage between the two races was forbidden. The attitude toward the Negroes was unmistakable, in the explanation of the need for such a law: "And for a further prevention of that abominable mixture and spurious issue, which hereafter may increase in this her majesty's colony and dominion, as well by English, and other white men and women intermarrying with negros or mulattos, as by their unlawful coition with them . . ." Any free English man or woman marrying a Negro, bond or free, was to be committed to prison or pay a fine. Further, any minister performing such a marriage was to pay a fine of 10,000 pounds of tobacco, at that time almost his total year's wages.[26] This law was not again enacted, as many others pertaining to slave behavior were. It was aimed primarily at white indentured servants, whose numbers were small in the eighteenth century. To the white society, marriage with a slave was unthinkable, not only because of his color, but because of his status. William Byrd expressed disgust because his neighbor's daughter had married an Irish overseer:

> . . . to stoop to a dirty Plebian, without any kind of merit, is the lowest Prostitution. I found the Family justly enraged at it.[27]

Byrd would hardly have thought about white-Negro marriages, no less considered them as a possibility.

Actually, any legislation regarding marriage of a slave to a white person was superfluous, for legal marriage did not exist for the slave. There were no instances in the parish records of marriages among Negro slaves. Some planters encouraged their slaves to live in family units; Robert Carter listed his Negroes in his will by family.[28] Others listed their slaves by name only.[29]

Bearing a child out of wedlock was a punishable crime for all free or indentured women, but not for slaves. The most severe punishment was given any white woman having a child by a Negro or mulatto father—a fine of £5 current money or sale into servitude for five years.[30] Furthermore, the child was to be bound to the church-wardens as a servant until thirty-one years of age. There are numerous instances in county court records of such indentures.[31] The existence of the illegitimate child was not proof of as great a crime as his color.

The exclusion of the Negro slave woman from such a law placed her outside the realm of white moral standards. It also condoned Negro-white relationships where the woman was a slave. Although the law on marriage outlawed all such relationships, they were tolerated as long as the children remained slaves. Such cases were more common than the law indicated. The report of a court dispute over slave property casually mentioned that the planter had left his wife, "carried off several of the Slaves and as it is say'd married one of them and has several children by her."[32]

On the whole, the slave's behavior was regulated by his owner; only misbehavior off the plantation, or serious crimes like murder and arson reached the county courts. On the plantation the owner, by law, had complete authority. In this respect, the attitude toward slaves was sharply different from that to servants. Although corporal punishments were considered "wholesome Severitys"[33] for both groups, the treatment of servants was legally regulated. Furthermore, the servant was entitled to complain of mistreatment to the justice of the peace.[34] In one instance, a servant accused of assaulting his master was found innocent on the basis of self-defense.[35] The same law specifically excluded the slave from this judicial recourse.

The law reinforced the owner's authority by exempting him from responsibility for his conduct toward the slave.

> And if any slave resist his master . . . correcting such slave, and shall happen to be killed in such correction, it shall not be accounted felony; but the master, owner, and every such other person so giving correction shall be free and acquit of all punishment and accusation for the same, as if such accident had never happened.

The same law also forbade any Negro, mulatto or Indian from lifting his hand "against any Christian, not being negro, mulatto, or Indian."[36] However, to prevent loss of property, the law allowed the owner to bring civil suit for damages against anyone causing the death of his slave. Only if a credible witness swore that the owner "wilfully, maliciously, or designedly" killed the slave could he be brought to trial; and even in this case, a verdict of manslaughter was not to be punished.[37]

That there was perhaps a need to provide protection to the slave against his owner was shown by the orders given Alexander Spotswood when he became governor. He was instructed, in Britain, to try to get a law passed restraining inhuman severities by ill planters or overseers toward servants and slaves, and making the wilful killing of Indians and Negroes punishable by death.[38] The law regulating behavior of servants was already in effect;[39] one that protected the slaves equally was never passed during this period.

While some planters consciously tried to be fair in their authority over slaves, others were, by the accounts of their own neighbors, unjust and cruel. William Byrd painted an idyllic picture of the slave's life in an invitation to a Jamaican.[40] His private journals of the same period told another story.

> The poor Negroes upon them [Jones' plantations] are a kind of Adamites, very Scantily supply'd with cloaths and other necessaries; . . . However, they are even with their Master, and make him but indifferent crops, so that he gets nothing by his injustice, but the Scandal of it.[41]

Byrd disapproved of Colonel Jones' treatment of his slaves, not only because of its injustice, but also because of its inefficiency in causing the loss of crops and scandal.

On another occasion, when Byrd stopped overnight at a public house, he commented on the landlady's mistreatment of her Negroes. "Between the Husband and the Wife, the Negroes had a hard time of it."[42] Yet even a humane man like Byrd was more severe to his slaves than he wished to be, out of necessity, he explained.

> Numbers make them insolent & then foul means must do what fair will not . . . these base Tempers require to be rid with a tort rein, or they will be apt to throw their Rider. Yet even this is terrible to a good natured Man, who must submit to either a Fool or a Fury.[43]

Thus, although he regretted the severity, Byrd accepted it as his right of authority; he was even able to rationalize it by blaming the "insolent" behavior and "base Tempers" of the slaves. The important fact is that, whether a Byrd or a Col. Jones, the owner possessed a virtual life and death authority over his slaves. The attitude of a planter in 1778, who wished his slaves "treated as Human beings Heaven has placed under my care"[44] was not the same as the midcentury planter who spoke of "my people" and "poor creatures."[45]

Certain minor crimes seem to have been common in Virginia, as seen in laws against stealing hogs, killing deer out of season, mismanaging water mills. In some cases, punishment for slaves was harsher than for others. Thus, the penalty for stealing a hog, in 1705, was twenty-five lashes, but for a Negro, mulatto, or Indian, thirty-nine lashes.[46] In 1748, when a similar law was passed, the distinction was made not by color, but in terms of a slave and "anyone not a slave."[47] In an act to encourage the building of water mills, slaves or servants were equally punished for not using the mill properly;[48] in this case, the servile status was the basis of legislation. Similarly, equal punishment was meted out to a servant or a slave killing a deer out of season.[49]

When it came to capital crimes, slaves were treated differently from any other group in Virginia society. Their rights in court consisted of being granted a trial, and being allowed to speak in their own defense, nothing more. There were no appeals and no lawyers, unless the owners wished to provide defense or petition for leniency.

For the general population, capital cases were tried by the General Court, or by special courts of oyer and terminer held twice yearly at Williamsburg. The county courts concerned themselves with all civil matters and lesser criminal cases. All decisions of the county courts could be appealed to the General Court, or by petition to the General Assembly.[50]

Over the slave, however, the county court had jurisdiction without right of appeal. In the case of a capital offense, the governor issued a commission of oyer and terminer to persons of the county, whom he deemed fit, usually justices of the county court. Provision for this special tribunal was first made in 1692. The title of the law indicated its purpose: in 1692, "An Act for the more speedy prosecution of slaves committing Capitall Crimes,"[51] and in 1705, ". . . the Speedy and easy prosecution of slaves . . ."[52] The goal was to eliminate the need of bringing the slave to Williamsburg for trial. Trial was to be held without jury; if convicted, the slave could be executed after ten days, except in cases of conspiracy or insurrection, when sentence could be carried out earlier.[53]

The slave suffered an additional liability, either as defendant or witness, for there were severe restrictions on his testifying. In 1705, a law was passed which appeared to take away his right to serve as a witness, or to call other slaves as witnesses; ". . . popish recusants convict, negroes, mulattoes and Indian servants, and others, not being Christians, shall be deemed and taken to be persons incapable in law, to be witnesses in any cases whatsoever."[54] However, Negroes who professed to be Christians were still allowed to testify after this act was passed; such was not the intent of the Burgesses, according to an amended law of 1732. They expressed the planter's feeling that slaves lied and were not to be trusted. ". . . They are people of such base and corrupt natures, that the credit of their testimony cannot be certainly depended upon . . ." This law therefore forbade the testimony of any Negro, mulatto or Indian, except in the trial of a slave for capital offense. The law further revealed its author's distrust of Negroes by requiring the judge to read a statement to such witnesses describing the penalty for false testimony: thirty-nine lashes and ears nailed to the pillory, without trial for perjury.[55]

The court records revealed frequent use of the special commission of oyer and terminer to try slaves in the county courts. In Goochland County, in 1733, six Negroes were tried for murder. Two were found guilty, sentenced to be hanged within the week.[56] Such rapid executions were perhaps the cause of the requirement, in 1748, that ten days elapse between sentencing and hanging; although the slave had no right of appeal, his owner might wish to petition the assembly to reconsider the verdict. In another instance, a slave was convicted of arson and hanged.[57] Even an acquittal was no guarantee that a slave would be unpunished; in the case of the six slaves tried for murder, one of those acquitted was whipped because she knew of the murder and did not report it.[58] In another case, in Caroline County, a slave acquitted of poisoning was nevertheless transported out of the colony on suspicion of having given "powders" to other Negroes.[59]

There was only one grant of additional rights to slaves during this time, and it occurred in the judicial area. The question of whether a slave was entitled to benefit of clergy arose in a capital case in 1732. To clarify the matter, the legislature passed a statute allowing clergy to Negroes in appropriate cases. Even in this instance, certain crimes within benefit of clergy by Virginia law were not allowed for slaves.[60]

In everyday life, the slave's freedom of movement away from his plantation was severely restricted by both his owner and the law. In effect, he was not permitted to leave his home without permission. The planter sought thereby to prevent two misfortunes—loss of slave property, and insurrections. Repeated laws dealing with runaways and insurrections attest to the persistent concern with these matters.

Fugitive slaves often took shelter in obscure parts of Virginia, near the North Carolina border.[61] A planter reading the *Virginia Gazette* would find frequent advertisements for runaway slaves; other announcements described runaways who had been apprehended.[62]

To encourage people to take up runaways, the law allowed anyone to take into custody any Negro suspected of being a fugitive slave. If court examination proved him to be a runaway, the captor was rewarded in tobacco. The public paid the reward, and was later reimbursed by the owner.[63] The unfortunate runaway was then whipped by order of the justice of the peace. His owner was empowered, by the same law, to mete out such punishment as he saw fit.[64]

In one case of this type, the county court of Northampton certified that "Alexander Bagwell & Jno Waggeman with one

Isaac Smith'' brought before them two runaways, who were returned to their owners. However, Bagwell and company had not been paid for this "Service;" the court therefore referred the matter to the General Assembly "for allowance according to Law."[65] Apparently, the planters were in no hurry to pay the reward, until it had first come from public supplies.

When a slave ran away, the justices of his county issued a proclamation against him, which was read on two Sabbath days at the parish church. If he did not return after such proclamation, it was lawful for anyone to kill him by any means.[66] Furthermore, if he were apprehended, the county court could, at the owner's request, punish him "by dismembering, or any other way, not touching his life." The purpose of this punishment was not to reclaim an "incorrigible slave," but to terrify others so they would not run away. If, by chance, the slave died because of his punishment, no one was held responsible for his death.[67]

There was no concern among the owners about what caused a slave to run away. From the planter's point of view, the slave had flouted his authority and had to be punished. On the plantations of Landon Carter, runaway slaves were a chronic problem. Carter routinely had the runaway announced in public, outlawed after two Sunday proclamations, and sought by militia, according to law. He also set up watchmen on the plantation, who, in at least one instance, shot the runaway when he was sighted and refused to return.[68] The usual reason for running away was, according to Carter, a whipping or threat of whipping for disapproved behavior. Carter felt that slaves would be "spoiled" by kindness and must be strictly disciplined to prevent dishonest behavior. Accordingly, he administered physical punishment routinely.[69] To Carter, he had the right to treat his slaves as he deemed proper, and they did not have the right to protest by words or action.

Similarly, where plots of insurrection were discovered, no one questioned the reason for the slaves' discontent. The crime was viewed in one way, as being directed against the white society, and the menace was considered raised by the Negroes against the whites.

Within such an authoritarian framework, revolts by slaves were increasingly feared as the slave population grew. The danger seemed especially great in times of crisis, when French and Indian attackers menaced the Virginia frontier. One of the planters asked for British fortifications in the western Virginia mountains, not only to prevent French settlements and defenses, but to stop Negroes from taking refuge there, where the French would supply them with arms to use against the English.[70] The link here between runaway slaves and revolt was direct. In the 1750's, the House of Burgesses refused Governor Dinwiddie's request for men and money to join the Crown Point expedition, because they were needed for border defense and to quell slave uprisings.[71]

Conspiracies and plots by slaves were more feared as possibilities, than experienced as actual events. The law was severe, and a strong deterrent to insurrection. If more than five slaves conspired to rebel, or plotted murder, the act of conspiracy carried the death penalty, even if the plan were not executed.[72] Slaves were not allowed to congregate in groups off their own plantations, except for specified types of meetings. Even on the plantation, the owner or overseer was not to allow more than five slaves to visit from other places. Further, slaves were forbidden to keep weapons of any kind, except on frontier plantations, with permission.[73] County militia patrolled the roads to enforce these regulations.[74]

Thus, although there were periods when conspiracies seemed to be threatening, the court action taken involved the discovery of such plots, rather than the violence itself. Early in the eighteenth century, the Council received reports from several counties about dangerous conspiracies. The justices in the counties were instructed to interrogate the slaves being held, and to report to the Council.[75] Other orders were issued for the arrest of certain Negroes for trial.[76] The records were quite vague on the circumstances of the multiple conspiracies, the prime concern being to squelch them.

Even a slave visiting alone was strictly supervised. He was required to have a certificate of leave from his owner when off his plantation. He could not remain on another plantation more than four hours without permission.[77]

The slave's family life was sometimes sacrificed, for many had mates or children on other plantations. William Byrd told of a neighbor's slave who had come to show Byrd's people how to destroy some rocks in a canal. Although he did very little work, Byrd gave him a small sum of money. Thereupon, the planter related, the slave bought rum and made the "Weaver and Spinning Woman, who has the happiness to be called his Wife, exceedingly drunk." To punish him, Byrd ordered him banished from his plantation "forever, under the penalty of being whipt home, from Constable to Constable, if he presum'd to come again."[78] Thus, the law intended to prevent conspiracy was invoked for a relatively minor infraction.

Even in lesser, private matters, the slave could not control his life. The law determined what he could possess. Servants were guaranteed the right of ownership of private "effects."[79] The only laws dealing with slaves in these terms denied them property: any cattle, horses, or hogs belonging to slaves were to be taken by the owner or forfeited to the parish.[80] When flocks of sheep were being diminished by dogs, slaves were forbidden to carry dogs from one plantation to another in the affected counties.[81] They were later further restricted to two dogs in any Negro quarter.[82]

While set apart from the non-slave Virginians in property rights, the slave was included in the total populace for revenue purposes. He was titheable, as all men were, with the slave's tax paid, of course, by his owner. The tithe base for the slave differed from that of the free man. All males over sixteen were titheable, but in addition, all female slaves were also chargeable at sixteen.[83] The laws regulating tithes were carefully followed. Parish and court records listed the names of titheables. Births, christenings, and burials were recorded for the same reason. Children who had not been born in the parish had to appear at court and have their ages judged, for tithing records. The Northampton County Court, for example, listed a number of slave children, with their ages, at each court session.[84]

These records indirectly illustrated the low social status of the slaves. Often they were not listed as "slave," but as "negro." Nevertheless, it was clear which records were those of free men, and which of slaves, for the slave alone had no last name. He was referred to by first name and by his owner's name. Last names for slaves were non-existent.

There was as much legislation dealing with the slave as property, as there were laws regulating his behavior. The very existence of such laws and court actions revealed the attitudes of their makers. For the most part, there was no introspection on the morality of dealing with people in terms of goods. The evaluation of the slave as an item to be measured in pounds and shillings was so accepted that there was no need to justify it, during the first half of the eighteenth century. Even William Byrd, one of the few who bewailed the slave trade, had engaged in it himself.[85]

One of the uses of the slave as property was to raise revenue, through import duties. At the beginning of the century, servants and slaves were both taxed upon import.[86] After 1705, all laws laying a duty on slaves involved slaves alone, or slaves and liquor. Although some of the established planters wished to stop the import of slaves, new planters needed them for the additional lands being brought under cultivation.[87] In addition, British merchants dealing in slaves opposed a high import tariff.[88] The result was that the import duty was used for revenue, and did not restrict the numbers imported. The laws often specified their purpose: to defray government expenses,[89] to aid in protection of the colony.[90] During times when colonial expenses increased, as in the 1750's, the duties were higher. One additional tariff of 10% of the price of the slave, above the other duties, laid during the French wars,[91] proved so burdensome that it prevented the import of slaves, thus lessening the income from the duty; it was therefore repealed a few years later.[92] When additional money was needed to pay treasury notes, in 1763, a 5% duty was again added. These laws were enforced as well as possible; when one form of collection allowed fraud, another type was tried.[93] Failure to pay the duty resulted in court action.[94]

Once slaves had been imported, then they became goods in various business transactions. They were viewed as investments of capital. One planter in need of money decided to sell most of his horses, ''and turn them into slaves,'' that is, trade them for slaves, because cash was scarce.[95] William Byrd, investigating the expenses of setting up an iron works, was given figures which included ''Land, Negroes, and Cattle'' in the basic costs.[96]

In business dealings, slaves were legally the same as cattle. In a case where a man had paid a high price for a slave, only to find him incurably ill, the buyer sued the seller for fraud. The court, however, found for the seller, citing the sale of horses as a case in point; in transactions in cattle, the seller was not liable for fraud. The judge then explained.

> This case of a Horse I take to be directly in Point for where is the difference between a Horse and a Slave as to this Matter. If an Action will not lie in one Case nither will it in the other as I conceive.

He went on to describe how slave dealers concealed illness in their merchandise. ''Numbers of these distempered Slaves have been sold and the consequences sometimes very fatal.'' Yet, he pointed out, there were no court actions brought in such cases.[97] The humanity of the ''very fatal'' consequences was irrelevant to the subject at hand.

The most frequent legal activity involving the slave was related to land. Dozens of private bills were passed by the Burgesses allowing the sale of entailed lands;[98] one type authorized the sale of slaves and land which were both entailed, for the payment of debts.[99]

The use of the human being as property created difficult legal problems. In wills, intestate estates, distraint for debt, attempts were made to treat the slave as part of the land. The problems arose when the human aspects of slavery intervened. Over the years, the legislature wrestled with the problem of the slave's status in his owner's estate.

In 1705, the first of a series of laws dealing with the question was passed: "an act declaring the Negro, Mulatto, and Indian slaves within this dominion, to be real estate." Its purpose was the "better settling and preservation of estates." In the legal sense, slaves became real estate rather than chattels, to descend to heirs according to the custom of land inheritance. However, slaves could still be taken for payment of debts, like other personal estate. At the same time, ownership of slaves without other real estate did not give the privilege of a freeholder.[100] Ambiguity as to whether the slave was real or personal estate led to another law, in 1727, to explain that of 1705; it was here declared that since the true design of the original law was to preserve the slaves for the use of those who inherited estates, slaves could be settled on entailed land, to descend, with their increase, as part of the freehold. However, because slaves were the "greatest part of the visible estates" of Virginians, they had to be available to maintain credit, and could thus be sold for payment of debts.[101]

Confusion still persisted over the nature of slave inheritance. Robert Carter I, who had written a will leaving his slaves to his sons, revised it after the law of 1727; his sons were now to have the use and profit of the slaves and their increase; the slaves themselves were to be annexed to his lands, so that his sons could not sell them.[102] Many cases came before the county courts and the General Court, concerning the inheritance of slaves. In one case, where the increase of entailed slaves were taken for debt, the action was appealed on the basis of the laws on real estate. The judge ruled, however, that although the act made slaves real estate, they remained chattels for payment of debts, like cattle.[103] In another instance, the General Court ruled that the law on slaves as real estate applied only to cases where a person died intestate; the law had altered the nature of the slave, which was that of chattel.[104]

Finally, in 1748, another act declared slaves to be personal estate, and repealed the two earlier laws. When this one was disallowed, the legislature drafted a lengthy explanation of the need for such a law. Slaves were, by their nature, personal estate. Making them real estate and annexing them to land produced many lawsuits. Additionally, some plantations became over-stocked. The slaves became mixed with others, and without sur-names could not be distinguished after several generations.[105]

In one important respect, the law combined both the personal and the property views on the slave. If a slave died as a conse-quence of the action of the law, the owner was reimbursed for his loss. Thus, if a slave were killed as a runaway, or executed for a capital crime, his owner was paid his assessed value by the public.[106] The expenses incurred by county courts in slave tri-als, or by sheriffs in punishing slaves, were reimbursed by the colonial treasury.[107] Planters whose slaves had been acquitted of crimes, but who had died or become ill due to jail confine-ment, could petition the legislature for damages.[108]

The law thereby strengthened the institution of slavery in two ways. It prevented slave owners from hiding the misdeeds of their slaves, out of fear of loss of property. It also provided a kind of subsidy to slaveholders, making the use of slaves even more attractive. In effect, the men who made the laws were helping themselves as slave owners. So, too, the laws they made reflected their own attitudes toward Negro slaves.

That these attitudes were based on both race and servile posi-tion is clear, but which of these attributes of the slave was the more important one? The legal status of the free Negroes, who shared the race of the slaves, but the social and legal standing of the free white population, reveals the basic importance of color, rather than status, as a molder of attitudes of the white planter class.

Free Negroes shared the same legal rights and obligations as the white population in some respects. In other instances, how-ever, they had severe legal disabilities placed on them, includ-ing some of the same restrictions imposed upon slaves. Their position in society was determined and limited not by their free status, but by their color. Within color ranks, free Negroes were more severely discriminated against than Indians. The definition of a mulatto, and hence the determinant of whether a person of mixed heritage was to be accounted white or colored stated that ". . . the child of an Indian and the child, grand child, or great grand child, of a negro shall be deemed, accounted, held and taken to be a mulatto."[109] Thus, a person who was one-fourth Indian and three-fourths white was considered a full-fledged white citizen, while an individual with any Negro ancestry had to be able to claim only one Negro and fifteen white great great grandparents to achieve the rights and status of a Caucasian.

The free Negro had the same access to the courts as the white man. The records of Northampton County Court contain numerous cases of suits initiated by Negroes. Many of these cases were disputes over the freedom of the plaintiffs. One such petition, in 1732, by "Nanny Webb Negroe," maintained that she and her two children were being "Illegally detain'd in Servitude by Mrs. Sophia Savage." Subsequently, "the Orphans Law as well as the law of Servants and Slaves being produced," the court found for the Negro mother and her children, set them free, and ordered Mrs. Savage to pay costs and attorney's fee for the plaintiff.[110]

In another instance, a free Negro mother, Anne Toyer, claimed that her three children, born free, were being illegally held in slavery by three separate men. What the record called slavery probably referred to servitude, for the court ruled that one of the children was not free and must serve until thirty years of age. The other two were freed by the court.[111]

As free men and women, Negroes were brought into court for violations of the law. They were sued for debt.[112] Negro women were prosecuted for bearing illegitimate children. In such cases, the prime concern was to prevent the child's becoming a charge upon the parish; accordingly, the punishment was dependent on the mother's ability to provide for the child. If she, or someone else, gave financial assurance of supporting the child, and paid a fine, no further action was taken. In all such cases—and they occurred frequently—there was no difference in the treatment of white and Negro mothers.[113]

In many important areas of civil rights and citizenship, free Negroes were classified with slaves. The white society viewed them first as Negro, then as free. The laws against manumission were designed to keep the number of free Negroes a small one. Laws which exempted the free Negro from obligations required of the white man set him apart from the white free population. Thus, while virtually all free males between twenty-one and sixty were to serve in the militia, free Negroes, mulattoes and Indians were specifically exempted. In time of invasion or insurrection, however, they were obliged to serve, but only to perform "servile labour."[114]

The reason given by the legislators for restricting manumission and militia service was their fear that free Negroes would aid slaves in rebelling against their masters. However, other restrictions were placed on the free Negro because of his color. He was forbidden, after 1705, to serve in any ecclesiastical, civil or military office or hold "any place of public trust or power."[115] After 1723, he could not vote at any election, even if he fulfilled freehold qualifications.[116] The white society thus prevented any Negro from reaching a position of social or political importance. For tithing purposes, free non-whites were classified with slaves.[117]

Until 1744, the free Negro was restricted as a witness in court in exactly the same way as the slave.[118] In 1744, his right was seemingly extended, for now any free Negro who was a Christian, could testify in any case involving a Negro, mulatto, or Indian. However, the reason for this law was to protect the white creditor who previously could not call Negroes as witnesses in civil cases of debt.[119]

The vast majority of Negroes, as slaves, lived under a legal-social system which dehumanized them. Treated as property, they did not have even the dignity of family names. The direction of their lives—where they lived, what kind of work they performed, with whom they associated—was in the hands of white masters. Free Negroes, while having control of their own activities, were condemned to a permanently inferior social status little higher than that of the slave. The laws pertaining to Negroes in colonial Virginia of the eighteenth century reflected the attitudes of the white planter class toward the Negro race.

Notes

1. *Virginia Magazine of History and Biography* (Richmond), V (1897), 409; VI (1898), 8.

2. Louis Morton, *Robert Carter of Nomini Hall* (Williamsburg, 1941), 251.

3. Jack P. Greene (ed.), *The Diary of Colonel Landon Carter of Sabine Hall, 1752–1778* (2 vols., Charlottesville, 1965), I, 133, 295.

4. *Ibid.*, I, 27.

5. Helen T. Catterall (ed.), *Judicial Cases Concerning American Slavery and the Negro* (2 vols., Washington, D.C., 1926), I, 57.

6. John Fiske, *Old Virginia and Her Neighbors* (2 vols., Boston, 1925), II, 191.

7. R. A. Brock (ed.), *The Official Records of Robert Dinwiddie* (2 vols., Richmond, 1883–841), II, 345.

8. Robert McColley, *Slavery and Jeffersonian Virginia* (Urbana, 1964), 71.

9. William W. Hening, *The Statutes at Large, Being a Collection of All the Laws of Virginia, from the First Session of the Legislature, in the Year 1619* (13 vols., Richmond and Philadelphia, 1809–1823), III, 447–48.

10. Catterall, *Judicial Cases Concerning American Slavery and the Negro,* I, 3.

11. Hening, *Statutes,* III, 460.

12. *Ibid.*, II, 260.

13. "Commissions and Instructions to the Earl of Orkney for the Government of Virginia," Jan. 15, 1714, *Virginia Magazine of History and Biography,* XXI, (1913), 354.

14. Greene (ed.), *The Diary of Colonel Landon Carter,* I, 292, 295.

15. *Journals of the House of Burgesses of Virginia, 1761–1765* (Richmond, 1907), 370.

16. Maude H. Woodfin (ed.), *Another Secret Diary of William Byrd of Westover,* 1739–1741 (Richmond, 1942), 8–9.

17. *The Parish Register of Christ Church, Middlesex County, Virginia, from 1653 to 1812* (Richmond, 1897), 49–74.

18.   Hening, *Statutes,* III, 450.

19.   *Ibid.,* 460.

20.   H. R. McIlwaine (ed.), *Executive Journals of the Council of Colonial Virginia* (5 vols., Richmond, 1925–1945), III, 332.

21.   Byrd to Lord Egremont, July 12, 1736, *Virginia Magazine of History and Biography,* XXXVI (1928), 221.

22.   Hening, *Statutes,* III, 87.

23.   *Ibid.,* 537.

24.   John W. Wayland, *A History of Shenandoah County, Virginia* (Strasburg, 1927), 113.

25.   "Journals of the Council of Virginia in Executive Sessions, 1737–1763," June 10, 1741, *Virginia Magazine of History and Biography,* XV (1907), 130.

26.   Hening, *Statutes,* III, 453–54.

27.   John S. Bassett (ed.), *The Writings of "Colonel William Byrd, of Westover in Virginia, Esqr."* (New York, 1901), 338.

28.   *Virginia Magazine of History and Biography,* VI (1898), 368.

29.   *Ibid.,* II (1894), 199.

30.   Hening, *Statutes,* III, 452–53.

31.   *Virginia Magazine of History and Biography,* IV (1896), 278.

32.   Sir John Randolph and Edward Barradall, *The Reports of Decisions of the General Court of Virginia,* 1728–1741 (2 vols., Boston, 1909), I, R37.

33.   Bassett (ed.), *The Writings of Colonel William Byrd,* 337.

34.   Hening, *Statutes,* III, 448–49; V, 549.

35.   *Northampton County Order Book No. 17, 1719–22* (Richmond), 14.

36.   Hening, *Statutes,* III, 459.

37.   *Ibid.,* IV, 133.

38.   "Commissions and Instructions to the Earl of Orkney," *Virginia Magazine of History and Biography,* XXI, 354.

39. Hening, *Statutes,* III, 448.

40. Byrd to Peter Beckford, Dec. 6, 1735, *Virginia Magazine of History and Biography,* IX (1901), 235.

41. Bassett (ed.), *The Writings of Colonel William Byrd,* 348.

42. *Ibid.,* 288.

43. Byrd to Lord Egremont, July 12, 1736, *Virginia Magazine of History and Biography,* XXXVI (1928), 220.

44. William Lee to Mr. Ellis, June 24, 1778, *Virginia Magazine of History and Biography,* XXXVII (1929), 299.

45. Bassett (ed.), *The Writings of Colonel William Byrd,* 383; Byrd to Lord Egremont, July 12, 1736, *Virginia Magazine of History and Biography,* XXXVI (1928), 220.

46. Hening, *Statutes,* III, 276.

47. *Ibid.,* VI, 122.

48. *Ibid.,* III, 403.

49. *Ibid.,* III, 463; IV, 425.

50. George L. Chumbley, *Colonial Justice in Virginia* (Richmond, 1938), 63.

51. Hening, *Statutes,* III, 102.

52. *Ibid.,* 269.

53. *Ibid.,* VI, 106.

54. *Ibid.,* III, 298.

55. *Ibid.,* IV, 127, 327.

56. *Virginia Magazine of History and Biography,* I, (1893), 328–330.

57. *Caroline County Order Book,* Dec. 10, 1743, in David J. Mays, *Edmund Pendleton, 1721–1803, A Biography* (2 vols., Cambridge, 1952), 35.

58. *Virginia Magazine of History and Biography,* I, 329.

59. Mays, *Edmund Pendleton,* 35.

188 ADELE HAST

60. Hening, *Statues*, IV, 326.

61. Bassett (ed.), *The Writings of Colonel William Byrd*, 47.

62. "Virginia Gazette, 1752–1755," *Virginia Magazine of History and Biography*, XXIV (1916), 415; XXV (1917), 12.

63. Hening, *Statutes*, III, 456.

64. *Ibid.*, 457.

65. *Northampton County Order Book No. 17*, 27, 93.

66. Hening, *Statutes*, III, 460; VI, 110.

67. *Ibid.*, III, 461; VI, 111.

68. Greene (ed.), *The Diary of Colonel Landon Carter*, I, 289.

69. *Ibid.*, 27.

70. William Byrd to Mr. Ochs, 1735, *Virginia Magazine of History and Biography*, IX (1901), 226.

71. Brock (ed.), *The Official Records of Robert Dinwiddie*, II, 394.

72. Hening, *Statutes*, IV, 126.

73. *Ibid.*, 129–131.

74. *Ibid.*, 202.

75. McIlwaine (ed.), *Executive Journals of the Council of Colonial Virginia*, III, 234–236.

76. "Order for Arrest of Negroes, 1709", *Virginia Magazine of History and Biography*, XVII (1901), 34; Philip Ludwell to Edmund Jennings, March 19, 1709, *Ibid.*, XIX (1911), 23–24.

77. Hening, *Statutes*, III, 459.

78. Bassett (ed.), *The Writings of Colonel William Byrd*, 385–86.

79. Hening, *Statutes*, V, 549; VI, 358.

80. *Ibid.*, III, 450.

81. *Ibid.*, VI, 295.

82. *Ibid.*, VI, 489.

83. *Ibid.*, III, 258–59.

84. *Northampton County Order Book No. 17*, 18, 24.

85. Byrd to Lord Egremont, July 12, 1736, *Virginia Magazine of History and Biography*, XXXVI, 221; Louis B. Wright and Marion Tinling (eds.), *The Secret Diary of William Byrd of Westover, 1709–1712* (Richmond, 1941), xii.

86. Hening, *Statutes*, III, 7.

87. Mays, *Edmund Pendleton*, I, 107.

88. "Commissions and Instructions to the Earl of Orkney", *Virginia Magazine of History and Biography*, XXI, 351.

89. Hening, *Statutes*, IV, 21.

90. *Ibid.*, VII, 1.

91. *Ibid.*, VI, 16.

92. *Ibid.*, VII, 5.

93. *Ibid.*, IV, 27.

94. Randolph, *Decisions of the General Court*, II, B38.

95. John Baylor to John Backhouse, July 18, 1764, *Virginia Magazine of History and Biography*, XXI (1913), 91.

96. Bassett (ed.), *The Writings of Colonel William Byrd*, 345, 351.

97. Randolph, *Decisions of the General Court*, II, B45–50.

98. For example, see Hening, *Statutes*, IV, 19.

99. *Ibid.*, 29.

100. *Ibid.*, III, 333–34.

101. *Ibid.*, IV, 222–26.

102. *Virginia Magazine of History and Biography*, VI (1898), 8–9, 17.

103. Randolph, *Decisions of the General Court*, I, 5.

104. *Ibid.*, 16– 17.

105. Hening, *Statutes,* V, 433– 41.

106. *Ibid.,* III, 29.

107. *Ibid.,* V, 326.

108. *Journals of the House of Burgesses of Virginia, 1761 –1765,* 97, 102.

109. Hening, *Statutes,* III, 252.

110. *Northampton County Order Book No. 19,* 145; *No. 20,* 7.

111. *Ibid., No. 20,* 59– 60, 70– 71.

112. *Ibid.,* 68.

113. For example, *Ibid.,* 87, 89, 107, 114, 136; *No. 19,* 8, 68, 95.

114. Hening, *Statutes,* IV, 119; V, 17; VI, 531.

115. *Ibid.,* III, 250– 51.

116. *Ibid.,* IV, 134.

117. *Ibid.,* IV, 133; VI, 41.

118. *Ibid.,* IV, 327.

119. *Ibid.,* V, 245.

Georgia and the Negro Before the American Revolution

Darold D. Wax*

Settlers in Georgia, the youngest of the British North American colonies, were prohibited from importing blacks (slave or free) because the Trustees sought to set up a white utopian community of virtuous, hard working, small farmers. Many white Georgians protested the ban, petitioned the government for relief, and ultimately prevailed in having the regulations changed. By 1752, "Georgia was entering a new phase in its history," explains Darold D. Wax, "possessed of a new governmental form, significant adjustments in agricultural policies, and now able to exploit the labor of Negro slaves." Wax is a member of the History Department at Oregon State University; among his publications are A History of Colonial America *(co-authored) and articles in the* Pennsylvania Magazine of History and Biography *and the* Journal of Negro History.

GEORGIA'S EARLY HISTORY HAS much to offer by way of an understanding of the eighteenth-century slave trade and the beginning of slavery as an institution in the English North American colonies. The Georgia experience, for example, suggests something about the British role in the American slave trade, and the extent to which British commercial policy sought to

*Darold D. Wax, "Georgia and the Negro Before the American Revolution," *Georgia Historical Quarterly* 11 (1967), 63–77. Reprinted by permission.

encourage, without equivocation or compromise, the traffic in Negroes. Further, one feature of the Utopia of Georgia was a prohibition of black slaves and Negroes. The grandiose visions of the Georgia Trustees, however, projected from England 3,000 miles across the Atlantic, were not realized, and within a short while there was a growing dependence on slave labor. Thus, the attempt to avoid reliance on Negro slave labor ended in failure. Finally, those who debated the future of the Negro in Georgia provided a useful summary of the arguments for and against slavery; in no other colony were the slave trade and slavery, in their non-humanitarian aspects, so thoroughly discussed.

With respect to commercial policy, it has long been fashionable to charge the British, almost exclusively, with prosecution of the American slave trade. English merchants, the argument runs, visited the west coast of Africa, engaged in contacts with native chieftains, and, having acquired their human cargoes, carried them to America where they were sold to colonists eager to supplement their labor supply. To support this vast commercial enterprise, the home government developed policies which permitted no colonial interference with the slave trade. Colonial laws levying duties on newly-imported Negroes were, on this basis, nullified in England.

During the revolutionary era particularly, when the American spirit burned with a white heat, it was convenient to blame the British for having perpetuated the slave trade. Such was a part of the argument presented by "Antibiastes" in a pamphlet urging abolition of slavery published at Philadelphia in 1777. Aimed at the Continental Congress, the essay requested that Negroes should be granted their freedom in return for having rendered to the states valuable military service. It was through the efforts of the British, "Antibiastes" seemed to say, that Americans became involved in the Negro trade: "We, the members of the United States, have been—we still are, the accomplices of the Britons. We have received great emoluments from their profligacy, their insidiousness and savage cruelty, since they first undertook the slave trade . . . . Let us therefore acknowledge that, had not our own cupidity and indolence prepared us for the seduction of the wily Britons, no - - - not all their sophistry could have deluded us. - - - We never would have been tempted by them to purchase the Slaves they brought to us from the African shores!''[1] The following year Samuel Wetherell, a Quaker, revealed a similar point of view when accused by the Society of Friends of taking an oath of allegiance to a state in rebellion against the mother country. So openly to espouse violence, abhorrent to the Quaker way of life, as well as to take an oath, was to invite censure and perhaps disownment; it was to vindicate his actions that Wetherell addressed a committee of the Philadelphia Monthly Meeting. Like ''Antibiastes,'' he thought it expedient to impose on the British the guilt of promoting the slave trade:

> See the poor African! Stolen from every tender connection. Husband from Wife, & Wife from Husband, Parents from Children, and Children from parents; perhaps a whole village desolated, and all its inhabitants taken together, and sold into an unredeemable captivity, and what for? what is their crime? what have they done to the great King of England, & his Parliament, that they should merit so undescribable punishment? nothing is pretended, no crime is laid to their charge, and all the apology for this evil, altho of such prodigious Magnitude, is that the African trade is a profitable one to the nation. Oh! my friends, are ye so fond of a further connection in government with this people, that ye will deny Christian Communion to all who are weary of their cruelty? I cannot believe what ye do in this respect is approved in heaven.[2]

Better known, perhaps, is Jefferson's indictment of George III, a portion of the Declaration of Independence which was not included in the final draft:

> He has waged cruel war against human nature itself, violating its most sacred rights of life and liberty in the persons of a distant people who never offended him, captivating and carrying them into slavery in another hemisphere, or to incur miserable death in their transportation thither. This piratical warfare, the opprobrium of *infidel* powers, is the warfare of the *Christian* king of Great Britain. Determined to keep open a market where MEN should be bought and sold, he has prostituted his negative for suppressing every legislative attempt to prohibit or to restrain

this execrable commerce; and that this assemblage of horrors
might want no fact of distinguished die, he is now exciting these
very people to rise in arms among us, and to purchase that liberty
of which *he* deprived them, by murdering the people upon whom
he also obtruded them; thus paying off former crimes committed
against the *liberties* of one people, with crimes which he urges
them to commit against the *lives* of another.[3]

The notion that Britishers were solely responsible for the
slave trade into English North America found ready acceptance
among a people fashioning a revolutionary ideology which
would justify a violent break with authority.[4]

Yet for Georgia this view seems wholly inaccurate. If it was
the aim of British policy to encourage trade in Negroes, the
guidelines established for that colony could hardly have been
less appropriate. The product of a humanitarian impulse coupled
with an imperialistic drive to protect English interests along the
southern frontier, Georgia's early development was closely related to the schemes of its sponsors. The new colony was to be
a haven of refuge for the poor and oppressed of Europe, who, in
a land of almost oriental splendor, would find new outlets for
their energies and virtually inevitable prosperity. Equally significant was the military nature of the colony: in an area turbu-
lent with the competing ambitions of Spanish, French, and English, to say nothing of the Indians, Georgia would introduce an
element of stability. Those who came to Georgia must, therefore, be equipped to resist the expansionist designs of other
European powers. These two considerations, the humanitarian
and the military, together with what were believed to be the
physical characteristics of the region, account for the grand plan
for Georgia, a plan which gradually unfolded from the delibera-
tions of the Trustees.[5]

Given the *raison d'etre* for the colony of Georgia—a home
for the indigent, a military bastion preventing foreign encroachments on English territory, and a producer of exotic goods—the
Trustees' policy was not without some validity. Landholdings
were kept relatively small, both to provide sufficient acres for
new arrivals and to insure a population adequate to ward off

aggression. Ownership of lands under the system known as tail-male would, the Trustees reasoned, serve the interests of a community one of whose foundation stones was military. Strong liquors also were prohibited, for they would have little place in a settlement composed of yeoman farmers dedicated to bettering their lives. In addition to these restrictions on land and liquor, the Trustees forbade the use of certain types of labor, specifically that of Negroes.

The law relating to Negroes, titled "An Act for rendering the Colony of Georgia more Defencible by Prohibiting the Importation and use of Black Slaves or Negroes into the same," was drafted in 1734, and after approval by the Privy Council, became effective in June, 1735. There is evidence that the prohibition policy was enforced even before final ratification; as early as January, 1735, an informant reported that settlers in Georgia were in good health "but unneasie they are not allow'd the use of Negroes."[6] The law advanced several reasons in support of an exclusion policy. First, in those colonies where slaves were employed they "hath obstructed the Increase of English and Christian Inhabitants therein who alone can in case of a War be relyed on for the Defence and Security of the same"; second, the use of Negroes "hath Exposed the Colonys so settled to the Insurrections Tumults and Rebellions of such Slaves and Negroes"; and third, large numbers of Negroes might prove an internal threat "in Case of a Rupture with any Foreign State who should Encourage and Support such Rebellions." The law of 1735 prohibited, under pain of a fine totaling £50 sterling, the importation and use of Negroes in Georgia. Negroes found in the colony in violation of the law were subject to seizure and sale by the Trustees. It is important to realize that this act was favorably received by the Privy Council, and that the English government therefore approved a colonial law which could in no way be interpreted as an encouragement to the traffic in Negroes.[7]

Although Negroes were prohibited from legally entering Georgia after June 24, 1735, some in fact had already reached the colony and others would be smuggled in later. According to one account, Colonel Bull arrived from South Carolina in February, 1733, and "brought with him 4 of his Negroes, who were Sawyers, to assist the Colony."[8] Several years later, it was said of the first settlers at Savannah that "They work'd hard indeed, in Building some Houses in Town; but then they labour'd in common, and were likewise assisted by Negroes from *Carolina,* who did the heaviest Work."[9] In February, 1736, James Oglethorpe, having been informed by Indians that persons from Carolina had crossed the river into Georgia, bringing with them Negro slaves, issued orders to these individuals "to withdraw their horses, cattle, and negroes, out of Georgia."[10] Thus, despite what appears to have been a determined effort to prevent their illegal entry,[11] Negroes were smuggled in, at least in small numbers. More important, the settlers were insistent that the restrictions on Negroes be removed; to that end they conducted a ceaseless campaign.

Georgians claimed that the supply of white servants, sent over by the Trustees as employees of the Trust and also brought by private parties, was inadequate and an unsatisfactory solution of the labor problem.[12] Even friends of the Georgia experiment called attention to the labor crisis. William Stephens, who arrived in 1737 to assume his responsibilities as "Secretary to the Trustees," discovered that the labor shortage was acute. He wrote that while he required workers to harvest his crop, he could find none to work at a decent wage:

> for our common labouring People, who never cared to work as long as they had Money or Credit to live in Excess; when they were wanted for Hire, required such Wages as is hardly to be believed: One or two that I attempted had the Modesty to ask Half a Crown a Day, besides Provisions; and after all the Means I could use, I found I must think well of it if I could procure any at eighteen Pence, and their Food withal. This evil alone, without the Addition of others, I apprehend to be of pernicious Consequence to the Colony, unless some Cure can be had for it, and in my humble Opinion may be worth the Consideration of the honourable Trustees, in what Manner to regulate Labourers Wages: For so long as an idle Fellow can find one Day's Pay sufficient to maintain him two or three, he will work no more; and more than Half the Time of such a Man's Labour is lost to the Publick.[13]

Those eager to supplement their work force with Negro laborers claimed that the problem was more serious and the prohibition policy more senseless because of Georgia's climate, which was not suited for white workers. In a tract published in 1741 Negroes were referred to as "the only human Creatures proper to improve our Soil." It was folly, the authors continued, "to expect to live in this Part of America by Cultivation of Lands without Negroes."[14] Others, however, were convinced that the climate did not prevent the growth of a prosperous white community. One writer, describing himself as "A Gentleman Who Has Resided There Upwards of Seven Years, and Was One of the First Settlers," praised the climate, produce and soil, and predicted a bright future for the colony.[15] A number of Georgians in 1741 attested to the excellent climate and stated that whites could satisfactorily perform labor services.[16] Even those who favored the introduction of Negroes and who argued that whites were made indolent by the climate, sometimes, in apparent contradiction, were eloquent in their approval of conditions: "the [Georgia] Air healthy, always serene, pleasant and temperate, never subject to excessive Heat or Cold, nor to sudden Changes."[17]

The experience of South Carolina provided Georgians with an additional ingredient in their discussions over the desirability of Negro labor. Sharing with Georgia a common boundary, and with an economy forged out of several decades of growth, South Carolina might offer valuable and relevant lessons. In 1733, when the first settlers reached Georgia, the Negro population in South Carolina was near 20,000; during the decade of the 1730's new Negroes entered that colony at about the rate of 2,500 per year.[18] Inevitably there were comparisons with South Carolina, and it was argued that without slaves Georgia could never expect to compete effectively. Petitioners in 1738, for example, noted that "It is very well known, that *Carolina* can raise every thing that this Colony can; and they having their Labour so much cheaper will always ruin our Market, unless we are in some Measure on a Footing with them. . . ."[19] An observer not unfriendly to Georgia wrote in 1737 of the "Abundance of Lots untouched, and many which had little done upon them''; several settlers, he continued, ''are lately gone for Carolina to seek some Land there. . . .''[20] But if some took South Carolina as a shining example, others drew contrary conclusions from the experiences of the sister colony to the north. The Reverend John Bolzius spoke disparagingly of the treatment of Negroes at Charleston, where but few were baptized while the rest lived ''like Brutes, in relation to the Seventh Commandment.''[21] The Georgia Trustees also tried to make unattractive the Carolina dependence on Negro slaves, dwelling on reports of alleged Negro conspiracies and quoting with approval a memorial to the King signed by the President and Speaker of the South Carolina General Assembly in which was highlighted the danger associated with the use of large numbers of Negroes.[22]

Georgia was still in its infancy and the Trustees' policy with respect to Negroes was just emerging when settlers began challenging the wisdom of the prohibition law. A Georgia planter, Hugh Stirling, delivered a petition to the Trustees during the summer of 1735; signed by ''about *Seventeen* of the better Sort of People in *Savannah*,'' it set forth the ''Disproportion betwixt the Maintenance and Cloathing of white Servants and Negroes.'' This early too the Trustees revealed their determination to resist pressures of this sort, dismissing the plea with little consideration.[23] Such a rebuff did not dampen the hopes or lessen the desires of those who favored the introduction of Negroes.

Three years later, in December, 1738, 117 residents of Georgia lodged another formal protest with officials at home. Two causes only, the petitioners asserted, were responsible for the sad state of affairs. First, the type of landholding, which prevented acquisition of a free title. Second,

> The Want of the Use of Negroes, with proper Limitations; which if granted, would both occasion great Numbers of white People to come here, and also render us capable to subsist ourselves, by raising Provisions upon our Lands, until we could make some Produce fit for Export, in some Measure to Ballance our Importation. We are very sensible of the Inconveniencies and Mischiefs that have already, and do daily arise from an unlimited

Use of Negroes, but we are as sensible, that these may be prevented by a due Limitation, such as so many to each white Man, or so many to such a Quantity of Land, or in any other Manner which Your Honours shall think most proper.

While this statement apparently represented the views of settlers near Savannah, it was not endorsed by residents of two other settlements, Darien and Frederica.[24]

If residents of Savannah and Augusta took the lead in demanding the introduction of Negroes, much of the support for the Trustees was centered in the Scottish community of Darien and at Ebenezer, home of the Salzburgers. These latter made public their position in 1739, requesting Oglethorpe "not to allow that any Negroes might be brought to our place, or in our neighborhood; knowing by experience that houses and gardens will be robbed always by them; and white people are in danger of life from them, besides other great inconveniences."[25] The Salzburgers were praised by others as able and industrious: "not one Person has abandoned his Settlement, or sent over the least Complaint about the Tenures or the Want of Negroes."[26]

Perhaps the best statement in behalf of Negro labor, and also the most denunciatory comment on the Trustees' policy, was the essay prepared by Patrick Tailfer, Hugh Anderson, and Da. Douglas and printed at Charles Town, South Carolina, in 1741.[27] These men described a colony that was backward and undeveloped, plagued by a set of rules drawn up and enforced by persons who had little understanding of New World conditions. It was charged that when settlers had applied for redress, in an effort to create a prosperous Georgia, they had been "brow-beat, obstructed, threatened, and branded with opprobrius Names, such as proud, idle, lazy, discontented and mutinous People. . . ." Noting again and again the lack of white servants, the essay reviewed the attempts to procure Negroes. In a final summary there were listed, twelve in number, the "REAL Causes of the Ruin and Desolation of the Colony." Among these was the prevailing Negro policy: "But chiefly the Denying the Use of Negroes, and persisting in such Denial after, by repeated Applications, we had humbly remonstrated the Impossibility of making Improvements to any Advantage with white Servants.''

In two pamphlets published that same year, 1741, the Georgia trustees replied to these criticisms. *An Account, Shewing the Progress of the Colony of Georgia in America, from its First Establishment,* published by order of the Trustees, at once took issue with the authors of that "Scurrilious Narrative," "a Narrative founded in Lies and Misrepresentations, projected and published by a few Persons of no Estate, and as little Character, Persons sour'd in their Tempers, because not humour'd in their endeavours of subverting, or at least altering, the Constitution of a new settled Colony, even in it's Infancy. . . ." The Trustees presented a spirited defense of their program, paying particular attention to the demands for Negro slaves, and then concluded: "From these several Considerations, as the Produces to be raised in the Colony did not make Negro slaves necessary, as the Introduction of them so near to a Garrison of the *Spaniards* would weaken rather than strengthen the Barrier, and as they would introduce with them a greater Propensity to Idleness among the Poor Planters, and too great an Inequality among the People it was thought proper to make the Prohibition of them a Fundamental of the Constitution."[28]

The other statement of policy also took cognizance of the "principal objection" made by settlers in Georgia: "That it will be impracticable to render the colony of any value, without the use of Negroes." Once more the Trustees argued that Negroes were not consistent with the constitution of Georgia, that they were unnecessary for the produce to be raised there, and that they were "absolutely dangerous to Georgia in its present situation, as well as to the adjacent provinces." Scarcely a stone was left unturned in insisting that Negroes had no place in Georgia.[29]

By now the increasingly sharp debate over the use of Negroes, a part of a larger conflict pivoting around the Trustees' colonial policy, was arousing discussion in England, both in and out of Parliament. The House of Commons in 1733 had begun appropriating almost annual sums for the Trustees' use. In 1735 £26,000 had been granted, and there were appropriations of

£20,000 in each of the years 1737 and 1739. The amount of assistance dropped to £4,000 in 1740, but increased to £10,000 in 1741. The next year, however, the Commons for the first time since 1732 rejected the Trustees' application for funds.[30]

The examination of Georgia affairs in the House of Commons during the session of 1741–42 was marked by a scathing attack against the Trustees by Thomas Stephens, a one-time employee of the Trust, son of William Stephens and one of the so-called 'malcontents.' On May 14, 1742, John Percival recorded what seemed to be the impact of the younger Stephens' testimony: "My son acquainted me that Mr. Stephens Evidence made great Impression on the house, and that he perceived there was a disposition to take the Colony out of the Trustees hands, but not to drop the Colony, particularly that they thought Negroes are necessary and change of Tenure into absolute liberty to sell their lands at will."[31] Three days before, on May 11, the House had ordered the Trustees to lay before it certain documents deemed important in evaluating the request for funds. Among these was the petition for Negroes which had been received by the Trustees in 1735, but which they had rejected. Commenting on the parliamentary session, Percival wrote that "the chief and main Debate was whether the use of Negroes should be allowed or not. . . ." Although a vote to permit Negroes in Georgia failed in the House of Commons, sufficient support for the Trustees was lacking and the requested funds were not granted.[32] During the remaining years of the Trusteeship the Commons was never as generous as it had been before the crucial debate of 1742. Twelve thousand pounds were appropriated for the Trustees' use in 1743, but only slightly more than £3,000 were granted in 1750.[33]

Criticized for nearly two decades, the Trustees were preparing to remove the old restrictions on Negro labor. In 1750 the Crown approved a Georgia act repealing the earlier legislation prohibiting Negroes and "permitting the Importation and Use of them in the Colony under proper Restrictions and Regulations." The new arrangement required that there be employed "one white Man Servant . . . capable of bearing Arms and aged between sixteen and sixty five Years" for every "four Male Negroes or blacks."[34] This innovation, long resisted by the Trustees, was accompanied by revisions in land policy, all of which was merely a prelude to the transition from Trustee rule to the status of royal colony, which occurred in 1752. Georgia was entering a new phase in its history, possessed of a new governmental form, with significant adjustments in agricultural patterns, and able now to exploit the labor of Negro slaves.[35]

The legislation of 1750 opening the way for slavery in Georgia also legalized the importation of Negroes. Nevertheless, the slave trade did not at once burgeon into big business. Existing records suggest that Negroes were imported after 1750 in small groups—eight, twenty, perhaps as many as thirty-five—primarily from South Carolina and island colonies in the Caribbean. Moreover, it does not appear that Georgia merchants imported those Negroes who did reach the colony immediately after removal of the ban.[36] Among these first slave traders, however, was the very prominent James Habersham.

Habersham had arrived in Georgia from England in 1738 and had quickly established himself as a provincial leader; he was active in local political circles, and in 1744 he entered upon a mercantile way of life at Savannah. Besides owning several hundred Negroes, Habersham was a partner in the importation and sale of several large cargoes of slaves brought direct from Africa. One such cargo, consisting of "about one hundred and fifty, chiefly men," entered in from Gambia during the spring of 1769. In these slaving ventures Habersham was associated with the well-known Joseph Clay.[37]

Habersham and Clay were not the only Georgia merchants, who, by the 1760's, were importing Negroes. The largest of these slave traders and slave trading firms included George Baillie & Co., Lewis Johnson and Alexander Wylly, John Graham and Co., Inglis and Hall, and Basil Cowper and William and Edward Telfairs. Between November, 1767, and November, 1774, the firm of Cowper and Telfair imported into Georgia no fewer than eleven shiploads of slaves, procured in Africa and the West Indies and containing as many as "Two hundred and Thirty prime young healthy SLAVES" per cargo.[38] In four years, from July, 1766, to June, 1770, Inglis and Hall imported and sold eight cargoes of slaves, the largest of which, containing "Three Hundred and Forty healthy NEW NEGROES," was offered for sale beginning May 31, 1770.[39] A partner with Inglis and Hall in this particular sale was John Graham, one of the largest slaveowners in the province, a member of the merchant-planter class, and an active politician as well. James Wright, the last of Georgia's royal governors and among the wealthiest land-owners, also imported Negro slaves.[40]

Few of these men limited their mercantile activities to the importation of slaves; almost all were involved in the handling and sale of other goods. Cowper and Telfair, for example, informed the public in February, 1767, that they had just received from London "SUNDRY GOODS," such as Irish and printed linens, tea, sugar, and two neat riding chairs, and a very neat chaise. Johnson and Wylly sold a varied assortment of manufactured goods "for the Indian trade" and such colonial products as West India rum and Philadelphia flour.[41]

Through the efforts of the slave merchants, and also through natural increase, Georgia's Negro population grew considerably in the years immediately preceding the outbreak of the revolution. In a total population estimated at 9,578 in 1760, Negroes numbered more than 3,500. The percentage of Negroes increased over the next decade, for by 1770 they accounted for 10,625 of the total population of 23,375.[42] To regulate the expanding slave population Georgia had adopted its first slave code in 1755.[43]

The revolutionary era, then, found Georgia solidly in the ranks of those rebellious colonies which were seeking a separate existence outside the British empire and with social and economic structures which leaned heavily on the institution of Negro slavery. Although permitted by English authorities to satisfy their experimental appetites, the Georgia Trustees had failed; Georgians were determined to have Negro laborers. The decision to abandon earlier policy clearly influenced the later history of Georgia. It may even have been of significance for the future of the new nation born in the midst of revolution.

Recent scholarship has suggested that the slavery issue was of pivotal importance at the Philadelphia Convention of 1787. Led by South Carolina, the southern states would not accept any serious constitutional interference with their peculiar institution. Had South Carolina stood alone, the Founding Fathers might have confronted the issue squarely; instead that issue was left to divide a later generation of Americans. The delegation from Georgia aligned itself with South Carolina, however, and together they constituted an opposition formidable enough to escape challenge. Certainly the Georgia Trustees were unaware of the long-range repercussions which would follow their decision to permit Negroes in Georgia, but that decision did hold an unusual significance for the future.[44]

Notes

1.   *Observations on the Slaves and the Indented Servants, inlisted in the Army, and in the Navy of the United States* (Philadelphia, August 14, 1777), in Hazard Family Papers, in Historical Society of Pennsylvania (HSP).

2.   Samuel Wetherell's Letter to the Committee of the Mon. Meeting of Philadelphia—in vindication of himself, Oct., 1778, in Pemberton Papers, II, in Etting Collection, HSP.

3.   Quoted in Carl L. Becker, *The Declaration of Independence, A Study in the History of Political Ideas* (New York, Vintage Edition, 1958), 212–13. There are other early examples expressing this point of view. See the essay by Thomas Paine, *Pennsylvania Journal and the Weekly Advertiser,* March 8, 1775, reprinted in Philip S. Foner, ed., *The Complete Writings of Thomas Paine* (New York, 1945), II, 15–19.

4.   More recent writers have accepted much of this interpretation of the American past. See Clarence L. Ver Steeg, *The Formative Years, 1607–1763* (New York, 1963), 192.

5.   An able summary of the background of the Georgia colony can be found in Trevor Richard Reese, *Colonial Georgia, A Study in British Imperial Policy in the Eighteenth Century* (Athens, Ga., 1963), Chap. I.

6.   Robert G. McPherson, ed., *The Journal of the Earl of Egmont, Abstract of the Trustees Proceedings for Establishing the Colony of Georgia, 1732–1738* (Athens, Ga., 1962), 71.

7. Elizabeth Donnan, ed., *Documents Illustrative of the History of the Slave Trade to America* (Washington, D.C., 1930–1935), IV, 587–89.

8. "A Brief Account of the Establishment of the Colony of Georgia, under General James Oglethorpe," in Peter Force, comp., *Tracts and Other Papers, Relating Principally to the Origin, Settlement, and Progress of the Colonies in North America, from the Discovery of the Country to the Year 1776* (Gloucester, Mass., 1963), I, 10.

9. Patrick Tailfer and others, "A True and Historical Narrative of the Colony of Georgia, in America, From the First Settlement thereof until this present Period . . ." (Charles Town, South Carolina, 1741), *ibid.*, I, 21.

10. Francis Moore, "A Voyage to Georgia, Begun in the Year 1735," (London, 1744), in *Collections of the Georgia Historical Society*, I, 102.

11. H. B. Fant, "The Labor Policy of the Trustees for Establishing the Colony of Georgia in America," in *The Georgia Historical Quarterly*, XVI (1932), 7.

12. McPherson, ed., *Journal of the Earl of Egmont*, 17, 18, 20, 55.

13. "Stephens Journal, 1737–1740," in Allen D. Candler, ed., *The Colonial Records of the State of Georgia*, IV, 201.

14. Tailfer and others, "A True and Historical Narrative of the Colony of Georgia," in Force, comp., *Tracts*, I, iv, viii.

15. "A Description of Georgia, By a Gentleman Who Has Resided There Upwards of Seven Years, and Was One of the First Settlers," (London, 1741), *ibid.*, II, 3–6.

16. "An Impartial Inquiry into the State and Utility of the Province of Georgia," (London, 1741), in *Collections of the Georgia Historical Society*, I, 187.

17. Tailfer and others, "A True and Historical Narrative of the Colony of Georgia," in Force, comp., *Tracts*, I, 18.

18. U.S. Bureau of the Census, *Historical Statistics of the United States, Colonial Times to 1957* (Washington, D.C., 1960), 756; Elizabeth Donnan, "The Slave Trade into South Carolina Before the Revolution," in *American Historical Review*, XXXIII (1928), 807 and 808, notes. One writer in 1734 said of South Carolina, in what obviously was an exaggeration: "There are five Negroes to one White, and there are imported generally 3000 fresh Negroes every Year. There are computed to be 30,000 Negroes in this Province, all of them Slaves, and their Posterity for ever." See "An Extract of the

Journals of Mr. Commissary Von Reck, Who Conducted the First Transport of Saltzburgers to Georgia: And of the Reverend Mr. Bolzius, One of their Ministers . . ." (London, 1734), in Force, comp., *Tracts,* IV, 9.

19. Tailfer and others, "A True and Historical Narrative of the Colony of Georgia," *ibid.,* I, 39.

20. "Stephens Journal, 1737–1740," in Candler, ed., *Colonial Records of the State of Georgia,* IV, 59.

21. "An Extract of the Journals of Mr. Commissary Von Reck . . . And of the Reverend Mr. Bolzius," in Force, comp., *Tracts,* IV, 18.

22. "An Account Shewing the Progress of the Colony of Georgia, in America, From Its First Establishment." (London, 1741), *ibid.,* I, 44–49.

23. Tailfer and others, "A True and Historical Narrative of the Colony of Georgia," *ibid.,* I, 23.

24. This paragraph is based on Tailfer and others, "A True and Historical Narrative of the Colony of Georgia," *ibid.,* I, 37–44; the quotation appears on p. 40.

25. "An Impartial Inquiry . . . ," in *Collections of the Georgia Historical Society,* I, 166–73.

26. "An Account Shewing the Progress of the Colony of Georgia," in Force, comp., *Tracts,* I, 33.

27. Tailfer and others, "A True and Historical Narrative of the Colony of Georgia," *ibid.,* I; the quotations which follow are from pp. 1 and 79.

28. "An Account Shewing the Progress of the Colony of Georgia," *ibid.,* I, iii, 10.

29. "An Impartial Inquiry . . . ," in *Collections of the Georgia Historical Society,* I, 166–73.

30. See Richard S. Dunn, "The Trustees of Georgia and the House of Commons, 1732–1752," in *William and Mary Quarterly,* XI (1954), 553.

31. Quoted in Lee F. Stock, ed., *Proceedings and Debates of the British Parliaments respecting North America* (Washington, D.C., 1924–41), V, 144, note 79.

32. *Ibid.,* V, 143, 151, note 90.

33. Dunn, "The Trustees of Georgia and the House of Commons, 1732–1752."

34. Donnan, ed., *Documents Illustrative of the History of the Slave Trade to America,* IV, 608–11.

35. Willard Range, "The Agricultural Revolution in Royal Georgia, 1752–1775," in *Agricultural History,* XXI (1947), 250–55.

36. Donnan, ed., *Documents Illustrative of the History of the Slave Trade to America,* IV, 612–13.

37. "The Letters of Hon. James Habersham, 1756–1775," in *Collections of the Georgia Historical Society,* VI, 5–7; *Georgia Gazette,* March 23, 1768, April 5, 1769; W. W. Abbot, *The Royal Governors of Georgia, 1754–1775* (Chapel Hill, N.C., 1959), 22.

38. Donnan, ed., *Documents Illustrative of the History of the Slave Trade to America,* IV, 612–25. The tabulation for Cowper and Telfairs is based on advertisements appearing in the *Georgia Gazette;* see the issue for August 24, 1774.

39. *Ibid.,* May 23, 1770.

40. Ralph Betts Flanders, *Plantation Slavery in Georgia* (Chapel Hill, N.C., 1933), 44–45; Donnan, ed., *Documents Illustrative of the History of the Slave Trade to America,* IV, 620.

41. *Georgia Gazette,* July 7, December 1, 1763, February 4, 1767.

42. U.S. Bureau of the Census, *Historical Statistics of the United States, Colonial Times to 1957,* p. 756.

43. Flanders, *Plantation Slavery in Georgia,* 23.

44. Dwight Lowell Dumond, *Antislavery: The Crusade for Freedom in America* (Ann Arbor, Mich., 1961), 36–45; Staughton Lynd, "A Constitution Divided," in *Columbia University Forum,* VIII (Spring, 1965), 17–22; Staughton Lynd, "The Abolitionist Critique of the United States Constitution," in Martin Duberman, ed., *The Antislavery Vanguard: New Essays on the Abolitionists* (Princeton, N.J., 1965), 209–39.

Part 3

Red and Black Resistance

TO WHITES, BLACKS WERE inferior beings who were marked by appearance, origin, and racial traits for slavery. Native Americans were uncivilized savages, and many whites believed that "the only good Indian was a dead Indian." Almost all whites agreed that Indian lands should be taken and that the Indians should be moved westward or exterminated. Red and black reaction varied. A few accommodated by adopting white values, habits, and mores and by accepting an inferior position within white society. Others took one of many possible middle courses: "putting on the mask," focusing one's life upon religious concerns for another life, borrowing from white culture, or engaging in a subtle, covert action against their condition. A third remedy was overt resistance. This, too, could take many forms: revolt and warfare were the most extreme examples, but various attempts at arson, murder, kidnapping, theft, and individual escape also demonstrated a rejection of the dictates of the dominant society.

Native American reaction to European encroachments reflected the broad range of possibilities. At first they often aided the new and strange settlers, assuming that there was land and food enough for everyone, but white refusal to accept this accommodation soon led to an escalation of tension. Ultimately warfare broke out between red and white. The final results of the skirmishes, battles, and wars of the colonial era were inevitably the same: disease plus the aggressors' technical superiority and total commitment to the single-minded goal of land acquisition guaranteed white victory. Some Indians accepted white military superiority, ceded their lands through treaties, and then moved farther west with the unavailing hope that they would remain unmolested on their new lands. Others, the "Praying Indians" for example, adopted white culture and civilization and lived near or within white settlements on "reservations." Other Indians turned with renewed interest to their own culture and religious practices in an attempt to resist at least the usurpation of their inner lives by white civilization.

While Native Americans were primarily involved in defending their own land and environment, Africans were forced to react to a different set of circumstances. Their first instinct was survival, which was challenged initially during the breaking-in process whereby whites tried to create obedient slaves. A major question, as Gary B. Nash has asked, is "how did they respond to the loss of their freedom and the separation from all that was familiar in the native culture?" What seems very clear is that they were not Sambos, that is, fawning, cringing, smiling, childlike dependents. Rather, among recently imported slaves, referred to as "outlandish" or "saltwater" Africans, overt rebelliousness was rampant and group runaways were common. The "New Negroes," those who had become more assimilated by white culture, still reacted against their labor and their masters by malingering, feigning illness, breaking tools, destroying crops, burning barns and houses, stealing food and property, and by truancy (hiding out in the woods) and outlawry (the attacking of white masters and their property by runaways). Even the best assimilated slaves, such as skilled laborers and house servants, used their ability to function within white society to run away and pose as free blacks. White fears concerning black resistance centered mainly on poisoning, arson, and conspiracy against the master class.

For black slaves, as for Native Americans, the ultimate form of resistance to their situation was warfare; and during the colonial period numerous slave revolts and conspiracies took place. Herbert Aptheker, in *American Negro Slave Revolts,* reported that "the first serious conspiracy involving black slaves in English America occurred in Virginia in 1663." Rebellions or elaborate conspiracies such as those at New York in 1712 and 1741, the Stono Rebellion of 1739 in South Carolina, and the plot to destroy Annapolis in 1740 followed, and further indicated the extreme contempt of blacks for the institution of slavery. But compared to Caribbean and South American colonies, the number and size of slave revolts was small. This fact has on occasion given rise to the belief that blacks in the English colonies were more docile; but what it mainly indicates is that whites maintained greater control over the lives of blacks in the English mainland colonies and that there was no place for the slaves to escape to, thereby reducing the number of slave revolts while at the same time contributing to other forms of resistance.

The kind of resistance that whites feared most was an armed alliance between red and black; and whites used various stratagems for preventing such an occurrence, especially in the southeast where whites were in a decided minority. There, whites followed a policy of divide and conquer by setting red against black; as William S. Willis, Jr., put it, "whites wilfully helped create antagonism between Indians and Negroes in order to preserve themselves and their privileges." They accomplished this in part by using Indians to capture runaway slaves and to suppress black slave insurrections, and by using blacks as soldiers against the Indians.

Basically whites were too powerful; successful resistance to the white society seldom came from direct confrontation, but more subtle reactions brought some limited success. Slavery continued until 1865 when the North and the South fought a Civil War over the issue; and the depopulation and removal of red Americans continued throughout the nineteenth century. It is important to remember that in their resistance both red and black adopted portions of the white culture, and that both resisted total cultural annihilation by retaining portions of their own cultural heritage.

Unrest Among
Virginia Slaves

Thad W. Tate*

As Thad W. Tate demonstrates in this excerpt from his book, The Negro in Eighteenth-Century Virginia, *black opposition to the institution of slavery in Virginia was made evident by a high incidence of runaways, by occasional efforts at rebellion, and by periodic flareups of defiant activity. But no major insurrections occurred; rather, Tate found that "the volume of runaway slaves was large" and that "well-laid plots by slaves were much rarer in eighteenth-century Virginia than what could be more correctly described as periods of unusual restiveness." Tate is professor of history at the College of William and Mary and director of the Institute of Early American History. He has served as book review editor and has written several articles for* the William and Mary Quarterly.

THE EVOLUTION OF THE NEGRO'S legal status from ordinary indentured servant to servant for life to slave was followed by the development of a separate legal code, distinct trial procedures, and harsher punishments for Negroes accused of criminal acts. Inevitably the slave's lack of personal freedom would have necessitated some revision in the English legal system that had

*Thad W. Tate, "Unrest Among Virginia Slaves," in *The Negro in Eighteenth-Century Williamsburg* (Charlottesville: University Press of Virginia, 1965), pp. 91, 103–13. Reprinted by permission.

been transported to Virginia. But it was unrelenting fear of the Negro as a potential insurrectionist and constant determination to police his conduct rigidly that instigated most of the early laws affecting Negro slaves.

Only in the last two decades of the seventeenth century did anything more than the faintest beginning of a separate criminal law for Negroes begin to appear. An act of 1680 for preventing Negro insurrections was the first real "black code" in Virginia, providing specific punishments for the three crimes of leaving the master's property without permission; lifting a hand against a "Christian," that is, a white man; and for hiding or resisting capture after running away.[1] Conviction on the last charge required the death penalty. A 1691 statute that was of the greatest importance as the first legal restriction on manumission of slaves in Virginia also provided a systematic plan for raising a force of men to recapture "outlying slaves," or runaways who were in hiding.[2] Then in 1692 the legislature provided the first trial procedures, in particular the denial of jury trial, which applied specifically to Negro slaves.[3] . . .

Much of the crime committed by Negro slaves was to some degree one possible means of resisting the demands of slavery. It was, to be sure, a fairly desperate method, particularly if a slave resorted to anything so extreme as the murder of his master and so insured his own execution. There was a much safer way of refusing to accept bondage. That was simply to run away at the first opportunity. The chances of being retaken were good, but not good enough to deter great numbers of slaves from becoming fugitives.

For a slave to run away was as much a criminal act as for one to rob or kill. The owner did not have to rely solely on his own resources to recapture his man. He could count upon the machinery of law to assist him. The fugitive slave represented in a number of ways, however, a distinct problem from the ordinary slave criminal. His offense was too common to treat it as a felony, until it became habitual.[4] Ordinarily he stood convicted by his very act of flight; therefore provision for trial and punishment by the courts were largely unnecessary. Swift recapture and return to his owner were the basic needs, and these the law tried to provide. Punishment by whipping could be administered by the officials responsible for his return without a court decree.

Before the advent of slavery in a legal sense Negroes were dealt with under the laws that applied to all runaway indentured servants, white or black. These enactments required fugitives to serve extra time, usually twice the length of their absence, as compensation to the master for the loss of their labor.[5] It was, in fact, a revision of these laws that constituted the first legal recognition in Virginia that the status of the Negro was changing so that he could be held as a servant for life. This occurred in the statute of 1661/62 which referred specifically to "negroes who are incapable of making satisfaction by addition of time."[6]

Not much later, in 1669, a system by which recaptured servants were to be returned to their masters was defined by law. A fugitive who was retaken was carried before the nearest justice in order to determine the name of his master. Then the man was to be delivered from constable to constable along the route to his home.[7] The next year the law was modified to instruct each constable to give the fugitive a severe whipping as he passed through his jurisdiction, and at the same time runaway Negroes were specifically stated to be comprehended in these acts.[8] A reward was also established for recapturing a runaway—1,000 pounds of tobacco in 1669 but reduced in 1670 to a less attractive 200 pounds with much more stringent inquiry into the claimant's right to collect.[9]

After slavery was fully established, these arrangements, that is, the reward of 200 pounds of tobacco and the system of returning runaways through successive constables, remained in force with only minor variations. Thus the 1705 law, while largely repeating existing regulations, did omit the requirement that every constable through whom a man was returned should administer a whipping.[10] Now only the first constable gave his thirty-nine lashes; so a hapless fugitive might have gotten home with at least a little skin on his back.

The 1705 law also introduced another modification in which the Public Gaol at Williamsburg figured prominently. Before it had been more or less assumed that the recaptured man would identify the name and residence of his owner. The Assembly overlooked the growing number of Negroes, some of whom knew no English and could not give this information and others of whom pretended to be new and feigned a lack of understanding of English. Now, when it was impossible to identify the owner, a slave was to be brought down to Williamsburg to the Public Gaol of the colony.[11] Eventually it became permissible to sell Negroes unclaimed after a reasonable time. With the founding of a newspaper in Williamsburg, it also became possible for the jailer to advertise runaways he was holding.

Justices and constables immediately began to send unidentified runaways to the capital, at times in such haste that a slave taken only a few miles from his home plantation might well be sent a long distance to Williamsburg before anyone had a chance to identify him. So, after 1726, it was necessary to hold a Negro first for two months in the jail of the county where he had been captured. Then if he had not been claimed, the constable would pass him along through the other constables to the Public Gaol.[12] The volume of Negroes brought to Williamsburg under these laws was considerable, for the columns of the *Virginia Gazette* carried a more or less steady flow of advertisements.[13] Such runaways may have furnished an addition to the local labor force, since they could be hired out under proper safeguards. Not many of the unidentified ones were sold here, since the court of the county in which they had first been captured had this authority.

In 1748, the same year in which the main body of criminal law affecting Negroes was overhauled and consolidated, an attempt was made to do the same thing regarding runaways in an act on servants and slaves.[14] This latter enactment, however, failed to include a suspending clause, holding up its effective date until it had received the royal assent. For this reason Virginians received notice in 1752 that it had been disallowed, but the Assembly moved quickly to pass a similar law in the proper form in 1753.[15] It was essentially a restatement of the law as it had stood since 1726.

In the 1760s there was a final attempt to alter the means of handling captured fugitives. An act of 1765 provided for a captor who had determined the owner of a fugitive to carry the man before the justice of the peace of the county. Then the captor was to take the responsibility of returning the runaway to the master upon himself, for which he was entitled to payment of 5 shillings plus 4 pence a mile.[16] This method, while eliminating the use of the constables except for slaves whose masters could not be determined, had obvious shortcomings. It is no surprise to find the law altered four years later in 1769 on the ground that it had been ineffective. Now a captor could follow the procedure of 1765, receiving larger sums of 10 shillings plus 6 pence a mile; or he could simply take the runaway to the county jail, where the older arrangements that still applied to slaves of unidentified masters could be followed.[17]

The conclusion is inescapable that the volume of runaway slaves was large, large enough to sap a part of the economic advantage of a slave labor force. The small stereotype of a black figure hurrying along with a parcel of clothing tied on a stick and slung across his shoulder identified listings of fugitives in substantially every issue of the *Gazette*. From George Washington to the humblest master, few owners escaped the loss of Negroes in this way.[18]

The ease with which the slave community in Williamsburg hid fugitives must suggest that the capital was no more immune from runaways than anywhere else in the colony and that recapturing them was no easier. Williamsburg's share of the *Gazette* advertisements was large, and not even the printers themselves escaped the disagreeable necessity of using their own columns to attempt to recover a slave.[19]

Not all of these escaped slaves had an idea of achieving permanent freedom. Free soil did not yet exist to the north. If a slave really intended to live as a free man, the possibilities were limited and, in some cases, the hardships almost as unendurable as slavery itself. He had essentially two alternatives. He might make his way to one of the hidden, illegal communities of refugee Negroes on the western frontier of Virginia or in the

Dismal Swamp. Otherwise and with less risk, if he were a skilled craftsman or light-skinned, he might get to a settled community where he could pass without too many questions as a free Negro. For Virginia slaves in the eighteenth century North Carolina offered the best opportunity for this latter course.

Bob, a slave of the Williamsburg innkeeper William Trebell, is a good illustration.[20] Bob, a man of 26 described as having been "burnt when young, by which he has a scar on the wrist of his right hand, the thumb of his left hand burnt off, and the hand [turned] in," escaped on a Saturday night in April of 1767. It is his past which was, however, more relevant. Bob had just been brought back from Hertford County in North Carolina after being away eight years. Part of the time he had lived in Charleston, South Carolina. Then for the last three years he had lived in North Carolina under the name of Edward or Edmund Tamar, had married, and with the protection of a man named Van Pelt had passed as a freeman. The fact that he could read and write and was an able carpenter and tailor had certainly made his deception easier. Some of the Negro women in Williamsburg were also able to get away in the hope of passing as free, including Nanny, "a brisk genteel sensible wench," whom her owner, Jane Vobe, suspected of having gone off with the New American Company of actors.[21]

Very frequently runaway slaves were less concerned about a permanent escape than simply returning to a locale from which they had recently been purchased or moved. John Maclean, for instance, bought a slave girl, Judith, and her year-old child at the sale of slaves from Middlesex County held on April 30, 1773, at Williamsburg. The following day she slipped off and was advertised as having probably started back to her Middlesex master.[22] Another girl, only 14 or 15 years old, from this same lot of slaves escaped in October, presumably to return to her mother, who was still a cook for the planter who had sold the daughter.[23] John, "6 feet high, 17 years old, well grown, with remarkable long feet," was known to have returned from Williamsburg to Warwick, where he had a father and some other relatives.[24] Often the attraction of the slave's former residence was the fact that a wife or husband was still living there, as in the case of Peter, the property of John Fox of Williamsburg, who for this reason had returned to Gloucester County.[25] Running away for the sake of returning to a familiar location or rejoining relatives was a two-way street so far as Williamsburg was concerned; for there were also slaves who escaped into town after being sold or leased elsewhere. One instance of this is the case of Billy, a 20-year old slave advertised by his master in Amherst County as a runaway and suspected of having gone back to Williamsburg, since he had grown up and been trained as a shoemaker there.[26] In a number of instances slaves who had accompanied masters to Williamsburg took advantage of the busy atmosphere of the capital to make an escape.[27]

After a time it becomes distinctly noticeable how many runaway Negroes were drawn from the more highly skilled classes of labor. A high proportion seemed to be craftsmen, and some were able to read and write. The average runaway often seemed to be a slave like Johnny, a mulatto serving man, able to read and write, and once the property of Peyton Randolph, who escaped from Edmund Randolph in late 1777.[28]

It cannot be overlooked, however, that many runaway slaves were simply ordinary field hands, quite often so recently imported that they knew no English. This was more characteristic of the early eighteenth century and of other areas than Williamsburg, although most of the recaptured slaves brought into the Public Gaol, because their masters were unidentified, were "new Negroes."[29] There was one occasion when a group of fourteen recently imported Negroes fled in a body from a Hanover County merchant, John Burnley, who was probably holding them for sale.[30]

In the final analysis these runaways were perhaps a mixed lot, as mixed as their motives for escape. Some had genuine hopes of freedom, and a very few made good on them. Some fled from sheer desperation, not caring any longer about the risk of recapture. Others were more temporary absentees than real fugitives, seeking only a brief return to relatives from whom they had been separated. Whatever the reasons, the number of slaves who, in the eighteenth century use of the word, "eloped" is a powerful argument that few Negroes accepted the demands of slavery complacently.

There has already been occasion . . . to comment on the lurking fear of insurrection which haunted every slaveowner. As the number of slaves mounted steadily toward half the population of the colony—and, of course, more than half in areas where the slaves were really concentrated—it became possible to conceive of the destruction of society itself, if a Negro uprising were really to take hold. Newspapers all over the colonies were quick to publish every available detail of a real or rumored attempt of slaves to rebel; and much of the restrictive legislation against Negroes in the colony was admittedly aimed at this unwelcome possibility.[31]

To what extent was the alarm of the whites exaggerated? One count of uprisings or threats of uprisings during the entire course of slavery in Virginia lists 72 of which only 9 occurred before 1776.[32] The truth is difficult to measure; for instead of specific, brief episodes more often there were periods of general unrest lasting several years at a time. Judged on this basis, about a fourth of the years from 1700 to 1775 were marred by an abnormal degree of this uneasiness. The fact remains, however, that no white person was killed in an organized slave insurrection in Virginia before the Nat Turner rising of 1831.

The first recorded attempt at a slave uprising in Virginia occurred in the Northern Neck in 1687. As so often happened, one of the men involved confessed and the attempt was checked. The slave who had been leader was not executed but was whipped around Jamestown from the prison to the gallows and back, forced to wear an iron collar for the rest of his life, and forbidden ever to leave his master's plantation.[33]

A more serious plot, which centered in Surry and Isle of Wight Counties but also involved James City, was uncovered in March, 1709.[34] Once again it was a slave who betrayed the plan to the whites—a Negro named Will, the property of Robert Ruffin of Surry.[35] It fell to the Council to direct an investigation of the whole matter and issue instructions for the trial and punishment of the Negroes involved. The way in which they proceeded provides a good picture of the operation of all levels of government in the colony in the face of what, to these men, presented a serious crisis. First of all, the Council apparently issued warrants for the arrest of all suspects, similar to one issued for four Negroes in Bruton Parish, Angola Peter, Bumbara Peter, Mingo, and Robin.[36] Then the county justices of Surry and Isle of Wight were ordered to examine all suspected slaves, releasing those only slightly involved with appropriate punishment and holding the leaders in the county jail, until the record of their examination could be examined by the president of the Council, Edmund Jenings.[37] James City Negroes were not considered to be so deeply involved. Here, with a single exception, the slaves, who had been rounded up and held under guard, were to be tried at the next county court, punished, and released.[38] There is an account of the close cross-examination of several of these slaves in a letter from Philip Ludwell to Jenings. The questioning by Ludwell and three others had cleared Commissary Blair's slaves and a number of others of complicity, but it had also turned up the evidence against John Brodnax's Jamy, the one James City slave ordered held in prison.[39]

About a month later the Council ordered the principal culprits, those still held in jail, to be tried before the General Court, where three of them were presumably convicted and hanged. One of the "chief Actors," Peter, belonging to Samuel Thompson of Surry, had escaped, and a reward of £10 alive or £5 dead was offered for his recapture.[40]

The episode had a happier ending for Robert Ruffin's Will. After he had given away the insurrection, it became necessary to move him to the Northern Neck because some of the other Negroes threatened his life. Then at its meeting in the fall of 1710 the Assembly voted him his freedom as a reward for his service to the colony, the occasion being marred only by the complaint of his former master, Ruffin, that the £40 voted by the Assembly was less than he had been offered for the Negro by a prospective buyer.[41]

Another plan for an uprising was headed off in 1722, prompt-
ing Governor Drysdale to include in his first message to the
assembly a request for improving the militia and for passing
stricter laws as a protection against Negroes.[42] The slave code
was, in fact, strengthened that year.[43]

The years of 1729 and 1730 seem to have brought a relatively
longer period of unrest among slaves which may have continued
through most of the decade of the 30s.[44] The first incident
occurred in June of 1729 on a new plantation near the head of
the James River. There a group of about fifteen Negroes seized
arms, provisions, and tools and made off for the mountains. The
search party found them already settled in a secluded area,
where they had even begun to clear ground for crops. A brief
exchange of gunfire brought about the surrender of the slaves,
however, and their small colony was destroyed.[45]

There was more trouble the next year, touched off by a rumor
that former Governor Spotswood, just back from England, had
brought an order from the Crown to free all Christian slaves.
This was more a matter of general unrest than a concerted plot.
The governor, at the time Gooch, reported that by ''keeping the
Militia to their Duty, by Imprisonment and severe whipping of
the most Suspected, this Disturbance was very soon Quashed,
and until about six weeks afterwards we were easy . . .''[46]
Then there was more trouble. About two hundred slaves in
Norfolk and Princess Anne counties gathered on a Sunday at
church time and elected officers to lead an intended rebellion. In
this instance four of the Negroes involved were executed.[47] A
certain amount of continuing uneasiness is reflected in Gooch's
address to the assembly in 1736, in which he recommended
strengthening the militia as a means of policing the slaves; in his
proclamation of October 29, 1736, on the same subject; and in
the 1738 revision of the law requesting the militia to include a
system of four-men patrols to police slave quarters and suspected gathering places of Negroes in every county.[48]

Another unsettled period occurred in and near Williamsburg
during the 1770s. The number of runaways advertised seemed
noticeably large, and accounts of trouble with slaves in York,

James City, and Hanover counties circulated in newspapers as far away as New York.[49] This was in part responsible for the establishment of a night watch in Williamsburg in 1772 to consist of four people to patrol the streets, cry the hours, and "use their best Endeavours to preserve Peace and good Order, by apprehending and bringing to Justice Hall disorderly People, Slaves as well as others."[50] About the same time there was a strict patrol in Yorktown, and Negroes found on the street were picked up and held overnight.[51]

For suppression of an incipient revolt the colony relied largely on the county militia and, after 1738, the system of patrols, reinforced by such local activity as the Williamsburg night watch. From what we know about the colonial militia, it is not likely that these men were over-diligent, until there was an indication of trouble. Still, the colony proved able to act swiftly in an emergency. Real emergencies, however, were relatively infrequent; for well-laid plots by slaves were much rarer in eighteenth-century Virginia than what could be more correctly described as periods of unusual restiveness.

Notes

1.   William Waller Hening, (ed.), *The Statutes at Large Being a Collection of all the Laws of Virginia* (Richmond, Va., etc., 1810–1823), 2: 481–82.

2.   *Ibid.*, 3: 86–88.

3.   *Ibid.*, pp. 102–3.

4.   For slaves who became habitual runaways or remained in hiding committing various depredations—"lying out" as the eighteenth century expressed it—more drastic legal procedures evolved. Two justices of the peace could issue a proclamation permitting such offenders to be killed without quarter. The sheriff could collect a force to hunt them down, or an individual captor might collect a reward for killing a Negro outlawed in this manner. If an "outlying" slave were taken alive, he was not executed, however, but punished by dismemberment. Hening, *Statutes,* 3: 86, 210–11, 460–61; 4: 32; 6: 110–11; 8: 358, 522–23.

5.   *Ibid.*, 1: 254–55, 401, 440.

6. *Ibid.*, 2: 116–17.

7. *Ibid.*, pp. 273–74.

8. *Ibid.*, pp. 277–79.

9. *Ibid.*, pp. 283–84.

10. *Ibid.*, 3: 456–57.

11. *Ibid.*, p. 456.

12. *Ibid.*, 4: 168–75.

13. See, for example, *Virginia Gazette,* September 15, 1737; September 22, 1738; March 21, 1745; January 2, 1752.

14. Hening, *Statutes,* 5: 547–48.

15. *Ibid.*, 6: 356–69.

16. *Ibid.*, 8: 135–37.

17. *Ibid.*, pp. 358–61.

18. *The Negro in Virginia.* Compiled by the Writers' Program of the Work Projects Administration (New York, 1940), p. 128.

19. *Virginia Gazette* (Purdie and Dixon), November 24, 1768; (Dixon and Hunter), January 28, 1775; (Purdie), March 8, 1776.

20. *Ibid.*, (Purdie and Dixon), April 16, 1767. See also the advertisement by James Southall for his slave, Peter, *ibid.*, (Purdie and Dixon), January 8, 1767.

21. *Ibid.*, (Purdie and Dixon), June 30, 1768.

22. *Ibid.*, (Purdie and Dixon), May 6, 1773.

23. *Ibid.*, (Purdie and Dixon), January 27, 1774.

24. *Ibid.*, (Purdie), July 25, 1777.

25. *Ibid.*, (Purdie), October 17, 1777.

26. *Ibid.*, (Clarkson and Davis), October 30, 1779.

27. *Ibid.,* (Purdie and Dixon), March 31, 1768; June 29, 1769; November 14, 1771.

28. *Ibid.,* (Purdie), December 12, 1777.

29. *Ibid.,* September 2, 1737; September 15, 1737; September 28, 1738; January 2, 1752; (Purdie and Dixon), July 8, 1773; February 3, 1774; June 16, 1774; August 4, 1774.

30. *Ibid.,* (Purdie and Dixon), August 19, 1773. Two months later Burnley had recovered ten of the Negroes, but the others were still in hiding near West Point, *ibid.,* (Purdie and Dixon), October 28, 1773.

31. The pertinent Virginia laws are those of 1680, 1682, 1723, and 1748. See above, section 1 of this chapter. Gerald W. Mullin, *Flight and Rebellion: Slave Resistance in Eighteenth-Century Virginia* (New York, 1971), *passim,* is extremely important for the study of slave rebellions and other forms of resistance. Mullin also thinks the whites were less apprehensive and insecure than I have described.

32. *Negro in Virginia,* p. 175.

33. *Ibid.,* p. 174; "Randolph Manuscript," *Virginia Magazine,* 19 (April, 1911): 151.

34. H. R. McIlwaine and Wilmer L. Hall, eds. *Executive Journals of the Council of Colonial Virginia* (Richmond, Va., 1925–1945), 3: 234–35.

35. *Journals of the House of Burgesses,* 1702–1712, p. 270.

36. *Virginia Magazine,* 17 (Jan., 1909): 34.

37. *Executive Journals of Colonial Virginia,* 3: 234–35.

38. *Ibid.,* 3, p. 235.

39. *Virginia Magazine,* 19 (January, 1911), 23–24.

40. *Executive Journals of Colonial Virginia,* 3: 236; *Negro in Virginia,* p. 174.

41. *Journals of the House of Burgesses,* 1702–1712, 270, 276, 282, 284, 288, 292, 298; Hening, *Statutes,* 3: 537–38.

42. *Ibid.,* 1712–1726, p. 360.

43. *Ibid.,* 1712–1726, p. 395.

44.   *Executive Journals of Colonial Virginia*, 4: 462–63.

45.   *Virginia Magazine*, 28 (Oct., 1920): 299–300.

46.   *Ibid.*, 32 (Oct., 1924): 322–23. Also, see above, p. 70 for the relation between this unrest and Anglican missionary efforts among the Virginia Negroes.

47.   *Ibid.*

48.   *Journals of the House of Burgesses*, 1727–1740, p. 243; *Executive Journals of Colonial Virginia*, 4: 383, 470–71; Hening, *Statutes*, 5: 19, 24.

49.   *Maryland Gazette*, February 8, 1770; *New York Journal or General Advertiser*, February 15, 1770.

50.   *Virginia Gazette* (Purdie and Dixon), July 16, 1772.

51.   *Ibid.*, (Pinkney), August 10, 1775.

The New York Slave Revolt of 1741: A Re-Examination

Ferenc M. Szasz*

In 1741, one hundred and fifty New York City slaves were imprisoned; eighteen were hanged, thirteen burned, and seventy sent to the West Indies. Why? Some historians claim that there was an elaborate slave conspiracy to destroy the city of New York. Others emphasize white fears and a mass communal hysteria similar to that which occurred fifty years before during the Salem witch trials. In "The New York Slave Revolt of 1741: A Re-Examination," Ferenc M. Szasz argues that "there existed no Negro conspiracy in 1741 to take over New York." According to Szasz, some blacks were involved in burglary plots, and arson scares were prevalent. Soon blacks and their white supporters were arrested and charged with conspiracy. Whether a slave revolt was plotted, it is quite clear that a considerable amount of tension existed between many of the whites and black slaves of New York City. Szasz teaches history at the University of New Mexico; he has published articles in the Tennessee Historical Quarterly *and* Mid-America.

THE FIRST PART OF THE eighteenth century has been seen as the "forgotten period" of American history,[1] and in 1741 there occurred an incident which, for the most part, has remained

*Ferenc M. Szasz, "The New York Slave Revolt of 1741: A Re-Examination," *New York History* 48 (1967), 215–30. Reprinted by permission.

forgotten: the Negro slave uprising in New York City. During the winter and spring of that year, the colonists were astounded to uncover what they felt to be a conspiracy among the Negroes to set fire to the town and murder all the inhabitants. A series of mass arrests, mass accusations, and an extended period of trials and punishments followed. During these proceedings, which dragged out for over a year, the magistrates imprisoned 150 slaves and 25 whites; hanged 18 slaves and 4 whites; burned 13 slaves, and transported over 70 to the West Indies.[2] All of this was carried out entirely within the law.

Although historians have dealt sparingly with this revolt, those who have examined it have recognized the significance of the situation. Benjamin G. Brawley listed this incident as "in some ways the most important single event in the history of the Negro in the colonial period."[3] George W. Williams saw it as "one of the most tragic events in all the history of New York or of the civilized world,"[4] while to Roi Ottley it was "the biggest lynching in the history of America."[5]

It is noteworthy, however, that compared with the energy which has been directed toward the Salem witch hysteria of barely fifty years before, the New York Negro slave revolt trials—so similar in many ways—have passed by almost unnoticed.[6] Little has been written about that incident which dominated the colony for over twelve months and which must have been remembered for years afterward.[7] Testimony before the Supreme Court of the colony extended well into 1742 and produced several sources to which the historian can turn. Though the Supreme Court minutes for this period unfortunately appear to be missing, materials pertaining to the plot can be found in the Caldwallader Colden papers, O'Callaghan's invaluable collection of colonial New York documents, and most newspapers of the time.[8] The most important single source of information, however, is a 400-page, tightly printed, day-by-day journal account of the trial proceedings. This book was compiled in 1744 by Justice Daniel Horsmanden, of the New York Supreme Court, the court that sentenced the conspirators. Voted a grant to produce a digest of the colony's laws, this sometime friend of the powerful DeLancey family put together his trial journal instead. His reasons for making this change are not known, but foremost among them, surely, was his desire for personal vindication, for in the preface Horsmanden asserts, "There had been some wanton, wrong-headed persons amongst us . . . [who] declared . . . *that there was no plot at all!"* Any analysis of the revolt must begin and end with his volume.[9]

The New York Slave Revolt is significant enough in colonial history to warrant an investigation on its own merits, and this interest is further heightened by the air of mystery which still surrounds the whole affair. Disagreement is widespread as to whether the Negroes really did organize a conspiracy in 1741. While no one other than Horsmanden would dare suggest that the conspiracy involved every slave in the city,[10] several historians feel that the colonists did, in fact, stave off a potential massacre. Benjamin G. Brawley, Ulrich B. Phillips, L. J. Greene, Carter G. Woodson, and M. R. Eppse are of this mind. So, too, are F. S. Eastman, Theodore Roosevelt, and the anonymous editor of the 1810 edition of the trial journal. All share the opinion that there did exist a corps of slaves who secretly planned and executed an uprising.[11] Herbert Aptheker in *A Documentary History of the Negro People in the United States* is the most recent exponent of this position. He states that "It [the plot] provided hysteria leading to exaggeration of the extent of the actual conspiracy but that one existed is clear."[12]

From the same sources, however, other historians have derived the exact opposite conclusion. J. C. Carrol, Cleveland Rodgers and R. B. Ranken, E. F. Frazier, M. W. Goodwin, and W. F. Prince all hold that in spite of the flurry of testimonials and the rash of confessions by the slaves, a judicious re-examination of the evidence shows that all the fears of the colonists were imaginary.[13] In *Black Odyssey,* Roi Ottley states, "Conspiracy! Actually there was none . . ."[14] while to George W. Williams, "there was not a syllable of competent evidence to show that there was an organized plot."[15]

Both groups have touched upon the edge of the truth, but neither has followed the winding path through to its center. If conspiracy is defined in the way the *Oxford Dictionary* lists the eighteenth century as using it, "an agreement between two or more persons to do something criminal, illegal, or reprehensible," then a conspiracy existed in 1741. But it was not a conspiracy organized by the slaves to burn the buildings and take over the town. Instead, there existed several small groups— perhaps in contact with one another, although this is not certain—all of which were plotting to rob the richer citizens of New York City. While more were certainly involved in the robberies than appear in the records, conclusive evidence from Horsmanden's Journal can be marshaled against, *at most*, only five whites and three Negroes. And this is just for larceny, not for rebellion. What the third Chief Justice wrote 400 pages to prove is unquestionably false. There existed no Negro conspiracy in 1741 to take over New York. But before beginning the attack on Horsmanden's evidence, it may help to clarify the picture if a brief mention is made of the position of the slave in colonial New York, for it was against this backdrop that the unfortunate events of 1741 played themselves out.

The slave code of colonial New York was harsh. Unlike New England, which tended to follow the Hebrew pattern of making the slave a part of the household, New York had regulations barely less strict than those of South Carolina.[16] No New York slave could buy, sell, inherit, or own property, nor could he testify in court cases concerning whites. He was forbidden to have a church marriage or burial, to strike a white, or to congregate in groups of more than four. He could not be publicly entertained, and any Negro found loose forty miles above Albany could be hanged.[17] The normal penalty was a public whipping but legally the master was left to his own devices, restricted only by the fact that his punishment could not extend to life or limb.

The severity of these laws, unique in the North, can be traced directly to the early years of the eighteenth century. In 1708, in New Town, Queens County, a farmer and his family were murdered by their slaves and that same year there appeared on the law books the first "Act for preventing the conspiracy of slaves." But the year 1712 was even more significant regarding laws pertaining to slavery. That summer, in Maiden Lane Orchard, New York City, a group of Negroes arose in what was to be the only significant slave rebellion in the northern colonies. One night about fifty of them banded together and set fire to a barn. When the whites came running to extinguish the blaze, the slaves attacked from the shadows, killing nine and wounding six others. Then they fled to the woods. When retribution came, it was swift and brutal. Twenty-one were executed and the suspected leaders were horribly tortured beforehand. Six killed themselves rather than face capture. Immediately afterwards, a number of regulatory laws appeared on the lawbooks — laws which further were modified and strengthened by the superseding acts of 1717 and 1730. From 1712 on, the penalty for arson by a slave was death.[18]

There is doubt, however, as to how strictly these laws were enforced. New York City in 1740 had a population of about 12,000, including almost 2,000 slaves. Their number alone (one-sixth of the population) would make enforcement of the rule of four impossible without creation of a police state. Records do show that there were some slave marriages and property holders, and tavern owners were not long in devising the custom of selling liquor to the slaves in "penny drams." The common council of the city found it necessary to supplement the colonial laws by passing codes explicitly prohibiting the slaves from things they were obviously already doing: selling oysters, corn, and fruit in the city; gambling; traveling at night without a light, etc. Those slaves living within the city limits were used chiefly as cooks, maids, handymen, personal servants, and sometimes skilled artisans. The multiplicity of masters, the long winters, and the absence of any consistent patrol or pass system doubtlessly meant there existed a considerable gap between the legislation on the books and actual practice.[19]

It was in this atmosphere that the 1741 conspiracy unfolded. Late on the night of February 28, 1741, the home of the merchant James Hogg was robbed of linens and other goods worth about 60 pounds. Information derived from Mary Burton, a

young indentured servant, set the authorities onto the following:
John Hughson, keeper of a low-class tavern; Hughson's wife
and daughter; Peggy Kerry, a lodger and a prostitute; and Caesar and Prince, two Negroes who often drank there. Mary,
"spinster, aged about sixteen years," was serving out her period of indenture by working at the Hughsons. Soon Hughson
admitted receiving the goods stolen by the Negroes.

Over two weeks later, Wednesday, March 18, Fort George
caught fire and burned to the ground. This caused much alarm,
especially when the fire reached the boxes of hand grenade
shells. At the time, the cause of the fire was attributed to the
carelessness of a plumber who had been using live coals to
repair a gutter. Exactly one week later, Wednesday, March 25,
another roof broke into flames, blamed this time on a faulty
chimney. One week later, Wednesday, April 1, a storehouse
burned to the ground. The cause of this was laid to a careless
smoker in the hayloft, but by now the seeds of the future panic
were well laid. That weekend, April 4 and 5, four more small
fires erupted and someone reported live coals found under a
haystack. By this time, general fear had reached such a state
that many of the townspeople began loading all their belongings
onto ox carts to flee the city. To calm the situation Lieutenant-
Governor George Clarke issued, on the eleventh of April, a
proclamation of reward and pardon, if involved, to anyone able
to reveal the cause of the disasters.

In the meantime the constables had been examining Mary
Burton about the Hogg robbery, seeking, if possible, a connection with the fires. Horsmanden noted in his *Journal* that Mary,
initially reluctant to testify about anything, finally told authorities that "she would acquaint them with what she knew relating
to the goods stolen from Mr. Hogg's but would say nothing
about the fires."[20] The magistrates, however, felt from this
statement that she *could* say something about the fires but had
decided not to. Consequently, they intensified their questioning,
alternating between cajoling the girl with dreams of the
100-pound reward and threatening her with damnation on the
Day of Judgement. It wasn't long before she weakened and

disclosed to them the existence of a conspiracy to burn the town and murder the white inhabitants. The chief conspirators, she said, were the slaves, Caesar and Prince, and Peggy Kerry. And the whole affair was masterminded by John Hughson, who afterwards was to be made king!

Mary's disclosure was preposterous to begin with, and as she added to it over the course of the year, it became even more so. The best critique of her testimony can be found in the little-known study by W. F. Prince, and it will serve here simply to mention his conclusions. Not even Horsmanden's 400 pages can hide the absurdities in her story. For example, Mary claimed the fires were to be set at night (the plan of the 1712 revolt), yet all but two broke out during the day. She initially stated that there were only three whites involved in the plot but later expanded this to include many more. The time lag (a week between each of the first three major fires) was far too great for any organized rebellion. And no conspiracy involving so many Negroes would have had a chance of remaining undetected in an urban environment with five citizens to every slave. As for Hughson's desire to be king, W. F. Prince concludes, "No white man able to run a tavern could have been capable of such an infantile conception."[21]

But if the magistrates were astounded at the disclosure of such a plot, nobody was more so than those accused of heading it. Caesar, Prince, Peggy Kerry, and the Hughsons all stoutly protested their innocence, but their pleas were ignored. After some debate, it was decided to try all those accused before the New York Supreme Court. The reason for this decision was that both whites and Negroes were involved and it was felt that the colony's highest tribunal should handle any plot that seemed to extend deeper than just a mere slave uprising.[22] The court ordered that the two slaves be hanged on May 10 for their admitted larceny, which at that time was a capital offence in New York. It assumed that they were guilty of the conspiracy also, but it decided to execute them on the first charge. Yet Horsmanden records: "They died very stubbornly, without confessing anything about the conspiracy; and denied they knew anything of it to the last.''[23] On June 12, Hughson and his wife also were executed. Here it states in the *Journal* that ''[Hughson] always denied he knew anything of the matter; said he had deserved death for receiving stolen goods. The wife was ever sullen; said little or nothing but denied all.''[24]

Peggy, when first confronted with Mary Burton's story ''positively denied that she knew anything of the matter; and said that if she should accuse anybody of any such thing, she must accuse innocent persons, and wrong her own soul.''[25] Later, hoping to fall under the Lieutenant-Governor's pardon, Peggy said that she actually had been involved in the plot, but shifted the scene of the conspiracy from Hughson's to another low-class tavern, run by John Romme, who had in the meantime fled the city. When the magistrates finally decided that the prostitute was too deeply enmeshed to fall under the pardon, Peggy called Justice Frederick Philipse into her cell where she told him ''all that she had said about Romme and his wife was false, excepting as to their receiving the stolen goods of the Negroes.''[26] She then was hanged.

Mary set the scene of the conspiracy at Hughson's. Peggy, to protect Hughson, switched it to Romme's. When Mary claimed not to have seen at Hughson's any of the slaves accused by Peggy, the Justices, instead of noticing any contradictions in the two stories, concluded that both taverns and both sets of slaves were involved.[27]

Other evidence implicating the slaves readily came to hand. Two of the fires flanked the home of a man who had recently purchased some Spanish Negroes—men who objected to their new condition of slavery since they claimed to have been free men in their home land. A suspicious remark by a slave was overheard and a Negro was reportedly seen escaping from one of the burning buildings.[28] Under the existing conditions of tension, this was enough to initiate a mass arrest of the slave population of the city. Before long, the jails were so overcrowded that the magistrates feared a plague. A slave, Quack, was soon found who ''confessed'' to firing Fort George, but the story extracted from him held that a hidden firebrand had remained lit in a loft for over twelve hours and suggested wanton laxity on the part of the guards. In short, the "confession" is quite incredible and only a people paralyzed with fear could have believed it. Other confessions trickled in slowly until Lieutenant-Governor Clarke, on June 19, issued a proclamation promising pardon and transportation to those who should confess within a specified time. This produced sixty-seven more slave confessions.

The best way to get an idea of the terror which must have gripped the city is to read in Horsmanden's *Journal* the chaotic testimonies of the slaves. Not even the most permissive manipulation can establish a pattern of conspiracy from them. Bewildered, terrified, living on the very threshold of execution, the Negroes were offered pardons only for "telling the truth," which meant, of course, confessing and implicating someone else. Confession contradicted confession. Lists given by different witnesses showed only random correlation. Denial after denial went unheeded. Yet little notice was taken of these contradictions. Whatever the magistrates wanted to believe was believed, and they had set their minds beforehand.

To try to piece together details of an operative conspiracy from these statements is impossible. Only in the most general terms do they correspond. Each slave was to burn his master's home, kill the nearest whites, and then take over the town. But this vague correlation arises not from a simple framework set up by Hughson to appeal to simple slaves, but from the fury of rumor which must have swept through the crowded cells. Anyone living in New York in the Spring of 1741 would have known this basic information. Vital questions of operation remain unanswered. Where was the plotting done? Surely Hughson couldn't have met personally with many slaves. How were the others introduced to the conspiracy? Who were the ringleaders? No satisfactory answers emerge from the recorded statements.[29] In addition, no attention was paid to the means of exacting the confessions. The fact that all the key witnesses except Mary Burton confessed only when faced with imminent death was not considered.[30] Two of the slaves, Quack and Cuffee, were bound at the stake with the faggots lit when their confessions were written down.

The testimony of two of the chief Negro witnesses, Sarah and Jack, is typical. Sarah, facing imminent death, listed many of her friends as being conspirators. But as soon as she left the courtroom, she retracted all she said. She did this more than once.[31] Jack was more cooperative. When told that he would be hanged on the morrow if he remained silent, Jack told the judges that, were he pardoned, he would tell everything. Twice he testified, each time accusing a score of slaves. As a reward, he was set free by Lieutenant-Governor Clarke.[32] Horsmanden calls Jack "a fellow of most remarkable craft and subtlety," as indeed he was.[33]

Less dramatic but equally important was the fact that no cognizance was taken of the bewilderment that doubtlessly beset the slaves facing a court trial for the first time. The magistrates felt they were tempering justice with mercy by trying all those involved before the same court.[34]

Before the trials were over, however, a fresh element had crept into the proceedings and this gave to the whole incident a new and vicious twist: New York's fear of Roman Catholicism. In May of 1741, Lieutenant-Governor George Oglethorpe of Georgia had written Clarke a warning that Spanish emissaries had been sent out to burn the English towns, and disguised Roman Catholic priests were being used for this purpose.[35] Clarke must have made this news known. On June 24, four months after the Hogg robbery and after sixty witnesses had testified concerning the slave revolt, the word "popery" first appears in Horsmanden's chronicle. Immediately suspicion switched from Hughson and the Negroes to fall upon a Latin teacher, John Ury, who suddenly was accused of masterminding the rebellion as a disguised priest. What had been Black Magic in Salem in 1692 became the Black Conspiracy in New York fifty years later.

Ury, a non-jurying clergyman, had been working peacefully in the city when he found himself implicated in the proceedings. It was rumored that he had criticized Mary Burton, and, one day, she named him as a chief conspirator in the plot. When it was pointed out that he could not always be understood when he talked religion, had refused to toast the King by name, and had built two wooden altars, his doom was sealed. The magistrates resurrected an old law of William III's time which provided severe penalties for being a priest in New York and they soon sentenced him to death.[36]

It is noteworthy that the part of the testimony implicating Ury as a leader in the Negro uprising is much more cogent and easy to follow than the conflicting and contradictory testimonies of the frightened slaves, whose accusations, of course, were not acceptable against Ury. In his case there was cold, reasoned perjury by three witnesses: Mary Burton, Sarah Hughson, the daughter of John, and a soldier, William Kane. Mary, still the chief witness, volunteered information freely but the origin of the confessions of the other two is significant. Sarah, after hours of questioning, was told by the magistrates that she would be hanged immediately if she remained silent any longer.[37] Only then did she confess. Kane, too, denied any knowledge of the conspiracy until threatened in a similar way. Then, Horsmanden records, "his countenance changed and being near fainting, desired to have a glass of water, which was brought him, and after some pause, he said he would tell the truth, though at the same time he seemed very loth to do it."[38] These three then wove their story: Ury often drank at Hughsons where one day he enticed the band of Negroes into a ceremony, allegedly a Mass. He told them that they would be absolved from guilt and sin when they began to pillage the city, and that soon the Spanish would arrive to help them.

The unfortunate John Ury found himself serving as the focal point for a long-standing anti-Catholic phobia. The prosecuting attorney—all seven lawyers in the city volunteered to help prosecute—began his presentation against Ury by the following: "before we enter upon their examination, give me leave to say a few words concerning the heinessness of the prisoner's offenses, and of the popish religion in general."[39] He then devoted most of his speech to a relation of the evils of Douay,

Rheims, and Smithfield. Quoting frequently from the *History of
Popery* by Jurieu, the horrors of d'Alva, Bloody Mary, and Guy
Fawkes were once again brought to life. Comparatively little
was said specifically about Ury. It was Catholicism in general
that was under attack. To Horsmanden, the finding of a Catholic
conspiracy in New York served as the ultimate revelation,
". . . for upon this [the presence of priests] and no other footing," he wrote, "can it [the plot] be accounted for."[40]

Ury handled his own defense before the court in a vain attempt to refute the circumstantial evidence brought against him,
but it was to no avail.[41] In the first week of September, the
Boston News Letter reported that he kneeled very calmly at the
gallows "and as in his prayer to God he denied the facts witnessed against him, so he prayed that it would please Almighty
God to cause some visible constraint upon the witnesses to
manifest to the world, that what they had witnessed against him
was false."[42]

Ury was the last to be executed. After his death, uneasiness
about the trial proceedings and the general character of the witnesses became markedly evident. Mary Burton, still the center of
attention, responded by lashing back at her new set of accusers.
To the amazement of the magistrates, she suddenly began accusing people "in ruffles," that is, of high social position, of being
involved in the conspiracy. These fresh accusations served the
same purpose in New York as had the accusation of Governor
Phips's wife in Salem. The trials ceased abruptly.[43] With the
decline of the hysteria, most of the slaves went back to their
former masters. Hughson's father and brothers and the Rommes
all escaped further punishment by promising to leave the colony
permanently. William Kane hastily enlisted for the West Indies.
And, after receiving her promised reward, Mary Burton also
disappears from the records.

Only a few people such as Horsmanden and Clarke felt that
the trial proceedings had been cut unnecessarily short. Both
regretted the new attempt to discredit the witnesses, for each
believed there was still much information which could yet be
disclosed. Horsmanden felt that the recent abuse heaped on

Mary Burton was done deliberately by those who feared losing their slaves.

Lieutenant-Governor Clarke may have had more personal reasons for keeping the issue of the trials alive. In virtually every letter to England, he pleaded that his personal losses from the fires be brought to the attention of the Duke of Newcastle. It would serve his advantage if the threat of conspiracy loomed ever larger in English eyes. His use of his position to gain special favors shows that this, perhaps, might not be entirely foreign to his character, although, of course, it remains pure conjecture.[44]

Unlike 1712, no mass of new regulatory legislation appeared in the lawbooks after 1741. Nor, after the initial fears had passed, is there evidence that the existing laws were harshly enforced. Instead, New York's enthusiasm seemed to turn to other problems: the revivals produced by George Whitefield's visit, the colonial wars with France, and the agitation which led to the break with Great Britain. Race relations in the colony remained quiescent until they were peacefully altered by the manumission laws of the Revolutionary period.

While a psychological study of New York's *année terrible* lies beyond the author's training and the materials available, nonetheless, certain factors are suggestive as to why the hysteria arose and took the form it did. Very important is the fact that the winter of 1740–1741 had been long, cold, and harsh. Snow drifts six feet deep in the city were not uncommon. Ice clogged the Hudson and with the roads impassable, wood and food supplies often ran low. The New York *Journal* reported that the bakers organized a strike to protest the high prices of grain. The effects of the weather would be felt by people of every class but, paradoxically, would also serve to accentuate the existing class cleavage. In January, John Peter Zenger, editor of the New York *Journal,* reported a collection made in the city wards to help the poor survive the winter, but by late February this money had been used up.[45] The William Johnson papers attest to the trials of "ye hard winter and bad crop," and William Smith in his *History of the late Province of New York* noted how the winter of 1740–41 had ever since been called "the hard winter."[46]

Also, hardly an issue of Zenger's newspaper during this period was without extended stories of war preparations, tales of privateering, or detailed accounts of the exploits of Admiral Vernon in Spanish America. Zenger warned New York of the dangers from the French. Governor Oglethorpe warned them of dangers from the Spanish. What the Iroquois were capable of doing when aroused could not have been far from the colonists' minds either, for Clarke continually urged the Assembly that more attention be paid to the Six Nations to keep their loyalty. In 1740 there were rumors that the Negroes had poisoned the water supply, and the horrors of 1712 were less than a generation away.[47] What the Hogg robbery and the mysterious fires did was to bring all these general fears into sharp focus. What had been a vague and unassailable enemy at last assumed tangible form. Hughson, Ury, and the Negroes could easily be dealt with, and in doing so all the various and larger pressures of the preceding months could be circumscribed and resolved in what can only be called a cathartic action. The trials neatly served this dramatic psychological function.

But if the conspiracy thesis is explained away, how can we account for the fires? Some, surely, were deliberate works of arson. While proof to fill a volume the size of Horsmanden's doesn't exist, yet the hypothesis suggested at the outset of this article can explain them, randomness and all: an organized conspiracy for robbery.[48] The Hughsons reluctantly admitted receiving the stolen goods of the slaves. So did Romme and his wife. Of this there is no question. Both denied, of course, that more than three Negroes ever met at their taverns at one time. Given the economic situation which existed that winter, one part of Mary Burton's testimony is most probable. She reported that "Cuffee used to say that a great many people had too much, and others too little; that his old master had a great deal of money but that in a short time he should have less and that he (Cuffee) should have more."[49]

Horsmanden's *Journal* describes in passing how the fires and robberies were connected. Whenever a blaze broke out, all the available able-bodied men would run to the area to help carry goods away from the burning building. In the process many items inevitably disappeared. Arthur Price, a key witness in the trial proceedings, was in jail on this very charge. Lieutenant-Governor Clarke in several of his letters to England noted that robbery made up a large part of the conspiracy.[50] Horsmanden, too, noted in many places in his *Journal* how "stealing and plundering was a principal part of the hellish scheme in agitation . . ."[51] Each of these men, of course, expanded his vision to a belief in an organized Negro-Catholic conspiracy. But if the spectre of conspiracy is removed, then robbery is all that remains. It is not hard to imagine one or two more discontented gatherings such as Hughson's and Romme's. They might have congregated around any of several of the city's lower-class taverns. That many of these existed is shown by the number of fines which were levied against tavern owners for selling liquor to slaves.[52] The existence of a number of groups would account for the delay between fires. Success one week might well spur on more concerted effort the next, perhaps even call a new group into existence. Also it is probable that not all of the fires were incendiary; probably not more than four out of ten. It is unfortunate that more precise evidence is not available, for given the situation as it occurred in 1741, there is truth in W. F. Prince's statement that the pent-up fury unleashed on Hughson, Ury, and the Negroes was the "crowning perversion of criminal justice in the annals of American history."[53]

Notes

1. See especially the essay by Clarence L. Ver Steeg in W. H. Cartwright and R. L. Watson, eds., *Interpreting and Teaching American History* (Washington, 1961), pp. 24–32.

2. The figures are from Herbert Aptheker, *A Documentary History of the Negro People in the United States* (New York, 1951), p. 23.

3.   Benjamin G. Brawley, *A Social History of the American Negro* (New York, 1921), p. 43.

4.   George W. Williams, *History of the Negro Race in America from 1619–1880* (2 vols., New York, 1883), I, 170.

5.   Roi Ottley, *Black Odyssey, the Story of the Negro in America* (New York, 1948), p. 29.

6.   This comparison was first noticed in a perceptive, unsigned letter to Cadwallader Colden. The writer had read about the executions in a Boston newspaper and wrote Colden that "this occasion puts me in mind of our New England Witchcraft in the year 1692 which if I don't mistake New York justly reproached us for, and mockt at our credulity about . . .

"What ground you proceed upon I must acknowledge myself not sufficiently informed of; but finding that these 5 who were put to Death in July denied any Guilt, It makes me suspect that your present case, and ours heretofore are much the same and that Negro and Spectre evidence will turn out alike. We had near 50 Confessors, who accused multitudes of others, all alledging Time and Place, and various other circumstances to render their Confessions credible, that they had their meetings, form'd confederacies, sign'd the Devils book, etc. But I am humbly of Opinion that such Confessions unless some certain Overt act appear to confirm the same are not worth a Straw; . . .

"And if nothing will put an end hereto till some of higher degree and better circumstances and characters are accused (which finished our Salem Witchcraft) the sooner the better, lest all the poor People of the Government perish in the merciless flames of an Imaginary Plot."

Colden had this letter circulated, but did so to *prevent* the prevailing of such an opinion.

The letters and papers of Cadwallader Colden, 1711–1764 (9 vols., New York, 1918–23; 1934–35, volumes L–LVI; LXVII–LXVIII of *The New York Historical Society Collections,* LXVII, 270.

7.   T. Wood Clarke, "The Negro Plot of 1741," *New York History,* XLII (April, 1944), pp. 167–181, while thorough, is purely narrative. The best analysis of the incident is Walter F. Prince, "New York 'Negro Plot' of 1741," published in the "Saturday Chronicle" of New Haven, Conn., June 28–August 23, 1902. A typewritten copy is at the New York Public Library. George W. Williams also devotes a complete chapter to analyzing the testimony. Most other works tend to slide over the whole affair. C. L. Ver Steeg in *The Formative Years 1607–1763* (New York, 1964), ignores the incident even though it might help support his general thesis that upheavals such as Bacon's Rebellion, Leisler's Rebellion, and The Salem Witch Trials were all part of a general transition from colony to province where the old lines of authority, aims, and precepts were dissolving without new ones having yet formed.

8. *The letters and papers of Cadwallader Colden* in the *New York Historical Society Collections*, LI, 255–57, 253; LXVII, 265–66, 270–73, 280–89.
E. B. O'Callaghan, ed., *Documents Relative to the Colonial History of the State of New York* (15 vols., Albany, 1855–87), VI, 186–87, 196–202, 213; VII, 528.

9. See the *Dictionary of American Biography* for a short sketch (IX, 237). The edition used for this study was Daniel Horsmanden, *The New-York Conspiracy or a History of the Negro Plot with the Journal of the Proceedings against The Conspirators at New-York in The Years 1741–42* (New York, 1810).

10. Horsmanden, *The New York Conspiracy*, p. 274n. Lieutenant-Governor George Clarke felt the same way. See O'Callaghan, *Documents Relative to the Colonial History of New York*, VI, 197.

11. Brawley, *Social History of The American Negro*, pp. 43–44; Ulrich B. Phillips, *American Negro Slavery* (New York, 1929), p. 469; Lorenzo J. Greene, *The Negro in Colonial New England 1620–1776* (New York, 1942), p. 160; Carter G. Woodson, *The Negro in Our History* (Washington, 1922), p. 93; Merl R. Eppse, *The Negro too in American History* (Chicago, 1938), p. 100; Francis S. Eastman, *A History of the State of New York* (New York, 1828), p. 133; Theodore Roosevelt, *New York* (New York, 1918), p. 100.

12. Aptheker, *Documentary History of the Negro People*, p. 4.

13. Joseph C. Carroll, *Slave Insurrections in the United States 1800–1865* (Boston, 1933), p. 30; Cleveland Rodgers and Rebecca B. Rankin, *New York: the World's Capital City* (New York, 1948), p. 51; E. Franklin Frazier, *The Negro in the United States* (revised ed., New York, 1957), p. 86; Maud W. Goodwin, *et al.*, *Historic New York* (2 vols., New York, 1899), I, 16; Prince, "New York Negro Plot," p. 8.

14. Ottley, *Black Odyssey*, p. 29.

15. Williams, *History of Negro in America*, p. 170.

16. Greene, *Negro in Colonial New England*, p. 324; Edwin Olson, "The Slave Code in Colonial New York," *Journal of Negro History*, XXIX (April, 1944), p. 147.

17. See *The Colonial Laws of New York from the Year 1668 to the Revolution* (5 vols., Albany, 1894), I, 520ff., 582, 761ff.

18. O'Callaghan, *Documents Relative to the Colonial History of New York*, V, 341; Olson, "Slave Code," p. 149; Ottley, *Black Odyssey*, p. 18ff., *Colonial Laws*, I, 631, 763, 680.

19.   For treatment of these issues see Samuel McKee, *Labor in Colonial New York 1664–1776* (New York, 1935), *passim;* Edwin Olson, "Social Aspects of Slave Life in New York," *Journal of Negro History,* XXVI (January, 1941), pp. 66–77; Edwin Olson, "The Slave Code in Colonial New York," *Journal of Negro History,* XXIX (April, 1944), pp. 147–165; W. R. Riddell, "The Slave in early New York," *Journal of Negro History,* XIII (January, 1928), pp. 53–86; A. J. Northrup, "Slavery in New York," *State Library Bulletin* (May, 1900), pp. 243–310; William Smith, *History of the Late Province of New York* (2 vols., New York, 1829), II, 62.

20.   Horsmanden, *The New York Conspiracy,* p. 38.

21.   Prince, "New York Negro Plot," p. 15.

22.   Julius Goebel, Jr., and T. Raymond Naughton, *Law Enforcement in Colonial New York* (New York, 1944), p. 121.

23.   Horsmanden, *The New York Conspiracy,* p. 60.

24.   *Ibid.,* p. 143.

25.   *Ibid.,* p. 141.

26.   *Ibid.,* p. 144.

27.   *Ibid.,* p. 59, 71.

28.   The statement, harmless enough by itself, was "fire, fire, scorch, scorch, a little, damnit, by and by." It took little agitation for the townspeople to demand that the Spanish Negroes be put in jail immediately. Horsmanden notes that the cry of "A negro, a negro" (the one seen leaping from a burning building) "was soon improved into an alarm that the negroes were rising." Horsmanden, *The New York Conspiracy,* p. 29.

29.   Consider this confession: "[Cambridge] did on the ninth day of June last, confess to the deponent in the presence of the said Mr. Codwise and Richard Baker, that the confession he had made before Messrs. Lodge and Nicholls, was entirely false, *viz.* that he had owned himself guilty of the conspiracy, and had accused the negro of Richard Baker, called Cajoe, through fear; and said, that he had heard some negroes talking together in one jail, that if they did not confess, they should be hanged; and that was the reason of his making that false confession; and that what he said relating to Horsefield's Caesar was a lie; that he did not know in what part of town Hughson did live, nor did not remember to have heard of the man until it was a common talk over the town and country, that Hughson was concerned in a plot with the negroes." Horsmanden, *The New York Conspiracy,* p. 250.

30.   Sarah Hughson, Peggy, William Kane, Jack.

31. Horsmanden, *The New York Conspiracy,* p. 106, 121.

32. *Ibid.,* p. 127.

33. *Ibid.,* p. 369.

34. *Ibid.,* p. 97.

35. O'Callaghan, *Documents Relative to the Colonial History of New York,* VI, 198.

36. The law, passed in July, 1700, provided for perpetual imprisonment for any priest caught in the colony. Only if he escaped and was recaptured could the death penalty be invoked. Ury, however, was found guilty on two counts: conspiracy and that of being a priest. Smith, *History of New York,* II, 60; *Colonial Laws,* I, 428.

37. Horsmanden, *The New York Conspiracy,* p. 247.

38. *Ibid.,* p. 239.

39. *Ibid.,* p. 290.

40. *Ibid.,* p. 32; see also *The letters and papers of Cadwallader Colden* in the *New York Historical Society Collections,* LI, 222.

41. Here is an excerpt. Ury: "You say have seen me several times at Hughson's, what clothes did I usually wear?" Mary: "I cannot tell what clothes you wore particularly." Ury: "That is strange, and know me so well." Horsmanden, *The New York Conspiracy,* p. 292.

42. *Boston News Letter,* September 3– 10, 1741.

43. Horsmanden, *The New York Conspiracy,* p. 371.

44. O'Callaghan, *Documents Relative to the Colonial History of New York,* VI, 202, 203, 196, 198; see Edith M. Fox, *Land Speculation in Mohawk Country* (Ithaca, 1949), p. x.

45. See *The New York Weekly Journal,* January-February 1740/41, *passim.*

46. James Sullivan, ed., *The Papers of Sir William Johnson* (13 vols., Albany, 1921), I, 9; Horsmanden, *The New York Conspiracy,* p. 62; Smith, *History of New York,* p. 57.

47. Herbert Aptheker, *The Colonial Era* (New York, 1959), p. 44.

48. William Smith noted too that "The conspiracy extended no farther than to create alarms for committing thefts with more ease." See O'Callaghan, *Documents Relative to the Colonial History of New York*, VII, 528*n*.

49. Horsmanden, *The New York Conspiracy*, p. 29.

50. O'Callaghan, *Documents Relative to the Colonial History of New York*, VI, 196–202.

51. Horsmanden, *The New York Conspiracy*, p. 60, 27.

52. *Ibid.*, p. 280. Ten owners were convicted.

53. Prince, "New York Negro Plot," p. 3.

Governor Berkeley and King Philip's War

*Wilcomb E. Washburn**

White encroachments, land hunger, and destruction of Indian culture led Native Americans to retaliate. Often expressions of Indian discontent took the form of warfare. The result was a vast increase in white fears. In 1675 and 1676, for example, when King Philip's War broke out in New England, whites in Virginia, faced with enmity from the Susquehannocks, worried that a general Indian uprising would be forthcoming. As Wilcomb E. Washburn indicates in "Governor Berkeley and King Philip's War," "reports of New England's Indian war stimulated their fears just as reports of Virginia's Indian war frightened the New Englanders." Washburn is director of the American Studies Program at the Smithsonian Institution and has written widely on red-white relations in the United States. Among his many publications are American Indian and White Relations to 1830: Needs and Opportunities for Study *(co-author),* The Indian in America, The Governor and the Rebel: A History of Bacon's Rebellion in Virginia, The Indian and the White Man, *and* Red Man's Land, White Man's Law. *He also has published articles in professional journals including the* American Historical Review, Quarterly Journal of Speech, *and* Pacific Historical Review.

*Wilcomb E. Washburn, "Governor Berkeley and King Philip's War," *New England Quarterly* 30 (1957), 363–77. Reprinted by permission.

VIRGINIA AND MASSACHUSETTS had little official contact with each other in the seventeenth century.[1] However, a good deal of trade between the two colonies was carried on, consisting mostly in the exchange of Virginia corn and tobacco for New England fish and other commodities.[2] The trade was often "triangular" via the West Indies.

Despite the lack of official contact, the leaders of each colony followed developments in the other with great interest and no little partiality. Governor Winthrop noted in his journal for May 20, 1644, that a ship from Virginia had brought news of the great massacre there in which perhaps 500 English were killed. It was reported that an Indian confessed "that they did it because they saw the English took up all their lands from them, and would drive them out of the country. . . ." Winthrop commented soberly that

> It was very observable that this massacre came upon them soon after they had driven out the godly ministers we had sent to them, and had made an order that all such as would not conform to the discipline of the church of England should depart the country by a certain day, which the massacre now prevented: . . .[3]

The massacre, Winthrop noted also, had begun only one day before the fast day appointed by the Council and Governor Berkeley—"a courtier, and very malignant towards the way of our churches here"—for the good success of the King, then having his troubles in England.[4] As a result of the massacre, many "godly disposed persons" (among them Daniel Gookin, of Newport News) came to New England, "and many of the rest were forced to give glory to God in acknowledging, that this evil was sent upon them from God for their reviling the gospel and those faithful ministers he had sent among them."[5]

Edward Johnson, in his *Wonder-working Providence of Sion's Saviour in New England* (1653), similarly saw "the hand of God against this people, after the rejection of these Ministers of Christ." Wrote Johnson:

> now attend to the following story, all you Cavaliers and malignant party the world throughout, take notice of the wonderwork-

ing providence of Christ toward his Churches, and punishing hand of his toward the contemners of his Gospel. Behold ye dispisers, and wonder. Oh poor Virginia, dost thou send away the Ministers of Christ with threatning speeches? No sooner is this done, but the barbarous, inhumane, insolent, and bloody Indians are let loose upon them, who contrive the cutting them off by whole Families, ... This cruell and bloody work of theirs put period to the lives of five or six hundred of these people, who had not long before a plentifull proffer of the mercies of Christ in the glad tidings of peace published by the mouth of his Ministers, who came unto them for that end: but chusing rather the fellowship of their drunken companions,[6] and a Preist of their own profession, who could hardly continue so long sober as till he could read them the reliques of mans invention in a common prayer book; but assuredly had not the Lord pittied the little number of his people among this crooked generation, they had been consumed at once, for this is further remarkable in this massacre, when it came toward the place where Christ had placed his little flock,[7] it was discovered and prevented from further proceeding, ... assuredly the Lord hath more scourges in store, for such as force the people to such sufferings; . . . .[8]

Winthrop recorded in his journal on September 7, 1644, that a pinnace arrived from Virginia "with letters from the governor and council there, for procuring powder and shot to prosecute their war against the Indians, but we were weakly provided ourselves, and so could not afford them any help in that kind."[9] Soon, however, the governor began to have doubts that his decision had been in conformity with the will of God when, in the first week of April 1645, seventeen barrels of the country's powder and many arms, to the value of nearly £500, were "suddenly burnt and blown up" in the house of John Johnson, the surveyor general of the ammunition, at Roxbury. Winthrop thought the occurrence "observable" in two respects: "1. Because the court had not taken that care they ought to pay for it," and "2. In that, at the court before, they had refused to help our countrymen in Virginia, who had written to us for some for their defence against the Indians, and also to help our brethren of Plymouth in their want."[10]

When King Philip's War broke out in the summer of 1675 the Virginians were at last given an opportunity to find evidence of God's displeasure towards the Puritans. But before they could enjoy New England's discomfiture they were faced with a war of their own. By a series of blunders, Virginia, in the fall of 1675, fell into a war with the Susquehannock Indians of Maryland.[11] Operations commenced with a siege of the Susquehannock fort in Maryland. The Indians, outraged by the murder of five of their chiefs under a flag of truce, broke out of their fort, crossed the Potomac, and murdered about forty persons in outlying Virginia plantations in January 1676. The marauders immediately retired into the forests to the west of the settlements, and Virginia began to fear that its troubles with the Susquehannocks would turn into a general war with all Virginia's Indians.

In a letter of February 16, 1676, probably to Thomas Ludwell, Secretary of the Council of State of Virginia who was then in England as one of Virginia's agents, Berkeley expressed his apprehension and concern. Wrote the governor:

The infection of the Indianes in New-England has dilated it selfe to the Merilanders and the Northern parts of Virginia, and wee have lost about Forty men Women and Children in Patomocke and Rapahannocke kild as wee suppose by the sesquashannocks . . . our neighbour Indians are pretty well secured for it is no doubt but they alsoe would be rid of us if they Could but I thanke god they have not dard to shew themselves our Enemies yet. . . . Now Mr. Secretary you will thinke this Relation strange which I shall next give you. The Indians in New England have burned divers Considerable Villages (which they call townes) and have made them desert more then one hundred and fifty miles of those places they had formerly seated and a very understanding and sober Virginia Merchant that came lately hence does assure me that in most of their encounters where the numbers have beene very Equall the Indians have alwaise had the better of it. I beleeve it would not have beene soe if they had had two hundred of our Virginians with them. We now expect howerly to heare from them who have beseegd fower thousand Indians in a fort fowerscore miles to the South of boston which the New England men once enterd but were beaten out of it againe before they could distroy their smiths shopps of which they say they have seene many there. The new England men are in a deplorable want of Corne and if this warr continue two yeares longer many of them must be forc'd to desert the place which divers already had done But that they have made several lawes to the contrary. . . .[12]

Berkeley was evidently referring to the Great Swamp Fight of December 19, 1675. Contemporary accounts of the fight note that the Narragansett fort, near the present town of South Kingston, Rhode Island, was built under the direction of "Stone-wall John," an Indian engineer and blacksmith, and that his forge was demolished before the English retired from the fort coincidental with the arrival of Indian reënforcements.[13]

How might news of the Great Swamp Fight have arrived in Virginia? Berkeley attributes the information to a "sober Virginia merchant." The merchant might have come from any of the New England colonies, but he may very probably have come from Rhode Island where 150 of the English wounded were sent following the fight.[14] Governor Berkeley's view of the war, too, tended to have a Rhode Island flavor.[15]

By the time of the meeting of the Virginia Assembly on March 7, 1676, nerves were at the breaking point in that colony, both from fear of local Indians and because of the reports from New England. The Assembly passed an act declaring war against "all such Indians who are notoriously knowne or shalbe discovered to have comitted the murthers, rapins and depredations" that had occurred in the colony, as well as against any other Indians who could be suspected of aiding them. Forts were ordered to be established on the frontier, and 500 men (a quarter of them horsemen) were provided to garrison them. Trade with the Indians was severely limited and strictly regulated.[16]

Virginia's problem was to discover who were the colony's enemies. The Susquehannocks seemed most obviously to be arrayed against the Virginians, but what of the many strange tribes far beyond the English settlements, and what of the approximately twenty tributary tribes living side by side with the English? Were these various Indians friends or foes? The for-

eign tribes were the subject of wild rumors while the local tribes
were the object of cold suspicion among the fearful English.
This attitude is brought out in the address to the King from the
Governor and Assembly, March 24, 1676. The address discusses the mismanaged attack on the Susquehannocks, the subsequent murders in Virginia, and the meeting of the March
Assembly

> where all the Representatives of the Country are now mett to
> consult of the fittest and safest way to put the Country in Secu-
> rity for the future and to take a just revenge on those bloodie
> Villains, which we should not have doubted (by Gods assis-
> tance) in a short time to effect, had their appeared none other
> danger but from those Indians within our reach.
>
> But May it please your Sacred Majesty, to our griefe we finde
> by certain intelligence, within these few dayes, that those Indi-
> ans have been and still are endeavouring (with offering Vast
> Summes of their wealth) to hyre other Nations of Indians two or
> three hundred miles distant from us, and that a very considerable
> bodie of them are come downe upon James River, within fifty or
> Sixty miles of the plantations, where they lye hovering over us.
>
> And not being able to ghuesse where the Storme will fall, for
> that all Indians as well our neer neighbours as those more re-
> mote, gieving us dayly Suspitions that it is not any private
> grudge, but a generall Combination, of all from New-England
> hither, which we are the rather inclined to beleive, Since the
> defection their and here, though at least three hundred miles
> distant, one from the other happened neer the same time; and we
> much feare that those Indians of New-England haveing been
> unfortunately Succesfull their,[17] where yet by our latest intelli-
> gence we finde affaires to have an ill aspect; is and will be a
> great incouragement to ours here; which puts us on an absolute
> necessity, not only of Fortifieing all our frontiers more strongly;
> but of keeping Severall, considerable parties both of Horsse and
> foot still in motion to confront them wheresoever they shall
> attaque us. Which cannot be done without a Vast expence.[18]

Today we find it curious that the fears of Virginians should
have been so great as to suspect a gigantic combination of
Indians from New England to Virginia. The fear is explicable
not only in terms of the relative weakness of the English at the
time, but also in terms of the colonists' ignorance of what lay

beyond their tiny fingers of settlement, and of what relations Indian tribes had with one another. There were, in 1670, only forty thousand colonists scattered over the entire eastern half of the present state of Virginia.[19] Because the English clung closely to the rich and accessible lands along the tidewater rivers, it was not difficult for Indian marauders to slip undetected into the heart of the country. Uncertainty concerning the intentions of the neighboring "friend" Indians and dread of the possible hostility of the Iroquois and other "foreign" Indians, who yearly traveled along the "backside" of the colony on their way to trade and war with the Indians of the Carolinas, encouraged the English to suspect a far-flung plot against them. Reports of New England's Indian war stimulated their fears just as reports of Virginia's Indian war frightened the New Englanders. One example from New England will suffice to show that the fears were mutual. When a vessel from Virginia arrived in Rhode Island on August 12, 1676, with "newes of great destruction done there by the Indeans," William Harris concluded that it "shewes that the contrivance of a war against the English went far. . . ." Only God's Providence, the Rhode Islander suggested, prevented more Indian nations from joining "the plot."[20]

On April 1 Berkeley sent Thomas Ludwell a more detailed account of what Virginians had heard about King Philip's exploits in New England. Berkeley wrote that

> a new tax is layde uppon us for the Indians are Generally combind against us in al the northerne parts of America. They have destroyed divers Townes in New-England kild more then a thousand fighting men seldome were worsted in any encounter and have made the New-England men desert above a hundred miles of ground of that land which they had divers yeares seated and built Townes on. I have not heard from thence this fortnight but expect to heare no very good newes when I doe for they either have not or pretend not to have mony to pay their soldiers But what ever the successe be they wil not this next twenty yeares recover what they have lost and expended in this warr. They had taken in their last harvest before the Indians envaded them and declared the warr against them yet now they are in such Want of

provisions that they have sent to us aboundance of vessels to buy
of us great quantities of al sort as Porke beefe and Corne in so
much that I and the Councel first and since the General Assembly have beene forcd to promulgate a severe law that no more
provisions shal be exported from hence and I thinke al considering men conclude that one yeares want of provision does impov-
erish Kingdomes and states (of al natures) more then seaven
yeares Luxury but this is not halfe the New England mens mis-
ery for they have lost al their Beaver trade Halfe at least of their
fishing and have nothing to carry to the Barbadoes with whose
commodities they were wont to carry away our Tobbacco and
other provisions. Add to this the new tax of one penny per
pound on Tobbacco which my Officers rigorously exact of them:
to conclude this if this warr lasts one Yeare longer they in new
England will be the poorest miserablest People of al the Plantations of the English in America. Indeed it [sic] I should Pitty
them had they deservd it of the King or his Blessed father.[21]

The Governor and Council of Virginia, as Berkeley relates,
placed an embargo on the export of provisions on October 12,
1675.[22] Five months later, the March 1676 Assembly enacted
the embargo into law, a law repeated by the next assembly, in
June, with the proviso that it was to remain in effect until the
last day of the following assembly.[23]

Detailed records of ship sailings between New England and
Virginia are not available, but it seems probable that trade declined appreciably during the troubles of 1675–1676. "N.S."
(probably Nathaniel Saltonstall) wrote from the port of Boston
on February 8, 1676:

Our Trade to Virginia is quite decayed, not one Vessel having
gone from here thither since the Wars began, but by a small
Vessel arrived here from thence, we are informed that the Indians have fallen unexpected on the English, and destroyed many
of them, and done much harm with very little Loss to themselves, but this Report finds very little Credit with us; . . . .[24]

A significant aspect of New England-Virginia trade relations
in this period concerns the conviction for smuggling of Thomas
Hansford of Virginia, owner of the ketch *Hopewell,* and later
one of Nathaniel Bacon's leading lieutenants in the rebellion

against Governor Berkeley. Giles Bland, His Majesty's Collector of Customs in Virginia and another of Bacon's later lieutenants, complained to the General Court on March 21, 1676, that on or about June 21, 1675, there was transported out of Virginia to New England in the ketch *Hopewell* thirty-five hogsheads of tobacco for which customs duties were not paid. Hansford, the owner of the vessel, admitted the fraud in court, and acknowledged that he himself had sailed in the ship to New England. Hansford, so "keenly sensitive to honor" as the historian Bancroft was later to describe him,[25] was thereupon ordered by the court to pay the penny per pound duty for the tobacco he had illegally transported to New England and to pay the costs of the suit.[26] Perhaps Hansford was one of those who informed Berkeley of the New England troubles. It is also possible that he encouraged Bacon and his fellow conspirators to think of the New England and Virginia Indian troubles as part of a single plot against the English in America.

In addition to his letter to Thomas Ludwell, Governor Berkeley wrote two more letters on April 1, 1676: one to each of the Principal Secretaries of State of Charles II. In these he became philosophical about the war in New England, much as Governor Winthrop had about the 1644 massacre in Virginia. To Secretary Henry Coventry he wrote that

> The New-England men are ingaged in a warr with their Indians which in al reasonable conjectures wil end in their utter ruine and let al men feare and tremble at the justice of God on the Kings and his most Blessed fathers Ennimies and learne from them that God can make or find every where Instruments enoughe to destroy the Kings Ennimies. I say this because the New England men might as soon and as well have expected to have been envaded by the Persian or Mogul as from their Indians and yet what cannot God doe when he is provoked by Rebellion and undoubtedly the New England men were as guilty of the late Blessed Kings murther by their Councels Emissaries and wishes as any that most apparently acted in it.[27]

Berkeley's conception of New England's "guilt" can be explained in part by reference to the first act of the October 1649

Virginia Assembly, held following receipt of the news of the
beheading of Charles I on January 30, 1649. The Assembly,
under Berkeley's leadership, denounced the trial and conviction
of the "late most excellent and now undoubtedly sainted king"
and enacted that

> what person soever, . . . after the date of this act, by reasoning,
> discourse or argument shall go about to defend or maintain the
> late traiterous proceedings against the aforesaid King of most
> happy memory, under any notion of law and justice, such per-
> son . . . shall be adjudged an accessory *post factum,* to the death
> of the aforesaid King, and shall be proceeded against for the
> same, according to the knowne lawes of England: . . . .

The act also provided that to doubt the right of succession of
Charles II "in words and speeches shall be adjudged high
treason: . . . ."[28] No doubt New England's "reasoning, dis-
course and argument" commending the resistance to Charles I,
to say nothing of her toleration of regicides, stamped the colony, in Berkeley's eyes, as traitorous.

In his letter to Secretary Sir Joseph Williamson of April 1,
1676, Berkeley wrote that

> I hope it wil not be impertinent to give you the relation of our
> Neigbours as wel as of our selves and the more because their
> Troubles were the cause and beginning of ours: and first I wil
> say, that al Inglish planters on the Maine covet more Land then
> they are safely able to hold from those they have disposesd of it.
> This was the cause of the New-England troubles for the Indians
> complayning that strangers had left them no land to support and
> preserve their wives and children from famine the Very Gover-
> nors told them that those that could not live by them would doe
> well to depart farther from them. The Indians that had beene
> schoold by them askt them if this uncharitable expulsion of them
> (who admitted them frendly when they might easily have ex-
> cluded them from seating on their ground) were according to the
> Charitable doctrines they had learned from their God to which
> they replyed that God had given [the] land to them and they
> would hold it adding farther that the Indians were to weake and
> Ignerant to contend with them. This Answere so exasperated the
> Indians that they immediately resolvd to revenge or dye. The
> nearest to the Inglish communicated their sufferings to those

farther of and told them if they did not Joyne to resist the common Ennimie the next complaynt would be theirs for the Inglish sayd they bounded their oppressions with no other measure then their inability of not being able to doe more but as soone as their strength and numbers encreased the more remoter parts should find how farr their Avarice extended to those that hindred the effects of it. These and other considerations so much enraged the Indians that presently their were Leauges made with those that were formerly Ennimies and on a sodune they assault the Inglish in their Townes and farmes kil many men women and children and an incredible number of horses and cattle and on my faith Sir I cannot learne that since in the numerous encounters they have had the Inglish have seldome had the better of them but have often lost whole parties (to a man or two) that have beene sent out against them.[29] What ever the event be (for I have not heard from them this five weekes at least) The New-England men wil not recover their wealth and Townes they lost thes twenty comming yeares.

And now Sir because I sayde the beginning of the New-England troubles were the cause of ours I must proceed to say that when the New England Indians resolved to attaque the New-England men they sent Emmissaries as farr as our parts to enduce our Indians to doe the like and it is almost incredible what intelligence distant Indians hold with one the other. Most certain it is that a Nation called the Sesquasahannocks murdered some people in Maryland and in our parts Joyning to Maryland but we quickly destroyed most of those that were got into a fort But since that in one night some of the same nation murthered six and thirty weomen and children in one of our frontier plantations and then fled towards the mountains from whence we have heard no more then this from them that they live only on Acornes that they have Robd other lesser nations of the Indians of and so made them their Ennimies and we have now such a strength on the frontiers of al our Plantations that we Cannot feare them if they were ten times more in Number then they are. But most honord Sir as I sayde at first al English Planters hold more land then they are able to defend this we al complayne of but no power of ours can redresse because they have this priviledge by his Majesties Grant. . . .[30]

Berkeley's suggestion that English greed for land was the specific cause of King Philip's War seems to have been based on misinformation. Plymouth Colony, in whose territory the

Wampanoags still lived in 1675, had expressly forbidden Philip
to sell more of his land.[31] Governor Winslow asserted in a letter
of May 1, 1676, defending Plymouth against such charges as Governor Berkeley's, that Plymouth Colony had not only obtained all
its land by fair purchase of the Indian proprietors, but had made a
law that no one should purchase, or receive as a gift, any lands of
the Indians without the knowledge and allowance of the court.[32]

Berkeley's view of the cause of the war, however, tends to be
in harmony with that of the Deputy Governor of Rhode Island,
John Easton, whose "Relacion of the Indyan Warre" in 1675
was sympathetic to the Indian fear that "thay had no hopes left
to kepe ani land."[33] It is also not basically different from the
views of John Eliot writing on July 24, 1675, to Governor John
Winthrop, Jr., of Connecticut.[34] Roger Williams, writing of the
attitude of Massachusetts following the Pequot conquest, spoke
of the "depraved appetite" of the English for "great portions
of land, land in the wilderness. . . ." "This is one of the gods
of New England," wrote Williams, "which the living and
most high Eternal will destroy and famish."[35] Although the
view that land hunger was the cause of war is not specifically
accurate in the particular case of King Philip's War, in its
general assumption of an underlying conflict over land it must
be given consideration.[36]

The similarity between Governor Berkeley's impression of
King Philip's War and Governor Winthrop's impression of the
Virginia Indian War of 1644 is striking. Both saw the hand of
God applied to chasten the pride of man. In Winthrop's eyes,
however, the pride was in the willful refusal of Virginia's royal
governor to allow the Church of England to be purified as it had
been in New England. In Berkeley's eyes, the pride was in New
England's perverse denial of the principle of royal authority.
Berkeley was not only an upholder of the right of the Stuarts to
sit undisturbed on the throne of England, however; he was also
a champion of the right of the American Indians to hold undisturbed the land they occupied. It is not too much to say that
Winthrop might have learned a few lessons in piety from the
cavalier governor.

Notes

1.   This assertion can be verified by examination of the public records of the two colonies. To give a significant example: in Vol. 2 of the Massachusetts Archives in the State House at Boston, a volume which deals with inter-colonial relations, 1638–1720, there is only one document relating to Virginia.

2.   For trade in the 1630's see, for example, John Winthrop's *Journal,* ed. James Kendall Hosmer, Original Narratives of Early American History series (New York, 1908), entries for April 27, 1631, March 14, 1633, April 16, 1633, June 1, 1634, August 29, 1634, and August 3, 1636; see also John Winthrop, Jr. to his father, April 30, 1631, in Massachusetts Historical Society, *Collections,* 5th ser., VIII (Boston, 1882), 31; for trade in the 1670's see, for example, proceedings of a court of June 17, 1675, in *Records of the Court of Assistants of the Colony of the Massachusetts Bay: 1630–1692* I (Boston, 1901), 40; proceedings of a court of November 30, 1675, in *Records and Files of the Quarterly Courts of Essex County, Massachusetts,* VI (Salem, 1917), 87–88; William Harris's "Account of New England, April 29, 1675," in the *Harris Papers,* Rhode Island Historical Society, *Collections,* X (Providence, 1902), 142–147; for trade in other periods see, for example, William Aspinwall, *A Volume relating to the Early History of Boston containing the Aspinwall Notarial Records from 1644 to 1651* (Boston, 1903), Howard W. Preston, ed., *The Letter Book of Peleg Sanford of Newport Merchant (later Governour of Rhode Island), 1666–1668* (Providence, 1928), Howard W. Preston, *Rhode Island and The Sea* (Providence, 1932).

3.   Winthrop, *Journal,* II, 167–168. In 1642 letters had arrived from Virginia requesting ministers be sent there from New England. The elders of Boston met the request (Winthrop, *Journal,* II, 73). The ministers were later ordered expelled from Virginia by an act of March, 1643 (William Waller Hening, *The Statutes at Large; being a Collection of all the Laws of Virginia,* I [New York, 1823], 277).

4.   There seems to be no record of such a fast day in the existing records of Virginia although it might well have been proclaimed.

5.   Winthrop, *Journal,* II, 168.

6.   Virginians—or at least the Anglican clergy in Virginia—were not noted for sobriety in seventeenth-century New England. Winthrop, writing in 1640 of the New Englander Nathaniel Eaton who had gone to Virginia and become a minister, noted that he was "given up of God to extreme pride and sensuality, being usually drunken, as the custom is there" (Entry of December, 1640, *Journal,* II, 20–21).

7.   Mostly in Upper Norfolk or Nansemond County.

8. Edward Johnson, *The Wonder-working Providence of Sion's Saviour in New England,* ed. J. Franklin Jameson, Original Narratives of Early American History series (New York, 1910), Bk. III, ch. xi, 265–267.

9. Winthrop, *Journal,* II, 194.

10. Winthrop, *Journal,* II, 220–221.

11. See my 1955 Harvard Ph.D. dissertation on "Bacon's Rebellion, 1676–1677" for a discussion of these blunders. The University of North Carolina Press will, this winter, publish a revised version of the thesis.

12. Contemporary copy of letter from Governor Sir William Berkeley to [Secretary Thomas Ludwell?], February 16, [1676], library of the Marquis of Bath at Longleat, Wilts, England, the Henry Coventry Papers, Vol. LXXVII, folio 56 (hereafter cited as Longleat, LXXVII, fol. 56, etc.). I am at present editing the papers in this collection which bear on the subject of Bacon's Rebellion for publication by the Virginia Historical Society. Microfilm copies of the documents were made by the British Manuscripts Project of the American Council of Learned Societies and are available in the Library of Congress.

13. "A Continuation of the State of New-England, by N. S., 1676," in Charles H. Lincoln, ed., *Narratives of the Indian Wars, 1675–1699,* Original Narratives of Early American History series (New York, 1913, reprinted 1952), 58–59.

14. "A New and Further Narrative of the State of New-England, by N. S., 1676," in Lincoln, *Narratives,* 79. Berkeley's account agrees in several particulars with *News from New-England,* . . . *as it was sent over by a Factor of New-England to a Merchant in London* (London, 1676, reprinted Boston, 1850). Although this account was later than Berkeley's, it may have been based on the same source, for it gives 4,000 as the number of enemy Indians, exactly the figure reported by Berkeley, and describes the Great Swamp Fight in similar terms, even to the temporary expulsion of the English from the fort, a happening denied by some.

15. See later, pp. 374–375.

16. Hening, *Statutes,* II (New York, 1823), 258–260.

17. This was correct. Although the Narragansetts had been defeated at the Great Swamp Fight on December 19, 1675, Philip and the Nipmucks were on the rampage in central Massachusetts, burning settlements and killing the inhabitants, and two days after Berkeley wrote, Capt. Michael Pierce's force was wiped out on the Seekonk plain. For Pierce see George Madison Bodge, *Soldiers in King Philip's War* (Leominster, Mass., 1896), 347–350.

18. Address to the King from the Assembly, signed by Governor Berkeley and Speaker Augustine Warner, March 24, 1676, Longleat, LXXVII, foll. 66–67.

19. Berkeley's answer to the Lords of Trade and Plantations' "Enquiries," in Hening, *Statutes*, II, 515.

20. William Harris to Sir Joseph Williamson, August 12, 1676, in the *Harris Papers*, Rhode Island Historical Society, *Collections*, X (Providence, 1902), 174. Another writer believed that Philip had created a "Confederacy [of] all the *Indians* from Cape *Sables* [Nova Scotia] to the *Mohawks*, which is about three hundred Miles or upwards." See "A further brief and true Narration of the late Wars risen in *New-England* . . . Boston, December 28, 1675," in Samuel G. Drake, ed., *The Old Indian Chronicle* (Boston, 1867), 316. In 1653 New England was in similar fear of a vast Indian conspiracy. The Commissioners of the United Colonies of New England, on April 19, 1653, considered an alleged Dutch plot "to engage the Indians to cutt of the English within the united Collonies and wee heare the Designe reaches alsoe to the English in Verginnia. . . ." See David Pulsifer, ed., *Records of the Colony of New Plymouth in New England: Acts of the Commissioners of the United Colonies of New England*, Vol. II: *1653–1679* (Boston, 1859), 22.

21. Public Record Office, London, Colonial Office, Series I, Vol. 36, no. 37 (hereafter written C. O. 1/36, no. 37, etc.). This letter, with several significant errors of transcription, has been printed in the *Virginia Magazine of History and Biography*, XX (1912), 246–249.

22. H. R. McIlwaine, ed., *Minutes of the Council and General Court of Colonial Virginia, 1622–1623, 1670–1676* (Richmond, 1924), 428.

23. Hening, *Statutes*, II, 338–339, 361.

24. "A Continuation of the State of New-England, by N. S., 1676," in Lincoln, *Narratives*, 68. See also McIlwaine, *Minutes of the Council*, 434–435.

25. George Bancroft, *History of the Colonization of the United States*, II (Boston, 1868), 229.

26. McIlwaine, *Minutes of the Council*, 449.

27. Longleat, LXXVII, fol. 68.

28. Hening, *Statutes*, I, 359–361.

29. A week before Berkeley wrote, Captain Michael Pierce, with sixty-three English and twenty friendly Indians, lost almost his entire force in a fight at Seekonk plain. See "A New and Further Narrative of the State of New-

England, by N. S., 1676," in Lincoln, *Narratives,* 84–85, and Bodge, *Soldiers in King Philip's War,* 347–350.

30.   C. O. 1/36, no. 36. This letter, with several very serious errors of transcription, has been printed in the *Virginia Magazine of History and Biography,* XX (1912), 243–246.

31.   Agreement of Philip and his Council, September 29, 1671, in Nathaniel B. Shurtleff, ed., *Records of the Colony of New Plymouth in New England: Court Orders,* Vol. V: *1668–1678* (Boston, 1856), 79; see also court order of July 7, 1674, committing Thomas Joy of Hingham to jail for breaking the law against purchasing or receiving as a gift any Indian lands without the permission of the court, *ibid.,* p. 151; for the laws to this effect see David Pulsifer, ed., *Records of the Colony of New Plymouth in New England: Laws, 1623–1682* (Boston, 1861), 41, 129, 183, 185.

32.   Quoted in Drake, *Old Indian Chronicle,* 4–5. See also Josiah Winslow and Thomas Hinckley, "A Brief Narrative of the begining and progresse of the present trouble between us and the Indians," in Pulsifer, *Records of the Colony of New Plymouth: Acts of the Commissioners of the United Colonies,* II, 362–364.

33.   Lincoln, *Narratives,* 11. William Harris of Rhode Island, in his letter of August 12, 1676, to Secretary Sir Joseph Williamson, discussed the accusation that the English caused King Philip's War by their desire for the Indians' lands, but rejected it as false *(Harris Papers,* Rhode Island Historical Society, *Collections,* x, 165).

34.   Eliot professes ignorance of the causes of the war in this letter, but speaks frequently of doing the Indians "justice about theire lands" (Massachusetts Historical Society, *Collections,* 5th ser., I [Boston, 1871], 424–426).

35.   Williams to Major Mason, June 22, 1670, in John Russell Bartlett, ed., *Letters of Roger Williams, 1632–1682,* Narragansett Club, *Publications,* 1st ser., VI (Providence, 1874), 342. Williams speaks again of "God Land" in his letter of May 28, 1664, to Governor John Winthrop, Jr., of Connecticut, *ibid.,* VI, 319. For a study of Connecticut's land hunger, see Richard S. Dunn, "John Winthrop, Jr., and the Narragansett Country," *William and Mary Quarterly,* 3d ser., XIII (January, 1956), 68–86.

36.   For a study of the causes of King Philip's War, see Douglas Edward Leach, "The Causes and Effects of King Philip's War," a 1950 Harvard Ph.D. dissertation. George W. Ellis felt that "The differences over land have, as a rule, been given too much importance, though the land question was a contributory cause to a growing estrangement" between English and Indian in the period preceding King Philip's War (George W. Ellis and John E. Morris, *King Philip's War* [New York, 1906], 22).

The Delaware Nativist Revival of the Mid-Eighteenth Century

Charles E. Hunter*

The effects of the European conquest began to make themselves felt on the Delaware Indians in the early seventeenth century. By the mid-eighteenth century they had been uprooted from their homelands, and their numbers had been decimated through the effects of war, disease, and rum. One result was a nativist religious revival which developed two branches, both of which combined elements of native and non-native culture. In 1763, the revival declined in the wake of the defeat of Pontiac. The Delaware revival indicated, according to Charles E. Hunter of Franklin and Marshall College in "The Delaware Nativist Revival of the Mid-Eighteenth Century," that "the Delawares had internalized white culture to the extent that they could no longer distinguish it from their own."

THE INDIANS OF EASTERN North America reacted to the initial advance of European culture in several ways: some nations simply moved west, away from the white men; others battled to preserve their homelands; still others gave rise to secret societies, formed to drive out the whites. Among the Delawares, originally of eastern Pennsylvania, New Jersey, and southeastern New York, the reaction to the European and his ways led, in

---

*Charles E. Hunter, "The Delaware Nativist Revival of the Mid-Eighteenth Century," *Ethnohistory* 18 (1971), 39–49. Reprinted by permission.

time, to an attempt to restore the nativist traditions, as expressed
in the rise of a religious revival in the 1750's and 1760's. That
this nativist revival was not successful is not surprising. By the
mid-eighteenth century the European's advanced technology, as
well as his force of numbers, had irrevocably altered the Delawares' material culture; moreover, nearly a century-and-a-half
of white contact had substantially altered the Indians' social
structure and system of values as well.

The Delawares first came in contact with white men in the first
quarter of the seventeenth century, having their first dealings
with the Swedish and Dutch fur traders along the Hudson River
and Delaware Bay. The Indians exchanged their furs for kettles,
clothing, firearms, and other elements of white material culture,
gradually becoming more and more dependent on European
goods, while simultaneously losing many native arts of subsistence. Later, in the 1670's and 1680's, and especially with the
establishment of William Penn's colony in 1681, a tide of white
settlers began to occupy the margins of Delaware lands. Subsequently, continued European demand for furs and the Indians'
adoption of firearms led to the decimation of game in the Delawares' homeland. Hunters were forced to range farther afield,
and the Indian population began to move westward. The position
of the Indian, who by now largely depended on white trade, was
becoming less secure. This, coupled with the importation of the
white man's rum and his diseases, seriously disturbed the Delawares' economic and social system (A.F.C. Wallace 1949:2–6).
As the Indians relinquished more land to the Europeans, and as
they absorbed more of the European's culture and its appurte-
nances, so their situation steadily worsened.

By the 1720's and 1730's, the Delawares had largely left their
homes in the Delaware Valley, and had moved to the north and
west branches of the Susquehanna. By 1724, a band of Delawares had migrated to the Allegheny River, and further westward
drift continued. The terms of the Walking Purchase of 1737 and
the Albany Treaty of 1754 document white pressure and Delaware departure from eastern Pennsylvania as a growing tide of
refugee Delawares moved north, among the Iroquois, or west, to

the Allegheny and Ohio valleys (P. A. W. Wallace 1961:138). The psychological impact of these events on the Delawares was perhaps greater than that upon the Iroquois, for, while the latter maintained their residence in western New York State for a time, the Delawares were uprooted from their homelands. Further, in 1755, the Delawares found themselves caught up in the conflict of the French and Indian War and, electing to support the French, necessitated English expeditions, such as that of Colonel John Armstrong against Kittaning in September, 1756, which further reduced the Indians' numbers (Hunter 1956:376–407).

By the middle of the eighteenth century, reaction to this sequence of sorry events arose among the Delawares in the form of a nativist religious revival, whose thesis was that the Indian's lot had been much happier before the arrival of the European, and would once again improve if, by some means or other, the Indian could again live without the white man. The nativists further asserted that the Delaware's present sad state resulted from their corruption by the Europeans, and that, if the old ways were revived, the Indian would regain his former strength and resume his previous, happy condition.

The message was clearly anti-white, but beyond this, the Delaware nativist revival may be interpreted not as an outgrowth of indigenous tradition, but rather as a basically European innovation expressed in native idiom. Indeed, an Indian religious movement, replete with crusading "prophets", suspiciously suggests its being adapted from contemporary white missionary activities, and, in fact, a model for such activity is close at hand. In 1744 and 1745, David Brainerd, a Presbyterian missionary, was active among the Delawares (Brainerd 1822:149–201). Moreover, the nativist movement may have been further encouraged by exposure to the Quaker "inner light" principle which held that God might speak to the Indian as well as to the white (Zeisberger 1912:52). Consequently, while the stated object of the nativist revival was to eliminate the white influence from Delaware culture (if such were possible by 1750), and, while many of the forms of this revival, such as feasts, were native in origin, others were European in style as will presently be seen. In addition, the content of the movement was expressed in terms of white belief concepts somewhat adapted to Delaware forms, and in many respects demonstrated that, by this time, the Delaware conception of the "old ways" was distorted, if not virtually lost through some five generations of European contact, and showed that the Indian could no longer define the influence he wished to expel.

The nativist revival among the Delawares was not a unified, organized program, and, in fact, developed along two divergent lines, each of which was represented, by May and June of 1760, by a community along the upper Susquehanna (Post 1760:May 19–21, 28; Hays 1954:76–77). The first of these was a band of Munsees headed by Papounhan, who had been preaching at Lackawanna from about 1752 until 1756, when, in consequence of the French and Indian War, he and his band moved north beyond Tioga. In 1758 they returned downstream to Wyalusing, where, in 1760, a Pennsylvania embassy to the western Indians found them "strictly adhering to the ancient Customs and Manners of their Forefathers" (Post 1760:May 19). Papounhan differed from other Delaware nativists in his Quaker-like pacifism, remarkable in a Munsee, such that his followers became known as the "Quaker Indians" (see Post 1853:743, clerk's endorsement on letter). He continued his nativist preaching until 1763, when, on the occasion of a visit by David Zeisberger, he was baptized a Moravian, and thereafter carried on Christian missionary work on the Muskingum from 1772 until his death in 1775 (P. A. W. Wallace 1961:177).

The second branch of the nativist movement among the Delawares did not, as will be seen, share Papounhan's pacifist nature, but may be characterized by its use of an "Indian Bible," or chart, outlining the major emphases of this variety of nativism. This bible, as well as the teachings it represented, were first encountered at Asinsing, on the Chemung, in May and June of 1760, by the Pennsylvania embassy. John Hays wrote in his diary:

> [June] 2 The old Preast Goes Round the houses Every Morning and Eveng Sayes Sum Sort of Prayers and he hase a Book of Pickters he Maid him Self and there is Heaven and Hell and

> Rum and Swan hak [Swannock = white men] and Indiens and
> Ride Strokes for Rum and he would Read Like Mad ofe it in the
> Morning and Sing to the Sune Rising. . . . [June 3] He keepes
> count of the Week for the Hole Town and he Workes 5 Days and
> Keepes the 6 Day and they way That he ceepes count he has a
> Litel Stick with 12 holes in it and He Putis it up a Hol Every
> Morning and Reades his Picter Book till Noon and then Gose to
> his Work A Gain . . . (Hays 1954:76–77).

During this same visit, Frederick Post also observed:

> At Sun-rise the Old Teacher of this Place went from House to
> House and wish'd both Old and Young Peace and a joyful good
> Morning and Thank'd God, who had suffer'd them to behold the
> Light of ye Sun once more (Post 1760: May 28).[1]

At the time the embassy was at Asinsing, its members witnessed the revival of several old Delaware ceremonies, presumably as part of the nativist program (Hays 1954:74–75; Post
1760: May 24–25). Failing in its mission to the western Indians, the Pennsylvania embassy left the upper Susquehanna, and
the "old Preast" and his band disappear from the record.

In 1767, however, David Zeisberger encountered at Goshgoshing, a Delaware refugee town on the upper Allegheny, one
Wangomen, whose views on nativism were in conflict with
those of Zeisberger (Zeisberger 1912:22, 27–30; Deardorff
1946:8; De Schweinitz 1871:333–335). As Wangomen used a
"bible" similar to that of the "old Preast" at Asinsing, and as
he had once lived at that place (before 1764, when it was
destroyed), it is reasonable to conjecture that Wangomen and
the "old Preast" were identical (Zeisberger 1912:22; Hays
1954:76n.).

Of Wangomen, John Heckewelder writes:

> I was also well acquainted with another noted preacher, named
> *Wangomend,* who was of the Monsey tribe. He began to preach
> in the year 1766 [?] . . . When Mr. Zeisberger first came to
> *Goschgoschink* town on the Allegheny river, this Indian prophet
> became one of his hearers, but finding that the Missionary's
> doctrine did not agree with his own, he became his enemy. This
> man also pretended that his call as a preacher was not of his own

choice, but that he had been moved to it by the great and good
Spirit, in order to teach his countrymen, who were on their way
to perdition, how they could become reconciled to their God
(Heckewelder 1876:293–294).

Earlier, in about 1762, another nativist preacher, the Delaware Prophet, had appeared in the Cuyahoga and Muskingum
valleys (McCullough 1808:321–322, reprinted in Peckham
1947:98–99; Kenny 1763:171–172, 175, reprinted in Peckham 1947:99–100; Heckewelder 1818:291–293). John McCullough, a captive of the Delawares at the time, later wrote:

> My [Indian] brother was gone to *Tus-ca-la-ways* [Tuscarawas, in
> the Muskingum Valley] . . . to see and hear a prophet that had
> just made his appearance amongst them; he was of the Delaware
> nation; I never saw nor heard him. It was said by those who
> went to see him, that he had certain heiroglyphics marked on a
> piece of parchment, denoting to probation that human beings
> were subject to, whilst they were living on earth, and also,
> denoting something of a future state. They informed me that he
> was almost constantly crying whilst he was exhorting them. I
> saw a copy of his heiroglyphics, as numbers of them had got
> them copied and undertook to preach, or instruct others. . . . It
> was said that their prophet taught them, or made them believe,
> that he had his instructions immediately from *Keesh-she-la-mil-
> lang-up,* or a being that thought us into being, and that by
> following his instructions, they would, in a few years, be able to
> drive the white people out of their country (McCullough
> 1808:321–322).

In none of the early writings is the Delaware Prophet named;
they were his teachings, widely circulated among the Delawares, which brought him to attention, and it was sufficient to
identify the man himself, simply and uniquely, as "the Delaware Prophet." Writings of the period after Pontiac's War,
however, and particularly those of Charles Beatty, mention one
Neolin, a Delaware from the Muskingum, who experienced a
vision and became a nativist preacher. It has been possible, on
this basis, to identify him with the Delaware Prophet, particularly since, in 1766, Beatty noted that Neolin had his vision
"about six years ago or about 1760" (Beatty 1962:57–59).[2]

The Delaware "Indian bible" is of some interest, as it provided a visual ground for the preachings of both Wangomen and Neolin. Descriptions of this bible are to be found in Hays (1954:76–77), Kenny (1913:171), Zeisberger (1910:133, 1767:25), McCullough (1808:321, 324–325), and Heckewelder (1876:291–293).[3] The last provides perhaps the most lucid account of the chart:

> The size of this map was about fifteen inches square, or, perhaps, something more. An inside square was formed by lines drawn within it, of about eight inches each way, two of those lines, however, were not closed by about half an inch at the corners. Across these inside lines, others of about an inch in length were drawn with sundry other lines and marks, all which was intended to represent a strong inaccessible barrier, to prevent those without from entering the space within, otherwise than at the place appointed for that purpose. When the map was held as he directed, the corners lay at the left hand side [of the speaker]. . . . He called the space within the inside lines "the Heavenly Regions," or the place destined by the great Spirit for the habitation of the Indians in future life; the space left open at the south-east corner, he called the "avenue," which had been intended for the Indians to enter into this heaven, but which was now in the possession of the white people, wherefore the great Spirit had caused another "avenue" to be made on the opposite side, at which, however, it was both difficult and dangerous for them to enter, there being many impediments in their way, besides a large ditch leading to a gulf below, over which they had to leap; but the evil spirit kept at this very spot a continual watch for Indians, and whoever he laid hold of, never could get away from him again, but was carried to his regions . . . (Heckewelder 1876:291–292).

Such were the general outlines of the "Indian bible." In addition, some of these charts were further embellished with pictures of deer and turkeys (Heckewelder 1876:293), balances (Zeisberger 1910:133; 1912:25) or a "Little God" who carried the Indian's petitions to the Great Spirit (Kenny 1913:173).

The Delaware Prophet taught that the Indian had lost his "avenue" to heaven by allowing the white man into his country and by adopting the white man's ways. He asserted, moreover, that the Indian could regain his previous state by returning to the ways of his pre-contact ancestors. Neolin preached that this could be done by making sacrifices, by reviving the "old" ceremonies and customs, by renouncing rum, firearms, and other European imports, by refusing to co-operate with white traders, and by returning to the supposed ethics and moral standards of previous times. In this manner the Indians, and particularly the Delawares, could regain their strength and identity, and drive out the whites (Heckewelder 1876:292–293; Kenny 1913:175; Zeisberger 1910:133–134; McCullough 1808:321–322; Zeisberger 1912:25). To help the Indian remember these teachings, Neolin "advised" his hearers to obtain a copy of the "bible," which he offered to reproduce at the fixed rate of one buckskin or two doeskins each (Heckewelder 1876:293).

The teachings of Wangomen, Neolin, and other nativist preachers had their effect on the Delawares: ancient ceremonies, or rather, supposed ancient rituals were "revived" in several places (Kenny 1913:172, 196–197; Hays 1954:74–75). But, more importantly, the nativist revival helped lead to a new stirring of anti-European sentiment, a sort of "Indian nationalism" which was harnessed by Chief Pontiac of the Ottawas. Pontiac and others proposed an Indian uprising, aimed at reducing the British strongholds in the west, and to that end, described to his council his interpretation of the words of the spirit of life to the Indians, as given through Neolin:

> Do not drink more than once, or at the most twice in a day; have only one wife and do not run after the girls; do not fight among yourselves; do not "make medicine" but pray, because in "making medicine" one talks with the evil spirit; drive off your lands those dogs clothed in red who will do you nothing but harm. And when ye shall have need of anything address yourselves to me; and as to your brothers, I shall give to you as to them; do not sell your brothers what I have put on earth for food. In short, become good and ye shall receive your needs. When ye meet one another exchange greeting and proffer the left hand which is nearest the heart (Ford 1912:30–32, reprinted in Peckham 1947:115–116).

The phrase, "dogs clothed in red," would seem to be of Pontiac's invention, in order to restrict his indictment to the English, and demonstrates a reinterpretation of the nativist movement to suit more political needs.

Pontiac and his allies, including many Delawares, opened their attacks on the British posts in the spring of 1763. However, in October and November of the following year, Colonel Henry Bouquet led a force of British troops in a show of strength to the Muskingum, and Delaware participation in the conspiracy was suspended (P. A. W. Wallace 1961:149).

The Delawares supposed that more favorable terms of peace could be obtained if they could deal with the Quakers of Pennsylvania rather than by dealing directly with British authorities. Consequently, Neolin apparently incited attempts to stall any dealings with Colonel Bouquet at Fort Pitt (Croghan 1852:47; 1943:208). George Croghan recorded that talks were slowed, since

> One of their Men having been called up to Heaven by the Great Spirit of Life, who told him that he must acquaint his Nation that before they made peace with the English they must first consult with the Quakers of Philadelphia, who would direct them how to make a lasting peace . . . (Croghan 1852:47).

The maneuver failed, however, and the Delaware chiefs were compelled to come to terms, first with Bouquet and finally with the Indian agent, Sir William Johnson, at his headquarters on the Mohawk River in New York (Johnson 1856:718–738).[4]

The collapse of Pontiac's rebellion was accompanied by a decline of the nativist revival which had helped arouse such anti-European sentiment. The native preachers, however, continued their activity for some time in a somewhat modified manner. Charles Beatty noted in his diary an encounter in September, 1766, with Neolin, who recounted the story of his vision and his preaching. Beatty further observed that the Indian had expressed an interest in the Christian teachings (Beatty 1962:57–59, 68–69).

In the following year, as previously noted, Zeisberger arrived at Goshgoshing, and there debated with Wangomen (Zeisberger 1912:22, 27–30; De Schweinitz 1871:333–335). Somewhat later, according to Heckewelder (1876:294–295), Wangomen exchanged his nativism for a campaign against "witches and sorcerers" among his people. In 1775 he traveled to the Muskingum to consult with the council of the Delawares, who charged him to investigate the spread of this witchcraft. This Wangomen did, says Heckewelder, but, finding the practice to be so widespread, he gave up his witch hunt and "returned to his former mode of preaching" (Heckewelder 1876:295). According to Zeisberger, the Delaware preachers were still somewhat active along the Muskingum in 1772, when the Moravian mission was established there. Soon afterwards, however, they disappeared (Zeisberger 1910:136).

The momentum of the Delaware nativist revival was destroyed in the collapse of Pontiac's rebellion, and the movement subsequently disappeared. Although to some extent it may have influenced later revivals of Handsome Lake among the Senecas and of the Prophet of the Shawnees, these, too, passed from the scene.

The Delaware revival was self-contradictory. Aimed at ridding the Delawares of white culture, it drew much of its inspiration from a Quaker principle; it was propagated through methods modeled after those of frontier missionaries; it employed a characteristically un-Indian chart or "bible" in its exposition and even sold, for a fixed price, copies of this plan; it systematized, after Christian fashion, concepts of Earth, Heaven, and Hell; and it generated an almost Mosaic pattern of ethics. In short, the nativists sought to eradicate European influences on the Indian, but, for this purpose, unconsciously employed, or unconsciously assented to the overt employment of a basically European innovation in order to eradicate that influence. In other words, by the mid-eighteenth century, the Delawares had internalized white culture to the extent that they could no longer distinguish it from their own. The Delaware's path was irrevocably tied to that of the white man, as was perhaps most aptly demonstrated in the character of his very attempt to separate the paths.

Notes

1. In light of the "old Preast's" morning ritual, it is interesting to note that the name Wangomen (introduced just hereafter) derives from the Delaware verb "to great."

2. This identification is further supported by marginal notes on a letter from Colonel Henry Bouquet to lieutenant colonels Francis and Clayton: "The Prist Delaware Negowland viz *Four* in English lives as [sic] Wakatowmike . . ." (Bouquet 1943:142). This note, which comprises part of a list of hostile Indians, further supplies a partial derivation of Neolin's name.

    Once this identification is made, a few data on this Indian can be assembled. Beatty, as noted, dates his revelation to about 1760, and he gained prominence as a preacher by 1762 (Kenny 1913:171; McCullough 1808:321). He is placed by Heckewelder at Cuyahoga in 1762 (Heckewelder 1876:291), although he later lived along the Muskingum (Bouquet 1943:142; McCullough 1808:321; Gibson 1943:244). Neolin figured in Pontiac's Rebellion, as discussed hereafter, and is described in 1765 as "an Indian of good repute among the Delawares" (McKee 1765). His influence thereafter waned, and his activities are unrecorded after 1766.

3. Included with McCullough's narrative is a representation and explanation of the chart (1808:324–325). This appears to be a later editorial insertion, and does not square with McCullough's, or any other writer's, account of the bible.

4. For the text of this treaty, see Johnson (1852:277–280).

References

Beatty, Charles
   1962   Journal of Beatty's trip to the Ohio country in 1766. In *Journals of Charles Beatty, 1762–1769,* edited by Guy S. Klett, pp. 41–75. University Park, Pennsylvania State University Press.
Bouquet, Henry
   1943   To Lt. Cols. Francis and Clayton, Sept. 22, 1764. In *The papers of Col. Henry Bouquet,* edited by S. K. Stevens and D. H. Kent, series 21650, II, p. 142. Harrisburg, Department of Public Instruction, Pennsylvania Historical Commission.
Brainerd, David
   1822   *Memoirs of the Rev. David Brainerd.* Edited by Jonathan Edwards. New Haven, S. Converse.
Croghan, George
   1852   Journal of transactions with the Indians at Fort Pitt. *Colonial Records of Pennsylvania,* Vol. 9, pp. 250–264. Harrisburg, T. Fenn.

1943   To Col. Henry Bouquet, May 12, 1765. In *The papers of Col. Henry Bouquet,* edited by S. K. Stevens and D. H. Kent, series 21651, p. 208. Harrisburg, Department of Public Instruction, Pennsylvania Historical Commission.

Deardorff, Merle H.
1946   Zeisberger's Allegheny river Indian towns: 1767– 1770. *Pennsylvania Archaeologist,* Vol. 16, no. 1 (January), pp. 2– 19. Harrisburg, Society for Pennsylvania Archaeology.

DeSchweinitz, Edmund A.
1871   *The life and times of David Zeisberger.* Philadelphia, J. B. Lippincott and Company.

Ford, Richard C., *tr.*
1912   *Journal of Pontiac's conspiracy. 1763.* Edited by M. Agnes Burton. Detroit, Speaker-Hines Printing Company.

Gibson, John
1943   Indian reply to Col. Henry Bouquet, October, 1764. In *The papers of Col. Henry Bouquet,* edited by S. K. Stevens and D. H. Kent, series 21655, p. 244. Harrisburg, Department of Public Instruction, Pennsylvania Historical Commission.

Hays, John
1954   John Hays' diary and journal of 1760. *Pennsylvania Archaeologist,* Vol. 24, no. 2 (August), pp. 63– 84. Honesdale, Society for Pennsylvania Archaeology.

Heckewelder, John G.
1876   *History, manners and customs of the Indian nations who once inhabited Pennsylvania and the neighboring states.* Revised edition. Philadelphia, The Historical Society of Pennsylvania.

Hunter, William A.
1956   Victory at Kittanning. *Pennsylvania History,* Vol. 23, no. 3 (July), pp. 376– 407. University Park, Pennsylvania Historical Association.

Johnson, William
1852   Treaty of peace with the Delaware nation . . . *Colonial Records of Pennsylvania,* Vol. 9, pp. 277– 280. Harrisburg, T. Fenn.

1856   Proceedings of Sir William Johnson with the Indians. *Documents relative to the colonial history of the state of New York,* edited by E. B. O'Callaghan, Vol. 7, pp. 718– 738. Albany, Weed, Parsons and Company.

Kenny, James
1913   Journal of James Kenny, 1761– 1763. *Pennsylvania Magazine of History and Biography,* Vol. 37, pp. 1– 201. Philadelphia, Historical Society of Pennsylvania.

McCullough, John
1808   McCullough's narrative. In *A selection . . . of narratives of outrages . . . ,* edited by Archibald Loudon, Vol. 1, pp. 297– 355. Carlisle, A. Loudon.

McKee, Alexander
1765   [Enclosed in Lt. Col. John Reed to Gen. Thomas Gage, July 15, 1765, in Gage Papers, William L. Clements Library, University of

Michigan.] Microfilm copy in Pennsylvania Historical and Museum Commission, Harrisburg.

Peckham, Howard H.
1947   *Pontiac and the Indian uprising.* Princeton, Princeton University Press.

Post, Frederick
1760   ''Journal . . .'' Manuscript on file with the Historical Society of Pennsylvania; microfilm copy at Pennsylvania Historical and Museum Commission, Harrisburg.
1853   Relation of Frederick Post of conversation with Indians, 1760. *Pennsylvania Archives,* 1st series, Vol. 3, pp. 742–744. Philadelphia, Severns and Company.

Wallace, Anthony F. C.
1949   *King of the Delawares: Teedyuscung, 1700–1763.* Philadelphia, University of Pennsylvania Press.

Wallace, Paul A. W.
1961   *Indians in Pennsylvania.* Harrisburg, Pennsylvania Historical and Museum Commission.

Zeisberger, David
1910   David Zeisberger's history of the northern American Indians. *Ohio Archaeological and Historical Quarterly,* Vol. 19, pp. 1–189. Columbus.
1912   Diary of David Zeisberger's journey to the Ohio . . . *Ohio Archaeological and Historical Quarterly,* Vol. 21, pp. 8–32. Columbus.

Part 4

Red, Black, and White
in the Revolutionary Era

THE HISTORIES OF BLACK AND red Americans constitute an ideological embarrassment for the American Revolution. Generally, the revolutionary era is viewed as a time of hope and expanded opportunities for Americans, but it brought no improvement to the lives of most blacks and Native Americans. Ultimately, the era accelerated the expansion of white landholding at the expense of Native Americans and strengthened the institution of black slavery. This fact appears to contradict the proud assertions of the Declaration of Independence concerning the natural equality of all men and to make the founding fathers vulnerable to charges of hypocrisy. In fact, the Revolution defies understanding when considered on the basis of its ideological rhetoric alone. However, if one takes into account the social reality of the era, the relationships between red, white, and black begin to make some sense. The American Revolution was largely instigated, led, and controlled by a relatively small white elite who wished to free themselves from British restrictions and interference. The freedom they sought was, at least in part, a freedom to pursue their own individual and collective happiness. With this in mind, the fate of black and red Americans during the revolutionary era appears less surprising.

At the beginning of the Revolution, most black Americans were enslaved. While the largest portion of the black population inhabited the southern colonies, slavery existed throughout British North America. But in spite of the pervasiveness of slavery, the institution came under attack throughout the new nation. One source of the attack on slavery was a set of religious objections which had developed during the preceding century. The claim of Quakers and others that slaveholding was incompatible with Christian brotherhood had been given added force by the widespread conversion of slaves during the Great Awakening of the 1740s. The religious attack was augmented by the obvious inconsistency between slavery and the natural-rights rhetoric of the revolution. Another source of judgment against the institution came from slaveholders themselves who began to question the economic future of slave labor. Tobacco and indigo, two major crops produced by slave labor, were in economic decline during this era, and rice culture could not be expanded for geographic reasons. Hard hit by the general postwar depression and shaken by religious and natural-rights criticism, many southern plantation owners began to assess slaveholding in negative terms and to talk of the development of a free labor system. Yet another element in the debate stemmed from the initiative taken by slaves themselves. During the war thousands of slaves were enrolled in the rebel and British forces, and many were granted freedom in return for their service. Others brought suit in court to obtain a freedom they claimed as their natural right.

Given the numerous attacks on slavery, the results appear small. There was an increase in voluntary manumission by individual masters. The importation of slaves was prohibited first by individual states and ultimately in 1808 by Congress under Article I, Section 9 of the Constitution. All the states north of Maryland had abolished the institution by 1786, most of them through legislation providing for gradual emancipation. Nevertheless, ninety percent of American blacks, numbering some seven hundred thousand, remained enslaved at the end of the revolutionary era. The southern states maintained, strengthened, and expanded the institution, and the internal slave trade flourished. The United States entered the nineteenth century as a house divided, part slave and part free.

The reasons for the failure of the southern states to abolish slavery during the revolutionary era reveal much about the nature of the institution. Despite the doubts and bad conscience of southern slaveholders, powerful forces perpetuated the institution. Slavery was more than a labor system. It was a form of capital investment which most slaveholders could not bring themselves to lose. It was a system of social control whereby the master class could protect itself against the interracial warfare which it feared. It was also the basic ingredient in a way of life which southern planters did not wish to relinquish. The final blow to any hopes for southern abolition was provided by the rapid expansion of cotton culture in the new states of the gulf south following the invention of the cotton gin in 1793. White southern leaders could not imagine an economy without slavery; nor could they imagine an interracial society based on an equality of natural rights. Ultimately the social and economic values of these men prevailed over their own revolutionary rhetoric.

The social and economic aims of the American revolutionaries also had much to do with the pattern of red-white relations in the revolutionary era. When the war came both the rebels and the British were anxious for alliances with the Native Americans. The inclination of most Indian nations was to remain neutral or to side with the British. Their distaste for the rebel cause is not difficult to understand. In 1763, the British government had temporarily stemmed the avarice of white settlers and speculators for Indian lands by a policy which prohibited white settlement beyond the Allegheny mountains. This policy, designed to keep peace and promote trade, was a deep source of grievance to many of the rebels; and it was clear to many Indian leaders that a rebel victory would reopen the floodgates for white expansion.

The policy of the American Congress during the war was largely one of trying to arrange treaties of neutrality with major Indian nations while at the same time circulating tales of atrocities committed by Loyalist Indians as a device for recruiting support for the rebel cause. Both along the southern frontier and in the Ohio Valley, Indian allies of the British created a second front which occupied the energies of a major portion of the rebel forces. In many areas frontier warfare merged imperceptibly with white attempts to take new lands.

At the Treaty of Paris of 1783, the British recognized United States independence and agreed to boundaries for the new nation which encompassed not only the thirteen rebel colonies but also the entire area between the Alleghenies and the Mississippi River which previously had been shielded from white settlement. The British made no provision for their Indian allies in the treaty. American settlers moved rapidly into the new lands, interracial warfare was renewed, and many state governments moved to dispossess Native Americans through treaty and legislation. The American Congress made some attempts to restrict this orgy of expansion, particularly in the Northwest Territory, but it was often unable to control the more aggressive actions of individuals and state governments.

Two Indian policies developed in the United States during the Confederation Period. The "civilization" policy, backed by the Congress and many national leaders, involved the seizure of large parcels of Indian lands, parts of which were then to be granted back to their former owners as small farms. The policy was designed to limit frontier violence and to create a deculturized population of Indian small farmers. The rival policy of frontiersmen and many state governments was simply to remove the Indian and seize his land using all necessary force up to and including the extermination of entire nations. The Congressional approach was deemed more humane, but both policies had the same aim: white seizure and settlement of Indian lands.

Clearly, the revolutionary era which brought dreams of a better life to many Americans offered no such hope for most blacks and Indians. The rhetoric of equality of natural rights which many whites were able to translate into social reality was to stand as an unfulfilled promise for other Americans.

The Use of Indians in the War of the American Revolution: A Re-Assessment of Responsibility

Jack M. Sosin*

Jack M. Sosin points out that during the American Revolution both the English and the colonists tried to enlist the active support of Native Americans in their respective war efforts. Previously, historians have argued over the reasons for Indian participation in the Revolution; some have asserted that the English were responsible, some that the colonists were responsible, and others that Indian participation was self-induced. But Sosin persuasively points out that both sides "actively tried to obtain warriors for offensive operations, but the British were more successful than the Americans in enlisting them." Sosin is a professor of history at the University of Nebraska; he has published Whitehall and the Wilderness, Agents and Merchants, The Revolutionary Frontier 1763–1783, *and articles in the* Journal of Ecclesiastical History, Huntington Library Quarterly, *and* Pennsylvania Magazine of History.

ONE OF THE MOST CONFUSED polemical aspects of the War for American Independence concerned the decision by the British and Americans to employ Indian warriors as combatants. The question was, and is, tinged with emotion for the very nature of

*Jack M. Sosin, "The Use of Indians in the War of the American Revolution," *Canadian Historical Review* 46 (1965), 101–21. Reprinted from *Canadian Historical Review*, vol. 46, 1965, by permission of the author and University of Toronto Press.

savage warfare resulted in the barbaric slaughter of unarmed men and innocent women and children by the ''hell hounds of death,'' as the warriors were called. Any discussion almost automatically brings to mind Henry Hamilton who purportedly paid the Indians for white scalps, the murder of Jane McCrae by Burgoyne's Indians, and the Wyoming and Cherry valley ''massacres'' conducted by John and Walter Butler of Ranger fame. Traditionally the excesses have been associated with the British side and American historians, imputing blame on Canadian partisans among others, have forgotten that at times Indians were the innocent victims of frontier violence. There were white as well as red savages. Late in the revolutionary conflict one British official complained that numbers of Cherokee ''women and children have been butchered in cold blood or burnt alive. . . .''[1] While almost all writers agree that Indian warfare was brutal they disagree on assigning responsibility for instigating this type of combat. Some blame the British, some the Whigs, and finally some argue that there can be no imputation of guilt since it was probable that the natives would engage in adjacent combat areas whether solicited by the whites or not.

The first of these interpretations is best illustrated by John Haywood who charged, in his *Civil and Political History of Tennessee,* that the British superintendent for Indian affairs in the southern district and his agents instigated the Cherokee attack on the southern frontier settlements in the summer of 1776. Some recent writers still follow this view,[2] despite studies disputing this judgment by John P. Brown, John R. Alden, Philip M. Hamer, and Helen Louise Shaw who contend that the superintendent, John Stuart, was the victim of circumstances: the efforts of the Whig governments to influence the natives, the orders issued him by the commander-in-chief, General Thomas Gage, and provincial politics. Stuart's political opponents in South Carolina instituted the charge that through his agents he sought to incite the Indians. While Gage did order the use of the savages, Stuart realized that innocent men, women, and children would suffer and sought to prevent an indiscriminate attack unless carried out in conjunction with a regular British force.

The Cherokee attack in 1776 was the result of encroachments by whites on Indian lands and not of the efforts of the British agents, Henry Stuart and Alexander Cameron. Hamer contended that one of the Watauga settlers forged a letter purportedly from Stuart and Cameron indicating that a British force would penetrate to the Indian country from Pensacola and in conjunction with the savages attack the frontier.[3] Although Hamer, Shaw, and Brown used the correspondence of the superintendent and his agents to prove their case, other historians remained unconvinced. Judge Samuel C. Williams, for example, argued that the fact remained that British agents and Tories in the back country did instigate the Indian attack.[4]

Historians are equally divided in assessing responsibility for the use of Indians in the north, particularly over the roles of Gage, Guy Johnson (the superintendent in the northern district), and various military officials such as Henry Hamilton at Detroit. Much has been written to determine if Hamilton did buy scalps,[5] but the larger issue relates to the use of the Indians. Although both James A. James and Orville John Jaebker disagree on their estimates of Hamilton, they do concur in blaming British Crown officials for urging the use of Indians and attacking the frontier. James dismissed as spurious Gage's argument that the Americans had employed the savages first in the siege of Boston.[6] Allen French in his study of the first year of the conflict condemned Gage even more strongly claiming that his efforts to arouse the Indians predated the efforts of the Massachusetts patriots. Moreover, while they used the domesticated Stockbridge Indians in "civilized" combat, Gage sought to employ savages indiscriminately against the frontier. On orders from the British commander, Guy Carleton was plotting to bring in the Six Nations of New York and the Seven Nations of Canada. Hence the New Englanders were justified in attempting to raise the Stockbridge and the Iroquois.[7] The opposite view is found in the work of Nelson Vance Russell who argued that the New England rebels had secured the services of such Indians as were willing to join them before the British employed the savages, but that the two efforts followed so closely that historians have been confused as to who first tried, and actually did, use the warriors.[8]

The confusion also stems from the fact that scholars have not examined all of the evidence. To understand fully what transpired it is essential to separate fact from rumour and propaganda, to distinguish between the intentions of men and what later happened, and to realize that responsibility on both sides was divided among many men on different levels. Moreover, a critical distinction should also be made (and participants in the Revolution often did not make it) between efforts to hold the Indians so that the enemy could not benefit from their help and an effort to bring the Indians actively into the conflict. Furthermore, developments along various sections of the frontier influenced events elsewhere so that decisions made with the southern tribes had an effect on the Canadian Indians and *vice versa*.

In seeking to influence the natives the British for several reasons had an initial advantage. They already had personnel in the Indian departments—superintendents, agents, and commissaries with long experience and, in some cases, married into leading Indian families. They were in a better position to supply the natives with necessities and munitions. Moreover the natives had for some time resented the white settlers encroaching on their lands and the personnel of the British Indian departments had for the most part been active in attempting to restrain illegal settlements. John Stuart emphasized these factors when addressing the Creeks and Cherokee. Only the authority of the royal government, he argued, could preserve the Indian lands from the acquisitive frontiersmen.[9] Even before the outbreak of the Revolution, Indian resentment over invasion of their hunting grounds had led to bloodshed. Both sides had been guilty of murders on the South Carolina and Georgia frontier.[10] Early in 1775 the Shawnee killed several settlers who had ignored their warning to leave Kentucky.

For some years the Shawnee and Delaware had attempted to form a general coalition of the tribes to unite against the whites in case of an outbreak brought on by encroachments. When such a war did erupt between the Virginians and the Shawnee in the summer of 1774 the British superintendents had played a decisive role. Not anticipating the outbreak of the Revolution and that they might later be requested to use the savages, John Stuart and Guy Johnson had disrupted the coalition and isolated the Shawnee.[11] In the fall of 1774 Lord Dunmore of Virginia and his agent, John Connolly, had then forced the Shawnee to sign a temporary truce, the Treaty of Charlotte. The tribes of the upper Ohio were to conclude a definite treaty the next spring. By that time the development of the revolutionary crisis had altered the situation.

In order to confirm the Treaty of Charlotte John Connolly with the assistance and advice of the committee of safety of the Virginia frontier district of West Augusta sent out an invitation to the Ohio Indians. Virginia also sent Thomas and John Walker, James Wood, Andrew Lewis, and Adam Steven to attend this conference at Pittsburgh. At the same time the frontiersmen west of the mountains, fearing that the provincial governments could not deal with the situation, asked the Continental Congress to appoint commissioners to meet with the tribal delegates. Since Congress had also received information from New York concerning the Six Nations it set about establishing its own machinery by creating three departments for Indian affairs and appointing commissioners. But it delegated to the South Carolina committee of safety the power also to appoint officials. South Carolina for practical purposes was acting independently of Congress in Indian affairs as were the revolutionary governments of Massachusetts, Connecticut, and New Hampshire.

The members of the Continental Congress were initially puzzled as to the course of action they should adopt with regard to the French Canadians and Indians to the north. Despite rumours circulating in Philadelphia, New York, and New England, they had not obtained any "certain evidence" that either Guy Carleton, the governor of Canada, or Guy Johnson had directly attempted to persuade the Indians to "take up the Hatchet." According to information given by John Brown and James Price (a merchant from Montreal), the Canadians were not unfriendly to the rebel cause and the northern Indians inclined toward neutrality.[12] Brown, a lawyer of Pittsfield, Massachusetts, had been sent to Canada as a spy for Samuel Adams. He brought back word that the Seven Nations, on receiving a letter from Israel Putnam of Connecticut, had refused to serve with the British. If they fought at all, they would side with the Whigs.[13]

The rebel governments had other agents among the Six Nations, resident missionaries from New England. Samuel Kirkland,[14] who lived among the Oneida for some years, had received instructions dated April 4, 1775, from the provincial congress of Massachusetts to deliver an address to the Iroquois. Since the Whigs had been informed, or so they claimed, that those in Canada inimical to their cause had been tampering with the Six Nations, they asked the Iroquois to "whet your Hatchet, and be prepared with us to defend our liberties and our lives." The Whigs had already enlisted the local Stockbridge Indians for service about Boston and in May they asked the Micmac and Penobscot of Maine to join the conflict.[15] Kirkland failed, however, to enlist the Six Nations of New York. The Oneida declared their neutrality and asked the rebel governments not to apply to the Indians of New England: "Let us Indians be all of one Mind & live in peace with one another, and you white people settle your own Disputes betwixt yourselves."[16]

As far as the Whig agents could ascertain, therefore, the Six Nations and Canadian tribes at this time were neutral. On this assumption Congress determined its initial policy of negotiating treaties of neutrality. It further resolved, however, that if British officials were to induce the Indians to commit hostilities or enter into any offensive alliance, then the colonies ought to avail themselves of the aid of such tribes as would be willing to join the revolutionary cause.[17] Ostensibly Congressional policy was contingent on British action. At this point the attitudes of the various British officials became crucial for within a year Congressional authorities, claiming that the British had incited the Indians, were to abandon neutrality and attempt to engage the savages.

In assessing the responsibility for British action it is essential to bear in mind several levels of authority—the Secretary of State in London (initially the Earl of Dartmouth and then Lord George Germain), the successive commanders-in-chief in America (Thomas Gage and Sir William Howe), the superintendents of Indian Affairs (Guy Johnson and John Stuart), various colonial governors (Guy Carleton of Quebec, Dunmore of Virginia, Patrick Tonyn of East Florida), commanders of the forts in the Indian country (Henry Hamilton and Richard Lernoult at Detroit), and such frontier loyalist leaders as John Connolly of Virginia and Thomas Browne of South Carolina.

As early as the summer of 1774 Gage from Boston wrote to the commanders of the interior posts putting them on their guard and asking them to cultivate the friendship of the tribes.[18] Did Gage want them to bring in the savages against the rebels or merely attach them to the royal cause to prevent the Whigs using them? From the reply of Captain Richard Lernoult, Gage seems to have had the latter object in mind. Lernoult replied to Gage's letter as follows: "I have represented to the several savage nations how much it is their interest to hold fast by government and advised them not to interfere in any disputes in the colonies, all of which they assure me they will observe." But as the crisis intensified, Gage found himself confined to Boston with an inadequate force. He then wrote to Guy Carleton in September, 1774, that as he had to anticipate the worst "I am to ask your opinion whether a Body of Canadians & Indians, might be collected & confided in for the Service of this Country, should matters come to extremeties. . . ." *Six months later* in a secret dispatch Carleton replied that the Canadian Indians "are very much at your Disposal whenever you are pleased to call upon them and what you recommend shall be complied with."[19] From this correspondence it is clear that until the spring of 1775 Gage was not even sure of the dependability of the Indians and that he had not yet ordered that the savages be brought into the conflict.

Disturbing news had come from the superintendent of Indian affairs in the northern district. Since the summer of 1774 Guy Johnson had been active with the Six Nations in an attempt to isolate the Shawnee in their warring with the Virginians on the upper Ohio. In September he had scheduled a conference for the following summer to conclude a general peace between the whites and Indians. The revolutionary crisis intervened. During the winter he complained repeatedly of the activities of the New England agents and missionaries among the Six Nations. Rebel emissaries had told the Indians that the royal government was the common enemy of both the colonists and the red men. Late in March, 1775, he informed Gage that the Yankees had threatened the Mohegan of Connecticut if they did not actively join their forces.[20] Shortly after, the rebels engaged the Stockbridge and issued calls for the Six Nations, the Micmac, and Penobscot. From all the evidence it appears that up to this point Gage had only sounded out Carleton and the interior commanders on the *possibility* of using the Indians. He had not attempted to enlist them.

The capture of Ticonderoga and the use of Indians by the rebels were the decisive developments for the British commander-in-chief. Gage feared that these were but a prelude to further attacks on Ontario, Niagara, Detroit. Since his communications were imperilled he placed Carleton in direct command over the interior posts. Colonel John Caldwell at Niagara, Captain Arent De Peyster at Michilimackinac, and Lernoult at Detroit were to take their orders from Quebec. They were also to cultivate the tribes and to raise them as they *might* be wanted for the royal service. On May 10, he secretly wrote Johnson of the situation and ordered him to keep Carleton informed of all developments and to concur with him in all measures for assembling the Indians and other "proper means to be taken for the support of that part of the country. . . ."[21] From these instructions it seems Gage intended only a defensive disposition of the Indians of New York and Canada to keep open the British line of communication.

When Johnson received these instructions he was not completely free to act. Already tension had developed between Whigs and Tories in the Mohawk Valley. The patriots had organized first in August, 1774, at Stone Arabia in the Palatine

District of Tryon County. The following March Johnson attempted to offset them by mobilizing his loyalists at Johnstown, particularly his Highland tenants. On March 20, he complained to the local magistrates that the patriots were planning to seize him. To protect his person and to keep open his communications, Johnson in May fortified his residence and brought in an armed guard of 150 Highlanders and a few Mohawks. Rumours circulated among the Whigs that the superintendent planned to use the Tories and Indians to attack them. Johnson branded this a "gross and notorious falsehood." At a conference called by Johnson for May 25, 1775, at the German Flats, the Indians informed the patriot delegation from Albany and Tryon counties of their attachment to their superintendent and insisted that they wanted no quarrel with the settlers.[22] Johnson was in a difficult position for the Whigs could cut off the provisions necessary for him to retain the Indians and were threatening to capture him. At this point, he received Gage's secret instructions of May 10. With a party of 250 loyalists and Mohawks Johnson left the valley at the end of May. Assembling a body of 1,500 Indians at Lake Ontario on June 17 he obtained from them a promise to assist in maintaining the line of communications in conjunction with British troops. He concluded a similar agreement with some 1,700 Canadian Indians at Montreal the following month. At this point a disagreement developed between Johnson and Guy Carleton who would not allow the Indians to be employed outside Quebec. The governor apparently had little faith in the Indians who seemed to have vacillated in their allegiance. Furthermore, he could not expect anything more of them than "cutting off a few unfortunate Families, whose Destruction will be but of little Avail towards a Decision of the present Contest."[23] Except for a small detachment retained to defend Canada against the invading Whig forces, Carleton dismissed the Indians in August. The delegates from the Six Nations returned to the Onondaga council after assuring Johnson that they would be willing to return whenever the British proposed vigorous action.[24]

Although some doubt may arise as to what fully transpired at the Oswego and Montreal conferences, the evidence indicates that Guy Johnson asked the help of the Indians in defending the British and in keeping open their line of communication. "There is no evidence that he asked them to fall upon the frontiers or fight anything but a defensive war."[25] So wild were the rumours in the Mohawk Valley that even before Johnson reached Montreal on July 17, the patriots claimed to have intelligence that he was already planning to march with eight or nine hundred Indians to attack their settlements.[26]

The American threat against Canada pressed by Arnold and Montgomery with the aid of Indians presented Gage with another crisis. With the rebel forces in possession of the British forts on Lake Champlain and operating as far north as the St. John River, Gage for the first time issued orders to Carleton to raise all the troops and Indians he could collect to retake Ticonderoga, secure the lake, and raid the frontiers of the New England colonies. This diversion would relieve his own force at Boston. Seeking to justify this harsh expedient the commander-in-chief wrote his superior in London that "we need not be tender of calling on the Savages, as the rebels have shewn us the example bringing as many Indians down against us here as they could collect." But this was a weak rationalization as Gage must have known for he admitted to Carleton that the natives used by the New Englanders "are not distant Indians but what the French would call Domiciliés, and not of great worth."[27] Far removed from the scene and dependent on Gage for information, the Secretary of State approved of his decision to employ Indians since the rebels had initiated the practice.[28] As Gage's military position deteriorated, he grew more desperate. Early in September he again urged Carleton to raise a savage army. The sooner the Indians were committed to the British side the better, for the rebels would not have it in their power to seduce them.[29] Unknown to the commander-in-chief, Carleton would not allow the savages to operate outside Canada. The tribesmen already assembled at Montreal had been dismissed and were no longer a military factor. Guy Johnson departed shortly for London, not to return to America until July, 1776.

He would not be in a position to determine events at the scene of operations.[30]

Gage received encouraging news from another quarter, however. Operating independently, Governor Dunmore of Virginia had written the home government on May 1, 1775, that with an adequate supply of arms and ammunition from Gage he could hold Virginia for the Crown by raising a force of loyalists, negro slaves, and Indians. A key aide in this hare-brained project was John Connolly, a rascally adventurer who had served the governor as agent and leader of the Virginia forces in wresting control of the forks of the Ohio from the proprietary government of Pennsylvania and the Shawnee in 1774. Connolly was scheduled to ratify the peace with the Indians in the spring of 1775. With the advice and assistance of the committee of safety of the district of West Augusta, Connolly met with delegates of the Six Nations, Mingo, and Delaware at Pittsburgh on June 19, 1775, when he ratified the peace. There is no reliable evidence that in his negotiations with the Indians up to this time he had been double-dealing or inciting the savages against the whites. Connolly later claimed that not only had he secretly obtained the support of prominent frontier leaders for a loyalist *coup* but had also evaded the Virginia commissioners and won over the Indians to support the British.[31] Whatever the case, on July 25, Connolly left the forks of the Ohio to join his patron, who after fleeing Williamsburgh, had taken refuge on the *William* in the Elizabeth River.

During the next two weeks Dunmore and his agent concocted their scheme to hold Virginia with a motley force while Connolly drew together the British garrisons from the interior forts and brought them down on Pittsburgh where the neighbouring tribes and loyalist frontiersmen would support him. On August 9, 1775, he sent to John Gibson, an Indian trader at Pittsburgh, a message from Dunmore to Captain White Eyes of the Delaware. Cornstalk of the Shawnee and the other chiefs of the Mingo and Six Nations were also to receive this message: the Indians were not to listen to the rebel commissioners but wait for further news from the royal governor.[32] Dunmore then dis-

patched Connolly to Boston to obtain military aid from Gage.
According to the governor, Connolly had convinced the Indians
on the upper Ohio to espouse the royal cause. Speed was essential since rebel emissaries, already on the scene, would no doubt
attempt to win over the natives.[33] On arriving in Boston early in
September, Connolly informed Gage that by Dunmore's orders
he had already prepared the Ohio Indians and frontier loyalists
to act. He now wanted the assistance of the Indian department,
military supplies, and the army units in the interior for a strike
on the Ohio so as to alarm the frontiers of the rebel colonies and
obstruct communications between the northern and southern
provinces.[34] Gage, unable to supply munitions and doubtful of
the ability of the commanders in the interior to do anything but
maintain defensive positions, none the less authorized them and
the Indian superintendent to give any assistance they could.[35]
Connolly's ill-conceived plot was doomed from the start when
his servant, William Crowley, notified the Whig authorities of
the scheme. Unaware of the leak Connolly returned to Portsmouth, Virginia, on October 12, received a commission from
Dunmore, and then started north again to put his plan into
operation. At Hagerstown, Whig officials apprehended him and
discovered the incriminating documents. So ended the haphaz-
ard scheme to bring in the Ohio Indians.[36]

Unaware of this development Gage was making a more real-
istic effort to employ the Indians in the south where for some
months British and rebel officials had been vying for the friendship of the Cherokee and Creeks. John Stuart and his agents had
to re-form the tribal coalition they had disrupted but a few
months before in an effort to prevent a general Indian attack
against the frontier. They had not predicted either the outbreak
of revolutionary hostilities or that they might be ordered to use
the savages against white settlements. Concurrently they had to
counteract the efforts of rebel officials such as William Henry
Drayton and George Galphin. Drayton, representing the South
Carolina council of safety had contacted the Cherokee that summer. He asked the natives not to listen to the British.[37] Officially the Whigs urged the Indians to remain neutral, but at the

same time they charged that Stuart and his agents were instigating the savages to attack the frontier. This was not the case, for as Alexander Cameron, Stuart's deputy among the Overhills, reported, the Indians were "in the best disposition to live in peace and harmony with all His Majesty's subjects." None the less, he was forced to withdraw temporarily from the Indian country early that summer to keep from falling into the hands of rebel officials seeking to capture him.[38]

The Whigs during the summer and fall of 1775 continued to propagate the rumour in the back country that on Stuart's orders, Cameron had collected 1,500 Indians to fall on the settlements as soon as he received word that royal troops had arrived.[39] These confused rumours increased when word reached Charleston of the fighting at Lexington and Concord. Fearing that the Whigs would seize him, Stuart fled to Savannah, but when rebel agents pursued him to the Georgia capital he travelled to St. Augustine. From this sanctuary in East Florida he protested that he had never received any orders from his superior "which by the most tortured construction could be interpreted to spirit up the Indians to fall upon the Frontier Inhabitants or to take any part in the disputes between Great Britain and her colonies."[40]

Ironically Stuart's account of his flight to St. Augustine and his disavowal of the patriot charges against him brought a direct order from the commander-in-chief to use the savages. The arrival of Stuart's report in Boston coincided with the American drive on Canada and the proposal by Connolly to raise the Ohio tribes. Since Stuart was now in a position at St. Augustine to communicate with the southern Indians, Gage ordered him, whenever opportune, "to make them take Arms against His Majesty's Enemies," and to distress the rebels with all their power "for no terms is [sic] now to be kept with them; they have brought down all the Savages they could against us here, who with their Rifle men are continually firing on our Advanced Sentries. . . . no time should be lost to distress a set of people so wantonly rebellious."[41]

Stuart did not implement these orders for the indiscriminate use of Indians. The exposed positions of the loyalists in the

southern back country led him to question Gage's policy. By the
time the superintendent received Gage's instructions early in
October, Tory leaders from the back country had joined him and
Governor Patrick Tonyn in East Florida. Among them were
Moses Kirkland and Thomas Browne. Kirkland was involved in
an unsuccessful attempt to form a loyalist association in the
Ninety-Six District of South Carolina. Browne, a recent immi-
grant to the upper Savannah, had been abused by the Sons of
Liberty in Augusta who had tarred and feathered him, burned
the soles of his feet, and driven him out for ridiculing the
Whigs. Embittered by this harsh treatment he had fled to St.
Augustine where he hoped to obtain aid for his almost defence-
less followers in the back country. Stuart realized that these
frontier loyalists might suffer in an indiscriminate attack by the
Indians as Gage had ordered. To prevent this he hoped to use
the Indians only under white leaders and in an operation in
concert with, and under the control of, a regular British force. It
would take time to transport such a force south, to settle a peace
between the warring Choctaw and Creeks, and to organize the
Indians to act with the British troops. Consequently, the superintendent did not execute Gage's orders, but dispatched his
brother Henry Stuart *via* Mobile to the Indian country with
enough ammunition to strengthen his hand with the savages
against the rebel emissaries and to dispose the Creeks and
Cherokee to act under the direction of British agents when required. They were not to take any step "except in the execution
of some concerted plan, jointly with the Friends of Government
[the Tories], or to favor the Operations of His Majesty's Forces
by drawing the attention of the Rebels."[42]

The British took no action until 1776, however, when various
plans were proposed to Sir Henry Clinton, commander of a
force intended for the southern campaign. Clinton himself was
under Sir William Howe who had replaced Gage as commander-
in-chief. During March and April, Clinton conferred off Cape
Fear with Stuart, Browne, and Captain Frederick Mulcaster, an
officer from East Florida. Initially Clinton hoped to land the
troops expected from Britain later in May, and open communi-

cations with the back-country Tories by way of the Savannah River. He realized, however, that the poorly armed loyalists would not hold out against the Whigs until he could reach them. Mulcaster suggested that to relieve the loyalists until the main body of troops landed, a subsidiary force from Pensacola secretly penetrate up the Alabama River to the Indian towns and then overland to the back country. Browne offered another plan: supplying the back-country Tories with ammunition and opening a passage to the Ninety-Six District directly from St. Augustine. He assured Stuart that he could organize the loyalists in time and provide him with men to lead the Indians. They could thus restrain the savages from indiscriminate acts of violence. The superintendent was dubious, pointing out to Clinton the great logistical problem involved in marching a force from West Florida and the time requisite to organize the Indians for such an expedition.[43] While Browne returned to St. Augustine in March, Stuart remained with Clinton off Cape Fear until the arrival of the British troops on May 8 when he too departed for the capital of East Florida. During this time neither Clinton nor Howe had ordered him to use Indians; nor had they decided to send a British expedition from West Florida to the Indian country. The superintendent was still adhering to the policy contained in his instructions of the previous fall to his deputies: to keep the Indians disposed to aid a British force *if* a campaign in the back country was directed.[44]

The superintendent was not the only official involved in the decision. Governor Tonyn, chaffing at the delay in using the Indians, accused Stuart of holding back for fear of Whig reprisals against his wife held hostage in Charleston. The superintendent "stands in need of a strong Spur," Tonyn wrote Clinton. He advised sending Browne to the Carolina back country and raising the Indians without delay. By April Browne actually was among the Indian towns, first among the lower Cherokee and then the Creeks hoping to offset the efforts of the Whig commissioners, Edward Wilkinson and George Galphin, open a line of communication to supply his hard-pressed followers, and raise a force to join the Indians.[45] The loyalist leader felt strongly about his mission. "The wanton outrages which have been committed upon my person & property will be a spur to my endeavours & tho I sincerely lament the misfortunes to which an attack will subject an infatuated multitude, their savage unparalleled cruelty would justify the severest reprisals. . . ."[46]

During the spring of 1776 there were then *two* groups operating for the British in the Indian country, Browne and his followers, and the agents of the Indian department, Henry Stuart, David Taitt, John Buchanan, and Alexander Cameron. Stuart's officials had not stirred up the Indians for Buchanan wrote Stuart late in May that none of the warriors had gone out, even to hunt, but waited word from the superintendent. But in June Tory leaders from the Carolina back country visited Henry Stuart and Cameron in the Overhill towns wanting to know if they could expect a British force from Pensacola or St. Augustine to penetrate to the Indian country and then relieve them.[47] Evidently Browne had informed his followers of the plan he had proposed to Clinton and Tonyn earlier that year—a plan which had not been adopted.

But even without British encouragement the southern Indians were disposed against the frontiersmen. The younger Cherokee warriors already resented the white settlers who encroached on their hunting grounds under title of buying and leasing land from the older, infirm chiefs. In March the Cherokee Dragging Canoe had warned Henry Stuart at Mobile that he intended to drive off the whites in the Nolichucky and Watauga settlements who had leased these lands from Attakullakulla. At the request of the younger Stuart the Cherokee deferred their attack until the agent wrote the settlers, warning them of the danger, and offering them free land and safe passage to West Florida. Instead of removing, the Wataugans sent to Virginia for aid, enclosing a letter purportedly from Henry Stuart warning the Tories of an impending attack by a British force from West Florida in conjunction with parties of Cherokee, Choctaw, and Creeks. Stuart denounced this letter as a forgery. When the Upper Cherokee under Dragging Canoe did attack in July after the expiration of the period allotted the settlers to remove, it appeared as if the charges made by the Wataugans against Stuart were true and that the British agents had instigated the onslaught.[48]

This charge did not tell the whole story. First, the proposed British force from the Gulf to the Indian towns was only discussed by Clinton and Stuart off Cape Fear; it had not been agreed upon, much less organized, and could not therefore have been imminent as the Wataugans claimed from the purported letter from Henry Stuart. Both Cameron and Stuart tried to prevent the Cherokee attack which seems to have been precipitated by the arrival at Chote of a delegation from the Shawnee, Delaware, and other northern tribes to ask the aid of the Cherokee in a united war against the frontiersmen who were occupying Indian lands and fortifying the Ohio. John Stuart and Guy Johnson had frustrated a similar attempt by the Shawnee two years before. In 1776 Henry Stuart and Cameron sought to prevent the Overhill Cherokee from joining the coalition and raiding the Watauga and Nolichucky settlements. While the warriors of the Upper towns agreed to wait, news arrived that the braves of the Lower towns had gone out against the Carolina frontier. This precipitated the attack by the Overhills. Although Cameron and Stuart could no longer restrain them, they extracted a pledge that the Indians would not raid beyond the boundary line, would not injure loyalists or women and children, and would not continue hostilities when ordered to halt by the superintendent. Henry Stuart then left for Mobile by way of the Creek towns where he persuaded the Creeks not to aid their northern neighbours and to remain quiet until they heard from his brother.[49] The Cherokee, thus isolated, could not withstand the greatly superior forces sent against them by Virginia and the Carolinas later that year.

One other critical question remains. Was there another factor precipitating the attack by the Lower Cherokee? The evidence is not conclusive but loyalists from the Carolina back country were in the Cherokee villages seeking aid against the Whigs before the Indian attack. Moreover it was reported in the Yadkin country of North Carolina before the Cherokee onslaught that the Indians were being incited by some forty whites from the Congaree River and not by orders of the royal officials.[50] Finally, one loyalist in his account of this episode made it clear that South Carolina Tories participated in the Indian raids.[51] Possibly Thomas Browne with the encouragement of Governor Tonyn of East Florida had led his followers in the back country to incite the Lower Cherokee—or the frontier loyalists, goaded by the Whig militia and rangers, resorted to the Indians for relief. From the correspondence of John Stuart it is clear that at no point in 1776 had the agents of his department organized the Indians to raid the frontier. Stuart had no plan for offensive action involving the Indians before he left Clinton off Cape Fear. Even when he arrived at St. Augustine in June, it was only at the strong insistence of Tonyn that he continued on to West Florida. He arrived at Pensacola on July 24 shortly after his brother who had just returned from the Indian country. At the end of August the superintendent wrote Clinton that he would attempt to keep the Creeks quiet until he received further orders. Not until October was he able to effect a truce between the Creeks and the Choctaw which would enable them to act if and when requisitioned by Clinton or Howe. Such a request did not reach Stuart that year.[52]

Late that summer the Secretary of State in London urged the superintendent and the military commanders to be vigilant in counteracting the efforts of the Whig agents to win over the Indians. He suggested to Stuart that possibly Howe might use the savages if he undertook a campaign in the southern colonies.[53] Howe was planning to use Indians, but in his campaign in the north where he depended on the influence of Guy Johnson with the Six Nations. Johnson, however, did not return to America until July, and it was not until late in November that he was able to send his Mohawk agent, Joseph Brant, in disguise through the American lines from New York City to the Indian country to organize the Iroquois. Consequently the New York tribes were not a military factor in 1776.[54]

Despite all the rumour and negotiations throughout 1776, the British had only used a few Indians defensively in East Florida and Canada.[55] Yet American policy had undergone a radical shift. Initially Congress had decided in 1775 on a policy of neutrality with the Indians pending proof that the ministerial officials had employed the savages. Philip Schuyler, a commissioner of Indian affairs in the northern department, provided apparent evidence when, in December, 1775, he reported what delegates from the Six Nations claimed was a British effort to bring them into the conflict. Johnson's purported invitation at Oswego and Montreal for the savages "to feast on a Bostonian and drink his blood," created a sensation in Congress.[56] But irrespective of the purported attempt by the British, Washington felt that with the defeat of Arnold and Montgomery before Quebec, the Canadians and their Indians must take sides. Since they would be used by one belligerent or another, and the British would certainly make an effort, he left it to the discretion of Schuyler to employ a party of Canadian Indians who offered to abandon neutrality and fight with the continental forces.[57]

Late in May, 1776, Congress itself took the final step. After conferring with Washington it resolved that it was highly expedient to engage the Indians for offensive operations against Niagara and Detroit. The commander-in-chief was also empowered to use up to 2,000 Indians against Canada.[58] The congressional commissioners for the middle department had proposed an expedition against Detroit the previous summer, but Congress, expecting that the conquest of Canada by Arnold and Montgomery would also result in the fall of the interior posts, had then rejected the plan. It was now taken up again.

The British commanders had appreciated the threat against the interior forts since Gage had warned them in the fall of 1775 to be on their guard. Lieutenant-Governor Henry Hamilton had to slip through an American blockade on the St. Lawrence before he could reach his post at Detroit on November 9, 1775. The neighbouring Indians immediately applied for permission to go against the frontier. Since he had no orders at the time sanctioning such attacks he did not comply. Instead he deterred the warriors and wrote the rebel authorities at Pittsburgh cautioning them against violating Indian territory. Such transgressions would probably result in a rupture with the savages.[59] By the summer of 1776 Hamilton discovered that the Americans at Fort Pitt were contemplating a campaign against Detroit and, through such agents as the Delawares, White Eyes, and the trader, William Wilson, were tampering with the neighbouring Indians. At a conference with delegates of the leading tribes Hamilton pointed out that the past performances of the rebel frontiersmen contradicted their current profession of friendship. Heretofore he had restrained the Indians since he had not received orders and Carleton had sent back a band of Ottawa raised at Michilimackinac the previous fall for the defence of Canada. When the Indians left this council at Detroit early in September Hamilton suspected that they would send out small parties against the scattered settlers on the Ohio in what he termed a "deplorable sort of War," but one "which the arrogance, disloyalty, and imprudence of the Virginians has justly drawn upon them." The warriors, he reported to the Secretary of State, were inclined toward war.[60]

When Hamilton's dispatch relating the sentiment of the interior tribes reached London, the British ministry had decided to utilize the Indians for the first time in extensive, offensive operations. Their military aid was necessary, so it was thought, for the comprehensive campaign of 1777 in the north. Burgoyne advocated using a thousand Indians to establish communication posts, protect his supply lines, and carry out a diversionary operation from Lake Ontario, Oswego, and the Mohawk River to Albany. Since Hamilton indicated in his dispatch of September 2, 1776, that the Indians were eager for war, and would probably send out small parties on their own initiative, Germain in March, 1777, issued instructions for significant numbers of Indians to be used for offensive action against New York, Pennsylvania, and the Virginia frontier along the upper Ohio. The southern tribes were to protect West Florida from a rebel invasion down the Mississippi and tie up rebel forces in the south by diversionary attacks on the frontier. White leaders were to conduct all Indian parties and they were not to molest loyalists or innocent persons.[61]

As far as the British government, and most of the men who executed its policy were concerned, there was to be no terrorism on the frontier. Few agreed with Colonel La Corne St. Luc, the Canadian partisan in charge of the Indians with Burgoyne, who purportedly stated that "Il faut lacher les sauvages contre les miserables Rebels, pour imposer de terreur sur les frontiers; . . . qu'il faut brutalizer les affaires. . . ."[62] Thomas Browne, Henry Hamilton, and John Graham who led parties of Choctaw and Chickasaw testified that they always sent white leaders with the Indians to prevent atrocities and barbarous treatment of prisoners. But it was not always possible to wage war with such calculated nicety. As Edward Abbott, Lieutenant-Governor of Vincennes, noted, savage warfare was by its very nature indiscriminate and barbarous "as it is not people in armys that Indians will ever daringly attack; but the poor inoffensive families . . . who are inhumanely butchered sparing neither women or [*sic*] children." It might be necessary to prevent the Indians serving the rebels but keeping them neutral would also serve the same purpose.[63]

Given the emphasis on war in the Indian culture and the proximity of the Indians to the scene of conflict, it was probable that the warriors would *to some extent* engage in the war. As the Whig leader in the Mohawk Valley, Marinus Willett put it, they would be fighting "for somebody and that they may better be fighting for us than against us needs no argument."[64] Ultimately both sides so rationalized. Although each was prone unduly to suspect the other, the Whigs of Massachusetts and the loyalists of the Carolina back country apparently could not resist the temptation to use Indians. But to Gage belongs the major blame for exaggerating the involvement on the patriot side and encouraging the wide-scale employment of the savages. Fortunately for the American frontier, Carleton and John Stuart did not initially follow his orders and the settlers were thus given two years to prepare. At that point both sides, seeking to increase their manpower, actively tried to obtain warriors for offensive operations, but the British were more successful than the Americans in enlisting them.

Notes

1. Lt. Col. Thomas Browne to General Guy Carleton, Oct. 9, 1782, British Army Headquarters Papers (Guy Carleton Papers), no. 5822, microfilm, Colonial Williamsburg, Williamsburg, Virginia.

2.   Stephen B. Weeks, "General Joseph Martin and the War of the Revolution in the West," American Historical Association, Annual Report for 1893 (Washington, 1894), p. 422; and William H. Nelson, The American Tory (Oxford, 1961), p. 144.

3.   John Richard Alden, John Stuart and the Southern Colonial Frontier (Ann Arbor, 1944), pp. 169 and 171, note 75; John P. Brown, Old Frontiers; The Story of the Cherokee Indians from Earliest Times to the Date of Their Removal to the West, 1838 (Kingsport, Tenn., 1938), pp. 140–9; Helen Louise Shaw, British Administration of the Southern Indians, 1756–1783 (Lancaster, Pa., 1931), pp. 88–105; Philip M. Hamer, ed., "Correspondence of Henry Stuart and Alexander Cameron with the Wataugans," Mississippi Valley Historical Review, XVII (Dec., 1930), 451–57; Philip M. Hamer, "The Wataugans and the Cherokee Indians in 1776," East Tennessee Historical Society, Publications, III (Jan., 1931), 114–26; and Philip M. Hamer, "John Stuart's Indian Policy during the Early Months of the American Revolution," Mississippi Valley Historical Review, XVII (Dec., 1930), 351–9, 363–66.

4.   Samuel C. Williams, Tennessee During the Revolutionary War (Nashville, 1944), p. 25 and note 4.

5.   The most exhaustive work is by Orville John Jaebker, "Henry Hamilton: British Soldier and Colonial Governor," unpublished Ph.D. dissertation, Indiana University, 1954; John D. Barnhart, "A New Evaluation of Henry Hamilton and George Rogers Clark," Mississippi Valley Historical Review, XXXVII (March, 1951), 643–52; and John D. Barnhart, ed., Henry Hamilton and George Rogers Clark in the American Revolution, With the Unpublished Journal of Lieut. Gov. Henry Hamilton (Crawfordsville, Ind., 1951). They conclude that the evidence against the British officer was hearsay and circumstantial and that we must presume that he did not pay Indians for white scalps. Hamilton himself charged that "every sort of misrepresentation . . . [had] been used to paint us in the blackest colour" (Hamilton to Captain Richard Lernoult, Feb. 28, 1778, British Army Headquarters Papers, no. 9826). He repeatedly urged the Indians to save their captives and bring in prisoners, not scalps. See Hamilton's narrative, April 2, 1782, Shelburne Papers, 66: 179, William L. Clements Library, Ann Arbor, Michigan; and Hamilton to Lord George Germain, Sept. 5, 1777, Colonial Office Records (Q series), vol. 14, p. 225, transcripts, Public Archives of Canada (P.A.C.).

6.   Jaebker, "Henry Hamilton," p. 102; and James Alton James, "Indian Diplomacy and the Opening of the Revolution in the West," Wisconsin State Historical Society, *Proceedings for 1909,* LVII (Madison, 1910), 129.

7.   Allen French, *First Year of the American Revolution* (Boston, 1934), pp. 403– 8.

8.   Nelson Vance Russell, "The Indian Policy of Henry Hamilton: a Re-evaluation," *C.H.R.,* XI (March, 1930), 20– 23.

9.   See the two speeches by John Stuart filed among the undated items for 1775 in the Sir Henry Clinton Papers, Clements Library.

10.   Col. William Thomson to the South Carolina council of safety, Sept. 29, 1775, *South Carolina Historical Magazine,* II (July, 1901), 171; and John Stuart to General Frederick Haldimand, July 5, 1775, Thomas Gage Papers, Clements Library.

11.   On the role of the superintendents in disrupting the Indian confederation see Guy Johnson to General Thomas Gage, July 12, 16, Aug. 11, 19, Sept. 29, 1774, Gage Papers; Johnson to Governor John Penn, July 22, 1774, in Peter Force, ed., *American Archives,* series 4 and 5 (9 vols., Washington, 1837– 53), 4th series, I, 645– 6; Johnson to the Earl of Dartmouth, Sept. 10, 1774, in Edmund B. O'Callaghan, ed., *Documents Relative to the Colonial History of the State of New York* (15 vols., Albany and New York, 1853– 87), VIII, 490; John Stuart to Haldimand, June 25, 1774, Gage Papers; John Stuart to Gage, Nov. 19, 1774, Jan. 18, 1775, Gage Papers; and Stuart to Haldimand, Nov. 20, 1774, Haldimand Papers, vol. 12, p. 397, transcripts, P.A.C.

12.   Entry for June 7, 1775, John Adams Diary, in Edmund C. Burnett, ed., *Letters of Members of the Continental Congress* (8 vols., Washington, 1921– 36), I, 113– 14. On June 29, 1774, Richard Henry Lee wrote Washington: "We are this day informed in congress that the Six Nations and the Canada Indians are firmly disposed to observe a strict neutrality." *Ibid.,* I, 147. On the activities of James Price see the Connecticut delegates to William Williams, May 23, 1775, in Nathaniel Bouton, *et al.,* eds., *Documents and Records Relating to the Province of New Hampshire (1623–1800)* (40 vols., Concord, 1867– 1943), VII, 490.

13.   French, *First Year of the Revolution,* p. 147.

14.   During the Revolution James Deane and Kirkland were agents for the northern department of Indian affairs under Congress. See their letters to Philip Schuyler in item 153, Papers of the Continental Congress, National Archives, Washington, D.C.

15.   Address to the Six Nations, in Force, ed., *American Archives,* 4th series, I, 1350; and the Massachusetts Provincial Congress to the eastern Indians, May 15, 1775, in Frederic Kidder, *Military Operations in eastern Maine and Nova Scotia during the Revolution . . . from the journals of . . . Col. John Allan . . .* (Albany, 1867), pp. 51–2. Captain Solomon of the Stockbridge told the provincial congress on April 15: "One thing I ask of you if you send for me to fight, that you will let me fight in my own *Indian* way. I am not used to fight *English* fashion. . . ." Force, ed., *American Archives,* 4th series, II, 316.

16.   Message of the Oneida, interpreted and written by Kirkland, to the New England governors, June 19, 1775, in Bouton, *et al.,* eds., *New Hampshire Provincial Papers,* VII, 534.

17.   Resolution of July 1, 1775, in Worthington C. Ford, *et al.,* eds., *Journals of the Continental Congress, 1774–1789* (34 vols., Washington, 1904–37), II, 123.

18.   Gage to Carleton, Aug. 18, 1775, Gage Papers.

19.   Lernoult to Gage, May 14, 1775; Gage to Carleton, Sept. 4, 1774; and Carleton to Gage (secret), Feb. 4, 1775, Gage Papers.

20.   Johnson to Gage, Jan. 14, March 31, April 7, 1775, enclosing the address of the Mohegan Joseph Johnson, March 25, 1775, Gage Papers.

21.   Gage to Carleton, May 20, 1775 with extract of Gage to Johnson, May 10, 1775; Gage to John Caldwell, May 10, 1775; Gage to Caldwell, Arent De Peyster, and Lernoult, May 20, 1775, Gage Papers.

22.   Force, ed., *American Archives,* 4th series, II, 637–8; Mabel G. Walker, "Sir John Johnson, Loyalist," *Mississippi Valley Historical Review,* III (Dec., 1916), 321–3; and New York (State) University, Division of Archives and History, *The American Revolution in New York* (Albany, 1926), pp. 208–9.

23.   Carleton to Gage, Aug. 5, 1775, Gage Papers. See also Carleton to Gage, May 31, June 4, and July 27, 1775, Gage Papers.

24.   In December the Iroquois delegation told Philip Schuyler that Johnson after offering them a war belt and hatchet, had invited them to "feast on a Bostonian and drink his blood—an ox being roasted for this purpose and a pipe of wine given to drink." To Schuyler this constituted "full proof that the Ministerial servants have attempted to engage the savages against us." Schuyler to John Hancock (President of the Continental Congress), Dec. 14, 1775, in Force, ed., *American Archives,* 4th series, IV, 260.

25. Marc Jack Smith, "Joseph Brant, a Mohawk Statesman," unpublished Ph.D. dissertation, University of Wisconsin, 1946, p. 19.

26. See Nicholas Herkimer, chairman of the Canojoharie Committee of Safety to the Schenectady Committee of Safety, July 12, 1775, Tryon County Commiteee of Safety Papers, New York Historical Society, New York. For the superintendent's own accounts of his activities see "Extracts from the Records of Indian Transactions under . . . Guy Johnson during the year 1775," Supplementary volume, Lord George Germain Papers, Clements Library; Guy Johnson's journal printed in O'Callaghan, ed., *New York Colonial Documents,* VIII, 658; and Johnson to Dartmouth, Oct. 12, 1775, *ibid.,* VIII, 636–37.

27. Gage to Dartmouth, June 12, 1775, in Clarence E. Carter, ed., *The Correspondence of General Thomas Gage* (2 vols., New Haven, 1931–3), I, 404; and Gage to Carleton, June 3, 1775, Gage Papers.

28. Dartmouth to Gage, Aug. 2, 1775, in Carter, ed., *Gage Correspondence,* II, 204.

29. Gage to Carleton, Sept. 5, 1775, Gage Papers.

30. The superintendent's cousin, Sir John Johnson, had remained in Tryon County. Despite his assurances to the Whigs that he would not take offensive action, it is clear that by the end of 1775 he was planning to raise a force of five hundred Indians and a body of loyalists on the Mohawk frontier. See Governor William Tryon to Dartmouth, Jan. 5, 1776, in O'Callaghan, ed., *New York Colonial Documents,* VIII, 651. The Whig militia disarmed his retainers, however, and with John Butler and other loyalists, Sir John fled to Canada.

31. On this episode see the *Virginia Magazine of History and Biography,* XIV (July, 1906), 56–58; Percy B. Caley, "Dunmore, Colonial Governor, New York and Virginia, 1770–1782," unpublished Ph.D. dissertation, University of Pittsburgh, 1940, pp. 569–76; Percy B. Caley, "The Life Adventures of Lieutenant-Colonel John Connolly: The Story of a Tory," *Western Pennsylvania Historical Magazine,* XI (April, 1928), 101–6; and Isaac S. Harrell, *Loyalism in Virginia* (Durham, N.C., 1926), p. 35. Connolly obtained a memorial from three hundred frontier leaders which he claimed contained their support of the royal cause. But the document he later submitted to Gage merely indicated the approval of the frontiersmen of Dunmore's policy of protecting the frontier against the Indians which had been criticized by some Virginians. At best, these frontier leaders were noncommittal in this memorial concerning the course they would adopt in the dispute with Great Britain. The address is enclosed in Dunmore to Gage, Aug. 22, 1775, Gage Papers.

306 JACK M. SOSIN

32. Connolly to Gibson, Aug. 9, 1775, and the enclosed message to Captain White Eyes, in Samuel Hazard, ed., *Pennsylvania Archives,* 1st series (13 vols., Harrisburg, 1852–6), IV, 683–84.

33. Dunmore to Gage, n.d. [Aug. 22, 1775?] but endorsed as received on Sept. 5, 1775, Gage Papers.

34. Connolly's "Proposals . . . ," Sept. 11, 1775, *ibid.*

35. See "His Excellency General Gage's answer to Major Connolly's proposal," Sept. 11, 1775; Gage to Dunmore, Sept. 11, 1775; Gage to Lernoult, Sept. 10, 1775; Gage to Carleton, Sept. 11, 1775; and Gage to Captain Hugh Lord (at Kaskaskia), Sept. 12, 1775, *ibid.*

36. Caley, "Dunmore," p. 147; and Clarence M. Burton, "John Connolly, A Tory of the Revolution," American Antiquarian Society, *Proceedings for 1909,* new series, XX (Oct., 1909), 86–87.

37. Drayton's talk to the Cherokee, Aug. 21, 1775, Clinton Papers; and Drayton's speech of Sept. 25, 1775, Ayer Collection, Newberry Library, Chicago.

38. John Stuart to Gage, July 20, 1775, Gage Papers.

39. Alexander Cameron to John Stuart, Nov. 8, 1775; and Cameron to Stuart, July 21, 1775, Clinton Papers.

40. John Stuart to the South Carolina Committee of Safety, July 18, 1775, enclosed in Stuart to Gage, July 20, 1775, Gage Papers. See also Stuart to Gage, May 26, and July 9, 1775, Gage Papers.

41. Gage to John Stuart, Sept. 12, 1775, *ibid.* (copy in Clinton Papers).

42. John Stuart to Clinton, March 15, 1776, Clinton Papers. See also Stuart to Gage, Oct. 3, 1775, in Force, ed., *American Archives,* 4th series, IV, 316.

43. See Mulcaster's plan for an expedition, 1776; Browne to John Stuart, Feb. 24, 1776; Clinton's memorandum for a conversation with Stuart and Mulcaster, April 16, 1776; Stuart to Clinton, May 9, 1776, Clinton Papers.

44. John Stuart to Lord George Germain, May 20, 1776, in William L. Saunders, ed., *Colonial Records of North Carolina* (10 vols., Raleigh, 1888–90), X, 607–8.

45. David Taitt to Tonyn, May 3, May 8, 1776; Tonyn to Taitt, April 20, 1776; Browne to Tonyn, May 2, May 8, 1776, enclosures to Tonyn to Clinton, June 8, 1776, Clinton Papers. See also Tonyn to Clinton, May 21, 1776, Clinton Papers.

46. Browne to Tonyn, Feb. 27, 1776, enclosed in Tonyn to Clinton, May 21, 1776, *ibid.*

47. Henry Stuart's account, Aug. 25, 1776, in Saunders, ed., *North Carolina Colonial Records,* X, 771.

48. For the activities of Henry Stuart and Cameron prior to and during the Cherokee attack see Hamer, "The Wataugans and the Cherokee Indians in 1776," pp. 114–23; Hamer, "John Stuart's Indian Policy during the early months of the American Revolution," pp. 363–66, Brown, *Old Frontiers,* pp. 140–1; and Shaw, *British Administration of the Southern Indians,* p. 100.

49. Henry Stuart's account, Aug. 25, 1776, *North Carolina Colonial Records,* X, 771–85. The following month in Pensacola, Attakullakulla confirmed the influence of the delegates from the northern tribes in precipitating the Cherokee attack and also the decision of the Indians not to raid beyond the white boundary line. Governor Peter Chester of West Florida to Howe, Aug. 30, 1776, British Army Headquarters Papers, no. 261.

50. Entry for June 6, 1776, Salem Diary, in Adelaide L. Fries, ed., *Records of the Moravians in North Carolina* (7 vols., Raleigh, 1922–47), III, 1065.

51. *The Narrative of Colonel David Fanning (A Tory in the Revolutionary War with Great Britain) Giving an Account of His Adventures in North Carolina from 1775 to 1783 As Written by Himself* (Richmond, Va., 1861, reprinted by Joseph Sabin, New York, 1865), p. 4.

52. Tonyn to Clinton, June 8, 1776, Clinton Papers; and Governor Chester to Howe, Nov. 21, 1776, British Army Headquarters Papers, no. 330. Howe, the commander-in-chief, did concur that summer in the request of Tonyn to use Indians in the defence of East Florida or an invasion of the Indian country by the rebels. Howe to Tonyn, Aug. 25, 1776, British Army Headquarters Papers, no. 259.

53. Germain to Stuart, Sept. 5, 1776, British Army Headquarters Papers, no. 263; and Germain to Burgoyne, Aug. 23, 1776, Germain Papers.

54. Guy Johnson to Germain, Nov. 25, 1776, in Force, ed., *American Archives,* 5th series, III, 839; and Howe to Germain, June 7, 1776, Germain Papers. Brant arrived in Niagara in December, 1776, and from there circulated messages to the Canadian and Lake tribes to induce them to help free the Mohawks held hostages by the Whigs of New York. He promised them that "You may depend on having your own way of making war." Brant's message dated Dec. 26, 1776, Haldimand Papers, Vol. 39, pp. 360–1. Carleton, learning of Brant's plan and disapproving strongly of indiscriminate war by the Indians, ordered Lernoult and John Butler at Niagara to divert the savages from Brant. See Carleton to Lernoult and Butler, Feb. 9, 1777, Haldimand Papers, vol. 39, pp. 356–57, 358–59.

55.   The Ohio tribes had raided in Kentucky that year, but the British had not instigated these attacks. Randolph C. Downes, *Council Fires on the Upper Ohio: A Narrative of Indian Affairs in the Upper Ohio Valley until 1795* (Pittsburgh, 1940), 190.

56.   Schuyler to John Hancock, Dec. 14, 1775, in Force, ed., *American Archives,* 4th series, IV, 260; and entries for Dec. 22, 23, 1775, "Diary of Richard Smith in the Continental Congress, 1775–1776," *American Historical Review,* I (Jan., 1896), 298–99.

57.   Washington to Schuyler, Jan. 27, 1776, in Force, ed., *American Archives,* 4th series, IV, 872–73. As a result of the efforts of the rebel committees in Maine, six hundred warriors of the St. John and Micmac tribes were raised later that year. Both sides claimed the other had initiated overtures to the eastern Indians. See Kidder, *Military Operations in Maine,* pp. 55–56, 62–65; Maine Historical Society, *Collections,* 2nd series, XXIV, 190–91; and Governor Michael Francklin of Nova Scotia to Clinton, Aug. 2, 1779, British Army Headquarters Papers, no. 2158.

58.   *Journals of the Continental Congress,* IV, 394–96.

59.   See Hamilton's narrative, April 9, 1782, Shelburne Papers, 66:78–79.

60.   Hamilton to Germain, Sept. 2, 1776, Colonial Office Records, vol. 12, pp. 218–19, 221 (extract in Germain Papers).

61.   "Thoughts for conducting the War, from the Side of Canada," Burgoyne to Germain, Feb. 20, 1777, Shelburne Papers, 66:131; Germain to John Stuart, Feb. 7, 1777, Germain Papers; Germain to Stuart, April 2, 1777, British Army Headquarters Papers, no. 472; and Germain to Carleton, March 26, 1777, Germain Papers.

62.   Governor William Tryon of New York to William Knox, April 21, 1777, in O'Callaghan, ed., *New York Colonial Documents,* VIII, 707.

63.   Browne to Carleton, Oct. 9, 1782, British Army Headquarters Papers, no. 5822; Hamilton's narrative, April 9, 1782, Shelburne Papers, 66:179; Graham to Carleton, Oct. 20, 1782, British Army Headquarters Papers, no. 5936; and Abbott to Carleton, June 8, 1778, Haldimand Papers, vol. 122, p. 50.

64.   Willett to Schuyler, April 29, 1778, Ayer Collection.

The Southern Indians in the War for American Independence, 1775–1783

James H. O'Donnell, III*

As Jack M. Sosin pointed out in the previous article, both sides sought Indian support in the Revolutionary War. For the Indians the choices were difficult and the consequences were often devastating. In "The Southern Indians in the War for American Independence," James H. O'Donnell, III, argues that the reason for their dilemma centered on the incessant colonial demand for land and the consequent fear of rebel victory. By the end of the war their fears proved correct, and no matter what the individual southern tribes did during the war, the rebels indiscriminately regarded "the southern Indians as the defeated allies of the British, who, as conquered enemies should give up the spoils of war, in this case land." As a result, many Indians lost their land and were forced to move. O'Donnell is a member of the History Department at Marietta College; he has published Southern Indians in the American Revolution, *and articles in the* Georgia Historical Quarterly *and in the* Journal of Southern History.

AT THE OUTBREAK OF THE War for American Independence, the Indian tribes living along the western frontiers of the colonies had reason to be concerned. In the ten years before the

*James H. O'Donnell, III, "The Southern Indians in the War for American Independence, 1775–1783," in *Four Centuries of Southern Indians,* edited by Charles M. Hudson (Athens: University of Georgia Press, 1975), pp. 46–64. Reprinted by permission.

Revolution, schemes by frontiersmen and speculators for grab-
bing Indian lands had been rampant. War now might mean more
demands for land, particularly if the colonials emerged victori-
ous, for their land hunger seemingly could not be satisfied.
While the tribal leaders in the past preferred to play off one
proponent of war against another for the good of the tribe, care
now had to be taken, for there was the simple and basic matter
that their lands and lives were at stake. Since choosing sides
was indeed a calculated risk, most tribes waited and watched for
more than a year after the war began.

It was in the South that the warriors struck first. By the spring
of 1776 the Cherokees were faced with the unhappy predicament of the continued encroachment by settlers on lands too
close to their villages. Cherokee leaders had hoped that the sale
to the Transylvania speculators in 1775 would give them breath-
ing room for a time, but the settlers could not be satisfied. In
the western stretches of the Carolinas and Georgia the frontiersmen pushed up the rivers into the Cherokee lands, ignoring
threats from the tribe and warnings from royal officials. West of
the mountains the Overhill Cherokees enjoyed no sanctuary because of their transmontane location. Moving south along the
valleys and west through gaps, settlers had entered Eastern Tennessee, again in defiance of threat of violent death and legal
sanctions.[1]

Since the Overhill Cherokees held a traditional place of
leadership in the tribe, their reactions both to the pressure on
their lands and to the war would be watched by the tribesmen at
large as well as by the colonials. Indeed when the Overhills
considered their own accumulated grievances with the colonies
as well as the rebellion against the king, it seemed logical that
they should be actively pro-British. But their friend John Stuart,
the British Indian superintendent in the South, thought otherwise, for he wanted the Cherokees to remain inactive until they
could be used as auxiliaries in conjunction with troops. He was
afraid that they would kill rebel and Loyalist alike. His policy in
1775–1776 then was to keep the southern tribes loyal and
ready to act when called upon.[2] But the Cherokees were impa-

tient, angry, and aggravated in the extreme. The long history of abuses by the Virginians (as all southern frontiersmen were called) alone justified action, but if that were not enough, they were displeased that the colonials had abused John Stuart and Alexander Cameron, the principal Cherokee deputy in the Indian department, and, worse yet, the Americans had reduced the trade to a mere trickle of goods.

In large measure the dilemma faced by the southern tribes in 1775–1776 is more than epitomized in the predicament of the Cherokees who seemed damned if they did and damned if they did not. If they did try to drive the settlers out of the mountains, they would risk both the anger of Stuart and the retaliation of the Americans, while if they did not strike, the Americans would continue advancing. The councils of the Cherokees were long and troubled in the winter of 1775–1776. A group of young men under the leadership of Dragging Canoe (who had gained some fame already at the Transylvania purchase by warning that the land would prove "dark and bloody") insisted that tribal leadership was lacking, that the principal chiefs had grown "too old to hunt," and that the young men should lead the nation to honor by driving out the settlers. By April of 1776 the council fires burned almost constantly. To the beloved town of Chota journeyed the leaders of the towns, including Dragging Canoe and his followers, the British agent Alexander Cameron, and, as the superintendent's personal representative, his brother Henry Stuart, who arrived in April with fifteen hundred pounds of powder.[3]

Dragging Canoe urged war; the Raven, the Great Warrior, and the Little Carpenter proposed patience, discussion, and deliberation; the Englishmen requested patient vigilance. But the war faction became so persuasive that finally Cameron and Stuart despaired and sought a chance to mediate with the settlers in the hope that they could forestall war. Their position, although they could hardly state it publicly, was that action in the spring before British troops arrived below the Chesapeake held little hope of success, for both frontier and tidewater would be alarmed, and Indian attacks would thereby profit the Patriots who could scream "villainy" and persuade the undecided that the American cause was more noble. The two agents did not reckon with frontier guile, however, for when their letters warning of impending attack if the settlers did not withdraw were received, the frontiersmen redrafted these and recast them as warnings for the king's friends only.[4] The Cherokees were infuriated by this treachery and by the obvious fact that the frontiersmen were making no preparations to move but were gathering the people into the blockhouses. As a result the war faction completely prevailed and were much pleased therefore when a group of northern tribesmen appeared in early May to report that they also were preparing for war.[5]

During May the Cherokees laid their plans; in June they took action. First the Lower Town warriors advanced, carrying axe and torch into the backcountry of South Carolina and Georgia. Within a month the North Carolina settlements as well as the outposts at Watauga and Holston had been attacked.

The most immediate effect of the Cherokee attacks was to arouse the frontier, sending a thrill of alarm across the four southern colonies. For the Cherokees there was satisfaction that the encroachments of the frontier folk had stopped for a time. Many families had retreated to safer districts. But quickly Patriot militia captains mustered their forces, state governments cried out against British treachery, and plans were laid for punitive expeditions. In South Carolina the alarm was more strident because Charleston was under British attack. To the minds of colonials accustomed to think in terms of British conspiracy, the coincidence of the Indian attacks and the coastal assault seemed all of a piece, a plot launched by the royal military command. It is true that Superintendent Stuart had visited General Clinton at Cape Fear in early May but no arrangements were made. Patriot leaders believed, however, that the plans laid had called for the Cherokee actions in conjunction with the British strike which would then be followed by a Creek attack.[6]

The Creeks, however, were still in a period of uncertainty. The British asked them to stand firm, while, among the Lower Creek towns, American agents led by George Galphin preached neutrality. Also there was Georgia's somewhat confused Indian policy. While on the one hand Sir James Wright, the royal governor, and the Patriot leaders competed with one another, on the other hand they cooperated in Indian affairs, for neither party wanted war with the Creeks.[7] But to the Creeks, most Georgians appeared no different from the other land-hungry colonials. Along the Georgia frontier the settlers schemed to grab the tribal lands, even at times provoking the Creeks in hope of a war for which the frontiersmen could retaliate and gain satisfaction by more demands for land. Thus the Creeks heard assurances from the British that all would be well if they supported the king, blandishments from the Americans urging neutrality, and at the same time threats from colonials eager for land.

While the tribal leaders had reason for resentment, nevertheless the cabins of the settlers had not pushed so far into Creek territory as onto Cherokee lands. Other problems also stood in the way of Creek assistance to the British. For a number of years there had been a war with the Choctaws, a war which the British supplied and at times fomented on the ancient principle of divide and conquer. But if the British now wished their assistance or that of the Choctaws, British policy would have to change. Early on, then, the Creeks urged that peace be made between the two tribes. In addition to the Choctaw problem the Creeks worried over supplies for their warriors and also about reports circulated that a detachment of British troops would be moved through the Creek country against the South Carolina frontier. Supplies they would welcome in their villages, soldiers they would not.[8]

Having no immediate and pressing reason to attack the colonials as did the Cherokees, the Creeks had adopted a wait-and-see attitude through the first six months of 1776. Then came word of the Cherokee attacks and requests for aid from their brethren. Reluctant still the Creeks asked the advice of John Stuart, who as of August was still advising neutrality. Then the superintendent got firsthand reports that the Cherokees had to be supported or they would be crushed by the Patriots. Accordingly he asked the Creeks to move against the frontier, but the Creeks by then knew more of what was happening in the Cherokee country than did Stuart or his deputies.[9] The refugees from the Cherokee towns had come with tales of destruction by the Patriot armies.

What drove the Cherokees south were the expeditions organized by the four southern states. Within two weeks after the first Cherokee attack against South Carolina the militia was being rallied, although everything in the state was rather confused because of the double alarm in what appeared to be simultaneous attacks from east and west. It was therefore some weeks before the Cherokee Lower Towns were attacked, but when the troops from South Carolina came they struck with a vengeance, levelling most of those villages.[10]

In the meantime North Carolina forces had marched to the frontier where they waited for supplies and then crossed into the mountains headed for the Cherokee Middle settlements.[11] Most of the Cherokees wisely had melted away into the mountains, leaving behind empty villages which the Americans put to the torch. Beyond the mountains the Overhills were still untouched but there was a Virginia expedition gathering. In the Overhill towns there was much discussion over the proper course of action. Dragging Canoe wanted to lie in wait for the Patriots at an advantageous spot, perhaps at a river crossing, and give battle. But the chiefs who argued for strategic withdrawal and application for a truce prevailed. No band of fifteen hundred warriors, however courageous, could stand the fire of five or six thousand Americans.[12]

Early in October the Virginians crossed the Holston and marched toward the heart of the Overhill country and the beloved town of Chota. After the Virginia army crossed the French Broad they met messengers who came in under a sign of truce asking for a cease-fire. By November a truce was granted, but this was too late to save many villages and the thousands of bushels of corn and potatoes cached for winter provisions.[13]

Now the Cherokees faced a bleak winter and a dismal spring. From north, east, and south their enemies had come to lay waste to their towns, and as the tribal leaders guessed, the treaty conferences proposed for the spring would mean demands for more land, a prospect not pleasing to the Cherokees. In May of 1777 the Lower and Middle town representatives journeyed to Dewitt's Corner, South Carolina, where they agreed to peace and of course a land cession. Two months later at the Long Island of the Holston River the Overhill Cherokee reached a similar settlement. The first of a long series of penalties forced on the Cherokees by the new nation was now being exacted.[14]

The fate of the Cherokees was a lesson not lost on the Creeks. Through the winter of 1776–1777 they had exchanged messages with John Stuart about attacking the Georgia and South Carolina frontier, but they committed themselves only on the condition of constant assistance in the form of supplies from Stuart and the mediation of a peace with the Choctaws.[15]

The Choctaws, alas, had problems enough that the Creeks need not fear warfare. In the spring of 1777 visitors to the Choctaw villages found a woeful scene. Excessive drinking was decimating the nation, for rum literally flowed into every town. The sober chiefs cried out for relief, for rum came in not only by the bottle but also by the keg and barrel. The British traders from Pensacola and Mobile kept the Choctaws in a state of intoxication. By one account women sat weeping over the unconscious forms of their husbands lying in the streets. Charles Stuart said the passion for rum was alcoholic: "It [rum] is like a woman—when a man wanted her and saw her—He must have her!"[16]

As much as anything else then, if the British wished the help of the Choctaws they had to try to plug the cask. This would have to be taken up at the meeting of the Choctaws and the Chickasaws scheduled for Mobile in May of 1777. Even then care would have to be taken for on such occasions it was expected that some rum would be distributed. In Mobile the superintendent heard the Choctaws promise peace and assistance for the Mississippi river patrol, but their strongest words, indeed their pleas, were requests that the rum be curtailed. John Stuart assured the Choctaws of his good intentions, but when he returned to Pensacola he found that the royal governor, Peter

Chester, listened to traders more than to the superintendent, so
the rum continued to flow.[17]

As a result of the Mobile conference the Creek-Choctaw War
was brought to a close. Choctaw parties could now aid in scout-
ing the Mississippi River for American expeditions, while the
Creeks could prepare for an assault against the colonies. Many
of the Creeks in the meantime had been persuaded to move east
against the settlements once the crops were gathered. One part
of the tribe, however, was meeting with the Patriots in the
summer of 1777. They were urged to drive the British Creek
deputy, David Taitt, and Alexander Cameron, temporarily in
the Creek country, out of the Creek towns. Upon leaving the
Americans, a group of these Lower Creeks, filled with "rum
and good words" moved west with the intention not just of
driving Taitt and Cameron away but of killing them. But if the
rum made them daring it also made them talkative, and Alexander McGillivray, the assistant British commissary in the
Upper Creek towns, learned of the plot and warned Taitt and
Cameron. When the two Englishmen eluded them, the Lower
Creeks chased the pro-British traders out so that by December
of 1777 the Creek towns were empty of British representatives
and traders.[18]

During the winter of 1777–1778 a major policy change in
overall war strategy was undertaken by the British command, a
change which would directly involve the southern Indians.[19]
Foiled in their plans to stamp out rebellion by isolating New
England, the British leaders decided to move the major theater
of operations south of the Chesapeake, where the Indians and
Loyalists could be of aid in restoring the colonies. According to
the official orders issued from London in March, the southern
Indian warriors were to be brought to the frontier of Georgia
and South Carolina where they could strike at the same time that
a British expedition attacked Savannah.

Accordingly the Cherokees and the Creeks were approached
by officials of the British Indian department and were asked to
prepare for war. Unfortunately the Creeks were finding it difficult to unite because of the strong pro-American faction among

the Lower Creeks plus the fact that the governor of East Florida regarded the Seminole Creeks as his personal troops, an attitude which infuriated John Stuart.[20] Thus Stuart could count on only the Upper Creeks where he had the assistance of David Taitt and the rising influence of Alexander McGillivray, the assistant commissary, whose blood connections in the tribe made him politically powerful.

The Cherokees on the other hand continued to make pledges of affection but they had not yet recovered from the war of 1776 or the treaties of 1777.[21] Goods promised had not been delivered, the boundary agreed upon had not been surveyed, and the frontiersmen still took up tribal lands at will. The Cherokee simply were not ready to make war in 1778.

When the British invasion of Georgia came in late 1778 one of the first moves made by the British was to send a column inland toward Augusta to meet the Indians under John Stuart and to rally the Loyalists.[22] When the British reached Augusta the commander was dismayed. Where were the numerous friends of the king so long described by the exiles as being in the majority in the backcountry? Few Loyalists emerged and no Indians were to be seen. In a rage the British officer led his men away toward Savannah.

Indeed where were the forest warriors and their British friends at the time the column was in Augusta? They were busy with life as usual, waiting for the word to come from Stuart. The failure was not of design or intention but a matter of communication. Messages to inform John Stuart were not sent until after the British landing so that it was late January before the word reached Pensacola. As soon as the dispatches came, Stuart sent word to the Creeks, but even so it was early March before about four hundred Creek warriors and fifty departmental officials and Loyalist traders reached the Ogeechee to wait for the expected British force. They were two months too late. Soon troops did approach but they were American, not British. The Creek leaders protested that they had no intention of doing battle without the aid of the king's troops. The majority of the Creeks thus went home, while a few joined Alexander McGillivray in slipping through the Patriot lines to reach the British at Savannah. There they served as raiders for some weeks before returning home.[23]

If the Creeks were frustrated in their attempts to help crush the colonial rebellion so were the other tribes in the South.[24] Some Choctaw had patrolled the Mississippi, but when they relaxed their watch early in 1778 a party of Americans slipped past to raid the settlements at Natchez and Manchac and reach New Orleans. In the Cherokee country the failure of the tribe to aid the British aroused bitter feelings within the tribe. For this and other reasons Dragging Canoe and his followers emigrated southward to establish new towns which would come to be known as the Chickamauga Cherokee villages. In those villages the British agents moved freely and in the winter of 1778–1779 the Chickamaugas were persuaded to prepare for action with the coming of spring. When the warriors moved away in April a raiding party from the Virginia overmountain settlements came south and destroyed their towns. After rebuilding their dwellings, the Chickamaugas went back toward the frontier only to be met by a large force of South Carolinians who chased them back once more.

The years 1778 and 1779 were not fruitful for the southern tribes in their efforts to aid the British in crushing the colonial rebellion. Disappointed also were John Stuart and certain members of Parliament, particularly those among the opposition to the war, who questioned spending thousands of pounds sterling on Indian affairs without visible results.[25]

But for John Stuart the frustrations and labors of public office came to an end in March 1779, when he died in Pensacola after a tedious and painful illness.[26] The southern Indians had reason to mourn, for they had lost a powerful advocate and a man who grasped something of the predicament in which the tribes were placed as the colonials pressed against them. With Stuart gone there was no one who could argue effectively with the officials in London over treatment of the tribes. Although Stuart was perhaps never so influential as Sir William Johnson in the North, he did have the respect of the southern Indians.

In addition to the changes which would come in Indian affairs as a result of Stuart's death, there were also the shifts taking place in the military conflict. After 1779 the Spanish moved against British outposts on the Mississippi and the Gulf, which made it imperative to call on the Creeks, Chickasaws, and Choctaws.[27]

In 1780 Mobile fell but Pensacola held out until a relief fleet came, a success credited in part to the presence of nearly two thousand Creek warriors led by Alexander McGillivray and William McIntosh. When the Spanish expedition arrived, the Spanish commander was unhappy about the odds and sought to reduce them by accusing the British of using uncivilized barbarians in warfare against the army of a Christian prince. The British commander informed his adversary that he would defend his post with whatever means at his disposal. On that occasion the Spanish chose to wait and when a British relief fleet appeared, the dons withdrew. In letters to Alexander McGillivray, Brig. Gen. John Campbell, the commandant at Pensacola, was fulsome in thanking the Creeks for their aid, crediting them with saving the post.[28]

While the Creeks served at Pensacola, some Cherokees had gone to the assistance of the British outpost at Augusta.[29] The commander there was Thomas Brown, a Loyalist from South Carolina who had fled to East Florida, joined the East Florida Rangers, gotten into the good graces of Gov. Patrick Tonyn, and now was not only the commander of the British outpost at Augusta but also the superintendent of the newly created Atlantic Division of the Southern Indian Department. (This division had been decided upon after the death of Stuart, with Brown given the Atlantic Division and Alexander Cameron, to his great dismay, the Mississippi Division.) The Patriots had been drawn to Augusta in part by the supplies cached there for conferences with the Cherokees and Creeks. After some weeks of siege a British rescue force arrived and the Americans had to withdraw.

The Cherokees who fought with the superintendent at Augusta reflected the tribe's first steps at renewing their support of the British against the Americans. Four years had passed since the conflict of 1776, and the painful memories had dimmed. In addition the British had succeeded in recovering Georgia and South Carolina, and so the Cherokees reasoned that the presence of royal troops in the South would give them protection. Of course the encroachment of their land by the frontiersmen had never stopped. The warriors who came home from Augusta loaded with goods and covered in glory now urged their comrades to act upon Thomas Brown's request that the tribe attack the frontiers once again.

There were however few secrets in the Cherokee country. Patriot traders soon passed word of the proposed raids and when some warriors started out against the South Carolina frontier in the fall of 1780 their action provided an excuse for the frontiersmen to strike. Down the Holston came the Patriots raiding and burning villages. Although the destruction was by no means as systematic as it had been in 1776, a number of towns were burned including the principal Overhill town of Chota.[30]

It was evident from these raids to many Cherokee leaders that their towns now lay so close to the frontiersmen and so open to punitive expeditions that the course of accommodation was the most sensible. Reports of these intentions reached the Virginia frontier early in 1781. Accordingly, one of the frontier leaders suggested that the commander of the Continental forces in the South, Gen. Nathaniel Greene, use this opportunity to seek some permanent settlement with the tribe, for by Patriot definition the Cherokees had broken the treaty of 1777 and by Cherokee definition the treaty had never been fulfilled.[31] A new treaty would give the Cherokees temporary security against renewed warfare and give the frontiersmen freedom to oppose the British army in the South. Of course the Cherokees were not willing to give up all hope of British aid so that at the same time that the word went to the Virginia frontier, talks promised the aid of the tribe to the British in any new offensive. Cherokee motives seem clear. They were unwilling to see the door closed to cooperation with the British if for some reason Patriot resistance collapsed and British control was restored.[32]

There seemed little likelihood, however, that the British would recover the colonies. Everywhere in the South British arms were pressed by their adversaries. In the Southwest the Spanish had taken Mobile, attacked Pensacola once, and were preparing for a second and successful siege. The Choctaws and Creeks had become disgusted with the inconsistent policy of General Campbell and would no longer rally at his call. Like the proverbial shepherd Campbell found that when his enemy did actually materialize there were very few Choctaws and Creeks present. With the fall of Pensacola the Gulf coast was closed to British communication with the Creeks, Choctaws, and Chickasaws.[33]

Now the messengers would have to move overland along the old trading paths to Augusta where Thomas Brown was located and where Alexander Cameron headed after the fall of Pensacola. But soon this post was no longer in British hands either, for the Patriots overwhelmed Augusta in the spring of 1781 and the British were soon reduced to the environs of Charleston and Savannah.[34] Even then the southern tribes tried to get through to the British. In the course of one such cross-country expedition, the principal warrior of the Upper Creeks, Emistisiguo, was killed, leaving a power vacuum that would be filled by Alexander McGillivray, now fully committed to life with his mother's people.[35]

By the end of 1781 the southern tribes were faced with hard choices. They remained essentially where they were at the beginning of the war though they had lost some lands by cession during the war. Their British allies had been driven away from the Gulf and now held two enclaves on the southern coast (plus of course East Florida). Commmunication with either Charleston or Savannah became impossible so that tribal representatives would have to travel the paths to Saint Augustine if they chose to remain loyal to the British.

On the other hand there was the option of making peace with the Americans, the choice eventually taken by the Cherokees and the Chickasaws.[36] The Choctaws wavered, but the Creeks remained firm. Then in 1782 they were slapped with the news that the British were evacuating the Floridas. Some chiefs would not believe it: they protested that it was a Virginia lie;

others demanded to be taken along in the British ships. Eventually they faced the hard reality, and led by Alexander McGillivray the tribe sought a marriage of convenience with the Spanish.[37]

No matter what each tribe chose at war's end, they all faced the same American demand. The Patriots looked upon the southern Indians as the defeated allies of the British, who, as conquered enemies should give up the spoils of war, in this case land. The Patriot attitude is summed up well in the outlook of the North Carolina legislature, which seems to have been struck by an epidemic of land fever. By rights, said the North Carolinians, we now own *all* the Cherokee lands, but out of our generosity the Cherokees may live on them until we can provide a reservation for the tribe.[38]

The policy and attitude assumed by the states during and just after the war thus becomes the basis for federal policy and attitude to a large degree. The defeated enemy should never be allowed to forget, their land should become part of the public domain. The demand for Indian land, indeed, would never cease. If the American Revolution was a time of national beginnings in politics and society, it was equally so in Indian policy, for with the nation's beginnings emerged the ideas of displacement and removal, ideas which came to fruition in the nineteenth century and have not died in the present century.

Notes

1.   Thomas P. Abernethy, *From Frontier to Plantation in Tennessee,* (Memphis, Tenn.: Memphis State Press, 1955), chap. 9 and 12; Louis De-Vorsey, Jr., *The Indian Boundary in the Southern Colonies, 1763–1775* (Chael Hill: University of North Carolina Press, 1966), chap. 2; and Jack M. Sosin, *The Revolutionary Frontier, 1763–1783* (New York: Holt, Rinehart and Winston, 1967), chap. 4 and 5.

2.   Philip M. Hamer, "John Stuart's Indian Policy during the Early Months of the American Revolution," *Mississippi Valley Historical Review* 17 (1930–1931): 351–366; *idem,* "The Wataugans and the Cherokee Indians in 1776," *East Tennessee Historical Society Publications* 3 (1931): 108–126.

3. Henry Stuart to John Stuart, 7 May 1776, British Public Record Office, Colonial Office Papers, series 5 (Film from the Library of Congress), 77: 145; same to the same, August 1776, in William L. Sauders, ed., *The Colonial Records of North Carolina,* 14 vols. (Raleigh; 1886–1890), 10: 763–785. The British Public Record Office papers are hereafter cited CO5, vol.: page.

4. Henry Stuart and Alexander Cameron to the Wataugans, 7 May 1776, CO5, 77: 143; John Carter to Cameron and Stuart, 13 May 1776, *ibid.,* p. 149; Saunders, Report of Isaac Thomas, n.d., *Colonial Records,* 10: 769; and Henry Stuart to Edward Wilkinson, 28 June 1776, CO5, 77: 156.

5. Henry Stuart to John Stuart, August 1776, CO5, 77: 145ff.

6. John Stuart to Henry Clinton, 9 May 1776, CO5, 77: 111; Frederick Mulcaster to Clinton, 16 April 1776, Clinton Papers, William L. Clements Library, University of Michigan; John Stuart to Henry Clinton, 8 May 1776, Clinton Papers, Clements Library. For contemporary opinion in South Carolina about the existence of a plot see Henry Laurens to John Laurens, 14 August 1776, in Henry Laurens, *A South Carolina Protest against Slavery* (New York, 1861), pp. 26–27, and in David Ramsay, *The Revolution of South Carolina from a British Province to an Independent State,* 2 vols. (Trenton, N.J., 1785), 1: 334–335.

7. Sir James Wright to Lord Dartmouth, 20 June 1775, in G. W. J. De-Renne, ed., "Letters from Governor Sir James Wright to the Earl of Dartmouth and Lord George Germain. Secretaries of State for America, from August 24, 1774, to February 17, 1782," *Collections of the Georgia Historical Society* 3 (1873): 189–190; Council held at the Governor's House, 31 October 1775, in Lilla M. Hawes, "Proceedings and Minutes of the Governor and Council of Georgia, October 4, 1774, through November 7, 1775, and September 6, 1779, through September 20, 1780," *Georgia Historical Quarterly* 34 (1950): 208–226, 288–312; *ibid.,* 35 (1951): 31–59, 126–151, 196–221. Information on Creek affairs before 1775 may be found in David Corkran, *The Creek Frontier, 1540–1783* (Norman: University of Oklahoma Press, 1967).

8. David Taitt to John Stuart, 1 August 1775, CO5, 76: 177; talk of John Stuart to the Creeks, 15 August 1775, CO5, 76: 181.

9. Talk of Emistisiguo to John Stuart, 19 November 1776, CO5, 78: 81; John Stuart to Lord George Germain, 24 November 1776, CO5, 78: 72.

10. Journal of an Expedition in 1776 against the Cherokees under the Command of Captain Peter Clinton, Lyman C. Draper Collections, Wisconsin State Historical Society (microfilm), Thomas Sumter Papers, 3: 164–175; Andrew Williamson to Griffith Rutherford, 14 August 1776, Saunders, *Colonial Records,* 10: 745–748; same to William H. Drayton, 22 August 1776, in R. W. Gibbes, ed., *Documentary History of the American Revolution, 1774–1782,* 3 vols. (New York, 1853–1857), 2: 32.

11. Griffith Rutherford to the North Carolina Council, 1 September 1776, Saunders, *Colonial Records*, 10: 788–789; William Lenoir, "Journal of the Cherokee Expedition, 1776," *Journal of Southern History* 6 (1940): 247– 249.

12. William Christian to Patrick Henry, 27 October 1776, "Revolutionary Correspondence," *Virginia Magazine of History and Biography* 17 (1908): 61–64, 170–173.

13. *Ibid.;* Captain Joseph Martin's Orderly Book of the Cherokee Expedition, Draper Collections, Virginia Papers, 8: 72–73; *Virginia Gazette* (Purdie's), 29 November 1776, p. 2.

14. Proceedings of the Virginia Commissioners with the Cherokee, April 1777, Draper Collections, Preston Papers, 4: 122–149; Treaty of Dewitt's Corner, John Steele Papers, 1777–1779, Southern Historical Collections, University of North Carolina; Archibald Henderson, "The Treaty of Long Island of Holston," *North Carolina Historical Review* 8 (1931): 55–116.

15. John Stuart to George Germain, 10 March 1777, CO5, 78: 105.

16. Charles Stuart to John Stuart, 4 March 1777, CO5, 78: 126; Charles Stuart's Report of his visit to the Choctaw Country, 1 July 1778, CO5, 79: 196–202.

17. John Stuart to Germain, 14 June 1777, CO5, 78: 143; William Howe to Stuart, 12 July 1777, CO5, 94: 401; Meeting of Chester, Stiell, and Stuart (concerning trade and rum), 10 April 1777, CO5, 78: 157.

18. Alexander McGillivray to John Stuart, 21 September 1777, CO5, 79: 33; John Stuart to George Germain, 6 October 1777, *ibid.*, p. 29.

19. George Germain to Henry Clinton, 8 March 1778, in Benjamin F. Stevens, ed., *Facsimiles of Manuscripts in European Archives Relating to America, 1773–1783*, 25 vols. (London, 1890), 11; no. 1062; same to Stuart, 5 November 1777, CO5, 78: 180; and Paul H. Smith, *Loyalists and Redcoats: A Study in British Revolutionary Policy* (Chapel Hill, N.C.: Institute of Early American History and Culture, 1964), chap. 6.

20. Patrick Tonyn to Henry Clinton, 8 June 1776, CO5, 556: 683–688; same to Germain, 29 April 1778, CO5, 558: 279; John Stuart to Tonyn, to July 1778, *ibid.*, p. 451; same to Germain, 23 February 1777, *ibid.*, pp. 19– 22, and same to the same, 19 May 1778, *ibid.*, p. 160.

21. Talks from the Cherokee to LeRoy Hammond and Edward Wilkinson, 26 September 1778, Laurens Papers, Bundle 46, South Carolina Historical Society.

22. Augustin Prevost to David Taitt, 14 March 1779, CO5, 80: 246; Archibald Campbell to the Creeks (1779), Clinton Papers, William L. Clements Library.

23. John Stuart to David Taitt, 1 February 1779, CO5, 80: 158; Taitt to Germain, 6 August 1779, *ibid.*, p. 234; Andrew Williamson to Benjamin Lincoln, 19 January 1779, Andrew Williamson Papers, South Carolina Library, University of South Carolina; James Keef to David Holms, 27 April 1779, CO5, 80: 205.

24. Hardy Perry to Farquhar Bethune, 4 February 1778, CO5, 79: 116; John W. Caughey, "Willing's Raid Down the Mississippi," *Louisiana Historical Quarterly* 15 (1932): 5–36; William Thompson to Cameron, 14 November 1776, CO5, 94: 157; Walter Scott to Cameron, 27 March 1779, CO5, 80: 179; Henry Hamilton to Stuart, 25 December 1778, CO5, 597: pt. 1, 121; Patrick Henry to Richard Caswell, 8 January 1779, Richard Caswell Papers, North Carolina Department of Archives and History; Cameron to Germain, 10 May 1779, CO5, 80: 171; *Gazette of the State of South Carolina,* 24 September 1779, p. 2.

25. John Almon, ed., *The Parliamentary Register; or, History of the Proceedings and Debates of the House of Commons,* 17 vols. (London, 1775–1780), 12: 255, 257, 258ff; Germain to Stuart, 3 March 1779, CO5, 81: 18; Murray S. Downs, "British Parliamentary Opinion and American Independence, 1776–1783," paper given at the Thirteenth Conference on Early American History, Columbia, S.C., March 1962.

26. Alexander Cameron and Charles Stuart to George Germain, 26 March 1779, CO5, 80: 109.

27. John R. Alden, *The American Revolution, 1775–1783* (New York: Harper and Row, 1962).

28. Extract of a letter from William McIntosh, 20 March 1780, CO5, 81: 167; Alexander McGillivray to Thomas Brown, 25 March 1780, *ibid.*, p. 169; same to same, 13 May 1780, *ibid.*, p. 240; John Campbell to Thomas, 15 November 1780, Clinton Papers, William L. Clements Library; same to McGillivray, 22 November 1780, CO5, 82: 451.

29. Charles Shaw to George Germain, 18 September 1780, CO5, 82: 318; *Royal Gazette of South Carolina,* 27 September 1780, *ibid.*, p. 2.

30. Thomas Brown to Cornwallis, 17 December 1780, Clinton Papers, Clements Library; Joseph Martin to Thomas Jefferson, 12 December 1780, Draper Collections, Tennessee Papers, 1: 41; Arthur Campbell to Thomas Jefferson, 15 January 1781, William P. Palmer et al., *Calendar of Virginia State Papers and Other Manuscripts, 1652–1781,* 11 vols. (Richmond, 1875–1893), 1: 434–437. Much to his surprise Colonel Campbell found in a

chief's baggage "which he left behind in his fight, various manuscripts, Copies of Treaties, Letters, and other Archives of the nation, some which shews the double game that people has been carrying on during the present war." Among the papers are included a copy of the King's Proclamation of 1763 and the Great Warrior's certificate of membership in the St. Andrew's Society of Charleston, S.C., dated 30 November 1773. In connection with this unique collection see John R. Alden, "The Eighteenth-Century Cherokee Archives," *American Archivist* 5 (1942): 240–244.

31.   Arthur Campbell to Nathanael Greene, 8 February 1781, Nathanael Greene Letterbook, Library of Congress; same to Jefferson, 27 January 1781, Palmer, *State Papers,* 1: 464–465.

32.   Thomas Brown to Cornwallis, 17 December 1780, Clinton Papers, William L. Clements Library; A Talk from the Cherokee Nation Delivered by the Raven of Chota at Savannah, 1 September 1781, CO5, 82: 287.

33.   Talk of Frenchumastabie, Great Medal chief of the Choctaw, to Alexander Cameron, 1 April 1781, CO5, 82: 210; *Royal Gazette of South Carolina,* 12 May 1781, p. 2; John W. Caughey, *Bernardo de Galvez in Louisiana, 1776–1783* (Berkeley: University of California, 1934), chaps. 11 and 12.

34.   Thomas Brown to Germain, 9 August 1781, CO5, 82: 252; Cameron to Germain, 27 May 1781, *ibid.,* p. 204.

35.   Anthony Wayne to Nathanael Greene, 24 June 1782, Papers of the Continental Congress (National Archives), no. 155, 2: 491–495; James H. O'Donnell III, "Alexander McGillivray: Training for Leadership, 1777–1783," *Georgia Historical Quarterly* 49 (1965): 172–186.

36.   A Talk from us (Poymace Tauhaw, Mingo Homaw, Tuskau Pulasso, and Paymingo) to be delivered by Mr. Simon Burney to the Commanders of every different Station between this Nation and the falls of the Ohio River, 9 July 1782, Draper Collections, Tennessee Papers, 1: 50; A Message sent to the middle Grounds by Charles Beaman a half breed & by a fellow called the Horn to the Vallies (by General Andrew Pickens), 25 September 1782, Force Transcripts, Georgia Records, Library of Congress; A Talk delivered by General Pickens to the Head Men of the Cherokee Nation, 17 October 1782, *ibid.;* A Talk to Colonel Joseph Martin by Old Tassel, 25 September 1782, Saunders, *Colonial Records,* 16: 415–416; William Christian to Benjamin Harrison, 15 December 1782, Palmer, *State Papers,* 3: 398.

37.   John W. Caughey, *McGillivray of the Creeks* (Norman: University of Oklahoma, 1938), pp. 22–26.

38.   Alexander Martin to the Cherokees, 25 May 1783, Saunders, *Colonial Records,* 14: 810; *Laws . . . relating to Indians and Indian affairs, from 1633 to 1831 . . .* (Washington, 1832), pp. 170–171.

Negroes and the
American Revolution

Wallace Brown*

*For blacks as for other Americans, the revolutionary period
was a time of hope and decision. First the British led by Lord
Dunmore and later the rebels offered the black slaves freedom in
return for their support. As Wallace Brown indicates in "Negroes and the American Revolution," blacks "had indeed nothing to lose and everything to gain." Ultimately five thousand
blacks assisted the rebels, and a lesser number joined the British. But both sides feared arming of blacks and placed them
primarily in support services. Many additional thousands of
black slaves ran away during the war to seek their freedom in
Canada, East Florida, or the West Indies. However, at the end
of the Revolution, as Brown reminds us, most blacks "faced a
worse future than at the beginning." Brown teaches history at
the University of New Brunswick; he has published* The King's
Friends, The Good Americans, *and articles in* Nebraska History
and Pennsylvania Magazine of History and Biography.

ON MARCH 5TH, 1770 SOME British soldiers, part of a detachment sent to overawe the refractory port of Boston, were goaded
into firing from outside the Custom House in King Street into a
jeering, violent mob. The result: five Americans lay dead or

*Wallace Brown, "Negroes and the American Revolution," *History Today* 14
(1964), 556–63. Reprinted by permission.

dying. One of them, a runaway ex-slave named Crispus Attucks, who was laid out in state in Faneuil Hall alongside some of his white compatriots, has since gained an inflated reputation in patriot hagiography as the first "martyr" of the "Boston Massacre." But, whatever Attucks' merits, the incident foreshadowed the ticklish question of the role of the Negro that was shortly to face both sides during the Revolutionary war.

The immediate issue was whether to use Negroes in the armed forces. The British, with little to lose, acted first. On November 7th, 1775, Lord Dunmore, Governor of Virginia, proclaimed freedom for all rebels' slaves who would join him, and soon nearly three hundred Negroes, known as "Lord Dunmore's Ethiopian Regiment," with "Liberty to Slaves" inscribed across their chests, were in service. Dunmore's offer was extended throughout the colonies in 1779 by the Commander-in-Chief, Sir Henry Clinton.

Until the success of Dunmore's scheme was seen to be growing, according to Washington "as a snowball, by rolling," official American policy had been to forbid the enlistment of slave or free Negroes and to eject those already in service—many Negroes had been in the early Northern skirmishes including Lexington and Concord. In January 1776, Congress reversed itself and allowed the recruiting of free Negroes, a policy most states followed and sometimes extended to slaves. The patriots became much less coy as the war continued and manpower problems grew acute: in 1777 Virginia allowed free Negroes to enlist, and in 1778 Massachusetts extended this privilege to all Negroes. Everywhere blacks were employed as substitutes in the draft. The bulk of patriot Negro troops, however, came from the Northern States. South Carolina and Georgia never permitted the enlistment of any Negroes, but even these two recalcitrants employed them as auxiliaries—to spy, dig, build, drive waggons, and generally help behind the lines.

Actually, both sides used more Negroes in these civilian ways than in the fighting services; for both feared the arming of the blacks. Typical was the stipulation of the British General, Sir Guy Carleton, that a Negro artillery unit be armed only with swords and all N.C.O.'s be white. Conversely, both sides were far less apprehensive about Negroes on warships or privateers, and blacks were widely used as pilots and ordinary seamen— throughout colonial times there had been a tradition of skilled Negro seamanship. The Virginian navy made particular use of Negro pilots, including the famous Caesar. James Forten served on a Pennsylvanian privateer, was captured, imprisoned for refusing to change sides, and exchanged at the peace; after which he made a fortune as a Philadelphia sail-maker and supported William Lloyd Garrison's anti-slavery campaign. Many Loyalists put their slaves on board British privateers, not as a means to emancipation but to collect prize-money.

How important Negroes were in the war is difficult to decide. Some individual exploits stand out. On the patriot side: at Bunker Hill in June 1775, Peter Salem allegedly[1] shot and killed Major Pitcairn who was in the act of proclaiming victory over the rebels; for his part in the same battle, Salem Poor was officially commended by Massachusetts as a "brave and gallant soldier"; in July 1777, at Newport, Rhode Island, Jack Sisson facilitated the bold capture of General Richard Prescott, apparently by breaking down the door with his head; Jordan Freeman is commemorated for slaying Major William Montgomery with a spear at the battle of Groton Heights, Connecticut, in 1781. During the Yorktown campaign the Marquis de Lafayette was greatly aided by a "double agent" slave called James Armistead. The Virginian legislature later freed and pensioned the Negro who changed his surname to Lafayette and was reunited with his namesake when the Marquis returned to America in 1824—incidentally, Lafayette's experience in America converted him to strongly pro-Negro abolitionist views.

Individual Negro exploits for the British are less well known. Samuel Burke of Charleston, South Carolina, serving with the notoriously sanguinary Colonel Thomas Browne's King's Rangers, claimed to have killed ten men at the bitter internecine battle of Hanging Rock in 1780. He also used his command of the Irish brogue, acquired during a stay in the British Isles, to help raise an American Irish regiment. Scipio Handley, a Charleston fisherman, carried British intelligence, was wounded, captured, and only avoided the death penalty by a daring escape. At Dunmore's early victory at Kemp's Landing, it was runaway slaves who captured two rebel colonels. In New Jersey, one Tye, a former soldier under Dunmore, commanded a rather successful partisan gang. Quamino Dolly helped the British to capture Savannah, Georgia, in 1779 by guiding the troops through a swamp leading to a surprise rear attack.

Armed Negroes were not usually segregated. Patriot black units in Massachusetts—including the Bucks of America, which actually had a Negro commander—and Connecticut were exceptions. At most, Negroes were organized into such auxiliaries as the fifty-two "Black Pioneers" attached to the Loyalist King's American Dragoons; or occasionally they comprised a large proportion of a unit such as the three-quarters black patriot Rhode Island Regiment, which distinguished itself in 1778 at the battle of Rhode Island. Later, at the battle of Points Bridge, New York, in 1781 the British are said to have reached the fallen colonel of the regiment, Christopher Greene, only over the bodies of his black soldiers. Some Negroes were probably on one or both sides in every major battle of the war; and it is in the mass they must be judged. They seem to have made good, reliable soldiers. The Revolution as a fight for "liberty" was a slogan literally true for the slave combatant.

Perhaps five thousand of the thirty thousand patriot troops were Negroes. It is not known how many fought for the British; possibly a few thousand. Many more fled to the British lines— estimates include thirty thousand in Virginia, twenty-five thousand in South Carolina, more than eleven thousand in Georgia— and, as with the patriots, were used behind the lines, thus releasing whites for active duty. There is a report of the British perpetrating "germ" warfare. In July 1783, General Leslie wrote to Cornwallis: "About 700 Negroes are come down the River in the Small Pox. I shall distribute them about the Rebell Plantations." In spite of great Negro activity in the war, however, an educated guess is that the blacks were not a decisive factor for either side.

After the end of the war, what happened to the Negroes who

had fought for the patriots or the British? Most who had been slaves received their liberty—on the American side the owners were compensated—numbering perhaps several hundred. More than twenty thousand Negroes, at least, mainly Loyalists' slaves, but including some hundreds who had earned their freedom, were evacuated with the British who honourably resisted all American demands for the return of the runaways. Most slaves were taken to the Caribbean, sometimes via East Florida—temporarily held by Britain; most freemen went to Canada and a few to England. One interesting group who were not evacuated was a bandit gang known as "the King of England's soldiers," who roamed the Savannah river region for a few years.

Two ironies must be noted about the Revolutionary war. First, it was the British use of Negroes that goaded the Sons of Liberty into liberalizing their own policies, thus enabling some slaves to win freedom on the rebel side. Second, the defeat of the British meant that, while slavery was abolished throughout the Empire in 1833, it grew in strength in the United States and only collapsed with the Civil War.

The majority of Negroes were too uneducated, unsophisticated, or oppressed to take any personal part in the Revolution. But there were many exceptions, especially in the North; and it is clear that some Negroes were well aware of the Revolutionary issues. For example, typical names taken by Connecticut's black troops were Dick Freedom, Cuff Liberty, and Jube Freeman. In some northern states Negroes petitioned against slavery: "We expect great things from men who have made such a noble stand against the designs of their *fellow-men* to enslave them"—often using the same Lockeian arguments for their freedom as the patriots used against England. In 1783 a Massachusetts court declared slavery unconstitutional within the state, a decision stemming from the Negroes' own legal battles.

The Revolutionary era brought forth a crop of outstanding Negroes who provided a challenge to white racial theories. For example, Benjamin Banneker, astronomer and scholar; Lemuel Haynes, Congregationalist minister; Prince Hall, pioneer black Mason; Paul Cuffe, merchant, ship-builder, philanthropist and abolitionist; and Phillis Wheatley, a kind of eighteenth-century quiz-kid, brought as a child from Africa to Boston, where she wrote religious poetry, translated part of Ovid and, in 1773, on a visit to England, mixed with the nobility and published her collected poems, praised by Voltaire, but not by Jefferson.

To fight for "liberty," Georgia and some other states paid their soldiers partly in slaves;[2] but most American patriots recognized that, to the Revolutionary philosophy, slavery was a standing reproach, a basic contradiction. John Jay avowed: "To fight for liberty and to deny that blessing to others involves an inconsistency not to be excused," and Abigail Adams wrote to her husband, John, about the wickedness of fighting "ourselves for what we are daily robbing and plundering from those who have as good a right to freedom as we have." The Declaration of Independence proclaimed: "We hold these truths to be self-evident, that all men are created equal . . ." If the American Revolution brought forth the eagle as the national emblem for the world to see, it also produced a black albatross no less visible.

In the draft of his propaganda sheet, Jefferson had inserted a preposterous paragraph blaming George III for slavery in the colonies: "He has waged cruel war against human nature itself . . ." New Englanders, of course, had grown rich in the slave-trade; slavery was supported in all thirteen colonies, and in the South was widely regarded as an economic and social necessity. Southern congressional delegates, supported by a few Northerners, struck out the offending paragraph. But, apart from Jefferson, many Southern leaders, including Washington, Madison, and Patrick Henry, opposed slavery. The inability to reconcile slavery and the Declaration of Independence marks a clear stage in the South's progressing schizophrenia. Typically, Jefferson, if he trembled "for my country when I reflect that God is just," was equivocal, firmly believing in innate Negro inferiority, and remained a slave-owner. His famous "Committee of Revisors," which began reforming Virginia in 1777, drew up an emancipation bill; but opposition prevented its being considered. Only in Maryland was emancipation actually discussed by a Southern legislature; and even manumission was discouraged by all Southern states except Maryland and Virginia.

But the defence of slavery was far less wholehearted—although the tone was apologetic—than in the years soon to come, when cotton, partly through Eli Whitney's invention of the cotton gin in 1793, became King. In spite of the conservatism of the early years of the Republic—exemplified by the tacit approval of slavery in the three-fifths Constitutional Compromise over representation in 1789 and the Fugitive Slave Act of 1793—emancipation societies did exist in the South; many Southerners expected Slavery to die out; Southern approval of the banning of slavery in the old North-West was obtained in 1785, and only South Carolina and Georgia continued the overseas slave trade during the twenty years sanctioned by the federal constitution.

In the North the Revolution intensified abolitionist sentiment, which pre-dated the rebellion, especially in Quaker areas—for example, the activities of John Woolman in New Jersey and Anthony Benezet in Philadelphia, aided by the non-Quaker, Benjamin Franklin. The Northern States all had slaves, but in small proportions compared with the South; and the underlying fear for white supremacy was not prevalent. Fairly soon after the war, slavery was abolished throughout the North by legislation or judicial decision, New Jersey, with a gradual emancipation law in 1804, being the last to act. New Jersey, however, had not scrupled to free Loyalists' slaves at the end of the war; and this was done elsewhere.

At the end of the Revolution, apart from the few who had gained freedom, the Southern Negro faced a worse future than at the beginning. And in the North, if freedom had arrived or was on the way, social equality was not, nor is it yet, achieved. The Revolutionary period was probably the happiest time in the history of American race relations.

If the American treatment of the Negro left something to be desired, the actions of the British were certainly not beyond criticism. An American Loyalist noted that: "these poor crea-

tures [Negroes] are esteemed no better than cattle by those virtuous Sons of Liberty;'' and Dr. Johnson demanded: ''How is it
that we hear the loudest yelps for liberty among the drivers of
negroes?'' But the British, of course, with West Indian and
other slave interests to consider, had no more intention than
Lincoln (at a later date) of waging an abolitionist crusade, and
did not extend the offer of freedom to Loyalists' slaves. But the
black man did not always appreciate the distinction. A Virginian
Loyalist sadly related that he had been crippled ''by one of his
own slaves who mistaking the purport of the proclamation
issued by Lord Dunmore, wherein he Declared all the Slaves
free belonging to the Rebels, thought it extended to the whole
race.'' No more than many Whigs did the Tories quarrel with
the institution of Slavery and, when defeat came, either sold
their slaves or carried them off.

The majority of free, or emancipated, Negroes who had
fought for the British were taken to Canada; and there is evidence that they were not very happy there. Early in 1792, a
group of Negroes, led by a war veteran called Thomas Peters,
sailed to Sierra Leone, having found the British Government's
promise of farms in Nova Scotia disappointing.

Benjamin West's lost painting of the American Loyalists being welcomed to England in 1783 shows, among others, the
hand of an emancipated Negro raised up to meet the out-
stretched grasp of a benevolent Britannia. In one of his
sketches, Crèvecoeur has a patriot thus address a Negro: ''They
say you are a good fellow, only a little Toryfied like most of
your colour''; and a contemporary Tory testified that the Negroes were ''strongly attached to the British.'' There was a
widespread fear of Negroes among the Whigs, which was partly
an extension of the perennial dread of slave revolt, intensified,
since Dunmore's proclamation and the great desertion of slaves,
to a wholesale offer of freedom the patriots could never match.

It is impossible to say what proportion of Negroes were
Whigs and what proportion Tories. As in the Civil War, many
slaves must have remained attached to benevolent masters from

both sides. The Negro who was active during the Revolution joined one side or the other for reasons of advantage and freedom, rather than for any political philosophy. Few could have been politically aware. William Snow, for example, a Charleston tailor, signed the association, he said, without knowing what it was. And those who did know of the issues could not fail to be disillusioned with both sides.

The attitude of whites towards the Negro is quite well known; the outlook of the Negro, much less so. But there is one source of Negro attitudes: the records of the British claims commissioners who apportioned compensation for losses caused by the loyalty of Americans. They included about forty Negro claimants. By reaching England—usually as seamen or batmen—these Negro Loyalists were not typical; but in many ways they probably represent the attitudes of Negro Loyalists in particular, and, to an extent, all Negroes. Strangely enough, the structure of Negro Loyalism parallels white Loyalism: the Negroes seem to have been rather well-to-do, for their race, and came mainly from urban areas—there was the best opportunity for joining the invading British—and usually had trades.

The claims commissioners, being eighteenth-century gentlemen, took a supercilious, class-conscious attitude. They were not inclined to give much compensation to what they regarded as white "upstarts," who had moved up the social scale in America. The Negro they regarded in a similar, but severer, way. Loyalist claimants had to produce proof of their loyalty, in the form of witnesses and supporting letters. Often Negroes were unable to do this—about half their claims were dismissed; but when someone, such as Colonel Edmund Fanning of North Carolina, would vouch for them they usually got a trifling award—customarily £5 or £10 in full. A few also got annual pensions, the highest being £18 per annum awarded to Shadrack Furman of Virginia, who was blinded and wounded in the leg serving the British.

The gaining of freedom alone was often considered ample enough reward for loyalty: "he ought to think himself very fortunate in being in a Country where he can never again be reduced to a State of Slavery"—a reference to Somersett's case of 1771–2, in which Lord Mansfield ruled that slavery could not exist in Britain; or, "he is in a much better Country where he may with Industry get his Bread & where he can never more be a Slave," were the typical comments of the commissioners in dismissing the claims of Alexander Maurice, a Connecticut farmer, and John Provey, a North Carolina servant.

How successful the American Negroes were in getting their "Bread" in the home of freedom is not widely revealed in the commissioners' records. Eighteenth-century England did not contain enough coloured people, perhaps 14,000 in 1771, to create a racial problem or exacerbate racial prejudice. The Negro may even have had a novelty value as a servant; and, indeed, this had been the chief reason for the importation of slaves in previous decades. George Peters, at the time of his claim in 1786, reported "attending at a Gentleman's House" for eighteen pence per week—not as low a wage as it seems if, as is probable, it were "all found." John Provey, a veteran from Governor Martin of North Carolina's Black Pioneers, said he had married a white woman since arriving in England, which was perhaps a help in making ends meet.

Samuel Burke of Charleston reported being employed in London at the "Artificial Flower Garden at 1s. per Day," a not unreasonable wage at the time for unskilled labourers. Those Negroes who had trades may well have been able to continue them in England. William Snow, a tailor in South Carolina, had "got some Business here as a Taylor." John Robinson, a cook who had kept a shop in Charleston, was able to open a similar establishment in Newmarket Street, London; and Shadrack Furman, an allegedly free Virginia farmer blinded in British service, supported himself in England by playing the fiddle, which, added to his pension of £18 a year, must have provided a tolerable living. Although one Negro returned to Virginia, that conditions in England were favourable may be inferred from the letter written in June 1783 by an English Negro (not a claimant) to the military authorities in America:

Honoured Sir

It was my Misfortune to be Stole in England and Brought to Baltimore and Sold for four years as a Slave which I suffered with the Greatest Barbarity in this Rebelious Cuntry.

I have been Six Years what they call Free in this Cuntry and Never Had The Opportunity to Go Home to Old England as I am without Money or Friends I hope you will assist me in Going Home I cant Get two Days work in one week I was brought up at the Plough I thought it the Best Honnoured Sir to Acquaint you of these my Misfortunes So I remain

True Brittam
Towers Bell

Most Negroes probably agreed with William Snow, who, as the commissioners noted, "Does not think of going back again."[3]

There is evidence that some of the Negro claimants were taken advantage of in London. Two Londoners, John Williams and Thomas Watkins, kept a boarding house in which a number of the Negroes lived. The commissioners became suspicious when several black Loyalists arrived with memorials claiming exactly the same property, written and certified by the above-named landlords. Although Williams submitted an affidavit that he was receiving no compensation for this service, the commissioners believed that he and Watkins would probably get the bulk of any money awarded. Henry Brown, a South Carolina claimant, told the commissioners that for writing his memorial he paid Williams one shilling.

The most interesting question about Loyalists of all colours is why were they loyal? For Negroes the answer is probably much simpler than for whites. John Twine of Petersburg, Virginia, admitted that he was first a waggoner with an American regiment, but "was kept very bare in Cloaths & little Money & therefore he ran away from home when he heard there was more Money & better Usage in the British Army." George Mills, a Guinea Negro, testified that he ran away from his master, a Captain Avery of Portsmouth, Virginia, to join Lord Dunmore and gain freedom.

The claims commissioners judged, in the case of William

Prince, that he was "a great gainer by the troubles in America for being in a situation in which he could loose (*sic*) nothing he has gained his Liberty and comes in our Opinion with a very bad grace to plead sufferings . . ." Although unsympathetic, these words sum up the position of the slave who became a "Loyalist" (or for that matter, in different circumstances, a "Whig")—he had indeed nothing to lose and everything to gain.

Notes

1. There is much mythology regarding Negro war heroes: many hallowed stories are false, such as the belief that Deborah Sampson who, disguised as a man, became an honoured Massachusetts soldier, was a Negro.

2. This is reminiscent of the story told by an American Negro minister to the Halifax (England) anti-slavery society of a Southern lady so affected by an anti-slavery sermon that she sold one of her slaves and donated the money.

3. It must be remarked, however, that Negroes were a noted element in the London poor of the eighteenth century; Granville Sharp, the indefatigable, eccentric friend of Negroes, had 400 pensioners called St. Giles blackbirds on his hands; in 1787 a number were shipped to Sierra Leone, and as late as 1814 a Parliamentary committee reported on destitute London Negroes.

The Slave in Connecticut During the American Revolution

Gwendolyn Evans Jensen*

Gwendolyn Evans Jensen demonstrates that despite numerous assertions to the contrary, service in the army did not necessarily bring freedom for the black slave. Jensen maintains that in light of presently known evidence, "it is not possible to say that in Connecticut many slaves were freed by serving in the Revolutionary armies." Even Connecticut's 1784 emancipation legislation was more the result of pressures from a small group of Quakers than of the revolutionary rhetoric. Jensen, a member of the History Department at the University of New Haven, specializes in Modern European History; she has published articles in Essays in Arts and Science *and* Central European History.

To all you who call yourselves Sons of Liberty in America, Greeting:

My Friends, We know in some good measure the inestimable value of liberty . . . Surely, some foul monster of hideous shape and hateful kind, opposite in its nature to hers, with all its frightful appearances and properties, iron hands and leaden feet, formed to gripe and crush, hath intruded itself into her peaceful habitation and ejected her. . . . We that declare, and that with

*Gwendolyn Evans Jensen, "The Slave in Connecticut During the American Revolution," *Connecticut Historical Society Bulletin* 30 (1965), 73–80. Reprinted by permission. Note: this article, with footnotes, may be consulted at the Connecticut Historical Society.

much warmth and zeal, it is unjust, cruel, barbarous, unconstitutional, and without law to enslave, *do we enslave?* Yes, verily
we do! . . . Can we expect to be free, so long as we are determined to enslave?

(Signed)

Honesty

[*Norwich Packet,* July 7, 1774]

THE EIGHTEENTH CENTURY WAS a period of so-called enlight-
enment, and its dream of a rational, free life for all men contributed to the more materialistic sources of discontent in the thirteen
English colonies along the Atlantic coast. In Connecticut, as in
the other colonies, the existence of slavery in a nation seeking
freedom seemed hypocritical. "Honesty," writing in 1774, cried
out to those who called themselves Sons of Liberty and asked
them some embarrassing questions. This article will analyze the
archival evidence in Connecticut to see to what extent this state
faced up to those questions and attempt to understand the extent
of the correlation of the battle of freedom from Britain with the
struggle of the Connecticut slave for *his* freedom.

On the eve of the Revolution Connecticut had the largest
number of Negroes in New England, 6,464 out of a total New
England Negro population of 16,034. The slave trade was a
central part of the economy of New England, for upon it
centered such industries as sugar, molasses, shipbuilding, dis-
tilling, and fishing. The Negro, like the New England economy
itself, was highly diversified and his services were not tied to
one crop. The slave trade was not a significant part of Connecticut's economy, and during the pre-Revolutionary period there
was a decided tendency for owners to free their slaves. Because
she was self-governing, Connecticut went so far as to defy the
mercantile interests of the Crown and halt the importation of
slaves into its territory. Apparently slavery was not proving to
be in the best economic interests of the community, for the
October 1774 legislation ending the importation of slaves reasoned that "whereas the increase of slaves in this Colony is
injurious to the poor and inconvenient . . ." more slaves could
not be imported.

Combined with this happy picture of an enlightened colony searching for ways to free her oppressed people is the strict Black Code which was in force during the same years. The Connecticut Yankee, while having neither a vested interest in the slave trade nor a need for slaves in increasing numbers, at the same time was afraid of the Negro. He feared the Negro as an economic liability and as a source of insurrection. The Code provided that a freed slave must be provided for by his former owner if he ever came to want. At the same time the Code forbade the Negro, Indian or Mulatto from fighting in colonial armed forces. As early as 1660 at the Court of Election at Hartford it was recorded: "It is ordered by this Court, that neithr Indian nor negar servts shalbe required to traine, watch or ward . . ." This and similar laws were continuously disobeyed during the colonial period. Although he was feared, the Negro fought on land and sea, for the armies needed all the men they could get.

The American Revolution in Connecticut continued this Janus-faced tradition of colonial times. The Negro was forbidden to fight, and he fought. There was legislation specifying that the Negro was ineligible to serve. The history of the evolving legislation throughout the Revolutionary period never changes the basic fact that the Negro could fight only in defiance of the sanctions of his state.

Statistical information on the Negro in the Revolution must remain fragmentary, for no racial notation is made in the various military lists in the archives. Only when a Negro has just a first name is he given the designation Negro. Not only is it impossible to know how many Negroes fought; it is equally uncertain whether those designated as Negroes are slave or free.

Negroes participated in the earliest actions of the war. Timon Negro "March'd from Weathersfield for the Relief of Boston in the Lexington Alarm in April 1775." Titus, Cato, Dan, and Nero took part in the Siege of Boston in the summer of 1775. On the Pay List of the Brig *Defence* for 1776 George, a Negro seaman, is listed, and Peter is on the Pay Roll of "Captain Seth Warners Company of Seamen raised in the State of Connecticut for the Naval Service on the Lake in the Northern Department . . ."

In the months after Concord and Lexington the use of Negro soldiers came under sharp fire within many states and in the Continental Army, and by the summer of 1776 legislation and military orders had been put into effect specifically barring the Negro from service. The action of Lord Dunmore in the South, however, quickly stopped this exclusion movement, and the army decided there was more to fear from the Negro in the British army than in their own. In 1777 Congress began to fix troop quotas for each state, and Negroes were used to fill some of the quotas despite state laws. All over the colonies opportunities grew for the Negro to exchange freedom for service. Because of the substitution system, the Negro was encouraged to serve, especially in the long-term Continental Army which sent men farther away from home.

In Connecticut, town officials did not question color or civil status in recruiting, and in 1777 there was a legislative effort to induce slave owners to free their slaves in exchange for military service.

The practical need for fighting men was coupled with an earnest desire on the part of some Connecticut citizens to end the hypocrisy of slavery itself. On April 17, 1777, the town of Enfield "in Town Meeting Assembled" petitioned the General Assembly to free the slaves of Connecticut. The petition states that, despite the passage in 1774 of the non-importation act ". . . those Now in the State are still held in Slavery & thereby that freedom & Liberty is unwarrantably & unjustly Taken & withholden from them which by their Natural Birth they are Entitled To . . ."

One historian suggests that, as a direct result of this Enfield petition, a committee was appointed by the General Assembly to study the position of the slave in Connecticut. This committee presented a proposal for emancipating Negro and Mulatto slaves which provided that any slave who could "procure either by bounty hire or in any other way such a sum to be paid to their Masters, as such Negroe or Molattoe shall be Judged to be Reasonably worth by the Selectmen of the Town . . . shall be allowed to enlist . . . and shall thereupon be de facto free and emancipated; and that the Master of such Negroe or Molattoe shall be exempted from the support and maintainance of such Negroe or Mulattoe . . .'' The slave owner could receive the bounty and half the Negro's pay during the time he served and up to the time when he had received the slave's full value. The committee's report was rejected in the Upper House and ordered to be continued in the Lower House.

Perhaps the key provision in this bill is the change made in the liability laws of the Black Code. Masters feared to free their slaves because they were not able to give up their responsibility toward them and were required by law to maintain them if they could not support themselves. For example, on May 26, 1777, Silas Loomis of Wethersfield petitioned the General Assembly in behalf of his slave Dick, who was 23 years old and wanted to enlist in exchange for manumission at the end of the term. Loomis petitioned the Assembly to be free of liability for the support of Dick.

In the October session of 1777 the liability provision of the May report was made law. This act, working jointly with an earlier provision permitting two men to hire one to serve for them, made it possible for the Negro slave to be hired to serve in someone else's place in exchange for his freedom. The owner of the slave could apply to the selectmen of his town who would then judge whether freedom was to the slave's advantage. If the selectmen then gave their approval all the owner's responsibility toward the slave was at an end.

This legislation released the slave owner from the liability he had been under from the early years of the century. This new freedom to emancipate and to get a substitute for military service should have emancipated many young male Negroes. It is a curious fact that there are not more definite cases of a Negro's being freed by this enabling legislation.

Joseph Mun, "a poor African," petitioned the General Assembly for freedom in May of 1780 because he had been promised freedom and had been cheated of it by William Nicholls who had joined the enemy and before leaving had given Mun's bill of sale to another man. Mun lost his case, but he had enlisted, expecting to be free. Cato is on the Durham bounty list for December 9, 1777. He was hired by two men, and freedom was his bounty. This is the only place in all the bounty lists where freedom is specified as a condition of service. There are, however, a few other evidences of a Negro's being promised freedom in exchange for service. Joshua Austin of New Haven petitioned the General Assembly on January 21, 1784:

> Whereas Brister a Negro man Servant of mine that has served in the Connecticut Line during the late War, and has been a good Soldier and frugal of his Interest . . . Thinking that it is reasonable that he should be set free, as he has been fighting for the Liberties of the Country, and I being willing . . . I freely give up all my Right . . .

One final case is that of Selah Hart of Farmington who petitioned the state for the 44 pounds, 8 shillings, and 2 pence owed his ex-slave Pharoah. Hart had agreed to have Pharoah enlist, but he had never received the agreed-upon price of 50 pounds.

The legislation also made it easier for the state to emancipate confiscated Tory slaves. Pomp, who was such a slave, petitioned the General Assembly on October 20, 1779 for freedom and it was granted. The selectmen of Norwalk testified that he was able to support himself. Great Prince, Little Prince, Luke, Caesar, and Prue and her three children petitioned the General Assembly unsuccessfully in this way:

> That your memorialists, though they have flat noses, crooked shins, and other queerness of make, peculiar to Africans, are yet of the human race, free-born in our own country, taken from thence by man-stealers, and sold in this country as cattle in the market, without the least act of our own to forfeit liberty; but we hope our good mistress, *the free State of Connecticut,* engaged in a war with tyranny, will not sell good honest Whigs and friends of the freedom and independence of America, as we are, to raise cash to support the war: because the Whigs ought to be *free;* and the *Tories* should be sold.

There is no question that the two-man act did bring many Negroes into the army, for there are many specifically listed. The crucial question, however, is whether or not freedom was their bounty. Since the lists do not specify who received the bounty money, there is no way to determine how many of these Negroes turned over their money to their masters in exchange for freedom.

J. Hammond Trumbull, editor of *The Public Records of the Colony of Connecticut,* is less critical of the evidence. "In point of fact," he wrote "some hundreds of blacks—slaves and free-men—were enlisted . . . *How* many it is impossible to tell; for, from first to last, the company or regimental rolls indicate *no distinctions* of color. The *name* is the only guide: and . . . such surnames as 'Liberty,' 'Freeman,' 'Freedom,' &c. by scores indicate with what anticipations, and under what inducements, they entered the service."

The archival lists give the overwhelming impression that the Negro soldier was in no way a special case, for he was given equal bounty or hire money, the same rate of pay, and usually the same supply allowance. If it were not for the one use of the word "freedom" noted above, perhaps it would be possible to assume that it was everywhere implied. We can, however, assume no such thing. There are too many other ways a Negro could enter the lists. He could be a free man already, and his lack of last name explained as a mark of lower caste. The Negro could have been a runaway, seeking the bounty money and an opportunity to get far away. Finally, and most obviously, the Negro could have been a slave when he entered service for his master and still have been a slave when his three years were up.

Until someone goes through the selectmen's records in each town to see how many masters actually applied for authority to manumit their slaves for military service, it is not possible to say that in Connecticut many slaves were freed by serving in the Revolutionary armies.

Perhaps George W. Williams, in his *History of the Negro Race in America,* is right when he says:

Enlistment in the army did not work a practical emancipation of the slave, as some have thought. Negroes were rated as chattel property by both armies and both governments during the entire war. This is the cold fact of history, and it is not pleasing to contemplate. The Negro occupied the anomalous position of an American slave and an American soldier. He was a soldier in the hour of danger, but a chattel in time of peace.

If this is so, then any significant connection between the dreams of the colonists for independence and the Negro for emancipation must be sought in legislative measures for direct emancipation. The deliberate attempt of the Legislature in 1777 to make enlistment an acknowledged and respectable means of manumission had never been voted into law in Connecticut, and the Negro was still a slave and likely to remain so despite his service in the war.

On May 4, 1779 the Negroes of Stratford and Fairfield submitted an impassioned petition to the General Assembly which deserves to be quoted at length, for it is remarkably like the Declaration of Independence. Its effects upon the General Assembly cannot be measured, but it stands as another instance of the growing clamor for emancipation.

> . . . we are the Creatures of that God, who made of one Blood, and Kindred, all the Nations of the Earth; we perceive by our own Reflection, that we are endowed, with the same Faculties, with our Masters, and there is nothing, that leads us to a Belief, or Suspicion, that we are any more obliged to serve them, than they us, and the more we Consider of this Matter, the more we are Convinced, of our Right . . . to be free . . .

In January, 1780, there was passed in the Upper House of the General Assembly a bill for the gradual emancipation of the Negro slave. The bill would have freed, at the age of 28, any Negro, Indian, or Mulatto child then under the age of seven and all born after the passing of the act. The bill was apparently not acted on in the lower house.

The bill that finally did pass in 1784 provided for the same method of emancipation, although it lowered the age for freedom to 25 and did not include children already born. The curious thing about this bill is that it is, in effect, a restatement of the old Black Code and thus a further discouragement to any owner who might wish to continue to hold slaves. It requires every slave or servant (which probably refers to the indentured servant) to carry a pass if he should venture beyond the limits of his home or town. It instructs ferrymen not to give passage to Negroes without such a pass. It prohibits all barter with slaves and provides that any caught out after nine at night without permission shall be publicly whipped. It then reasserts the provisions of the 1777 law, stating that the master will continue to be responsible for the care of his slave unless he has applied to the selectmen for approval to emancipate him. Then, almost as an afterthought, gradual emancipation becomes the law:

> *And whereas sound Policy requires that the Abolition of Slavery should be effected as soon as may be, consistent with the Rights of Individuals, and the public Safety and Welfare.* Therefore,
> *Be it enacted . . .* That no Negro or Molatto Child, that shall, after the first Day of *March, One thousand seven hundred and eighty-four,* be born within this State, shall be held in Servitude, longer than until they arrive to the Age of twenty-five Years, notwithstanding the Mother or Parent of such Child was held in Servitude at the Time of its Birth; but such Child, at the Age aforesaid, shall be free; any Law, Usage, or Custom to the contrary notwithstanding.

In October, 1788, further legislation was passed providing for the registration of every child eligible for freedom under the provisions of the March 1784 act. This provision was an incidental part of a bill designed to enforce more strictly the prohibition of the slave trade. It was a direct outcome of the lobbying of a group of Rhode Island Quakers whose concern was that slave ships had been fitted out in Connecticut harbors in defiance of the law. The eloquence of the Quaker's petition deserves quotation:

> . . . ever bearing in Mind that He who is graciously favouring us with the enjoyment of Liberty Civil & religious, regardeth the Cry of the Oppressed, & requires that we be ever found in the due Observance of his Solemn injunction, 'whatsoever ye would that men should do to you, do ye even so to them.'

The preliminary assumption in the writing of this article was that the ideals of the American Revolution and the practical realities of the need for more fighting strength had helped bring

about the emancipation of the Negro in Connecticut. This conclusion is not justified by the evidence. The movement toward
freedom for the slave had begun in Connecticut long before the
Revolutionary years, and the first clear legislation in this direction was the law forbidding the importation of slaves a year
before the start of hostilities. The final emancipation of the
slave was a gradual thing and was probably the result of the
moral force of a small group of pacifist Quakers as much as it
was the military strength of the Negro at war. There was one
point during the Revolution when the Negro's dreams and war
aims may have coincided, in 1777, but this move probably
misfired, despite the advantages to be gained. The white man's
fear of the Negro was simply too powerful a force, and despite
all the enlightened appeals from white and black, the Connecticut General Assembly would not put into law an acknowledg-
ment of its need for Negro military strength.

If there are to be any conclusions drawn, therefore, they must
be qualified. The same ideals of brotherhood and freedom epitomized in much of eighteenth-century thought had their effect
upon the propagandists of both the Revolution and emancipation. The same pleas for recognition of the dignity of all men
prevailed in both movements, although there was little interaction between them. The Revolutionary War continued a long
standing American tradition of reluctance to let the Negro fight.
Although the contradiction in ideals of a slaveholding state
fighting for freedom became obvious to all, nothing very much
was done about it.

To the Negro, however, there is an importance in those isolated figures in the archives which in no way reflects their
significance as causal factors. The Negro fought, and apparently
he fought as well as the white man. In Massachusetts, Crispus
Attucks, Salem Poor, and Peter Salem were heroes in their own
right, and the Negro in his search for historical identity should
know about these men. He should know about the others, too,
who were not heroes, but fought for the freedom of their country, perhaps because they were forced to do so, or perhaps
because they wanted the bounty money. But they did fight. The

words of Lemuel Haynes, writing in his old age, point to possible sources of pride for the American Negro today, if he would but search them out:

> Perhaps it is not ostentatious in the speaker to observe, that in early life he devoted all for the sake of freedom and independence, and endured frequent campaigns in their defence, and has never viewed the sacrifice too great. And should an attack be made on this sacred ark, the poor remains of life would be devoted to its defence.

Selected Bibliography

Alden, John R. *John Stuart and the Southern Colonial Frontier: A Study of Indian Relations, War, Trade, and Land Problems in the Southern Wilderness, 1754–1755*. Ann Arbor: University of Michigan Press, 1944.

Averkieva, I. Pablovna. *Slavery Among the Indians of North America*. Translated by G. R. Elliott. Victoria, British Columbia: n.p., 1966.

Cooley, Henry S. *A Study of Slavery in New Jersey*. Baltimore: Johns Hopkins University Press, 1896.

Cope, Robert S. "Slavery and Servitude in the Colony of Virginia in the Seventeenth Century." Unpublished Ph.D. dissertation, Ohio State University, 1951.

Corkran, David H. *The Cherokee Frontier: Conflict and Survival, 1740–62*. Norman: University of Oklahoma Press, 1962.

Corkran, David H. *The Creek Frontier, 1540–1783*. Norman: University of Oklahoma Press, 1967.

Craven, Wesley Frank. *White, Red, and Black: The Seventeenth-Century Virginian*. Charlottesville: University Press of Virginia, 1971.

Crosby, Alfred W., Jr. *The Columbian Exchange: Biological and Cultural Consequences of 1492*. Westport, Connecticut: Greenwood Press, 1972.

Curtin, Philip D. *The Atlantic Slave Trade: A Census*. Madison: University of Wisconsin Press, 1969.

Davidson, Basil. *The African Slave Trade: Precolonial History, 1450–1850*. Boston: Little, Brown, 1961.

DeVorsey, Louis, Jr. *The Indian Boundary in the Southern Colonies, 1763–1775*. Chapel Hill: University of North Carolina Press, 1966.

Duncan, John Donald. "Servitude and Slavery in Colonial South Carolina, 1670–1776." Unpublished Ph.D. dissertation, Emory University, 1971.

Fenton, William N. *American Indian and White Relations to 1830: Needs and Opportunities for Study*. Chapel Hill: University of North Carolina Press, 1957.

Glasrud, Bruce A., and Smith, Alan M., eds. *Promises to Keep: A Portrayal of Nonwhites in the United States*. Chicago: Rand McNally, 1972.

Graymont, Barbara. *The Iroquois in the American Revolution*. Syracuse: University of Syracuse Press, 1972.

Greene, Lorenzo. *The Negro in Colonial New England*. New York: Atheneum, 1942.

Huddleston, Lee Eldridge. *Origins of the American Indians: European Concepts, 1492–1729*. Austin: University of Texas Press, 1972.

Hudson, Charles M., ed. *Red, White, and Black: Symposium on Indians in the Old South*. Athens: University of Georgia Press, 1971.

Jacobs, Wilbur R. *Wilderness Politics and Indian Gifts: The Northern Colonial Frontier, 1748–1763*. Lincoln: University of Nebraska Press, 1966.

Jernegan, Marcus. *Laboring and Dependent Classes in Colonial America, 1607–1783*. Chicago: University of Chicago Press, 1931.

Jordan, Winthrop. *White Over Black: American Attitudes Toward the Negro, 1550–1812*. New York: Penguin, 1968.

Kawashima, Yasuhide. "Indians and the Law in Colonial Massachusetts, 1689–1763." Unpublished Ph.D. dissertation, University of California, Santa Barbara, 1967.

Klingberg, Frank. *An Appraisal of the Negro in Colonial South Carolina*. Toronto: Associated Publishers, 1941.

Lauber, Almon W. *Indian Slavery in Colonial Times Within the Present Limits of the United States*. New York: Columbia University Press, 1913.

Leach, Douglas E. *Flintlock and Tomahawk: New England in King Philip's War*. New York: Norton, 1958.

Lynd, Staughton. *Class Conflict, Slavery, and the United States Constitution*. Indianapolis: Bobbs-Merrill, 1967.

McCarey, Ben. *Indians in Seventeenth Century Virginia*. Williamsburg: n.p., 1957.

McColley, Robert. *Slavery and Jeffersonian Virginia*. Urbana: University of Illinois Press, 1964.

MacLeod, Duncan J. *Slavery, Race and the American Revolution*. London: Cambridge University Press, 1974.

McManus, Edgar J. *Black Bondage in the North*. Syracuse: Syracuse University Press, 1973.

McManus, Edgar J. *A History of Negro Slavery in New York*. New York: Syracuse University Press, 1966.

Mannix, Daniel, and Cowley, Malcolm. *Black Cargoes: A History of the Atlantic Slave Trade*. New York: Viking, 1962.

Mellon, Matthew T. *Early American Views on Negro Slavery*. New York: Mentor, 1934, 1969.

Milling, Chapman J. *Red Carolinians*. Chapel Hill: University of North Carolina Press, 1940.

Morgan, Edmund S. *American Slavery, American Freedom: The Ordeal of Colonial Virginia*. New York: W. W. Norton, 1975.

Morris, Richard B. *Government and Labor in Early America.* New York: Harper, 1954.

Mullin, Gerald W. *Flight and Rebellion: Slave Resistance in Eighteenth-Century Virginia.* New York: Oxford University Press, 1972.

Nammack, Georgiana C. *Fraud, Politics, and the Dispossession of the Indians: The Iroquois Land Frontier in the Colonial Period.* Norman: University of Oklahoma Press, 1969.

Nash, Gary B. *Red, White, and Black: The Peoples of Early America.* Englewood Cliffs, N.J.: Prentice-Hall, 1974.

O'Donnell, James H., III. *Southern Indians in the American Revolution.* Knoxville: University of Tennessee Press, 1973.

Peckham, Howard H. *The Colonial Wars, 1689–1762.* Chicago: University of Chicago Press, 1964.

Peckham, Howard H. *Pontiac and the Indian Uprising.* Princeton: Princeton University Press, 1947.

Peckham, Howard, and Gibson, Charles, eds. *Attitudes of Colonial Powers Toward the American Indian.* Salt Lake City: University of Utah Press, 1969.

Quarles, Benjamin. *The Negro in the American Revolution.* Chapel Hill: University of North Carolina Press, 1961.

Robinson, Donald. *Slavery in the Structure of American Politics, 1765–1820.* New York: Harcourt, 1971.

Salisbury, Neal. "Conquest of the 'Savage': Puritans, Puritan Missionaries, and Indians, 1620–1680." Unpublished Ph.D. dissertation, University of California, Los Angeles, 1972.

Smith, Abbot Emerson. *Colonists in Bondage: White Servitude and Convict Labor in America, 1607–1776.* Chapel Hill: University of North Carolina Press, 1947.

Smith, Hale G. *The European and the Indian: European-Indian Contacts in Georgia and Florida.* Gainesville: University of Florida Press, 1956.

Smith, James Morton, ed. *Seventeenth-Century America: Essays in Colonial History*. Chapel Hill: University of North Carolina Press, 1959.

Smith, Warren B. *White Servitude in Colonial South Carolina*. Columbia: University of South Carolina Press, 1961.

Snell, William Robert. "Indian Slavery in Colonial South Carolina, 1671–1795." Unpublished Ph.D. dissertation, University of Alabama, 1972.

Tate, Thad W. *The Negro in Eighteenth-Century Williamsburg*. Charlottesville: University of Virginia Press, 1966.

Trelease, Allen W. *Indian Affairs in Colonial New York: Seventeenth Century*. Ithaca: Cornell University Press, 1960.

Vaughan, Alden T. *The New England Frontier: Puritans and Indians, 1620–1675*. Boston: Little, Brown, 1965.

Wallace, Anthony F. C. *The Death and Rebirth of the Seneca*. New York: Random House, 1969.

Wallace, Anthony F. C. *King of the Delawares: Teedyuscung*. Philadelphia: University of Pennsylvania Press, 1949.

Wallace, Paul A. W. *Indians in Pennsylvania*. Harrisburg, Penn.: Pennsylvania Historical Commission, 1961.

Washburn, Wilcomb E. *The Governor and the Rebel: A History of Bacon's Rebellion in Virginia*. Chapel Hill: University of North Carolina Press, 1957.

Wasserman, Maurice Marc. "The American Indian as Seen by the Seventeenth-Century Chroniclers." Unpublished Ph.D. dissertation, University of Pennsylvania, 1954.

Wood, Peter H. *Black Majority: Negroes in Colonial South Carolina from 1670 Through the Stono Rebellion*. New York: W. W. Norton, 1974.

Zilversmit, Arthur. *The First Emancipation: The Abolition of Slavery in the North*. Chicago: University of Chicago Press, 1967.